Wishing you Success —

Love,
Pops!

July. 2. 1979

A
Deskbook of
Business
Management
Terms

A
Deskbook of
Business
Management
Terms

Leon A. Wortman

A Division of American Management Associations

Calligraphy by Bonnie Bier

Library of Congress Cataloging in Publication Data

Wortman, Leon A
    A deskbook of business management terms.

      1. Management–Dictionaries. 2. Business–
Dictionaries. 3. Economics–Dictionaries. I. Title.
HD30.15.W67   658'.003   78-23257
ISBN 0-8144-5470-4

First Printing

To
Dorothy, Alan, and Chris

Preface

See how smart he must be!
One can hardly understand him.
(author unknown)

As with so many inventions, this book was created out of necessity. Many business managers, faced with the imbroglio of spending the major part of the long and dynamic day in moving from meeting to meeting, realize the mind becomes awash with words and terms whose meanings are too often subject to interpretation and loose translations that may lead to hazardous actions. This physical and mental locomotion is, however, an important part of the process of attempting to communicate with superiors, peers, and subordinates.

Although all meetings, letters, memoranda, and conversations among business people are characterized by volumes of words, terms, idioms, phrases, and jargon, the fact is that disappointingly few of them succeed in meeting their objectives; too often, the intent of the communication effort fails. Within the same company, within one department, section, or group, there often are language barriers—people talking *at* each other instead of talking *with* each other.

A fast-moving exchange of words can prove disastrous the moment sophistication enters the verbiage. I recall sitting in my boss's office one day—he was general manager, chief honcho of the division—when his boss, president of the corporation, called in by telephone from corporate headquarters. My boss listened, smiled, nodded periodically, added a few apparently appropriate erhums, suddenly looked puzzled, perplexed, a bit bewildered and distracted. He covered the mouthpiece and quickly whispered to me, "What's management by exception?" I whispered a brief explanation. He smiled and nodded his thanks. He probably would have accepted any explanation at the moment, if for no other reason than to get a warm feeling of self-confidence, a sensation of communication with his boss.

I am by no means a semanticist. I claim to be a thoroughly pragmatic business manager, student, and sometimes a teacher. However, I did become aware some time ago that people were using words and expressions that I did not always understand and whose relationship to the business at hand was often a mystery to me. But, more often than not, I was too proud to ask for clarification. To develop my resources in the language of the business community, I began to make secret notes each time I heard a new term; and I became especially aware that the same terms were sometimes used with different meanings in different contexts.

Some of my professor/teacher friends confess they aren't always certain their students know what they are being taught because of the special words and phrases habitually used in the classroom as an integral part of the dialect of the subject. I remember, as a student, some rather frantic searches in the library for definitions, some of which were relatively obvious, others somewhat misleading. For example, in studying the Federal Reserve System, I learned there were several kinds of *city banks* and other banks known as *country banks*. Unfortunately, the teacher assumed I knew the difference. And I made the wrong assumption based on the adjectives. Are country banks in the country and city banks in the city? But then, where does the "city" end and the "country" begin? I discovered it wasn't necessarily that way. I must have spent hours searching the library's books on economics and their descriptions of the Federal Reserve System for a definition of "country bank." Of course I found it eventually, and that's why it appears in its alphabetical order in this book. A country bank is not always out in the boondocks!

As I moved upward in management circles and gained greater exposure to the multiple disciplines of business operations, new words appeared with great regularity. Often these new words seemed to puzzle no one but me. I assumed that I must be the only naive person in the business environment. But in time I realized that some of the others—probably most of them—were merely better at concealing their ignorance. Because I don't have the memory of an . . . (can't recall that animal's name), I started a private cross-indexed file intended for my personal use and security, a self-confidence-building device. However, unintentionally, I soon became a dialectician to my peers, a mystery to my superiors, and somewhat of a nut to my subordinates.

Therefore, I issue a fair notice to those who expect to benefit from the contents of this book: Beware! Your new knowledge and ability to express and comprehend may make you appear as a threat to your superiors. And, behind your back, as is the common behavior of the intimidated, those who envy you will put you down as a "theorist."

Today's students of business administration are, most likely, the source of tomorrow's business managers. Managers and students must learn to use the many dialects of the business environment. And, if they are to succeed in communicating thoughts, concepts, and instructions, they must use these dialects and their terms with precision.

What are these "dialects"? They are known as the languages of finance, economics, marketing, insurance, law, industrial relations, human behavior, industrial psychology, real estate, transportation and distribution, data processing, statistics, and the broad field of general management. Each of these dialects contains idioms, words, or phrases that are uniquely applied to a vertical segment of business operations. Many of the words are found in the dictionary. There the semanticist can find strict, rigid, sterile definitions out of context. However, the idiomatic form peculiar to the language of the business community is rarely found in a standard dictionary.

One can find specialized dictionaries that are dedicated to vertical areas or specific disciplines. There are law, accounting, and economics dictionaries, for examples. However, given a new term, business students or managers must be equipped with a certain priceless prescience that tells them, on hearing that new term, exactly which discipline, or dialect, of the business world uses the term. If they are fortunate enough to have such wisdom, they may go directly to a pertinent dictionary or section of the library and find a definition. Unfortunately, this may not reveal the fact that the same, or a slightly modified, expression may also apply to another business discipline. In any case, the quest for knowledge and explanation is time-consuming, and often the seeker is unsatisfied or frustrated.

The business manager must move constantly from one discipline to another. A conference, a memorandum, a letter, or a telephone conversation with the production supervisor, industrial relations manager, insurance agent, marketing manager, traffic director, comptroller, legal department, chairman of the board, or a stockholder demands swift comprehension and the accurate use of terms and phrases. Each dialog may call for a change of dialect. The uses of special terms test the verbal communication skills of each participant. There's precious little time to research meanings, significances and values of words.

New managers or supervisors may become especially perplexed. For example, in conversations with the legal counsel whose intentions are to protect the corporation and the individual, they may be confronted by an entirely new world of "acts," "amendments," and "regulations," most of which appear to be preceded by the surnames of people—Norris-La Guardia, Miller-Tydings, Robinson-Patman, Clayton, or Sherman, to name but a few. Who are they? What did they do that makes their names so important to the business community?

Similarly, the financial department seems to delight in the use of special words, such as "ratios." There are so many of them! Just when "depreciation" seems to be comprehensible, we learn that it comes in several varieties, each with a different, qualifying word.

Move into the overtly friendly environment of industrial relations, and there you are, all over again, involved with verbal mysteries—Boulwarism, Hawthorne studies, leveling. Leveling? Is that the same as the term the boss used in our staff meeting—leveling effect? But no, they are quite different. One is used in evaluating work performance in motion studies, the other describes a phenomenon that occurs during group meetings.

Pity the marketing director who worked his way up through the ranks, promoted (possibly to his level of incompetence) on the basis of past performance as a sales manager or star salesman in the field. Suddenly he is assaulted with terms such as "price equilibrium," "elasticity of demand," "propensity to save," "propensity to consume," and other econometric terms that, when understood, can significantly improve the skills and accuracy of the professional manager. Ignorance of such terms can have a dramatic effect on this manager's career, especially if his boss has an advanced degree in business administration and tends to insist on scientific support for any gut-feel decision making.

One could go on and on citing examples that illustrate the need among students and business managers at all levels for a translation vehicle, a resource that briefly defines, explains, and perhaps gives examples of the practical usage of terms in different disciplines. With such a resource, how much greater would be the probability that communication and comprehension will prevail, that cohesive action will follow, and that the intended objective will be met!

This book is distinctly a reference book, one that the student and practitioner will want to keep close at hand—within arm's reach of the telephone for instant verification of knowledge; on the night table for quiet study; on the desk as a unique reference to assure the correct interpretation of incoming letters and memoranda; or for the writing of sophisticated, intelligent, meaningful, and accurate business communications. Advanced students will want to consult it regularly while researching study topics, and to improve their comprehension of the jargon of the professional community they aspire to enter.

When the contents of this book were in index-card format, the knowledge contained therein was not easily accessed. The cards were inconvenient and conspicuous on my desk, and they were too large and cumbersome for my night table. I am delighted to be able to share my cards with you, in an easy-retrieval book format that is readily moved from desk to night table, from office to home.

In closing, I acknowledge a personal debt to my superiors, peers, and subordinates. It was their use and misuse of the language of business management that made this book a necessity.

Leon A. Wortman
Palo Alto, California

A
Deskbook of
Business
Management
Terms

AAA
See AMERICAN ACCOUNTING ASSOCIATION.

AAAA
See AMERICAN ASSOCIATION OF ADVERTISING AGENCIES.

A&D rates
Published rates that apply to freight moving to *assembly* or consolidation points and from *distribution* points.

A&S insurance
See ACCIDENT AND SICKNESS INSURANCE.

AAR
Initials for *against all risks,* with special reference to freight insurance. Also, initials for *Association of American Railroads.*

ABA
See AMERICAN BAR ASSOCIATION.

abandonment
In accounting, the complete retirement of a fixed asset after it is removed from service. There are several legal applications: Abandonment of property is the giving up of all control over it with the intention of relinquishing all claim to it. Loss of property is involuntary; abandonment is a voluntary act. When used in connection with duty or responsibility, abandonment is synonymous with repudiation.

abatement
The cancellation of all or part of a past or prospective expenditure. A reduction or cancellation of an assessed tax. Also, any item of incidental income accounted for as a reduction of general cost.

1

abatement-of-rent clause
In a lease, a provision that the tenant will be released from his obligation to pay rent if the premises are made uninhabitable by such causes as flood or fire.

ABC
See AUDIT BUREAU OF CIRCULATION.

ABC classification
Inventory items are ranked according to annual usage in dollars. "A" items represent high-dollar-value items and are given close attention. "C" items are lower in value than "B" items, usually ordered less frequently but in larger quantities, and require less attention than do the "A" or "B" classified items. It can be expected that a small percentage of the items will account for the major dollar value (see EIGHTY-TWENTY RULE).

ability to pay
A wage theory that holds that the wage level should be based on a company's ability to pay. Under this theory, wage levels should increase as profits increase. Those who support this theory rarely recommend the converse, lowering wages as profits decline. Also, a theory of taxation holding that taxes should be based on the taxpayer's ability to pay, the rich paying proportionately more than the poor. See PROGRESSIVE TAX.

ab initio
Latin, "from the beginning." For example: A person who enters upon the land of another with permission and thereafter abuses the permission becomes a trespasser ab initio; that is, he has nullified the permission and is legally regarded as a trespasser from the time he first entered upon the land.

above par
As used in the securities market, a premium price, either paid or quoted, that is higher than the face value of the item.

above the line
Those items on a balance sheet or other financial statement that are given in support of the sum of the details. See BOTTOM LINE.

absentee ownership
An enterprise in whose operation the owners do not take an active part.

absolute address
In data processing, an address that indicates the exact storage location where specific data are to be found or stored in the actual machine code address numbering system. Also referred to as *specific address.*

absolute advantage, law of
The principle that a basis for trade exists between nations or regions when each of them, because of natural or acquired advantages, can provide goods or services that the other wants at a lower cost than each could provide for itself. This law accounts for much of the world's trade.

absolute component bar chart
See BAR CHART.

absolute liability
Legal liability for an act that causes harm, even though the doer of the harm is not at fault.

absorption
In transportation, the assumption by one carrier of the shipping charges of another, without any increase in charges to the shipper. This might include, for example, charges normally applied to switching from one conveyance to another.

absorption costing
In accounting, the allocation of all or a portion of fixed and variable production costs to work in process, cost of sales, and inventory.

abstinence theory of interest
The concept that interest gained by saving money in an interest-bearing savings account is a reward for not spending the money on goods and services. See BÖHM-BAWERK.

abstraction
In real estate, a method of placing a monetary value on land upon which improvements have been constructed. The value of the improvements is estimated and subtracted from the total. The remainder becomes the value of the land.

accelerated depreciation
Depreciation of an asset at a rapid, nonlinear rate, generally during the early years of its useful life.

acceleration clause
A section of a written legal document that provides that a balance or remainder of a debt becomes payable immediately under certain conditions, such as failure to make a scheduled payment.

acceleration principle
The theory in economics that investment is a function of the increase in consumer demand or sales and, therefore, of changes in income.

acceptable quality level
In manufacturing, the level of quality at which components, processes, or finished goods are considered good, to be continued without rework, or immediately shippable. See LOT TOLERANCE PERCENT DEFECTIVE.

acceptance
A promise to pay by the drawee of a bill of exchange, usually indicated by writing the word "accepted" followed by the date, the place payable, and the acceptor's signature across the face of the bill. See TRADE ACCEPTANCE and BILL OF EXCHANGE.

acceptance sampling
In statistical analysis, the use of samples, usually selected at random, to determine the acceptability of a lot of delivered merchandise.

accessorial service
A transportation service in addition to the line-haul service, usually at an added cost, such as heating, packing, loading, and storage.

accessory after the fact
A person who, after a felony has been committed, knowingly assists the felon.

accessory before the fact
A person who is not present during the commission of a crime but who aids and abets its commission.

access right
The right of an owner or his authorized agent to enter or leave his property without trespassing.

access time
The amount of time a computer takes to locate data on a storage device and make them available to a user. Also, the time interval between a request for data to be stored and actual storage.

accident
An event that occurs even though no reasonable person could foresee its occurrence. Because of this, the law holds no person legally responsible for any harm that may result from an accident, unless injury or damage is increased by negligence.

accident and sickness insurance
Intended to reimburse the insured for loss of income or for expenses incurred as a result of an accident or illness. Indemnity or reimbursement through A&S insurance may be purchased by individuals, or through other forms of contracts such as group insurance, disability insurance under a life insurance policy, workmen's compensation, and medical insurance provided by federal, state, and local governments.

accommodation note
A note signed by one person as the maker, endorser, or acceptor on behalf of another whose credit position is not strong enough to be self-supporting. Usually no consideration is involved. The signer acts as guarantor for the note.

accommodation paper
See ACCOMMODATION NOTE.

accommodation party
A person who signs a negotiable instrument as a favor to another.

accord and satisfaction
Legally, an agreement that is made and executed in satisfaction of the rights one has acquired under a former contract.

accountability
The obligation of an employee or a manager to perform a task or to fulfill an assignment and to bear responsibility for the effects of his or her effort. In government accounting, the designation of the account or the amount of a disbursing officer's liability.

accountant's report
See AUDITOR'S REPORT.

accounting period
The period of time for which an operating statement is customarily prepared. Typical periods are one month, four weeks, a quarter of a year, 26 weeks, 52 weeks, a fiscal or calendar year.

Accounting Principles Board
A committee of the American Institute of Certified Public Accountants. It was established in 1959 but discontinued in 1973. The board's function was to report on and recommend improvements in accounting principles and standards.

accounts payable
Moneys owed to others, but not yet paid, and considered payable within the next 12-month period.

accounts receivable
Moneys earned, but not yet received, and considered receivable within the next 12-month period.

accounts receivable insurance
A fire insurance policy that provides coverage against losses due to the inability to collect outstanding accounts receivable because of destruction of records. It may cover the difference between the amount actually collected and the amount that would have been collected had the records not been destroyed. See CONSEQUENTIAL-LOSSES INSURANCE.

accretion
In finance, an addition of principal or income to a fund as a result of a plan of accumulation. For example, in a pension fund, an accretion may arise from payroll contributions or from revenue received on fund investments. Also, an increase in economic worth from any cause; for example, the growth of timber, the aging of wines, the increases in flocks and herds that are bred for commercial purposes.

In real estate, the acquisition of title to additional land when an owner's land is built up by gradual deposits made by the natural action of water.

accrual basis of accounting
The method of accounting whereby revenues and expenses are identified with specific time periods, such as a month or year. Items are recorded as they are incurred, along with acquired assets, without regard to the date of receipt of payment of cash. See CASH BASIS OF ACCOUNTING.

accrual costing
In accounting, the expensing of goods and services as they are consumed.

accrued asset
In accounting, interest, commission, or revenue earned but neither received nor past due.

accrued depreciation
In accounting, the difference between the cost of replacement of equipment or real property as of the date of the appraisal at the time of acquisition and the appraised value at the present time.

accrued dividend
Unpaid and undeclared dividend on preferred stock. See DIVIDEND IN ARREARS.

accrued expense
In accounting, the liability of an expense incurred on or before a given date, payable at some future date. For example: accrued interest on notes payable, product warranty expenses, and accrued wages.

accrued income
See ACCRUED REVENUE.

accrued liability
See ACCRUED EXPENSE.

accrued revenue
Revenue that has been earned but not yet received and that is not yet past due.

accumulated distribution
In accounting, income that has been received and accumulated by a trust for future distribution.

accumulated dividend
See DIVIDEND IN ARREARS.

accumulated income
Net income retained and not paid out in dividends or dissipated by subsequent losses. Also referred to as *accumulated earnings* and *accumulated profit*.

accumulation bin
The place where a product is assembled; usually a physical location intended for the accumulation of all components that comprise an as-

sembly before the order to perform the assembly is sent to the production floor.

accumulation plan
An arrangement under which the purchaser of shares in a mutual fund (open-end investment company) agrees to acquire more shares over a given period of time.

accumulation schedule
A table in which computations are provided for the periodic write-up until maturity of the discount relating to an investment or obligation.

accumulator
The register and associated equipment in the arithmetic unit of a computer in which arithmetic and logic operations are performed. Also, a unit in a digital computer where numbers are totaled.

ACE
See ACTIVE CORPS OF EXECUTIVES.

acid test
The ratio of an enterprise's current assets minus inventories to its current liabilities. One of several factors used by credit analysts to judge an enterprise's financial position. Also known as the *quick ratio*. See LIQUIDITY RATIOS.

ACLU
Initials for *American College of Life Underwriters* (see CHARTERED LIFE UNDERWRITER). Also, initials for *American Civil Liberties Union,* an association of attorneys concerned with the practice and interpretation of the law with respect to civil rights.

ACME
See ASSOCIATION OF CONSULTING MANAGEMENT ENGINEERS.

acquisition cost
The funds required to acquire goods or services.

acquisitive need
A motivational factor; the desire to possess or hoard material possessions such as money, property, fancy automobiles, and clothing. The objects of the acquisitive need are often those that are esteemed by the individual's societal affiliations.

acre-foot
An amount of water equivalent to that covering one acre of land to a depth of one foot.

acronym
A word that is formed from the first letter or letters of the words in a name, term, or phrase. For example, NASA (National Aeronautics and Space Administration), NATO (North Atlantic Treaty Organization), or COBOL (Common Business-Oriented Language).

ACTION
See VOLUNTEERS IN SERVICE TO AMERICA.

action ex contractu
Legal action to recover damages for the breach of a duty arising out of a contract. There are two types of causes of action: (1) those that arise out of contract, *ex contractu,* and (2) those that arise out of tort, *ex delicto.* See ACTION EX DELICTO.

action ex delicto
Legal action to recover damages for the breach of a duty existing by reason of a general law. For example, an action to recover damages for an injury caused by the negligent use of machinery is an *ex delicto* action. Tort, or wrong, is the basis of the action. See ACTION EX CONTRACTU.

action of the sun
In real estate, a consideration in the selection of a retail store. The shadier side of the street is usually more desirable.

action to quiet the title
An action to clarify one's title to property by removing any interests or claims of others.

Active Corps of Executives
An organization of executives who are still employed and who have volunteered to offer expertise in many operational aspects of business. Formed in 1969 and sponsored by the Small Business Administration (SBA).

activity ratio
In production, the ratio of a number of actively used records in a file to the total number of records in the file. May also be used with reference

to electronic data processing. In finance, any one of a set of financial ratios that deals primarily with the utilization of assets entrusted to corporate management. These are especially useful in tracking the performance of operating managers responsible for specific functions such as inventory management, cash management, and credit policy. Activity ratios include: fixed asset turnover, or sales divided by fixed assets; total asset turnover, or sales divided by total assets; inventory turnover, or sales divided by inventory; and average collection period, or accounts receivable divided by sales per day.

act of God
An act of nature that is not reasonably foreseeable. In insurance, a natural event, such as flood, lightning, earthquake, or hurricane, that leads to a property loss and could not have been prevented by reasonable care or foresight. See VIS MAJOR.

Act to Regulate Commerce (1887)
A compromise of the divergent views of the Senate and the House of Representatives, the act was a product of the Cullom Report (1886). The act applied only to interstate and foreign commerce and, because the language lacked precision, there has been some controversy over the exact scope and interpretation of the act, which attempted to deal with reasonableness of rates, personal discrimination, undue preference and prejudice, and long and short hauls. The Act to Regulate Commerce created the ICC. See INTERSTATE COMMERCE COMMISSION.

actual cost
Cost data based on transactions that have been completed, as contrasted with costs that have been estimated.

actuary
One who calculates risks and rates, on the basis of statistical information, for an insurance company.

A/D
See ANALOG-TO-DIGITAL CONVERTER.

ADAMHA
See ALCOHOL, DRUG ABUSE AND MENTAL HEALTH ADMINISTRATION.

ADC
See ANALOG-TO-DIGITAL CONVERTER.

ad damnum clause
A clause in a legal declaration or complaint of a plaintiff that makes a demand for damages and sets out the amount.

added value tax
See VALUE-ADDED TAX.

address
In data processing, an identification, represented by a name, label, or number, for a register or location in a storage. A part of an instruction word along with commands, tags, and other symbols. Also, the part of an instruction that specifies an operand for the instruction.

ad hoc
Latin, "for this." Refers to a limited or particular situation. An ad hoc committee is one limited to a specific purpose and may be dismissed on completion of its task. An ad hoc decision means "for this purpose only." An ad hoc attorney is one appointed to perform a special task in a particular case.

adjective law
The rules of procedure used by and in courts for enforcing the duties and maintaining the rights defined by the substantive law. Adjective law primarily involves matters of evidence, procedure, and appeals. Also known as *remedial law*.

adjudicate
To exercise judicial power by hearing, trying, and determining the claims of litigants before the court.

adjustable peg
A system that permits changes in the par rate of foreign exchange after a nation has had long-run disequilibrium in its balance of payments. It allows also for short-run variation within a narrow range of a few percent above and below the par value.

adjusted basis
In federal income taxes, the basis used to compute depreciation or gain or loss on sales of fixed or noninventory assets.

adjusted cost basis
For accounting purposes, the value of property equal to the original cost plus improvements less depreciation.

adjusted gross income
For federal income taxes, the gross income of an individual less business expenses where applicable, deductions allowable for income-producing property, certain losses from sales or exchanges of property, self-employment expenses, and moving expenses. Adjusted gross income is the basis for determining the standard deduction, the possible use of the optional tax table, and the limitation on medical costs (except for persons over 65), contributions, and the childcare deduction for working wives.

adjuster
In the insurance industry, an employee of an insurance company authorized to study, and make recommendations to his employer relative to, the cause of an event that has resulted in a claim, the amount of the loss, and the extent of the insurance company's liability.

adjusting entry
Any change in an account required either by an auditor or by accounting policy and expressed in the form of a simple or compound journal entry.

administered price
A price that is purposely influenced by the government. For example, the interest rate for the use of money is determined by the demand for, and the supply of, loanable capital; it is not generally considered to be determined by a free market.

administration
The branch of management concerned with the supervision and operation of an organization.

Administration on Aging
A unit of the Office of Human Development of HEW, AoA is the focus within the federal government of all matters of concern to older people. AoA administers grants to states for planning, coordination, and provision of community services, including nutrition programs; grants to organizations, institutions, and individuals for research and demonstration projects; and grants to public and nonprofit organizations for training.

administrative accounting
That part of the accounting process generally associated with management. See also CONTROLLER.

administrative expense
Expense incurred in the general direction and management of an enterprise; contrasted with expenses incurred by specific functions such as selling or manufacturing.

administrator
A person skilled in administration. In the law, a person to whom letters of administration have been issued by a probate court, giving such person authority to administer, manage, and close the estate of a deceased person. See LETTERS OF ADMINISTRATION.

adoption notice
In transportation, notice given to the effect that one carrier has taken over the operations of another or that a carrier agrees that another carrier's tariff is also binding for it.

ADP
Initials for *automatic data processing.* See DATA PROCESSING.

ad valorem
A property tax or import or other duty computed as a percentage rate of the value of the property.

ad valorem subsidy
A fixed-percentage subsidy granted to producers of commodities as a form of financial aid or relief from hardships resulting from economic conditions beyond the control of the producers. The subsidy is calculated on the basis of the current or prevailing market value of the commodity.

advance bill
See PRO FORMA INVOICE.

advanced charge
A transportation charge advanced by one carrier to another to be collected by the latter carrier from the consignor or consignee.

adverse possession
The acquisition of legal title to the land of another through continuous possession for a period of time prescribed by statute. The possession must be actual, visible, known to the world, and with an intention by the possessor to claim the title as owner against the rights of the true owner. Usually, the claimant must pay the taxes and liens lawfully charged against the property.

adverse selection
The insuring of a group of risks that represents an above-average expectation of loss. Also, the tendency of poor risks to seek insurance.

AE
See ANONYMOS ETAIRIA.

AEA
Initials for *American Electronics Association.* See WEMA.

AEC
See ATOMIC ENERGY COMMISSION.

AECT
Initials for *Association for Educational Communications and Technology.*

"A" end of car
Referring to railroad cars, the end opposite the end with the hand brakes. See "B" END OF CAR.

AES
See AUDIO ENGINEERING SOCIETY.

AFDC
Initials for *Aid to Families with Dependent Children.* See SOCIAL SECURITY ADMINISTRATION.

affidavit
A voluntary statement of facts in writing sworn to before an officer authorized to administer oaths, such as a notary public.

affiliate
A corporation or other organization related to another by owning or being owned, by common management, by a long-term lease of its properties, or by other control devices.

affiliation
A connection existing between a holding or parent company and its subsidiary, or between two corporations or other organizations owned or controlled by a third.

affiliation need
A motivational factor, the desire to be associated with, or to be in the presence of, another person or persons. The need to "belong" to a group.

affirmative warranty
See WARRANTY.

affreightment
A contract for transporting goods by sea. Also known as *charter party* or *ocean bill of lading*.

afghani
Basic unit of currency in Afghanistan.

AFL
See AMERICAN FEDERATION OF LABOR.

AFL–CIO
See AMERICAN FEDERATION OF LABOR–CONGRESS OF INDUSTRIAL ORGANIZATIONS.

a fortiori
Latin, "by a stronger reason." The phrase is often used in judicial opinions to say that, because specific proven facts lead to a certain conclusion, other facts that strengthen the argument for the conclusion follow logically.

AG
See AKTIENGESELLSCHAFT.

AGA
See AMERICAN GAS ASSOCIATION.

age life depreciation
A method used by real-estate appraisers in estimating depreciation of a building, based on expected life.

agency
The relationship of trust in which one person (the agent) is authorized by another (the principal) to represent him in dealing with third parties. See FIDUCIARY.

Agency for International Development

Established in 1961 as part of the U.S. Department of State, AID administers the nonmilitary U.S. foreign aid programs. Congress votes funds; AID determines their use in assisting underdeveloped countries that have shown they want to help themselves become self-supporting. AID helps provide basic needs in areas such as agriculture, education, family planning, and health. The bulk of AID assistance is in the form of long-term, low-interest loans and technical advice. AID encourages U.S. business firms to make investments in underdeveloped countries by conducting surveys of investment opportunities and providing guarantees on certain investments.

agency tariff

In transportation, a tariff published by an agent on behalf of several carriers.

agent

One who represents, acts for, and is accountable to another. A contractual relationship may exist between a principal and an agent, forming an agency. The scope of the contract determines whether the agent is "special" (restricted in his activities) or "general" (equipped with broad powers).

aggregate demand

In economics, the flow of money and expenditures for goods and services during a given time period. The expectations of aggregate demand influence the aggregate supply. See AGGREGATE SUPPLY.

aggregate supply

The amount of goods and services produced by all firms in the economy during a given time period in response to demand expectations. See AGGREGATE DEMAND.

aging

An analysis of individual accounts receivable according to the time elapsed after the due or billing dates.

agribusiness

The sector of the economy involved with the processes and procedures of agriculture, including farming, services, and supplies.

Agricultural Adjustment Acts

In 1933 Congress passed an act designed to control the prices of farm products by regulating the production of those products. In 1938, a second act was passed by Congress which redefined and extended the agricultural policies of the 1933 act that were held unconstitutional by the courts in 1936. The 1938 Agricultural Adjustment Act is a basic U.S. farm law that provides for: (1) price supports of selected farm products at specified levels, to be implemented by purchases and non-recourse loans by the Commodity Credit Corporation; (2) production control through acreage allotments of certain crops; (3) marketing agreements and quotas between the Department of Agriculture and producers in order to control the distribution of selected commodities; (4) payments to farmers and others who follow soil conservation practices; and (5) parity payments to farmers for selected agricultural staples.

Agricultural Stabilization and Conservation Service
A major unit of the U.S. Department of Agriculture that has had, since 1961, direct responsibility for the administration of the nation's agricultural support program.

Agriculture Research Service
An agency of the U.S. Department of Agriculture, ARS provides the necessary knowledge and technology so that farmers can produce efficiently, conserve the environment, and meet the food and fiber needs of the American people. The service also conducts the USDA's basic research in human nutrition and national dietary levels.

AHAM
Initials for *Association of Home Appliance Manufacturers.*

AIA
Initials for *American Institute of Architects.* Also, see AMERICAN IN-STITUTE OF ACCOUNTANTS.

AICP
See ASSOCIATION OF INTERSTATE COMMERCE PRACTITIONERS.

AICPA
See AMERICAN INSTITUTE OF CERTIFIED PUBLIC ACCOUNTANTS.

AID
See AGENCY FOR INTERNATIONAL DEVELOPMENT.

AIDA
Acronym for four fundamentals of selling: *attention, interest, desire, action*. Often used as a test of the merits of an advertising or sales promotion program.

AIEE
Initials for *American Institute of Electrical Engineers*.

AIIE
Initials for *American Institute of Industrial Engineers*.

AIMCO
See ASSOCIATION OF INTERNAL MANAGEMENT CONSULTANTS.

air freight rates
Regulated by the Civil Aeronautics Board, not the Interstate Commerce Commission.

Air Quality Act
A 1967 act of Congress that authorized the establishment of federally funded interstate agencies to provide standards for measuring air pollution and to enforce such standards. The legislation also made funds available for research into sources of air pollution.

AJE
Initials for *adjusting journal entry*. See ADJUSTING ENTRY.

Aksjeselskap
A Norwegian joint stock company. Abbreviated A/S.

Aktiebolaj
A Swedish joint stock company. Abbreviated AB.

Aktiengesellschaft
A joint stock company under Austrian, German, and Swiss business laws; abbreviated AG. Also known in Switzerland as *Société Anonyme* (SA).

Aktieselskab
A Danish public company or corporation. Abbreviated A/S.

ALA
See ALLIANCE FOR LABOR ACTION.

Alcohol, Drug Abuse and Mental Health Administration
A unit of the Public Health Service, ADAMHA is the leading federal partner in the national effort to prevent and treat alcohol abuse and alcoholism, drug abuse, and mental and emotional illness.

Alcohol, Tobacco and Firearms Bureau
A unit of the Department of the Treasury, AT&F monitors the content, labeling, and reuse of alcoholic beverage containers and the classification and labeling of tobacco products. It also enforces and administers regulations for firearms and explosives.

Aldrich-Vreeland Act
A 1908 act of Congress that authorized associations of national banks to issue bank notes secured by commercial paper and state and municipal bonds. The act was intended to be temporary during a period of reorganization of the banking system. An outcome of the reorganization was the establishment of the Federal Reserve System.

Alford, Leon Pratt (1877–1942)
A pioneer in industrial management. See CHURCH, ALEXANDER HAMILTON.

Alger, Jr., Horatio (1832–1899)
Educated at Harvard; teacher, editor, minister, writer of popular fiction. Thought by many to be a fictional person, Horatio Alger, Jr., did exist and is considered to be one of the most widely read writers in American history. Approximately 250 million copies of his stories have been bought in book form. His heroes always rose from tattered poverty to riches and respectability. The "rags to riches" theme has been a symbol and inspiration to small-business entrepreneurs.

ALGOL
Acronym for *Algorithmic Language,* a computer format devised in 1958 and revised in 1960. It is an international algebraic procedural language for programming an electronic data processing system, used more widely in Europe than in the United States. ALGOL is most often used in the programming of scientific problems or as a reference and publication language.

alienation clause
A special type of acceleration clause that requires payment of an entire loan balance upon sale or other transfer of title to real property.

aliquot
A legal term meaning a subdivision or portion of the whole.

all commodity rate
A freight rate that generally applies to any and all commodities.

Alliance for Labor Action
A federation of unions started in 1968 by the United Automobile Workers (which dissociated itself from the AFL–CIO) and the International Brotherhood of Teamsters.

Alliance for Progress
A conference of 20 Latin American states convened at the Inter-American Economic and Social Conference at Punta del Este, Uruguay, in 1961 to formulate and adopt a program to hasten the economic development of Latin American states. The program included an agreement from the United States to provide loans and grants of $20 billion during the ensuing ten-year period in return for a pledge that the Latin American states would direct a greater flow of resources to their own social and economic development. The U.S. Agency for International Development (AID) was given responsibility for administering the program.

allied company
See AFFILIATION.

allocate
To spread a cost systematically over two or more time periods, objects, activities, processes, operations, or products. In government accounting, to transfer an appropriation, or a part thereof, from one agency to another.

allocated material
See RESERVED MATERIAL.

allodial system
Pertaining to allodium freehold. The system of ownership in the United States in which land is owned absolutely, without obligation to sovereigns or superiors.

allonge
An attachment to a document that provides for endorsements when no space for the purpose remains on the document proper.

all-or-none order
A market or limited-price order given to a stockbroker to be executed in its entirety or not at all. Unlike a fill-or-kill order, the all-or-none order is not to be treated as canceled if not executed as soon as represented on the floor of the stock exchange. Bids or offers on behalf of all-or-none orders may not be made in stocks, but may be made in bonds when the number of bonds is fifty or more. See FILL-OR-KILL ORDER.

all-risk cargo insurance
Preferred-risk ocean marine insurance covering all risks. Cargo insurance is usually written on a specified-perils basis.

all-risk protection
A contract that covers all causes of loss except those specifically excluded, and that presumes that the cause of any loss is not the deliberate action of the insured. A high percentage of inland marine insurance policies are written on all-risk basis.

alluvion
An accession to land by the gradual addition of soil or silt caused by the flow of a river or by tides, or sometimes by the gradual receding of a body of water from its banks; the new land belongs to the owner of the land to which the material was added. Also, land added to existing property by such action. Opposite of DILUVION.

alluvium
See ALLUVION.

alphabetic–numeric
In data processing, letters of the alphabet, numerals, and other symbols such as punctuation or mathematical symbols. Also known as *alphanumeric* and *alphameric*.

alphameric
A contraction of *alphabetic–numeric*.

alphanumeric
A contraction of *alphabetic–numeric*.

ALTA title insurance policy
A type of title insurance policy that expands the standard policy coverage to include such risks as unrecorded mechanic's liens, unrecorded

physical easements, facts a physical survey would reveal, water and mineral rights, and rights of parties in possession (such as tenants and buyers under unrecorded instruments). The initials stand for *American Land Title Association*. Formerly known as *ATA* (American Title Association) *title insurance policy*.

alter ego
Latin, "the other I." In law, an agent is the alter ego (or other person) for his principal.

AMA
See AMERICAN MANAGEMENT ASSOCIATIONS; AMERICAN MARKETING ASSOCIATION.

AMA/International
Formerly *International Management Association* (IMA). Set up in 1956 as an affiliate of the American Management Associations, with centers in Argentina, Belgium, Brazil, Canada, Mexico, and Venezuela; headquartered in New York City.

amalgamation
The act of combining under a single head all or part of the assets and liabilities of two or more business units by merger or consolidation.

AMC
See ASSOCIATION OF MANAGEMENT CONSULTANTS.

amenities
Conditions of agreeable living or beneficial influence arising from the location of, or improvements to, property, especially a home.

amenity value
The value of the pleasures of property, such as a good neighborhood location with desirable schools and parks.

American Accounting Association
AAA was formed in 1935 as the successor to the American Association of University Instructors in Accounting (AAUIA), which had been established in 1916. AAA is a professional association, primarily academic but open to accounting practitioners, economists, and others interested in the development of accounting principles and standards.

American Association of Advertising Agencies (AAAA)
A trade association whose function is to foster, strengthen, and improve the advertising agency industry, to advance the cause and purpose of advertising as a marketing vehicle, and to provide a forum for communications, education, and the exchange of knowledge among its members.

American Bar Association (ABA)
The ABA was founded at Saratoga Springs, New York, in 1878 as a voluntary association of lawyers, judges, and teachers of law in the United States and its possessions. Some of its primary objectives are to advance jurisprudence, to promote the administration of justice and uniformity of laws, and to foster high standards of legal education and ethics in the practice of law.

American Bureau of Shipping
Publishes the *Record,* which is both an annual compilation of technical information on American and foreign ships and a reference for rating bureaus and insurance companies in establishing rates for ocean marine insurance. The publication is similar to *Lloyd's Register of British and Foreign Shipping*.

American Federation of Labor
An organization of trade unions in the United States and Canada created in 1881. In 1955, the AFL merged with the Congress of Industrial Organizations (CIO) to form the AFL–CIO.

American Federation of Labor–Congress of Industrial Organizations
A federation of labor unions formed in 1955 by a merger of the AFL and CIO to improve wages, hours, and conditions of workers and to enhance the benefits of free collective bargaining. It exercises no control over member unions other than requiring them to abide by its constitution and code of ethical practices.

American Gas Association
A trade association of producers of gas-operated equipment and appliances.

American Hull Underwriters Syndicate
The syndicate developed a rating system for all major vessels as to their fitness for the type of work for which they are built, and has prepared uniform policies that are used by most marine insurance companies.

American Institute for Property and Liability Underwriters
The institute awards the designation of chartered property casualty underwriter (CPCU) to those in the field of property and casualty insurance who successfully complete a series of examinations, among other requirements. These individuals are principally agents, brokers, and employees of insurers.

American Institute of Accountants
A professional body incorporated in 1916; originally an integral part of the American Association of Public Accountants, which was established in 1887. AIA is now known as the AMERICAN INSTITUTE OF CERTIFIED PUBLIC ACCOUNTANTS.

American Institute of Certified Public Accountants
A professional association of accountants originally incorporated as the American Institute of Accountants (AIA); its present name was adopted in 1953. The AICPA formulates statements of policy and professional practice for its members.

American Institute of Marine Underwriters
An organization concerned primarily with the collecting of marine information and the passage of legislation beneficial to carriers with respect to reduction of hazards.

American Lloyds Association
Intended to provide a service in the United States similar to that performed by Lloyd's of London. See LLOYD'S OF LONDON.

American Management Associations
Founded in 1923 as a nonprofit organization dedicated to research and training in, and publication of information and materials about, numerous management disciplines.

American Marketing Association
An organization of professional people engaged in marketing activities whose purpose is the advancement of the discipline of marketing. The present organization resulted from the consolidation of the American Marketing Society and the National Association of Marketing Teachers.

American National Standards Institute, Inc. (ANSI)
Established in 1918 as the American Engineering Standards Committee, this institute represents the United States on the International

Organization for Standards. The institute's members include approximately 150 national trade associations and 900 companies and corporations. Generally referred to as ANSI.

American selling price
A method of customs valuation that is applied to several groups of U.S. imports. The ASP uses the domestic price of competing goods, which is generally higher than that prevailing in other countries.

American Society for Industrial Security (ASIS)
An association of manufacturers, suppliers, and individuals involved with hardware and techniques for assuring the security of information, property, and personnel in private enterprises.

American Society for Training and Development
A trade association for individuals engaged in training activities. Its primary purpose is the dissemination of knowledge and information pertaining to techniques for personnel training and development.

American Society of Certified Public Accountants
A professional body established in 1921, it merged with the American Institute of Accountants (AIA) in 1935.

American Stock Exchange
Abbreviated to ASE or Amex, sometimes referred to as the *curb*. See CURB EXCHANGE.

American Stock Exchange Index (ASEI)
Published hourly by the American Stock Exchange as an indicator of the performance of issues on the exchange, it is computed to provide the actual average price of all stocks and warrants listed.

AMEX
Acronym for *American Stock Exchange*.

AMHS
Initials for *American Material Handling Society*.

AMMI
Initials for *American Merchant Marine Institute*.

AMO
Initials for *Accredited Management Organization*.

amortize
To write off all or a portion of the cost of an asset; to depreciate or deplete. Also, to retire a debt over a period of years.

amortized cost
In accounting, the cost of an asset minus the portions written off or depreciated.

AMS
Initials for *Administrative Management Society*. Formerly the National Office Managers Association (NOMA).

AMTORG
The state trading agency of the Soviet Union.

analog
The representation of relative numerical quantities or values.

analog computer
A computer that represents variables by physical analogies and solves problems by translating physical conditions such as flow, pressure, temperature, voltage, current, and angular position into related mechanical or electrical quantities. In general, a computer that uses an analog for each variable and produces analogs as outputs. An analog computer measures continuously, whereas a digital computer counts discretely.

analog panel meter
A panel, mounted on a measuring instrument, that indicates relative values. The APM consists essentially of a low-mass coil of wire to which a pointer has been affixed. The coil is supported by miniature bearings and pivots between the poles of a permanent magnet. As current flows through the coil, the interaction of magnetic fields causes the coil to rotate, moving the pointer in an arc. Generally, the pointer is moved across an arc that has been calibrated in relative values with respect to the strength of the interactive magnetic fields. See DIGITAL PANEL METER.

analog representation
A representation that does not have discrete values but is continuously variable.

analog-to-digital converter
Any device, circuitry, or system that accepts analog representations and alters or converts them to discrete values or digital representations.

analyst
In management, a person skilled in the definition of problems and in the development of techniques for solutions. In data processing, a person skilled in the use of the computer as a problem-solving tool.

analytical forecasting
Forecasting gross national product by estimating the components of demand and then combining them into an overall estimate.

analytic schedule
See DEAN SCHEDULE.

anarchism
A theory of a society without any form of coercive government. The theory postulates that harmony among the members of the society, as well as the production of goods, can be attained by voluntary cooperation. There would be no privately held property, all being held collectively by cooperating groups.

anchor lease
A lease, usually favorable, given to a large or well-known retail business in order to attract the public to an area such as a shopping center.

anchor tenant
A tenant in an ANCHOR LEASE.

ANCOM
See ANDEAN COMMON MARKET.

Andean Common Market
An economic alliance of Bolivia, Chile, Colombia, Ecuador, Peru, and Venezuela. Abbreviated ANCOM.

and gate
A signal circuit with two or more input wires in which the output wire gives a signal only when all input wires receive simultaneous signals.

Animal and Plant Health Inspection Service
An agency of the USDA, APHIS conducts regulatory and control programs to protect the wholesomeness of meat and poultry products for human consumption. Areas covered by these programs include meat and poultry inspection, animal and plant quarantine, and disease and pest control.

annual audit
An audit by a professional accountant that covers transactions for a period of one year.

annual closing
In accounting, the posting of closing entries that takes place at the end of a fiscal year.

annual transit policy
Insurance obtained to cover incoming and outgoing commercial shipments. It is applicable to shipments via railroad, railway express, interstate or intrastate motor carriers, coastwise steamers, or the insured's own vehicles. This policy is usually written on a specified-perils basis.

annuitant
The recipient of an annuity.

annuity
A series of periodic and equal payments made at fixed intervals. In the case of a retired employee who receives such payments, the annuity is referred to as a *pension.*

annuity fund
The fund that is created as a result of an annuity agreement.

annuity method
A method of depreciating an asset. See DEPRECIATION.

anonymos etairia
A joint stock company under Greek law, in which shareholders are liable only to the extent of their capital investments. Abbreviated AE.

ANSI
See AMERICAN NATIONAL STANDARDS INSTITUTE, INC.

anticipated cost
An addition to operating costs that results from the use of LIFO inventory evaluation during a period of rising prices. Also known as *inventory profit*.

anticipated profit
A profit that is recorded before being realized; paper profit. Also known as *anticipatory profit*.

anticipatory repudiation
A breach of contract occurring when a buyer of real estate informs the seller before closing escrow that he does not plan to fulfill the transaction.

antidumping tariff
A tariff applied by a government to discourage market dumping of imported goods intended for sale in the importing country at prices significantly below those charged for similar goods produced in the country of import. See COUNTERVAILING DUTY and DUMPING.

Anti-Injunction Act
See NORRIS–LA GUARDIA ACT.

Antiracketeering Act
A 1934 act of Congress that, with its subsequent amendments, identifies the crimes of robbery and extortion as federal offenses when these have the effect of interrupting the free flow of interstate commerce.

Anti-Strikebreaker Law
See BYRNES ACT.

Antitrust Division
A unit of the Justice Department formed in 1890. It regulates all activity that could affect interstate commerce, from trade restraints and illegal agreements to mergers.

antitrust laws
Acts passed by Congress since 1890 to prevent monopoly and to maintain competition. The major acts are the Sherman Antitrust Act (1890), the Clayton Antitrust Act (1914), the Federal Trade Commission Act (1914), the Robinson-Patman Act (1936), the Wheeler-Lea Act (1938), and the Celler Antimerger Act (1950).

AoA
See ADMINISTRATION ON AGING.

AOQ
See AVERAGE OUTGOING QUALITY.

APA
See ASSISTANCE PAYMENTS ADMINISTRATION.

APB
See ACCOUNTING PRINCIPLES BOARD.

APCO
See ASSOCIATION OF PUBLIC-SAFETY COMMUNICATIONS OFFICERS.

APHIS
See ANIMAL AND PLANT HEALTH INSPECTION SERVICE.

APICS
Initials for *American Production and Inventory Control Society.*

APM
See ANALOG PANEL METER.

a posteriori
Latin, "from the latter." Relating to the process of reasoning whereby principles or other propositions are derived from observation.

Appalachia
An economically depressed region that encompasses parts of nine states from Pennsylvania to Alabama along the Appalachian highlands.

apparent effectiveness
Factors of managerial behavior which, although considered to be admirable, may not be related to or appropriate to the output requirements of the job. Examples include characteristics such as always maintaining a tidy desk, being good at public relations, making decisions quickly, and arriving promptly for meetings or work.

apparent title
See COLOR OF TITLE.

applied cost
In accounting, a cost that has been allocated to a product, process, or other specific activity of an enterprise.

apportionment
An equitable division of real estate charges and expenses between a buyer and seller at the date of the closing of title. Usually the seller pays expenses incurred up to that date and the buyer assumes expenses thereafter.

appraisal method
An obsolete method of depreciating an asset, wherein the annual depreciation expense is the difference between the appraised values of the asset at the beginning and at the end of the depreciation period.

appreciation
The increase in the value of a specific asset with reference to book value or acquisition cost.

appropriated retained earnings
Retained income that is earmarked for specific or general purposes, taking the form of a separate account to which retained earnings are transferred. The financial records and the statement of earnings of a corporation that has established such an account record the existence of such a fund or account.

appropriation
The earmarking of funds for some specific or general purpose; a distribution of net income to various accounts; the amount of future expenditures that has been approved.

appropriation account
In government accounting, the account of a government agency to which the amount of an appropriation is credited. Also, a British phrase for the account to which the profit-and-loss balance for the year is carried and taxes and dividends are charged; the balance is transferred to revenue reserves.

appropriation act
A law that provides funds for the operation of a government agency over a specified period, usually one year.

appropriation period
In government accounting, the period of time, usually one year, for the expenditure or obligation of an appropriation.

appropriation section
A section of an income statement that shows the disposition of net income between dividends, surplus reserves, and earned surplus.

a priori
Latin, "from the former." A generalization that rests on presuppositions, not on proven facts.

a priori probability
In statistics, if one designates a particular outcome as signifying success and the total number of possible outcomes is known and each is equally likely, then, in a large number of trials, the ratio of the number of possible successes to the total number of outcomes is the probability of success. For example, a die has six possible outcomes on any one throw. The probability of throwing any declared number is 1/6. There are six possible outcomes, only one of which can be declared "success." This class of probability is determined relatively easily whenever complete information is available to the analyst on the various ways an event may occur. See EMPIRICAL PROBABILITY.

APT
Acronym for *Automatically Programmed Tools,* a computer programming language that produces instructions for the control and operation of machine tools.

AQ
Initials for *any quantity.* In transportation, a rating of charges that applies to an article regardless of weight or quantity.

AQL
See ACCEPTABLE QUALITY LEVEL.

AR
Initials for *all rail.* A shipment made exclusively by railroad.

arbitrage
A technique used to take advantage of differences in market prices for shares of stock. If, for example, WXR stock can be bought in New

York for $10 a share and sold in London at $10.50, an arbitrageur may simultaneously purchase WXR stock in New York and sell the same amount in London, making a profit of 50 cents a share, less expenses. The technique also applies to the purchase and selling of commodities. Arbitrage tends to equalize prices of a commodity in different markets.

arbitration
Settlement of differences between a labor union and management by the use of an impartial third party, called an arbitrator, who is acceptable to both sides and whose decision is binding and legally enforceable on the participants. The arbitrator's decision is based entirely on his interpretation of the language of the contract between the parties as it applies to the specific disagreement.

arguendo
Latin, "in the course of an argument"; in law, to make a case by way of argument or in an argument.

Argyris, Chris
Born in 1923; professor of organizational behavior at Yale University; specialist in industrial relations. A prolific writer of books (17) and a frequent contributor to professional journals. Argyris reasoned that a basic drive of human beings is to experience success in living and in their human condition. By "success" Argyris means that the interpersonal relationships of human beings will tend to lead them to become more aware and accepting of themselves and others. Argyris goes on to argue that descriptive, nonevaluative feedback makes it possible for individuals to achieve their excellence. See IMMATURITY-MATURITY THEORY.

arithmetic mean
See MEAN.

armored car insurance
May be issued either as a separate policy or as an endorsement to a registered mail or first class mail contract. Rates are determined by an analysis of the individual hazards to which the goods may be exposed. The same conditions apply to messenger insurance.

ARS
See AGRICULTURE RESEARCH SERVICE.

artificial person

An enterprise, business firm, or organization that has powers, either granted by law or by custom, that resemble those of a natural person. See NATURAL PERSON and PERSONA FICTA.

artisan's lien

A legal claim against another's property as security by a person who has invested labor upon, or added value to, such property and who has not been reimbursed for the value of the labor and materials.

A/S

See AKTIESELSKAB and AKSJESELSKAP.

ASA

Acronym for *American Standards Association* and *Acoustical Society of America*.

ASCII

See USASCII.

ASCPA:

See AMERICAN SOCIETY OF CERTIFIED PUBLIC ACCOUTANTS.

ASE

See AMERICAN STOCK EXCHANGE.

ASEI

See AMERICAN STOCK EXCHANGE INDEX.

ASIS

See AMERICAN SOCIETY FOR INDUSTRIAL SECURITY.

as is

Phrase used to denote merchandise that is offered for sale just "as it is," without warranty and without recourse to the seller after the sale has been made.

asking price

The price at which a good or a security is offered for sale. In some circumstances, such as in local retailing, asking price is taken to indicate willingness on the part of the seller to negotiate the final selling price to some level below the asking price.

ASN
See AVERAGE SAMPLE NUMBER.

ASP
See AMERICAN SELLING PRICE.

aspect cards
See PEEK-A-BOO SYSTEM.

assemble
In data processing, to integrate subroutines that are supplied, selected, or generated into the main routine by means of preset parameters, by adapting, or by changing relative and symbolic addresses to absolute form.

assembly chart
See GOZINTO CHART.

assembly kit list
In manufacturing, a bill of material, assigned an order number, that contains the quantity and total number of parts needed to complete a specific job order.

assessed value
The value of property as appraised for taxation.

assessment
The process of valuing property for establishing taxation. Any recurrent tax levied by a government authority, such as for property or real-estate taxes. A special tax levied for improvements or repairs to community property under the direct control of a municipal authority; also known as a *special assessment tax* or *improvement tax*. A levy on stockholders, members of an organization, or owners of special beneficial interests for the purpose of raising additional capital.

assessment bonds
Municipal bonds that are to be repaid through assessments made against property—usually against the property that has benefited from the improvements financed by the bond issue.

asset
A physical (tangible) object or a right (intangible) that has economic value to its owner. For balance-sheet purposes, assets are broadly

grouped as current, fixed, or intangible, and within these groupings are descriptive titles, such as receivables, inventories, investments, plant and equipment, goodwill, and patents.

assigned material
See RESERVED MATERIAL.

assigned-risk pools
A group of insurance companies who jointly issue a policy to a firm or an individual considered to represent an undesirable, high risk. Such risks are assigned to companies within the pool on a pro rata basis.

assignee
One to whom an ASSIGNMENT has been made.

assignment
The transfer from one party to another of the right or interest in real property, or of the title to and interest in an item of personal property; for example, ownership of a patent or a receivable may be assigned or transferred. Also, the transfer from one person to another of a right that usually arises out of a contract. Such rights are called *choses in action,* or the right one person has to recover money or property from another by a judicial proceeding. Such a right might involve a contract, claims for money, debts, and property. Notes, drafts, stock certificates, bills of lading, warehouse receipts, and insurance policies are examples of choses in action and are called *tangible choses.* Book accounts, simple debts, and obligations not evidenced by formal writing are called *intangible choses.* Choses in action may be transferred by assignment.

assignment clauses
In insurance, clauses referring to the assignment of proceeds of a policy before a loss occurs. A collateral assignment is sometimes made, in which the policy is assigned as security for a debt. A life insurance policy may be assigned to a lender as collateral for a loan. After a loss has occurred, the benefits may be assigned like any other fund.

assignor
One who makes an ASSIGNMENT.

Assistance Payments Administration
A unit of the Social and Rehabilitation Service of HEW, APA makes grants to states to assist them in providing cash payments to needy

families with dependent children. APA is also responsible for assistance to elderly, blind, and disabled persons in Guam, Puerto Rico, and the Virgin Islands and to ill and destitute American citizens returned from foreign countries. It requires applicants and recipients to enroll in the Work Incentive Program (WIN)—with exceptions specified in the law—to gain guidance and assistance in getting a job or in being trained for a job.

associate broker
A licensed natural or legal person who acts for another in a real estate or related transaction.

associated company
A corporation wherein 50 percent of the voting capital stock is owned by another. In British usage, a corporation in which another company holds a trade investment. See TRADE INVESTMENT.

Associated Factory Mutual Fire Insurance Companies
An association of eight independent mutual companies organized to provide insurance coverage for real properties that meet high standards of building construction.

Association of Casualty and Surety Companies
An association active in preparing and recommending legislation intended to be helpful in loss prevention. The association also maintains an index division, which keeps a file on all personal injury claims. In cooperation with law enforcement agencies, it has assisted in breaking up fraudulent claims organizations.

Association of Consulting Management Engineers
Founded in 1929, ACME represents many large consulting firms in the field of management.

Association of Internal Management Consultants
AIMCO was founded in 1970 for those who hold staff positions as consultants to a corporation.

Association of Interstate Commerce Practitioners
A group of attorneys and practitioners who hold certificates permitting them to practice before the Interstate Commerce Commission. Its purpose is to maintain high standards of technical procedure and ethics among those who practice in or have an interest in this special field of law.

Association of Management Consultants
AMC was founded in 1959 to represent management consulting firms. One-man companies comprise about half the membership.

Association of Public-Safety Communications Officers
An association of individuals and business firms involved with the development of hardware and techniques for improving radio and telephone communications specifically related to public safety, as for police and fire departments.

assumed liability
The assumption of the payment of an obligation incurred by another.

assumpsit
Latin, "he undertook." An action at common law to recover damages for a breach of contract. Assumpsit is historically based on an implied undertaking to properly perform a duty.

assured
A beneficiary of an insurance policy; a person who would be indemnified by another against a risk of loss.

ASTD
See AMERICAN SOCIETY FOR TRAINING AND DEVELOPMENT.

ASTM
Initials for *American Society for Testing Materials.*

astronomical theory of the business cycle
See SUNSPOT THEORY and JEVONS, WILLIAM STANLEY.

ATA
Initials for *American Trucking Associations.*

ATAA
Initials for *Air Transport Association of America.*

ATA carnet
International customs document, recognized by countries that are parties to the ATA Convention, and used by firms that send or take goods abroad on a temporary basis as sales samples or exhibits at international conventions. Goods covered by the ATA carnet are imported and exported free of customs duties. See TIR CARNET.

AT&F
See ALCOHOL, TOBACCO AND FIREARMS BUREAU.

ATA title insurance policy
See ALTA TITLE INSURANCE POLICY.

ATMI
Initials for *American Textile Manufacturers Institute, Inc.* A trade association.

Atomic Energy Act
A 1946 act of Congress that provided for public assistance to private research, the dissemination of technical information and knowledge (consistent with national security), federal research and development, and control over the production, ownership, and use of fissionable materials. The act is administered by the Atomic Energy Commission.

Atomic Energy Commission
A five-member commission of the U.S. government charged by law with the development of policies that will promote public and private research into nuclear fission, the dissemination and exchange of scientific information on such research, government ownership and exploitation of fissionable materials in the interests of national security, and the application of atomic energy to industrial operations after proper international safeguards have been established. AEC administers the Atomic Energy Act of 1946; it was transferred to the U.S. Department of Energy in 1977.

atomistic society
An economy in which there is a distinct preponderance of small, independent producing units, as compared with large aggregates of capital in industry and trade.

at par
In securities trading, at par is the quotation or price that is equal to the face or nominal value of the security being traded; also a fixed transfer rate of foreign exchange.

attachment
A legal proceeding that accompanies a court action by which a plaintiff may acquire a lien on a defendant's property as a security for the payment of any judgment the plaintiff may recover. It is provisional and independent of the court action and is usually provided for by

statute. One person, for example, sues another and, before judgment, attaches property belonging to the one being sued in order to make certain of the payment that may eventually be secured by judicial action.

at-the-close order
A stock market order to buy or sell that is to be executed at or as near to the close of the trading day as is practicable; any such order or portion thereof not so executed is treated as canceled. See AT-THE-OPENING ORDER.

at-the-opening order
A stock market order to buy or sell that is to be executed at the opening of the stock or not at all; any such order or portion thereof not so executed is treated as canceled. See AT-THE-CLOSE ORDER.

attorney-at-law
A licensed practitioner of law. Also known as a *lawyer* or a *counselor.*

attorney in fact
A person to whom a power of attorney is given, authorizing him to act for another. See POWER OF ATTORNEY.

attorney's opinion of title
In real estate, a legal document written and signed by an attorney, stating his opinion as to whether a seller may transfer a good title. See GOOD TITLE.

attribute gage
See GO NO-GO GAGE.

Audio Engineering Society
A professional association of engineers and other persons interested or active in the design, development, or marketing of audio equipment.

audit adjustment
An adjusting entry to a journal resulting from an examination by a public accountant.

Audit Bureau of Circulation
An independent organization established in 1914, ABC provides certified evidence of the paid circulation of publications in the United States.

audit certificate
The certification of a financial statement by a certified public accountant; an *auditor's report*.

audit period
The period of time covered by an audit.

audit trail
A notation accompanying a transaction entry or posting that refers to its source records or documents.

audit year
The year covered in an annual or balance-sheet audit; usually the fiscal year. See FISCAL YEAR.

audited voucher
A voucher that has been examined and approved for payment.

auditor
A person engaged to examine the financial records of a firm and to report his observations and findings. He may be an employee of the firm whose records are being audited or an outside individual or member of a professional auditing group.

auditor's report
A written declaration prepared by an auditor following an audit conducted by him. Using standard language, it is addressed to the management of the firm whose financial records have been audited, and it contains details of the scope of the audit, comments on operating results and financial condition, a funds-flow statement, causes of changes as compared with preceding years, and procedural suggestions. The auditor may or may not express an opinion about the fairness or unfairness of the data as being an accurate representation of the financial condition of the firm. If the auditor is unable to express an opinion, he explains his reasons for this in a *disclaimer of opinion*.

authoritarian leadership
A style of management in which the leader plays a strong, directive role in setting group goals and in planning and directing the activities of the members of the group. The authoritarian leader delegates few of the functions of leadership to the members of the group. See LAISSEZ-FAIRE and DEMOCRATIC LEADERSHIP.

authorized capital stock
The number of shares and the par or stated value of the capital stock
that may be issued by a corporation under its articles of incorporation.
In some instances, the stockholders or directors may determine the
stated value per share.

autocrat
A basic style of management characterized by inappropriate emphasis
on task orientation at the cost of relationships orientation. The autocrat
is perceived as having no confidence in others, as unpleasant, and as
interested only in the immediate task. See RELATIONSHIPS ORIENTA-
TION and TASK ORIENTATION

automatic dividend-reinvestment plan
An agreement between a shareholder and a mutual fund, whereby dividends are automatically used to purchase additional shares of stock in
the fund.

automatic reinstatement
The continuance of the total effectiveness of an insurance contract,
after a loss has occurred, in an amount equal to the face value of the
contract.

automatic reinstatement clause
An insurance policy clause that brings coverage up to the full face
amount despite payments against losses, assuming the property has
been restored to its insured value. Some time ago, the payment of any
loss to an insured reduced the amount of insurance in force. Today,
most insurance policies either have automatic reinstatement clauses or
require a waiting period before the full coverage is reinstated.

automatic stop
An automatic halting of a computer processing operation as the result
of an error detected by built-in checking devices.

automobile dealers' direct damage insurance
A type of insurance policy that protects the interests of dealers for
automobiles in their care that have not been sold. Coverage automatically terminates for the vehicle when it has been sold. Usually written
to cover fire and theft, but collision may be included.

autonomous consumption
In economics, the minimum level of nominal expenditure people plan to make for consumable goods, regardless of their level of nominal disposable income.

autonomous transactions
See COMPENSATORY TRANSACTIONS.

auxiliary activities
In institutional accounting, the business operations carried for the service of employees and patrons but not necessarily directly related to the primary functions and purposes of the institution. Examples are found in a university that maintains dormitories, a bookstore, cafeterias, and so on.

auxiliary storage
In data processing, a supplementary storage that may take the form of a magnetic drum, disc, magnetic tape, or other similar storage medium.

availability
In industrial psychology, availability reflects the perceived limitations of the environment. It is determined by the accessibility of goals that can satisfy a given need, as perceived by the individual.

available assets
Assets that are free for general use, free of encumbrance or lien, and not serving as collateral for an obligation.

available quantity
In materials requirements planning (MRP), the available quantity of a given part is equal to the sum of the on-hand quantities in all stock locations.

average cost
Total cost divided by total quantity; a generally accepted basis for inventory valuation.

average demurrage agreement
In transportation, an agreement to offset detention debits with credits. See DEMURRAGE.

average outgoing quality
A term that applies to a 100 percent inspection procedure to remove all defective items from a rejected lot, which are then to be replaced by acceptable items.

average outgoing quality limit
The maximum AOQ value that is associated with a given sampling plan when inspection of each rejected lot of goods is practiced. It represents the poorest of the averaged quality levels that will exist in items passed into inventory under AOQ inspection procedures.

average sample number
The number of items, on the average, that an inspector can expect to examine from an incoming lot before he will be able to reach a decision whether to accept or reject the lot with respect to quality.

averaging
See DOLLAR COST AVERAGING.

avoirdupois pound
Equal to 0.45359237 kilograms.

avulsion
The tearing away of soil by the action of water.

A/W
Abbreviation for *actual or gross shipping weight.*

AW
Initials for *all water.* A shipment made exclusively by water.

AWS
Initials for *American Welding Society.*

Babbage, Charles (1792–1871)

An Englishman, specialist in production economics. He augmented Adam Smith's observations. Basically a mathematician who became interested in manufacturing, he questioned many existing practices and wrote *On the Economy of Machinery and Manufactures* (1832). In addition to the productivity advantages through the division of labor cited by Adam Smith, Babbage recognized the principle of levels of pay or compensation according to the utilization of skills. See SMITH, ADAM.

Babeuf, François Émile

Born in 1760, Babeuf was a product of the French revolution and a supporter of the Reign of Terror. He died in 1797 under the blade of the guillotine. Babeuf was an early socialist and held that "nature has given to every man an equal right in the enjoyment of all goods." He believed in national ownership of all large enterprises in the business world and eventual nationalization of all private property by the abolishment of inheritance. Production and distribution were to be directed by an elected government, nobody who refused to do useful work could have political rights, and teachings contrary to the regime were to be forbidden. He also referred to himself as "Gracchus."

backdoor financing

A means of financing first used in the 1930's by government agencies to obtain funds without congressional approval by borrowing directly from the U.S. Treasury.

backlog

Orders that have been accepted and entered in the financial, sales, and job records of performance but for some reason have not yet been shipped.

back order
The portion of a customer's order that has not been shipped against an accepted order that is in backlog. The usual reason for a back order is materials shortages, although there may be other causes; for instance, the customer may have exceeded his or her credit limit.

backward scheduling
A production-scheduling technique wherein the schedule is calculated by starting with the due date for completion and working backward to determine the date at which the job must be started.

bad debt
An account receivable that is uncollectible.

bad faith
In the law, the term means "actual intent" to mislead or deceive another. The important word is "intent." Misleading by a careless or inadvertently wrong statement does not constitute bad faith.

bad title
A defective legal document used as evidence of lawful ownership of land.

Bagehot, Walter (1826–1877)
A British banker and economist, educated at University College, London, Bagehot joined his father's banking and shipping business. He married the daughter of James Wilson, founder of the *Economist,* a London newspaper, of which he became the editor in 1860. A well-informed economist and a follower, with some reservations, of the philosophy of Ricardo, he described the English banking system in his book *The Lombard Street* (1873), considered to be a classic. In other writing, Bagehot discussed economic evolution and showed the force of customs and habits in economic behavior and their effects on competition. He came to the conclusion that competition does not always produce results that are in the best interests of humankind.

baht
Basic unit of currency in Thailand.

bail
The security that is pledged to enable an arrested or imprisoned person to be temporarily released until his appearance is required at a specified place and time.

bailee
A person who is entrusted with the possession of goods and, by a warehouse receipt, bill of lading, or other document of title, acknowledges such possession and contracts to deliver those goods. See BAILMENT.

bailment
A transfer of possession of goods without the passing of title, as on consignment for safekeeping, repair, or sale. The person making the delivery of the goods is the bailor, the recipient is the bailee. No one can become a bailee without his written consent. A bailor need not be the owner of the goods. A bailee has a property interest in the bailed goods. A bailee may not deny the bailor's title. The bailor must warn the bailee of any hidden dangers within the condition of the goods. The bailee must return the goods at the end of the bailment. The bailee must exercise ordinary care with the goods. A bailment constitutes a contract, express or implied, that the purpose of the delivery or transfer will be carried out.

bailor
See BAILMENT.

balanced budget
A budget in which the expenditures forecast for a given period of operations are equal to the expected revenues for the same period. See BUDGET DEFICIT and BUDGET SURPLUS.

balanced economy
When imports equal exports in dollar value, the national economy is said to be in balance.

balanced fund
A mutual fund that has an investment policy of balancing its portfolio, usually between bonds and common stocks.

balanced loading
Scheduling a mix of work in a department so that other departments are neither overloaded nor underloaded when the work is sent to them for further processing.

balance due
The quantity of material or parts ordered on a purchase order or requisitioned on a work order but not yet received.

balance-due bill
See DUE BILL.

balance of payments
A record of all transactions between the residents of one country and the rest of the world, with payments expressed in terms of the country's currency. In effect, the balance-of-payments summation is the country's balance sheet of receipts and disbursements for a given period. Overall deficits or surpluses are sometimes brought into balance by movements in the gold and foreign-exchange reserves.

balance-of-stores record
In production, a double-entry record system that shows at all times the balances of material on order and available for future orders in addition to the balance of inventory items on hand.

balance of trade
The difference between the money value of a country's merchandise imports and the money value of its merchandise exports. A country is said to have a balance-of-trade surplus if it exports more than it imports and a deficit if it imports more than it exports.

balance on current account
In economics, the net value of a nation's exports of goods and services, plus or minus all unilateral money transfers abroad, such as remittances, Social Security payments, and grants in aid.

balance sheet
A condensed statement that shows the nature and amount of a company's assets, liabilities, and capital on a given date. In dollar amounts, the balance sheet shows what the company owns, what it owes, and the stockholders' ownership interest in the company. See CONSOLIDATED BALANCE SHEET.

balboa
Basic unit of currency in Panama.

balloon mortgage
A mortgage with a large last payment. See BALLOON PAYMENT.

balloon payment
A large final payment on a note. Any final payment that is at least twice the smallest periodic or installment payment is considered to be a balloon payment.

Baltimore method
In real estate, a method for estimating the value of corner lots. It assumes that the corner lot is equal in value to the combined value of the two inside lots adjoining. See BERNARD RULE.

banana republic
A small, usually tropical, country that depends heavily on, and is dominated by, foreign capital. Some of these countries are economically dependent on their fruit-exporting trade, hence the name.

bank
In production, a quantity of materials awaiting further processing. "Bank" can refer to raw materials, semifinished stores or hold points, or a work backlog maintained behind a work center.

bank draft
An order issued by a seller's bank against a purchaser's bank directing payment of money, usually through an intermediary bank. Bank drafts generally are negotiable and are similar to the checks drawn against standard checking accounts except that they are drawn by one bank on its account in another bank.

banker's acceptance
An instrument used in financing foreign trade. It makes possible the payment of cash to an exporter for all or part of the amount of a shipment made by him. See BILL OF EXCHANGE.

bank note
A promise made by a bank to the bearer of a note, which is intended to serve as money. Since 1935, the issuance of bank notes has been confined to the FEDERAL RESERVE SYSTEM.

Bankruptcy Act of 1938
This act of Congress provided a procedure for reorganization of financially troubled firms. The Securities and Exchange Commission assists the courts to assure soundness and fairness in the reorganization plans.

bank statement
The formal, periodic statement of assets, liabilities, and net worth of a bank. Also, the statement issued periodically by a bank to its customer.

bar
A term used to refer to the entire body of the profession of practicing attorneys. Also, a railing in the courtroom separating the judges from the prisoners, witnesses, plaintiffs, defendants, and attorneys.

bar chart
A diagram for comparing the absolute magnitudes of several variables. Simple bar charts are one-dimensional comparisons composed of a number of bars that are spaced so that they do not touch each other. (see HISTOGRAM). An absolute-component bar chart uses a single scale for the different variables being measured with the heights or lengths of the bars varying in direct relation to the quantity each represents. On a relative-component bar chart the bars are equal to each other in height or length, representing the same total (100 percent, for example), but the bars are segmented into different relative-component values.

bargain and sale deed
In real estate, a written document that transfers title to the property described in the deed, but without any guarantees whatsoever.

Barnard, Chester Irving (1886–1961)
An American business executive, public administrator, and sociologist, Barnard specialized in the nature of corporate organization. His book *Functions of the Executive,* published in 1938, was widely influential in the teaching of sociology and business theory. Barnard stressed the cooperative nature of the business organization, observing that executive ability to deal with practical matters tends to diminish when the same problems are presented in theoretical terms. He is considered to have been one of the pioneers of scientific management, continuing where Henri Fayol left off. See FAYOL, HENRI.

barratry
An obsolete term in ocean marine insurance for the dishonesty of master and/or crew, such as absconding with the cargo. This coverage is actually a fidelity bond on the ship's officers and crew.

barter
The exchange of goods or services without the use of money or other medium of exchange.

base and meridian
Imaginary lines used by surveyors to find and describe the location of tracts of land.

base period
The period or moment of time chosen as a standard of comparison with other periods or moments of time. Under the average income concept which may be used for computing federal income tax, the base period

consists of the four taxable years immediately preceding the year for which averaging is elected. Under federal excess-profits-tax regulations, the base period used for computing the excess-profits tax may be the 48-month period ended March 31, 1950, for certain corporations, or the four-year period of 1946–1949.

In economics, the level of activity for the base period (usually a year) is commonly assigned an index value of 100. An index value of, say, 118 for another period would indicate a level of activity 18 percent higher than that for the base period.

base stock system
In production, a blend of the fixed-order-quantity and the fixed-reorder-cycle systems. The base stock system uses information regarding customer orders to establish demand at each stock point directly rather than passing the information through a chain of operations and stock points. Orders are placed to replenish inventories to the "base stock" level, which is sufficient for "buffer stock" plus a quantity calculated to cover current use. See BUFFER INVENTORIES.

base year
A reference year established for purposes of comparison and the indication of trends or changes. See BASE PERIOD.

BASIC
Acronym for *Beginner's All-purpose Symbolic Instruction Code*, a programming language closely resembling FORTRAN but simpler in design, making it suitable for beginners. It is used in time sharing and designed for easy data input and output.

basic motion-time study
See TIME AND MOTION STUDY.

basic producer
A manufacturer who uses natural resources to produce materials for other manufacturers. Examples include glass, rubber, and wood pulp producers and steel companies that process iron ore and produce steel ingots.

basic standard cost
In accounting, a standard cost that serves as a point of reference from which to measure changes in current standard cost as well as actual cost. Also, a standard cost that is developed from engineering studies, using specific assumptions.

basic style
The way in which a manager behaves or carries himself, as measured by the amount of task orientation and relationships orientation he uses. The four basic styles are referred to as integrated, dedicated, related, and separated. See RELATIONSHIPS ORIENTATION, TASK ORIENTATION, INTEGRATED MANAGER, DEDICATED MANAGER, RELATED MANAGER, and SEPARATED MANAGER.

basic time-motion study
See TIME AND MOTION STUDY.

basket purchase
See LUMP-SUM PURCHASE.

batch processing
A technique in data processing by which items to be processed are coded and collected into groups before processing. Each program in the batch is completed before the next program is started.

Batten system
See PEEK-A-BOO SYSTEM.

baud
A variable unit of telegraphic transmission speed (one-half dot per second) named after the French engineer Jean Baudot. The term is sometimes applied to the data transmission of a computer facility, with one baud equaling one bit per second. See BIT RATE.

Bayes, Thomas (1721–1761)
Reverend Thomas Bayes, a Presbyterian minister and mathematician who lived in England in the early part of the 18th century. Bayes's theorem for calculating probabilities is known as the Bayesian mode of reasoning, the Bayesian school, or most often simply as the Bayesian theory. The theorem is expressed in a lengthy mathematical formula.

Bayesian
See BAYES, THOMAS.

Bayesian statistics
A type of statistical analysis for management decision making, developed for translating subjective forecasts into mathematical probability curves. In many typical business situations there are no normal statistical probabilities because alternatives are unknown or have not

been tried before. Bayesian statistics use the best estimate of a given circumstance as if it were a firm probability.

BBB
See BETTER BUSINESS BUREAUS.

b-box
See INDEX REGISTER.

BCD
See BINARY CODED DECIMAL.

BDO
See BUSINESS DEVELOPMENT ORGANIZATIONS.

beam-right agreement
An agreement between the owner of an existing building and the builder of a new, adjoining structure to permit use of an existing wall as support for the new structure.

bear
Someone who thinks that the stock market prices or activity will decline. See BULL and SHORT SALE.

bearer bond
A bond that does not have the owner's name registered on the books of the issuing company and that is payable to the bearer. See COUPON BOND and REGISTERED BOND.

bearer stock
Corporate capital stock whose certificates are not registered in any name. They are negotiable on delivery without the requirement of endorsement and carry numbered or dated dividend coupons. Bearer certificates are used quite commonly in European countries but not in the United States.

bearing wall
A wall or partition that supports a vertical load in addition to its own weight.

below par
A term for an issue or a security that is currently priced at a discount, or at less than the face amount.

belt conveyor
A power-driven endless belt with terminal pulleys and idlers or slider beds, intended to convey constant or intermittent flows of materials from one point to another. A belt conveyor may be fixed or portable. It may be adjustable to operate horizontally or at an inclined angle.

bench
A term used to indicate a court or the judges of a court. It is also used to indicate the place where the judges sit. See BAR.

"B" end of car
The end of the railroad car on which the hand brake is located. See "A" END OF CAR.

beneficial interest
An interest in a property held in trust (as distinguished from legal possession) or in the benefit of an insurance policy or other contract. In its plural form, beneficial interests are the proprietorship represented by the outstanding shares of stock of a corporation.

Benelux
An economic union comprising Belgium, Luxembourg, and the Netherlands, formed in 1947 to develop trade and tariffs agreements.

benevolent autocrat
A manager who uses a high task orientation and a low relationships orientation where such behavior is appropriate, and who is, therefore, more effective and perceived as knowing what he wants and how to get it without creating resentment. See TASK ORIENTATION and RELATIONSHIPS ORIENTATION.

Bentham, Jeremy (1748–1832)
An English social philosopher. Son of a wealthy solicitor, he studied law. Bentham held the view that lack of money was responsible for misery but that, if the wealth of an individual exceeded a sufficiency, his pleasure did not increase proportionally. The amount of wealth in excess of sufficiency, if available to the poor, could bring a much larger sum of happiness. This concept was similar to the socialistic view of equality of wealth. He believed that every social institution should be judged by its usefulness in increasing the good to individuals. This gave the name *utilitarianism* to his doctrine.

Bernard rule
A widely used method of estimating the value of a corner lot. The lot is appraised first as an inside lot fronting on a side street, then as an inside lot fronting on a main street. The average value of the two hypothetical inside lots is the appraised value of the corner lot. Compare BALTIMORE METHOD.

Bernoulli, Jakob (1654–1705)
Swiss mathematician and professor at the University of Basel, he developed new material in the theory of probability, analytic geometry, and the calculus of variations. Bernoulli wrote the first extensive treatise on the law of large numbers.

Bernoulli, Johann (1667–1748)
Succeeded his brother, Jakob, as a professor at the University of Basel. He conducted further research into statistical theory.

Better Business Bureaus
BBBs have been established in more than 125 cities in the United States by privately owned business firms to promote ethical conduct in their communities. A Better Business Bureau acts as a monitor of local business mores, examining claims of unethical practices. The bureaus have no legal authority but can and do bring pressure on firms involved in unethical practices by exposing them to the public and, where there is evidence that a law has been broken, by notifying the appropriate authorities.

BI
Abbreviation for *bodily injury* covered by LIABILITY INSURANCE.

bicolumnar
A term used to describe a two-column balance sheet or income statement, or double-entry bookkeeping, wherein one column is used to display credits, and the second column, debits. See CREDIT and DEBIT.

bid
An offer to buy. A bid proposal may be presented by a vendor to a potential buyer, in effect stating that the vendor would accept a bid from the potential customer in conformity with the terms of the bid proposal.

Big Board
A popular term for the New York Stock Exchange. See NEW YORK STOCK EXCHANGE.

BILA
See BUREAU OF INTERNATIONAL LABOR AFFAIRS.

bilateral contract
A contract that contains mutual promises, with each party to the contract being both a promisor and a promisee. See UNILATERAL CONTRACT and CONSIDERATION.

bilateral monopoly
A market structure in which a monopsonist buyer faces a monopolist seller. The price of the merchandise will tend to be between the minimum price preferred by the monopsonist and the maximum price preferred by the monopolist.

bill of exchange
An unconditional order in writing signed by the drawer and requiring the drawee, the party to which it is addressed, to pay a certain sum in money to order or to a bearer at a fixed or determinable future time. A personal check is a bill of exchange drawn on a bank and payable on demand. See BANK DRAFT and TRADE ACCEPTANCE.

bill of lading
A receipt for any property received by a common carrier. The form and use of a bill of lading is regulated by the Interstate Commerce Commission. A "straight bill of lading" is a nonnegotiable document that cannot be bought, sold, or traded and states the destined consignee. An "order bill of lading" is negotiable and can be bought or sold, or conveyed by endorsement; the shipper retains title or control of the property until the invoice and charges are satisfied. "Export bills of lading" may be either "straight" or "order" formats and are used only on shipments for export that move through coastal ports rather than inland airports or seaports. See BILLS OF LADING ACT.

bill of material repetitions
The number of times a part number is referenced in a bill of material. This information can be useful in determining order quantities for specific part numbers, as for developing kits of materials for production.

bill of materials
In production, a list of components that combine to become a product. It is more complex than a list of parts in that the B/M details the materials that may have to be processed and assembled to create the parts.

bill of sale
A written document that confirms that the title or interest of one person in property, merchandise, or goods has transferred to another.

bill rate
See TREASURY BILL.

Bills of Lading Act
Enacted by the U.S. government in 1917, the act standardized the form and provisions of the bills of lading. It provides penalties for altering, forging, counterfeiting, or falsely making a bill of lading for criminal purposes. Also see BILL OF LADING.

bimetallic standard
A monetary standard that defines the national unit of currency (such as dollars) in terms of a fixed weight of two metals (such as gold and silver) in a specific ratio called the *mint ratio*. The United States was on this standard during the nineteenth century. See GRESHAM'S LAW and MINT RATIO.

binary
Relating to systems that have only two possible alternatives, such as go/no-go, on/off, yes/no, or the digits *0* and *1*.

binary code
A code, usually in communicating with computers, that makes use of only two distinct characters, such as *0* and *1*.

binary coded decimal
A number consisting of four-digit groups of binary numbers, where each such group is the binary equivalent of a decimal digit. For example, decimal *15* is expressed as the binary coded decimal *0001 0101* (decimal *1* = binary *0001;* decimal *5* = binary *0101*). BCD numbers have the advantage of being more readable than true binary numbers since they are more closely related to decimal numbers; however, more digits are required in this system to express a given number (for exam-

ple, the binary representation of decimal *15*, namely *1111*, uses only four digits, half the number of digits required for the BCD representation.

binary coded decimal notation
A method of representing each figure in a decimal number by a four-digit binary number. See BINARY CODED DECIMAL.

binary counter
In data processing, a counter that counts according to the binary system of numbers.

binary notation
Fixed radix (number base) notation, where the radix is two. For example, in binary notation the numeral 110.01 represents the number 1×2^2 plus 1×2^1 plus 1×2^{-2}.

binary-to-decimal conversion
The process of converting a binary number to the equivalent decimal number, that is, a base two number to a base ten number.

binder
In insurance, a document that is used extensively as a means for providing immediate insurance protection to an applicant for a policy. The binder—oral or, preferably, written—is evidence that a consideration has been given to purchasing a formal policy. In effect, the binder is itself a temporary insurance policy that is enforceable as though it were the final, formal policy.

In real estate, a temporary document, usually requiring a monetary deposit, executed by a buyer and a seller in contemplation of a more formal contract for the purchase of real property.

binomial distribution
In statistical analysis, a method that can be generalized to problems in which one wants to know how often, or what percent of the time, certain general events with known constant probability can be expected to take place. For instance, a doctor who knows the mortality rate associated with a certain disease may be anxious to know what percent of the time he can expect three out of ten afflicted patients to die from the disease. Similarly, a psychologist may want to know how many correct answers he can expect a student to give in an objective test if the student leaves the selection of his answers purely to chance;

or a gambler may want to know the probability that an unbiased die will show six *x* times out of *n* throws. When the number *n* of independent trials is specified and the probability of a given outcome (for instance, the probability that a die will show six in a single throw) is known for each trial, a binomial distribution indicates the theoretical frequency of each of all possible outcomes.

binomial expression
An algebraic expression consisting of two terms connected by a plus sign or minus sign; for example, $7bx + 9$. See MONOMIAL EXPRESSION, TRINOMIAL EXPRESSION, and POLYNOMIAL EXPRESSION.

biotechnology
See ERGONOMICS.

BIS
See BRITISH IMPERIAL SYSTEM.

bi-stable
In data processing, being capable of assuming either of two stable states, hence of storing one bit of information; for example, an on-off switch.

bit
Acronym for binary digit. A single character in a binary number or a single pulse in a group of pulses; a unit of information in a storage device.

bit location
In data processing, a storage position on a record that is capable of holding or storing one bit.

bit rate
In electronic data processing, the rate at which binary digits, or pulses representing them, pass a given point on a communications line or channel. Usually expressed in *bits per second*.

bits per second
The standard measure of data transmission speed. See BIT RATE.

B/L
See BILL OF LADING.

black capitalism
An effort begun in the late 1960s to increase the ownership and control of business by black people. Its objective is to improve the job market, the ghetto economy, and the condition and status of the black community.

black market
The purchase or sale of foreign exchange or commodities in violation of government restrictions. See GRAY MARKET.

Blake, Robert R.
See MANAGERIAL GRID.

Blanc, Louis (1811–1882)
The son of an inspector-general of finance in Spain appointed by Louis Bonaparte, Blanc became a journalist and founded the influential *Revue de Progrès,* in which he published serially in 1840 his chief work, *Organisation du Travail* (Organization of Labor). He proposed social workshops, to be established by the state so that everyone could be guaranteed a job. Intended to constitute the basis of a new society, these workshops were to be permanent institutions that, through efficient competition with private enterprise, would soon drive other businesses out of existence. The workers would form and control a national federation.

blanket coverage
An insurance policy that covers two or more items, and in which the full face amount may be applied to any one item. Blanket policies are often used to cover merchandise and goods stored at several different locations, or where the aggregate amounts are fairly constant but the locations or values of individual items may be changing.

blanket order
An order placed with a vendor, usually for large quantities of materials, such as for an annual supply, against which individual releases are made.

blanket rates
In transportation, rates that are generally designed to meet peculiar marketing requirements, usually of argicultural products. Blanket rates cover large geographic marketing areas for specified produce, offering through an average calculation a reduced rate for the entire market areas regardless of the distance between shipping points in that territory. See CLASS RATES.

blind entry
In accounting, a journal entry that states only the name of an account and the amounts debited or credited, without explaining the transactions or providing the information essential to an adequate record; a posting in a ledger that is not supported by a journal voucher or other evidence.

block
In data processing, a group of words, characters, or digits treated as a unit. A collection of contiguous records recorded as a unit; blocks are separated by interblock gaps.

blocked currency
Currency whose exchange for the currency of another country is legally restricted. See FREE CURRENCY.

blocked needs satisfaction
When the satisfaction of a need is blocked, a reduction in the strength of the need may result. Usually, there is a tendency for the "blocked" individual to engage in "coping behavior." This is an attempt to overcome the obstacle or blockage by trial-and-error problem solving. This individual may try a variety of behaviors in an effort to find the one that will accomplish his goal or that will reduce tension created by the blockage. See NEEDS SATISFACTION and COPING BEHAVIOR.

block scheduling
In production, a detailed scheduling technique that allows each operation a fairly long period, or "block" of time, for completion.

block sort
In data processing, a sort of one or more of the most significant characters of a key to serve as a means of making workable-size groups from a large volume of records to be sorted.

BLS
See BUREAU OF LABOR STATISTICS.

blue chip
Common stock in a company known nationally for the quality and wide acceptance of its products or services, and for its ability to make profits and pay dividends. Usually, such stocks are high-priced and offer relatively low yields; they are considered relatively stable and secure in capital value or market price.

blue laws
Laws that restrict the transaction of business on Sundays. See SUNDAY CONTRACT.

blue-sky laws
A popular name for the laws enacted by various states to protect the public against securities frauds. The term is believed to have originated when a judge commented that a particular stock had about the same monetary value as a patch of blue sky.

B/M
See BILL OF MATERIALS.

BM-T
Abbreviation for *basic motion-time study*. See TIME AND MOTION STUDY.

board of directors
The group of persons who are elected by the stockholders of a corporation to supervise the affairs of the corporation. The chief function of the board of directors is the formulation of policy, rather than the administration of the day-to-day operations of the firm.

board room
A room for customers in a broker's office where opening, high, low, and closing prices of leading stocks are posted on a *quote board*.

body shop
Slang term for *employment agency*.

bogey
In manufacturing, an unofficial production standard that a work group may set for itself in an attempt to control effort and output. In marketing, the level in an incentive or bonus program at which the payment rate is increased or augmented by the amount of the incentive or bonus.

Böhm-Bawerk, Eugen von (1851–1914)
An Austrian economist, Böhm-Bawerk was concerned with refuting Karl Marx. He is known primarily for his theory of interest based on marginal utility of capital, a theory that introduced comparison of present and future values.

boiler and machinery insurance
See POWER-PLANT INSURANCE.

boiler room
A room used for high-pressure peddling over the telephone of stocks of dubious value. A typical "boiler room" is simply a room lined with desks or cubicles, each with a telephone and a salesperson. The noise level generated by such frenzied activity gives it its name.

bolivar
Basic unit of currency in Venezuela.

BOM
Abbreviation for *beginning of the month.*

BOM
See BILL OF MATERIALS.

bond
An IOU or promissory note issued by a corporation, usually in multiples of $1,000 although $100 and $500 denominations are not uncommon. A bond is evidence of a debt on which the issuing company usually promises to pay the bondholder a specified amount of interest for a specific length of time, with the face amount of the bond to be repaid on the expiration date. A bondholder is a creditor of the corporation, not a part owner as is a stockholder.

bond and preferred stock fund
A mutual fund whose policy is to invest in bonds and preferred stocks.

bonded block loading
An effective and secure method for loading freight; the items are stacked in the manner of overlapping "bricks."

bonded debt
Outstanding bonds that are evidence of a debt. See FUNDED DEBT.

bonded warehouse
A warehouse, usually at a port of entry, in which imported goods can be stored until duties have been paid or the goods have been reexported.

bonus account
A savings account that pays a higher than normal rate of interest.

bonus formula
The formal provisions in an incentive bonus plan that determine the total funds available for bonus purposes in a given year. Individual bonus awards are made from this total pool.

bonus pool
The total amount of bonus funds generated by an incentive plan in a given year and available for awards. In most companies, the pool approximates the total bonuses that would be paid if all participants received "normal" awards.

book inventory
A statement of inventory that is not the result of a physical count. It is accomplished by adding the units and cost of incoming goods to previous inventory figures and deducting the units and cost of outgoing goods.

bookkeeper
A person who keeps the books in which the financial transactions of an enterprise are recorded. This work may be specialized, as in the case of the person who maintains the general ledger or works on accounts receivable or accounts payable. A bookkeeper may also be a public accountant, although the function of bookkeeping does not usually require the professional level of training and education of a public accountant.

book of final entry
In accounting, a record book to which the money amounts of transactions are transferred, or posted, from other books; a ledger. Also called *book of secondary entry*.

book of original entry
In accounting, a record book in which transactions are recorded and that serves as the source of postings to ledgers; a journal.

book of secondary entry
See BOOK OF FINAL ENTRY.

book value
The net amount at which an asset or a group of assets appears on the books of account, as distinguished from the market value or an intrinsic value. Also, the face amount of a liability less any unamortized discount and expense.

book value per share
An indicator of the financial status of an enterprise, BV/share represents the sum of the common stock, paid-in surplus, and retained-income accounts of the balance sheet, divided by the number of common shares outstanding. It is purely of historical interest and conveys no information about future performance.

Boole, George (1815–1864)
An Irish logician and mathematician, Boole developed a system of formulating logical statements symbolically so that they could be written and proved in a manner similar to that in ordinary algebra. His algebra of logic also has applications in engineering problems, such as in the design of electrical switching circuits. See BOOLEAN ALGEBRA.

Boolean algebra
A process of reasoning, or a deductive system of theorems, named after George Boole, which deals with classes, propositions, or on-off circuit elements. AND, OR, NOT, and IF—THEN, for examples, are operators represented by symbols to permit mathematical calculation.

bootstrap
In data processing, a technique for loading the first few instructions of a routine into storage, then using these instructions to bring in the rest of the routine. This usually involves either the entering of a few instructions manually or the use of a special key on the console.

bootstrap financing
A technique of generating capital by using a company's internal ability. Bootstrap financing may rely on the prudent use of trade credit, on turning fixed assets into cash, and on reducing operating expenses, especially those related to fixed overhead, to the very minimum.

bordereau
In insurance accounting, a tabular register or report that contains abstracts of insurance that has been written.

Boren's law
A satirical principle holding that when one is in doubt, it is best to mumble.

Boston ledger
A type of ledger in which the record on each account moves horizontally in columnar sections assigned to consecutive accounting periods.

Several accounts may be kept on a single page. This form of ledger may eliminate the need to prepare a separate trial balance.

bottomland
Low-lying land, especially grassland, along a watercourse.

bottom line
On a balance sheet or other financial statement, the sum or total of the details listed above the line. See ABOVE THE LINE.

Boulwarism
Lemuel R. Boulware, a vice president for employee relations, General Electric Company, introduced in 1948 a collective bargaining technique that became known as Boulwarism. Management's position was to present a "truthful offer" in labor contract negotiations that it considered realistic and final. In 1954, 1958, and 1960, the union charged General Electric's management in front of the NLRB with not bargaining in good faith, and lack of concession. The two earlier charges were dismissed by the NLRB. The later charge was resolved through successful contract development between GE and the union in 1963.

bourse
A word of French origin applied to any stock exchange or commodity market in continental Europe.

box car
A closed freight car.

BOY
Short for *beginning of the year*.

boycott
An effort to discourage people from dealing with a particular firm, or to discourage nations from dealing with a particular nation.

bps
See BITS PER SECOND.

branch instruction
An instruction to a computer that enables the computer to choose between alternative subprograms depending upon the conditions determined by the computer during the execution of the program.

Brannan Plan
A proposal made by Secretary of Agriculture Charles F. Brannan in 1949 to eliminate parity payments to farmers and give them direct payments instead. Under the plan, agricultural prices would be determined in a free market by supply and demand. Farmers would then be compensated by a subsidy from the government for the difference between the market price they receive and some higher target or parity price established according to a selected base period in the past. See PARITY and SUBSIDY.

break bulk
To unload and reship the contents of a freight car.

breakdown time distributions
A statistical method useful in formulating general policies concerning preventive maintenance of machinery. Breakdown distributions show the frequency with which machines have maintenance-free performance for a given number of operating hours, and are normally shown as distributions of the percentage of breakdowns that occur after an acceptable minimum operation time.

breakeven chart
In accounting, a chart in any form that graphically depicts the breakeven point in operations.

breakeven point
That level of output at which a firm's total revenue and its total cost (or its average total revenue and its average total cost) are equal. At this point the net profit is zero.

breakup value
The amount that can be obtained for assets in a forced sale. See SALVAGE.

Bridge of Fayol
See FAYOL LADDER.

British Imperial system
A system of units of measurement from which the U.S. customary system was derived. See U.S. CUSTOMARY SYSTEM and INTERNATIONAL SYSTEM.

broker
An agent, often a member of a stock exchange firm or an exchange member himself, who handles the public's orders to buy and sell securities or commodities. A commission is charged for this service.

Generally, a natural or legal person who, for compensation or in expectation of compensation, acts for another in a real estate or commercial transaction.

brokerage
A commission that accrues to a broker for having brought about an arrangement or transaction between a buyer and a seller. The commission may be paid by either the buyer or the seller, or in part by both, in accordance with custom or regulation. Also, the business or establishment of a broker.

broker's loan
A loan obtained from a bank by a broker or dealer in securities for the purpose of purchasing or carrying securities or, most often, for carrying a customer's margin account.

bubble memory
A computer memory device without moving parts. Each one-inch square of such a memory can store 92,000 bits of data in the form of magnetic bubbles that move in thin films of magnetic material. A bubble represents a *1* in computer language; the absence of a bubble stands for *0*. The tiny bubbles, measuring five microns across (five millionths of a meter), are cylindrical magnetic islands polarized in a direction opposite from that of the film. The bubbles appear, disappear, and move around on the surface of the crystalline chip (gadolinium-gallium garnet) under the control of a magnetic field.

buckets
Slang expression for the portion of computer storage specifically reserved for accumulating data or totals. Commonly used in initial planning of materials requirements for production; a possible use is "Throw it (the data) in bucket three."

bucket shop
Old and derogatory term for a stock brokerage of doubtful integrity.

budget
A financial plan; an itemized estimate of expected revenues and expenditures for a specific future period of time. The term may also be

applied to any proposed detailed plan for the utilization of manpower, material, or other resources.

budget deficit
An excess of total expenditures over total revenues in a company's or national budget. Some economists hold that a deficit in the U.S. national budget is not detrimental to the economy if the gross national product increases during the budget period. See BALANCED BUDGET and BUDGET SURPLUS.

budget loan
See BUDGET MORTGAGE.

budget mortgage
A mortgage loan under whose terms each monthly payment made by the borrower covers not only the interest and a payment on the principal but also one-twelfth of such annual liabilities as taxes and insurance. The lending firm keeps these payments in a reserve account and pays the charges as they become due. Also known as *budget loan.*

budget surplus
An excess of total revenues over total expenditures. The effect of a surplus in the national budget is to reduce the level of economic activity. See BALANCED BUDGET and BUDGET DEFICIT.

buffer
An internal portion of a data processing system serving as an intermediary storage between two storage or data handling systems with different access times or formats.

buffer inventory
A buffer stock is maintained as a safeguard against delays in deliveries of materials on order, strikes, or slowdowns for any unpredictable reason, or to cover sudden and unforecast increases in demand. The level of this inventory may be determined on the basis of scientific models or pure judgment growing out of past experience. Also known as *safety stock, reserve stock,* or *protective inventory.*

bug
A mistake in the design of a routine or a computer program; a malfunction.

builder's risk
Fire insurance written to cover the constantly increasing value of a building under construction. It may be written for a small initial face value and increased each month on the basis of regular reports from the insured. Alternatively, it may be written for an amount presumed to be the final value of the building when completed, with the rate being adjusted periodically.

building and loan association
See SAVINGS AND LOAN ASSOCIATION.

bulk cargo
Unpackaged cargo.

bulk freight
Material that is shipped loose rather than in packages or containers, as coal in a hopper car or sulfur in the hold of a ship.

bulkhead
A partition separating one part of a ship, freight car, aircraft, or truck from another part. Also, a wall or side of a structure intended to resist water flooding.

bulk items
Piece parts or raw material issued, on a regular basis, in excess of immediate manufacturing requirements. Such items usually have a low unit cost and high usage.

bulk pack
A group of small packages that have been inserted into a larger carton or box container.

bulk sales law
A law in some states that requires the sale of a business to be advertised beforehand for the protection of its creditors. Also known as *ten-day escrow law*.

bulk storage warehouse
A warehouse providing tank storage of bulk liquids such as oil, chemicals, syrups, and molasses.

bull
One who believes that the stock market prices or activity will rise. For example, a bullish operator on a stock exchange or commodities mar-

ket expects prices to rise and buys in the hope of selling at a later time for a gain. See BEAR.

bullion
Refined gold or silver in the form of bars or ingots.

bunched cost
See LUMP-SUM PURCHASE.

bunching
The accumulation of railroad cars for loading, generally at an industrial plant.

bunker charge
An extra charge that may be added to ocean freight charges, justified usually by increased fuel costs.

burden
The costs of manufacture or production that are not readily identifiable with specific products; examples are factory overhead, indirect costs, and employee fringe benefits.

bureaucrat
In organizational behavior, a manager whose style is to use a low task orientation and a low relationships orientation in a situation where such behavior is appropriate, and who is, therefore, more effective than other types of managers. He is perceived as being primarily interested in rules and procedures for their own sake, wanting to control the situation by the use of rules and procedure, and as being conscientious. See RELATIONSHIPS ORIENTATION and TASK ORIENTATION.

bureaucratic concept of organization
The traditional model of an organization, which emphasizes superior–subordinate relationships. Orders flow from the top down through a chain of command, and individuals carry out the orders.

Bureau of International Labor Affairs
A unit of the Department of Labor, BILA represents the interest of American workers in trade and tariff matters and administers a trade-adjustment assistance program for workers adversely affected by import competition. Such a program may take the form of skills-retraining activities to enhance the reemployment opportunities for those workers who may have become unemployed or whose skills have become less essential as a result of the import of finished goods.

Bureau of Labor Statistics
A unit of the Department of Labor, BLS collects, analyzes, and publishes data relating to wages, prices, productivity, employment, and the performance of the nation's economy. This bureau publishes a monthly consumer price index.

Bureau of Land Management
A federal agency within the Department of the Interior; responsible for the management of all federal lands. Formerly called the General Land Office.

Bureau of Motor Carrier Safety
A branch of the Department of Transportation, the bureau administers and enforces motor carrier safety regulations as well as regulations governing the transportation of hazardous materials.

burglary insurance
Basic protection against loss due to crimes committed by outsiders rather than by employees of an organization or authorized visitors. It applies only when there is physical evidence of forced entry. Coverage is provided for specific goods or property and damage incurred in the course of the burglary.

burning ratio
In insurance accounting, the ratio of an actual loss by fire to the total value of the combustible property.

business agent
In labor relations, the highest official in a union or labor organization operating on a local basis. The business agent is usually salaried and is either elected or appointed to perform the principal work of the local union, such as negotiating contracts, settling grievances, and building membership rolls.

business development organizations
Independent organizations that provide, free of charge, help to small businesses in solving operational problems and finding outside money when needed. Most BDOs concentrate on a particular minority group, but do work with nonminority entrepreneurs. See OFFICE OF MINORITY BUSINESS ENTERPRISE.

business interruption insurance
A type of insurance that covers the insured for loss of earnings sustained as a result of fire. See CONSEQUENTIAL-LOSSES INSURANCE.

business life insurance

Insurance on the life of a member of a partnership or on the officer or stockholder in a corporation payable so as to finance purchase by surviving owners of the insured's interest at his or her death. Insurance on the life of a sole proprietor payable so as to finance the purchase of the business by an outside interest at the owner's death. Insurance on the life of a key employee for the benefit of the enterprise. See PARTNERSHIP LIFE INSURANCE.

business trust

A form of organization for a business venture. Assets are held by a trustee, who will manage the business; the owners or those who contribute capital receive documents known as "certificates of beneficial interest," which serve as evidence of ownership. The extent of the owners' liabilities varies in accordance with the laws of the state in which the organization is registered; the business trust may be treated as a partnership or have complete status as a corporation. Also known as *Massachusetts trust* and *common-law trust*.

Buy American policy

To protect products manufactured in the United States, a law was passed in 1933 prescribing that the federal government and its agencies buy American-made goods for public use unless the cost is substantially higher than that of foreign-made goods. For example, if domestic prices are not more than 6 percent higher than foreign-made equivalents, the government may be obliged to buy domestically (the Pentagon uses a differential of 50 percent). The term also applies to similar provisions of later laws.

buyer

An employee responsible for buying goods and services from company-approved vendors.

buyer's market

A market in which supply is greater than demand, giving buyers considerable influence over prices and terms of sales. Prices generally tend to move downward in a buyer's market. See SELLER'S MARKET.

buyer's monopoly

See MONOPSONY.

buying subject to encumbrances

Purchasing property subject to encumbrances. If such encumbrances are valid and enforceable, the title and rights in the property are subject to and inferior to such encumbrances. An encumbrance may be a mortgage, mechanic's lien, lease, or any other claim or right.

BV/share
See BOOK VALUE PER SHARE.

bylaws
The rules adopted by the members or the board of directors of a corporation or other organization for its government. These rules must not be contrary to the law of the land, and they affect only the rights and duties of its members who are officially affiliated with the corporation or organization. They are not applicable to outsiders.

Byrnes Act
Passed in 1936, this act makes it a felony to transport in interstate commerce persons who are hired to interfere with peaceful picketing in a labor dispute over wages, hours, or working conditions or employee rights of self-organization or collective bargaining. Also known as the *anti-strikebreaker law*.

byte
In computer technology, a measurable portion of consecutive binary digits; for example, an 8-bit or a 16-bit group. A byte is a group of binary digits usually operated upon as a unit.

C
See CELSIUS

CAB
See CIVIL AERONAUTICS BOARD.

CACM
See CENTRAL AMERICAN COMMON MARKET.

CAD
See COMPUTER-AIDED DESIGN.

Cady test
See MULLEN TEST.

CAF
See COST AND FREIGHT.

Cairnes, John Elliot (1823–1875)
Taught economics at Queen's College in Galway and at University College, London. He limited his teachings to production and the distribution of wealth, excluding ideas of social policy. He favored the deductive method of thinking.

CAL
Acronym for *Conversational Algebraic Language,* a computer programming language developed at the University of California, Berkeley, and adopted widely in the United States for medium-size time-sharing systems.

call
See PUTS AND CALLS.

callable issue
A bond issue, all or part of which may be redeemed by the issuing corporation under defined conditions before maturity. The term also applies to preferred shares redeemable by the issuing corporation.

called loan
See CALL LOAN.

call loan
A loan that may be terminated at will by either party; primarily a loan made by a bank to a stockbroker. A loan that has been terminated in this way is known as a *called loan*.

call premium
The excess above par that is payable by the issuer of a bond if the bond is redeemed before maturity.

call price
The price at which a callable bond is redeemable.

CAM
See CONTENT ADDRESSABLE RANDOM-ACCESS MEMORY.

cameralism
A form of mercantilism extensively implemented by German governments during the eighteenth century with the chief objective of increasing the revenue of the state.

CAMP
See COMPUTER-AIDED MASK PREPARATION.

cancellation right
The assumption that both the insured and the company have the right to cancel the contract, unless otherwise defined in the terms of the contract. Rates for noncancellable insurance policies are generally higher than for those that are cancellable.

cancel order
A market or limited-price order given to a securities broker, to be executed in whole or in part as soon as it is represented in the trading arena. The portion not so executed is to be treated as canceled.

C&F
See COST AND FREIGHT.

C&SMFTA
Initials for *Central & Southern Motor Freight Traffic Association.*

capacity cost
The cost of operating a plant at full capacity.

capital
An inclusive term embracing plants, equipment, tools, inventories of materials, work in process, finished goods, and the financial resources for conducting business. All material values necessary to launch and maintain production are elements of capital. The meaning, therefore, is not confined to money, but also includes items that are evaluated in terms of money.

capital asset
An asset in continuous use or possession, including land, buildings, equipment, leaseholds, mineral deposits, goodwill, patents, trademarks, and copyrights.

capital bonus
A British term for STOCK DIVIDEND.

capital budget
In finance, the portion of a budget, or a separate budget, dedicated to proposed future additions to capital assets and their financing. In municipal accounting, it is a plan for municipal improvements during the budget period, including self-supporting activities such as municipal utilities. In the private sector of business enterprise, it is usual to evaluate projects that require capital budgets on the basis of estimated costs, priority of need for the project, and return on investment of capital.

capital deepening
An increase in capital relative to other resources, especially labor; usually applied to a nation, but can apply to a region or to a business firm.

capital dividend
In business finance, a dividend that is charged to, and thus paid from, the paid-in-capital account.

capital expenditure
An expenditure for an addition to, or betterment of, existing capital assets, charged to a capital assets account. The benefits of such an

expenditure are to be realized in a future accounting period. By contrast, the benefits of a *revenue expenditure* are realized in the period of the expenditure. See REVENUE EXPENDITURE.

capital gain
Profit from the sale of a capital asset. A capital gain under federal income tax laws may be either short-term or long-term. In 1977, short-term was defined as less than nine months between purchase and sale, and long-term as nine months or more. A short-term capital gain is taxed at the reporting individual's full income tax rate. A long-term capital gain is taxed at a maximum of 35 percent, depending on the reporting individual's income tax bracket. The amount of capital gain is reduced by the amount of capital loss, if any. (These are rules and regulations governed by the U.S. Internal Revenue Service and are subject to change.) See CAPITAL LOSS.

capital gains fund
An investment company that seeks profits primarily through capital gains.

capital goods
A term commonly used for fixed assets.

capital-intensive
A capital-intensive process of production is one that uses proportionately more capital than it uses labor or land. A nuclear power plant is a capital-intensive method of producing electricity when compared with a conventional coal-burning plant, because the cost of labor is a smaller proportion of total costs. See LABOR-INTENSIVE.

capitalism
In a capitalistic system the initiative to undertake any form of economic activity rests with the individual. Capitalism, as an economic system, is characterized by private ownership of the factors of production and by private initiative, guided by the profit motive, in the conduct of production. Capitalistic societies are relatively free of government control over economic activity, particularly over prices and production. Capitalism recognizes the concept of private property and the right of ownership and use of capital goods to gain income. See SOCIALISM.

capitalization
The total amount of the various securities issued by a corporation. Capitalization may include bonds, debentures, preferred and common

stock, and surplus. Bonds and debentures are usually carried on the books of the issuing company in terms of their par or face value. Preferred and common shares may be carried in terms of par or stated value. Stated value may be an arbitrary value decided upon by the directors or may represent the amount received by the company from the sale of the securities at the time of issuance. See PAR.

capitalization ratio
The total of fixed assets (after depreciation) divided by net worth; one of many ratios that are sometimes used in measuring quantitatively the effectiveness of an entrepreneurial effort.

capitalized expense
An expense item usually charged to profit and loss that is added to the capital-asset account because it is related to a period of construction. Examples of capitalized expense include taxes on property under construction, interest, and other expenses incurred on new construction before it is placed into operation.

capitalized surplus
Surplus capital of a corporation that has been transferred to capital stock through the issue of a stock dividend, by increasing the par or stated value of capital stock without an issue of additional shares, or by a resolution of the board of directors.

capital levy
In finance, a nonrecurring tax on capital. The term may be used in connection with a special nonrecurring tax that is placed on new capital values acquired during a particular accounting period. In this concept, the capital levy is similar to a capital-gains tax except that it is levied on appraised instead of realized gain.

capital loss
Loss from the sale of a capital asset. For tax purposes, a capital loss is reduced by the amount of any offsetting capital gains. Up to $1,000 of net capital loss is deductible from an individual's income tax during the year reported. If the capital loss is more than $1,000, as much as $1,000 may be deducted annually thereafter until the full amount has been deducted. (These are rules and regulations of the U.S. Internal Revenue Service and are subject to change.) See CAPITAL GAIN.

capital market
Collectively, securities exchanges, underwriters, and investment banks, usually concentrated in some financial center that may be a major city such as New York, Chicago, or London.

capital outlay
See CAPITAL EXPENDITURE.

capital/output ratio
A concept with two facets: (1) the "total" capital/output ratio is the economy's total stock of real capital divided by the level of its income or output; (2) the "marginal" capital/output ratio is the change in an economy's income or output resulting from a unit change in its stock of real capital; a ratio of 3/1 means that three units of additional capital produce one unit of additional output.

capital rationing
In corporate finance, capital rationing occurs any time there is a budget ceiling, or constraint, on the amount of funds that can be invested during a specific period of time, such as a year. Such constraints are particularly prevalent in firms that have a policy of financing all capital expenditures internally. Another example is when a division of a large company is allowed to make capital expenditures only up to a specified budget ceiling, over which the division usually has no control. By imposing the capital rationing constraint, the firm attempts to select the combination of investment proposals that will provide the greatest profitability.

capital reconciliation statement
See STATEMENT OF SOURCES AND APPLICATION OF FUNDS.

capital rent
A price paid for the use of improvements that are a permanent part of or are attached to the land. This is purely hypothetical, because the improvements cannot be used apart from the land to which they are attached. The concept is used when it may be desired to maintain separate accounts for the cost of rental, one for the *ground* and the other for the *improvements* that have been capitalized.

capital stock
All shares representing ownership of a business, including preferred and common stock. See COMMON STOCK and PREFERRED STOCK.

capital surplus
That part of the paid-in capital of an enterprise that is not assigned to capital stock. Contributions by stockholders in excess of par or stated value of shares, also known as *paid-in surplus,* are capital surplus. See PAID-IN CAPITAL.

capital value
Investment in capital goods (fixed assets), measured in terms of cost or other value.

CARAM
See CONTENT ADDRESSABLE RANDOM-ACCESS MEMORY.

career-average pension
A form of pension in which the benefit earned each year is calculated in terms of that year's income. This contrasts with pensions based on some form of final average pay, often the average of the five-year period immediately preceding the employee's date of retirement.

Carey, Matthew (1769–1839)
An early leader in American thinking; traveled with Lafayette, worked for Benjamin Franklin in Paris. He settled in Philadelphia as a publisher aided by a $400 gift from Lafayette and support from Franklin. One of the first to advocate conservation of natural resources, especially the soil.

car float
A barge equipped with tracks on which as many as 12 railroad cars may be carried and moved in harbors or inland waterways.

cargo ship tonnage
Defines either weight or volume. In the United States, the *weight ton* is 2,000 or 2,240 pounds; in British Commonwealth countries it is the English long or gross ton of 2,240 pounds. The *measurement ton* is usually 40 cubic feet.

carload
The minimum number of tons required for shipping at carload (CL) rates. These rates are lower than those quoted for less than a carload (LCL). The same principle applies to truckload (TL) and less than a truckload (LTL).

carnet
An international customs document intended to facilitate the import and export of a commodity used as a sample or for demonstration on a short-term basis. Carnets are issued in the United States by the U.S. Council of the International Chamber of Commerce, New York City. See ATA CARNET and TIR CARNET.

car pooling
In transportation, the use of individual carrier equipment through a central agency for the benefit of carriers and shippers.

carried value
The amount at which a property or other noninventory asset is recorded on the books, net after depreciation. Also known as *book value*.

carryback
The right, sometimes extended under tax regulations, to average out gains and losses over more than a one-year period. This enables the taxpayer to offset gains in one year with losses that have been accrued in an earlier year. The effect is to reduce the tax for the period in which gains were recorded.

carryover clause
In real estate, a provision in an "exclusive listing" (one that is given only to a single real estate sales agent) that, under specified and negotiated circumstances, assures the sales agent that he or she will be eligible to receive a commission should the real estate be sold after the tenure period of the exclusive listing period. It is usual to assign an exclusive listing for a specified period of time after which, if the property has not been sold, the listing may be offered to one or more other sales agencies that may simultaneously endeavor to sell the property.

car seal
Small metal strips and lead fasteners used to lock freight-car or truck doors. Seals are numbered for record-keeping purposes.

cartel
An association, often international, of firms in the same industry, established to limit competition by allocating markets among its members, regulating prices, and other means. Sometimes referred to as an *international monopoly*.

CASB
See COST ACCOUNTING STANDARDS BOARD.

cascade control
In data processing, an automatic control system in which various control units are linked in sequence, each control unit regulating the operation of the next control unit in line.

cascaded systems
In production, multiple operations in which the input of each stage is the output of a preceding stage.

cash-and-carry wholesaler
A merchant who requires that his customers come to his warehouse, select the products from the warehouse shelves, pay cash for what they select, and carry away the products they have thus purchased. This type of wholesaler operates much like a supermarket, dispensing with delivery and credit services in an effort to introduce operational methods that are expected to reduce costs.

cash asset
Cash and any asset that can be immediately converted into cash without disrupting day-to-day operations. Also known as *cash resource*.

cash basis of accounting
The method of accounting whereby revenues and expenses are recorded on the books of account when received and paid without regard to the period to which they apply. See ACCRUAL BASIS OF ACCOUNTING.

cashbook
A book of original entry for cash receipts and disbursements. See CASH JOURNAL.

cash discount
A reduction in the amount of an invoice given for prompt settlement of a sales debt.

cash dividend
A dividend paid in cash rather than in property, stocks, bonds, or any other substitute for cash.

cash flow
The cash inflow and outflow of an enterprise between two given dates or accounting periods. According to the AICPA, cash flow in financial analysis means net income after adding back expense items that currently do not *use* funds, such as depreciation, but it may also involve deducting revenue items that do not currently *provide* funds, such as the current amortization of deferred income. It corresponds to the *funds derived from operations* in a statement of source and application of funds. Cash flow is also known as *net cash income, net cash generation, cash income,* and *cash funds generated from operations.*

cash funds generated from operations
See CASH FLOW.

cashier's check
A bill of exchange drawn by the cashier of a bank, for the bank, upon the bank. After the check is issued or delivered to the payee or the holder, the drawer bank cannot put a stop order against itself. By delivering the check, the drawer bank has accepted the obligation to pay and may not cancel the obligation.

cash income
See CASH FLOW.

cash journal
In accounting, a cashbook; a columnar journal in which all transactions are entered, whether or not cash is involved. See LEDGER JOURNAL and CASHBOOK.

cash resource
See CASH ASSET.

cash sale
The delivery of goods or services with immediate receipt of cash in payment. In stock market terms, a transaction on the floor of the stock exchange calling for delivery of the securities the same day. In "regular way" trades, the seller is to deliver on the fifth business day after the purchase or sale has been made.

casualty insurance
Insurance providing coverage for a variety of specific situations in which chance, accident, or neglect may result in provable loss. Some of the usual types are: (1) burglary, robbery, theft, and larceny insurance, (2) automobile insurance, (3) workmen's compensation insurance, and (4) disability or accident and health insurance.

Catt concept
Observations made by Ivor Catt on certain techniques used by some employees to prolong their tenures of employment. These observations were published in *The Catt Concept* (New York: G. P. Putnam's Sons, 1971). Three basic methods, according to Catt, are: (1) the *incompleteness gambit,* which means essentially that one should not complete a project, because most layoffs occur at the completion of a project, (2) *secretiveness,* or making certain the superior does not have enough information about the job significance and function and, therefore, will

be afraid to terminate the employee, and (3) *semi-blackmail,* in which the employee has knowledge that can damage his superior if he attempts to fire him.

cause of action
Created when one's legal rights are invaded, either by a breach of a contract or by a breach of a legal duty toward one's person or property.

caveat emptor
Latin, "let the buyer beware." In commerce, the principle that if a customer buys a product without warranty, on an "as is" basis, or on "no refund or credit" terms, he assumes the risk of quality and of all losses due to defects in the product.

caveat venditor
Latin, "let the seller beware." In commerce, the principle that unless a seller by express language disclaims any responsibility, he shall be liable to the buyer if the goods he delivers are different in kind, quality, use, or purpose from those described in the contract of sale.

CBD
Initials for *cash before delivery.* Same as CIA and CWO.

CBEMA
Initials for *Computer and Business Equipment Manufacturers Association.*

CC
See CHAMBER OF COMMERCE.

CCC
See COMMODITY CREDIT CORPORATION.

CCR
See COMMISSION ON CIVIL RIGHTS.

CCS
See CENTRAL CERTIFICATE SERVICE.

CCTV
See CLOSED-CIRCUIT TELEVISION.

CD
See CERTIFICATE OF DEPOSIT.

CDC
See CENTER FOR DISEASE CONTROL.

CE
Initials for *civil engineer*.

CEA
Initials for *Council of Economic Advisors*. See EMPLOYMENT ACT OF 1946.

cedi
Basic unit of currency in Ghana.

ceiling price
The highest price obtainable or permissible in the sale of particular goods or services.

Celler Antimerger Act
A major antitrust law enacted in 1950, it was an extension of Section 7 of the Clayton Antitrust Act prohibiting a corporation from acquiring the stock or assets of another corporation if the effect would be a substantial lessening of competition or a tendency toward monopoly. Prior to the Celler Antimerger Act, only the acquisition of stock by competing corporations was illegal under the Clayton Act; the act prohibits the acquisition of assets as well as stock if the effect would be to substantially lessen competition.

Celsius
A thermometric scale calibrated so that, at sea level, the freezing point of water is 0° and the boiling point 100°. The Celsius scale was invented by Anders Celsius, a Swedish astronomer who died in 1744. It is also known as *centigrade*. The formula for converting Fahrenheit (F) to Celsius (C) is:

$$C = \frac{(F - 32) \times 5}{9}$$

Center for Disease Control
A unit of the Public Health Service, CDC provides leadership and direction in the prevention and control of diseases and other preventable conditions affecting health.

centigrade
See CELSIUS.

Central American Common Market
Five nations—Costa Rica, El Salvador, Guatemala, Honduras, and Nicaragua—who joined together to seek means for accelerating economic expansion through a movement toward a common external tariff and free interregional trade.

central certificate service
A department of a stock clearing corporation that conducts a central securities certificates operation. Through this service, clearing firms effect securities deliveries between one another via computerized bookkeeping, thereby reducing the physical movement of stock certificates. See STOCK CLEARING CORPORATION.

centralized data processing
Data processing performed at a single, central location on data obtained from several geographical locations or managerial levels.

central limit theorem
In statistics, any of several fundamental theorems of probability that state the conditions under which the distribution of a sum of independent random variables is approximated by the normal distribution. A special case of the central limit theorem is often applied in sampling; it states that the distribution of a mean of a sample from a population with finite variance is approximated by the normal distribution as the number in the sample becomes large. This theorem is applicable in establishing quality control standards; specifically, it permits calculation of the probability that a product will fall within acceptable quality levels.

central processing unit (CPU)
The central processor of a computer system. It contains the main storage, arithmetic unit, and special register groups. Also, that portion of a computer that is exclusive of the input, output, peripheral, and, in some instances, storage units. Also known as *mainframe*.

central reserve city bank
See COUNTRY BANK.

Central standard time (CST)
The time of the sixth time zone west of Greenwich that includes the central United States. Also known as *Central time*.

central tendency
In statistics, the center number (or numbers) of a distribution; notably the arithmetic MEAN, MEDIAN, and MODE. Also see SCATTER.

Central time (CT)
See CENTRAL STANDARD TIME.

CEO
Initials for *chief executive officer*.

cermet
Acronym for *cer*amic and *met*al, a material used in making thin-film electrically resistive components. Also called *ceramal*.

CERN
See EUROPEAN ORGANIZATION FOR NUCLEAR RESEARCH.

certificate
In stock market terminology, the actual piece of paper that is evidence of ownership of stock in a corporation. Watermarked paper is used to discourage forgery. The certificate is usually registered by the corporation or the transfer agent in the name of the owner of the certificate.

certificate of deposit
A special type of time deposit which, by agreement with the purchaser, is kept on deposit for a specified minimum time period in the bank that sold it. Many CDs are negotiable, and, because they offer both liquidity and yield, can be sold in a secondary market. Banks began to offer CDs in the 1960s at rates competitive with other money market instruments. This was initiated to discourage corporate accounts from withdrawing money for the purpose of investing in securities. Also known as *time certificate of deposit*.

certificate of incorporation
The document issued by an authorized official of state government (usually the secretary of state) establishing the existence of a corporation.

certificate of origin
A certified statement of where goods originated, often required for imported goods.

certificate of public convenience and necessity
Authority granted by a government regulatory body to operate as a common carrier.

certificate of release
A notice by a lender that a mortgage has been paid in full.

certificate of title
A written opinion of the condition of a title, based on available records and without guarantee. Certificates of title are used in several fields of business, such as real estate, marketing, and any other area of activity that involves proof of ownership of real property or goods.

certified check
A depositor's check guaranteed by the issuing bank to be fully covered by funds being held in suspension in the account of the depositor who has drawn the check.

certified financial statement
A statement of the financial position of a company attested to by an independent auditor who is a certified public accountant.

certified public accountant
An accountant who has been registered or licensed to practice public accounting and is permitted to call himself a certified public accountant and use the initials CPA after his name. Certification is obtained by passing a series of examinations given by the state, but certain additional requirements of education, experience, and moral conduct recommended by the AICPA may have to be met, depending on the state in which the accountant wishes to practice.

certiorari
A writ of a higher or appellate court to call up the records of an inferior court or other authority that has exercised a judicial function.

cession deed
A legal document transferring title to privately owned property, such as a private road, to a municipality.

cestui que trust
Old French, "he who trusts"; one for whose benefit a trust is created. A person entitled to the beneficial interest in property that is held in trust by a trustee.

CET
See COMMON EXTERNAL TARIFF.

ceteris paribus
Latin, "other things being equal." In economic analysis, the assumption that outside influences on an economic model remain constant. The economist uses this assumption because it is difficult to isolate economic variables from a variety of other influences.

CFA
Initials for *Canadian Freight Association.*

CFTC
See COMMODITY FUTURES TRADING COMMISSION.

CGL
Abbreviation for *comprehensive general liability insurance.* See LIABILITY INSURANCE.

chain
A unit of length equal to 66 feet. Also, a measuring instrument of 100 links used in surveying.

chain discount
A series of trade discounts, usually related to quantity purchases and indicated as a progression of percentages. For example, a series of 30 + 5 + 5 would be calculated from the published list price or the suggested end-user purchase price, taking first a 30 percent discount, then an additional 5 percent discount from the result, and once more a 5 percent discount from that result to arrive at a net purchase price. The progression of discounts increases with the quantity of items purchased. The use of chain discounts is a common practice among wholesalers.

chain of title
In real estate, history of the conveyances and encumbrances affecting a title from the original grant or patent, or as far back as records are available.

chamber of commerce
An association of businessmen formed with the purpose of promoting commercial and industrial interests in the community.

chance of loss
In insurance, the relative probability of specific property being destroyed. If the property is certain to be destroyed, the chance of loss is 100 percent. If the property cannot be destroyed, the chance of loss is zero. The greater the chance of loss, the more likely a person or a company will be to seek insurance.

change date
In accounting, the date the standard cost of material and labor for produced goods was last revised by the company official responsible for establishing standard costs.

changeover cost
The sum of the setup and tear-down costs for a manufacturing operation.

channel capacity
In data processing, the maximum number of binary digits or elementary digits to other bases that can be handled by a particular channel in a unit of time. Also, the maximum possible information transmission rate through a channel at a specified error rate. Channel capacity is commonly measured in bits per second or bauds. See BAUD and BITS PER SECOND.

character
One of a set of symbols such as those corresponding to the keys on a typewriter. In data processing, the symbols usually include the decimal digits 0 through 9, letters A through Z, punctuation marks, and any other symbols a computer may read, store, or write.

character density
In data processing, the number of characters that can be stored per unit of length on a magnetic tape.

character recognition
In data processing, the technology of using a machine to sense and encode into a machine language characters that are printed or written to be read by human beings.

charm price
The price affixed to merchandise, and ending in a "9" or any number other than "0," for the purpose of attracting the consumer. Retailers claim that price tags of $3.98 or $4.99 are more appealing to customers than the relatively similar $4.00 or $5.00.

chartered life underwriter
A designation awarded as professional recognition to insurance under-writers who have passed a series of five comprehensive examinations, among other qualifications. See ACLU.

chartered ship
A ship leased to others by its owners.

charter party
A form of contract between merchant and shipowner. See AF-FREIGHTMENT.

chart of accounts
A systematic listing of accounts by name and number serving as an index for recordkeeping and as rapid account identification for posting and other uses in bookkeeping.

chattel
An item of tangible personal property, movable or immovable.

chattel mortage
A mortgage on tangible personal property of a movable nature, such as automobiles or large appliances.

cheap money
A term signifying that the value of a particular currency is low compared with the value of goods and services. It describes a condition wherein the general price level is high and a relatively small amount of goods or services may be obtained for a relatively large quantity of money. Also, cheap money is money lent at low interest rates. The term is sometimes used to signify inflated currency.

check
In data processing, partial or complete testing of the accuracy of machine operations or of the correctness of a computer program.

Also, a bill of exchange drawn on a bank and payable on demand. The British spelling is *cheque*.

check indicator
In data processing, a device displaying or announcing that an error has been made or that a checking operation has determined that a failure has occurred.

checkoff
A procedure by which an employer, with written permission of a worker, withholds union dues and other assessments from his or her paychecks and transfers the collected funds to the union. This provides security for the union from the standpoint of prompt collections from its members.

check problem
A problem chosen to determine whether a computer or program is operating correctly.

check register
In accounting, a journal in which checks are recorded as issued.

   In data processing, a register used to store information temporarily so that it may be checked against the result of a succeeding transfer of the same information.

checkweighman
A worker in a coal mine whose job is to weigh the coal that each miner produces, a practice required when miners were paid according to the number of tons of coal they produced individually.

CHEMTREC
Acronym for *Chemical Transportation Emergency Center*. Operated by the Manufacturing Chemists Association to provide immediate information about hazards of chemicals involved in transportation accidents anywhere in the continental United States.

cheque
See CHECK.

children's bureau
See OFFICE OF CHILD DEVELOPMENT.

chi-square distribution
Usually written χ^2. A technique for estimating a standard deviation on the basis of a small sample.

chose in action
See ASSIGNMENT.

Christian socialism
A movement in the late nineteenth century by various church groups to preach the "social gospel" and promote social legislation and reform

that seeks to improve the well-being of the working classes by appealing to Christian ethical and humanitarian principles.

Christmas tree
In manufacturing, a bill of material in graphic form that displays the structure of a product and how its assemblies and subassemblies are related.

Church, Alexander Hamilton (1866–1936)
A pioneer in industrial management and the relationship between physical working conditions and employee morale. Associated with LEON PRATT ALFORD.

CI
Initials for *cost and insurance.*

CIA
Initials for *cash in advance.*

CIF
See COST, INSURANCE, AND FREIGHT.

CIF&C
Initials for *cost, insurance, freight, and commission.*

CIF&E
Initials for *cost, insurance, freight, and exchange.*

CIFCI
Initials for *cost, insurance, freight, collection, and interest.*

CIFI&E
Initials for *cost, insurance, freight, interest, and exchange.*

CIO
See CONGRESS OF INDUSTRIAL ORGANIZATIONS.

CIP
See COST IMPROVEMENT PROPOSAL.

circle charts
See PIE CHARTS.

circuit capacity
In computers, the number of communications channels that can be handled by a given circuit at the same time.

circular shift
See CYCLIC SHIFT.

circulating assets
British term for CURRENT ASSETS.

circulating capital good
In economics, a capital good that is destroyed in the course of use by a single use. Coal and similarly expendable fuels are examples.

circumstantial evidence
In law, facts establishing a set of conditions from which the principle at issue may be reasonably inferred.

civil action
A proceeding in a court of law or a suit in equity by one person against another for the enforcement or protection of a private right or the prevention of a wrong. It includes actions on contract ex delicto and all suits in equity. Civil action is in contradistinction to criminal action, in which the state prosecutes a person for an offense against criminal law.

Civil Aeronautics Act
See FEDERAL AVIATION ACT.

Civil Aeronautics Board
The CAB is vested with regulatory powers over civil aviation within the United States and between the United States and foreign countries. It has jurisdiction over tariffs and over the rates and fares charged for air transportation. Carriers initiate tariffs and fares, and the Board approves or disapproves them to ensure reasonable and adequate service to the public without unfair competitive practices or undue preference or advantage. The CAB is composed of five members who are appointed by the president for staggered six-year terms. The chairman and vice-chairman are designated annually by the president.

Civil Rights Commission
An agency of the U.S. government responsible for the development of recommendations to Congress of solutions to problems related especially to the rights of minorities.

CL
See CARLOAD.

Clark, John Bates (1847–1938)
An American economist, who founded the American Economic Association. His work *The Distribution of Wealth,* published in 1899, made him the first American theorist in his field to gain international recognition. He thought that workers should receive a fair share of all they produce. He became the leading exponent of the marginal productivity theory of distribution. See NEOCLASSICAL ECONOMICS.

classical economics
A body of economic thought dominant in the Western world from the late eighteenth century until the 1930s. It emphasized man's self-interest and the operation of universal economic laws that tend to guide the economy automatically toward a full-employment equilibrium if governments adhere to a policy of laissez-faire or noninterventionism. Among its chief proponents were Adam Smith, Jean Baptiste Say, Jeremy Bentham, Thomas Robert Malthus, David Ricardo, and John Stuart Mill.

class rates
Insurance rates established for large general classes of risks, according to the construction, occupation, and location of the insured property. Also known as *minimum rates* and *tariff rates.*

In transportation, a system of rates established by the ICC, and similar scales adopted by motor carriers. Virtually every community in the nation that has common carrier transportation service is linked with every other such community by an underlying rate structure. The system provides a basis for calculating freight charges on almost anything that is likely to be shipped from one place to another. See COMMODITY RATES and EXCEPTION RATES.

class struggle
According to Marxist theory, an irreconcilable clash between the bourgeoisie (capitalist class) and the proletariat (working class), arising out of the surplus value that capitalists appropriate from workers. The class struggle will be resolved when the proletariat overthrows the bourgeoisie and establishes a new and equitable economic order.

Clayton Antitrust Act
Enacted in 1914, the act is aimed at preventing unfair, deceptive, dishonest, or injurious methods of competition. Where the effect is to substantially lessen competition or tend toward a monopoly, the act

declares the following to be illegal: (1) price discrimination, except where there are differences in grade, quality, or quantity sold, cost differences in selling or transportation, or where lower prices are offered in good faith to meet competition; (2) tying contracts between buyers and sellers; and (3) intercorporate stockholdings or interlocking directorates among competing corporations.

clearing house
A central agency for the collection, classification, and distribution of information. In finance, an establishment maintained by banks for settling mutual claims and accounts among the members of the establishment.

clear title
A title to goods or property that is free of all encumbrances.

clock
A master timing device used to provide the basic sequencing pulses for the operation of a SYNCHRONOUS COMPUTER.

clock frequency
The master frequency of periodic pulses that schedules the operation of a computer. See SYNCHRONOUS COMPUTER.

clock rate
In computers, the time rate at which pulses are emitted from the CLOCK. The clock rate determines the rate at which logical or arithmetic gating is performed by the machine.

close
The actions that result in adjustments of entries and in the placing of the books of account in order at the end of a month (or any accounting period of less than one year) so that trial balances can be drawn and financial statements prepared.

closed account
An account the sum of whose debits and credits are equal.

closed-circuit television (CCTV)
The transmission of television signals through a cable or a microwave link. CCTV signals can be viewed only through TV sets connected directly to the cable or the microwave link and are intended for use by restricted audiences. CCTV is finding popular use among business organizations as a communications vehicle for interdivisional transmis-

sion of information, such as management meetings with participants at remote points. Also, CCTV is being used as an industrial education medium for training personnel in areas such as sales and in vertical aspects of business management. See OPEN-CIRCUIT TELEVISION.

closed corporation
A corporation whose stockholders are few in number and who are generally active in the management of the business.

closed-end company
A company that maintains an investment service for a limited group of stockholders, often specializing in a particular type of security, without redemption privileges. Its shares may be listed on a stock exchange.

closed-end investment company
An investment company that has a fixed number of shares of stock outstanding. These shares are traded like other shares of common stock and are not redeemed by the investment company. See INVEST-MENT TRUST.

closed-end investment trust
See INVESTMENT TRUST.

closed-end mortgage
A mortgage that has no provision for an increase of the loan to satisfy additional financing needs. Opposite of OPEN-END MORTGAGE.

closed mortgage
A mortgage that cannot be paid off before maturity.

closed shop
A firm which agrees that a person must be a labor union member before being employed and must remain a member of the union while employed. Closed shops were outlawed by the TAFT-HARTLEY ACT of 1947, which permits only a union shop, when agreed to by the employer and the union.

Also, a computer facility where programmers are not allowed to enter the computer room to run or oversee the running of their programs. See OPEN SHOP.

closing statement
A financial summary given to the buyer and seller at the close of a transaction involving the exchange of property for a specific considera-

tion. The statement accounts for all funds received and expended by the escrow holder.

cloud on title
In real estate, words used to express the idea that there is some evidence of record that shows a third party has some prima facie interest in the property in question.

CLU
See CHARTERED LIFE UNDERWRITER.

CMOS
Acronym for *complementary metal-oxide-semiconductor;* pronounced "seamoss." A technology in solid-state circuitry fabrication.

coalition bargaining
A method of bargaining by which a federation of unions (such as the AFL–CIO) tries to coordinate and establish common termination dates for contracts with firms that deal with a number of unions at their plants throughout the country. Its purpose is to enable the federation to strengthen union bargaining positions by threatening to close down all plants simultaneously.

coastwise
Water transportation along the coast.

co-ax
See COAXIAL CABLE.

coaxial cable
An electrical conductor, usually a copper wire, inside a metallic tube. Used as a transmission medium for high-frequency telephone, telegraph, and television signals. Commonly abbreviated and pronounced as *co-ax.*

COBOL
Acronym for *Common Business Oriented Language.* A specific language by which business data processing procedures may be precisely described in a standard form.

cobweb theorem
The generic name for a theory of cyclical fluctuations in the prices and quantities of various agricultural commodities. These fluctuations arise

because for certain agricultural products the quantity *demanded* of the commodity at any given time depends on its price at that time, whereas the quantity *supplied* at any given time depends on its price at a previous time when production plans were initially formulated. If the movements of prices and quantities are plotted on a conventional supply and demand diagram, the pattern of lines looks much like a cobweb—hence the name of the theorem.

COD
Initials for *collect* (or *cash*) *on delivery*.

code
A collection or a compilation of the statutes passed by a legislative body of a state. Such codes are often annotated with citations of cases decided by the state supreme courts. These decisions construe the statutes.

coded decimal
See BINARY CODED DECIMAL.

coded stop
A stop instruction built into a computer routine.

coder
In data processing, a person who prepares instruction sequences from detailed flowcharts and other algorithmic procedures that have been prepared by others; as contrasted with a programmer, who prepares the procedures and flowcharts.

codicil
A written change in a will.

coefficient of correlation
In statistics, a number that expresses the degree of relationship between paired measures. Usually designated by the letter r and calculated by dividing the COVARIANCE of the paired variables by the product of their STANDARD DEVIATIONS. A correlation coefficient indicates high positive correlation if its value is close to 1, high inverse correlation if its value is close to -1, and poor correlation if its value is close to 0.

coefficient of determination
In statistics, the square of the coefficient of correlation; a measure of the degree of relationship between two variables, x and y. The closer the coefficient is to 1, the greater the degree of relationship.

coefficient of elasticity
In economics, the ratio of a percentage change in quantity demanded to a percentage change in price. See ELASTICITY OF DEMAND.

coefficient of relative effectiveness
A term used in the Soviet Union to mean the expected payoff or percent rate of return on a capital investment. It is the equivalent of "marginal efficiency of investment" in the Western economic structure.

cognitive dissonance
A theory put forth by Leon Festinger, a behavioral scientist, dealing primarily with the relationships that exist between perceptions about oneself and one's environment. Dissonance is created when two perceptions that are relevant to each other are in conflict. This creates tension and causes the individual to try to modify one of the incompatible elements to reduce the tension or dissonance. For example, Festinger's research indicates that heavy smokers are less likely to believe there is a relationship between lung cancer and smoking than nonsmokers.

cognovit
In law, a plea by which the defendant, for the purposes of avoiding trial, admits the right of the plaintiff. It is an answer to the complaint often called a "narr" in the confession of judgment action. Often used to secure judgments on promissory notes.

coincident indicators
Time series that tend to move approximately in coincidence with the aggregate economy and that are measures of current economic activity. See TIME SERIES.

coinsurance
A coinsurance clause (often found in property insurance) which assumes that the insured will carry insurance equal to a certain percentage of the value of the property. In the event of loss, the insured will recover any partial loss in the proportion that the amount of insurance

actually carried bears to the amount of insurance required by the coinsurance clause. The effect of coinsurance is to limit the amount that will be paid on partial losses if the insured does not carry the required amount of insurance. If the insured carries the full amount of insurance required by the coinsurance clause, all partial losses will be paid in full up to the amount of insurance carried.

Colbert, Jean Baptiste (1619–1683)

Colbert entered the French public service at age 32 and rose to minister of finance under Louis XIV. He was intensely unpopular because of severe policies of tariffs on imports, bounties to French shipping, extension of French colonies, and public works at home. He forbade French workers from leaving France and attracted immigrants to maintain a plentiful supply of cheap labor. He granted monopolies, stimulated invention, doubled the king's revenues, and made France the most powerful nation in Europe, with a mighty navy. Taxes soared, but the spending habits of the king brought France close to bankruptcy.

cold storage warehouse

A refrigerated warehouse that provides controlled, low temperatures for the storage and preservation of perishable foods such as fruits and vegetables. Also used for storing furs, special chemicals, and other items requiring controlled, low temperatures.

collateral

Personal or real property pledged as security for an obligation.

collateral trust bonds

A debt issue that is secured by collateral such as other securities deposited with a trustee.

collecting officer

In government accounting, an employee who is bonded and authorized to receive, deposit, and report moneys owed to the government.

collective agreement

A collective bargaining contract agreed upon by management and a union, describing wages, working conditions, and other matters of mutual interest.

collective bargaining

Negotiation between a company's management and a union, which represents the company's employees as its bargaining or negotiating agent, for the purpose of agreeing on mutually acceptable wages and working conditions for the employees.

collective farms
Agricultural cooperatives in the Soviet Union, consisting of communities of farmers who pool their resources, lease land from the government, and divide the profits among themselves according to the amount and kind of work done by each. This type of farming, which is subject to detailed government regulation, dominates agriculture in the Soviet Union.

collusion
In law, a secret understanding between two or more persons to take advantage of a third with the object of depriving that person of a property or right.

colon
Basic unit of currency in Costa Rica and El Salvador.

color of title
In real estate, a title that appears to be good but is not. Also known as *apparent title*.

COM
See COMPUTER OUTPUT MICROFILM.

command
See INSTRUCTION.

command economy
An economic system in which an authoritarian government exercises primary control over decisions concerning what and how much to produce; the government may also decide for whom to produce.

Commerce Department
See DEPARTMENT OF COMMERCE.

commercial acre
That which remains of an acre of newly subdivided land after the area devoted to streets, sidewalks, and other rights of access has been deducted.

commercial bank
A financial institution chartered by federal or state government, primarily engaged in making short-term industrial and commercial loans by creating demand deposits or checking deposits, and in retiring loans by canceling demand deposits. It may also perform other financial functions such as holding time or savings deposits and making long-term mortgage loans.

commercial floater contract
An insurance policy issued to cover business property that is in the hands of the owner. Several of the most common commercial floaters are: contractor's equipment, installment sales, physicians' and surgeons', salesmen's, agricultural mobile equipment, livestock, and paraphernalia.

commercial law
The branch of law that relates to business enterprises and commercial transactions, including contracts, negotiable instruments, estates and trusts, sales, debtors, creditors, corporations, real estate, and securities.

commercial paper
Any form of negotiable instrument, such as a check, draft, or bill of exchange.

commission
Compensation paid to an agent, broker, or employee, related to services performed; usually based on a percentage of the gross amounts involved.

commission merchant
An agent or factor through whom goods, wares, and merchandise are sold or to whom they may be consigned for resale, for a compensation referred to as a commission. See FACTOR.

Commission on Civil Rights
An independent agency of the federal government, the commission's purpose is to encourage constructive steps toward equal opportunity for minority groups and women. It conducts fact-finding hearings, research, and investigations relating to the denial of equal protection under the law because of race, color, religion, sex, or national origin. The commission has no enforcement authority, but it refers complaints to agencies with enforcement responsibility. CCR has six citizen members and a staff director, all appointed by the president.

committee deed
An instrument used to transfer, with court approval, the title to property of an infant or an insane person.

committee of incompetent
A court-appointed guardian or guardians of the person or estate of one adjudged incompetent or insane.

Committee on Economic Security
Appointed in 1934 by President Franklin D. Roosevelt to study problems of unemployment, old-age dependency, and other aspects of the nation's economic security. The committee's report became the basis for the Social Security Act, which became law in 1935. See OASDI and SOCIAL SECURITY ACT.

commodity
Another word for an economic "good"; an article of commerce.

Commodity Credit Corporation
A credit organization operated by the U.S. Department of Agriculture. U.S. exporters may apply to the CCC for export financing of eligible commodities purchased either from privately owned stocks or CCC inventories.

Commodity Futures Trading Commission (CFTC)
An independent regulatory agency of five commissioners appointed by the president for staggered five-year terms, CFTC was established by the Commodity Futures Trading Commission Act of 1974 as successor to the Commodity Exchange Authority under the Department of Agriculture. CFTC regulates commodity futures markets, which involve purchases and sales of contracts for certain quantities of specified commodities at fixed prices for delivery at some future date. The Commission's function is to bring under regulation all commodities traded on commodity exchanges; to prevent price manipulation and the dissemination of false or misleading information that might affect prices; to protect against cheating, fraud, and abusive practices in commodity transactions; and to safeguard the handling of traders' margin money and equities by preventing misuse of such funds by brokers. Approximately 16,000 brokers and agents are registered with CFTC, which also supervises the activities of 14 exchanges.

commodity rates
A system of freight charges that takes into account the special characteristics of a particular commodity moving between specified points, as

related to volume and distance. For example, an economical rate may be established for automobile parts moving from Detroit to Cleveland because of heavy volumes between these two places. See CLASS RATES and EXCEPTION RATES.

commodity warehouse
A warehouse specializing in storing and handling commodities such as wool, cotton, potatoes, or tobacco. Commodity warehouses deliberately restrict their service to specific types of commodities.

Common Business Oriented Language
See COBOL.

common carrier
A transportation company, operating under a certificate of convenience and necessity, that provides service to the public at published rates. Familiar examples include buslines, airlines, railroads, and freight truckers. They must accept shipments from anyone who desires to use their services, must charge the same standard rate to all customers, and must maintain regularly scheduled service. They are limited in their ability to provide specialized services. See CONTRACT CARRIER.

common external tariff
A customs duty or tariff, charged in common by the member nations of a common trading area and customs union on goods imported from nonmember states.

common-law corporation
See JOINT-STOCK COMPANY.

common-law trust
See BUSINESS TRUST.

common market
An association of trading nations resulting from the agreement to: (1) impose no trade restrictions, such as tariffs or quotas, among its participants, (2) establish common external barriers to nonparticipants, and (3) impose no national restrictions on the movement of labor and capital among participants. See EUROPEAN ECONOMIC COMMUNITY.

Commons, John R. (1862–1945)
An American economist who was a highly controversial teacher of sociology and a critic of institutions. He is chiefly known for his work

History of Labor in the United States, published in 1918, which was later supplemented by additional volumes written by co-workers.

common stock
Securities representing ownership interest in a corporation. If the corporation has also issued preferred stock, both common and preferred have ownership rights, but the preferred normally has prior claim on dividends and, in the event of liquidation, on assets. Holders of common stock assume the greater risk, but generally exercise more control and may gain greater reward in the form of capital appreciation in addition to dividends. Claims of both stockholdings are junior to claims of bondholders or creditors of the company. The terms "common stock" and "capital stock" are often used interchangeably when the company has no preferred stock. The British term for common stock is *ordinary shares.*

common stock fund
An investment company whose investment policy is to seek profits by investing in common stocks.

Common Stock Index
The New York Stock Exchange (NYSE) computes the performance of all the common stocks traded on the exchange. Based on the close of the market on December 31, 1965, with a base index of 50.00, it is weighted according to the number of shares listed for each issue. Point changes are converted to dollars and cents as indicators of the overall performance of the NYSE.

Commonwealth v. Hunt
An 1842 Massachusetts court case; the first time a court held that a trade union was a lawful organization and that workers could form a union to bargain collectively with employers.

communism
According to the theories of Karl Marx, communism is: (1) a classless society in which all men live by earning and no man lives by owning, (2) a nonexistent state, and (3) an order in which the wage system is completely abolished and all citizens live and work according to the motto "from each according to his ability, to each according to his needs." In most communist countries, communism is an economic system based on social ownership of property, government planning and control of the economy, and programs of rewards and penalties to achieve maximum productive output. Leaders claim that today's communism is Marxist socialism, in preparation for full communism.

community property
All property acquired by a husband and wife after marriage, other than separate property acquired by bequest or from the proceeds of non-community property. Community property is a concept that has been inherited from the civil law. The relationship of husband and wife with respect to community property is somewhat similar to that of the members of a partnership in the ownership of property acquired during marriage.

company
Broadly, any group of people voluntarily united for performing jointly any activity, business, or commercial enterprise. Synonymous with *firm*. *Partnerships* and *corporations* are also considered to be companies.

company union
A labor union limited to a particular firm and usually unaffiliated with any other union.

compa-ratio
The mathematical relationship between the average actual salaries within a salary grade and the midpoint of that grade. If all salaries were at the mathematical midpoint of their respective ranges the compa-ratio would be 100. In most companies, the compa-ratio is about 95, meaning that average actual salaries in a grade are 95 percent of the range midpoint.

comparative advantage, law of
In economics, the principle that if one nation can produce each of two products more efficiently than another nation, and can produce one of these commodities more efficiently than the other, it should specialize in the product in which it is most efficient and leave production of the alternative product to the other country. The two nations will then have more of both goods by engaging in trade. This principle is applicable to individuals and regions as well as to countries.

compensatory transactions
Transactions among nations that are a direct response to balance-of-payments conditions. They may be thought of as balancing items that accommodate differences in money inflows and outflows resulting from so-called *autonomous transactions*. The two main classes are short-term capital movements and shifts in gold holdings.

competition
Rivalry among buyers and sellers of goods, services, or resources. Competition tends to be related to the freedom with which buyers and sellers may enter or leave a marketplace.

competitive bidding theory
The theory that the optimum bid in a competitive bidding situation may be determined by balancing the probability of success of each possible bid and the expected profits from each bid.

competitive price
The price that is established in a market through the independent actions of a number of buyers and sellers. Also, the price per unit of a commodity sold under conditions of perfect competition.

compile
In data processing, to produce a machine language routine from a routine written in source language by selecting appropriate subroutines from a subroutine library. The compiled routine is then ready to be loaded into storage and run; the compiler itself usually does not run the routine it produces.

complaint
The first paper filed in court by the plaintiff in a law suit. It is called a "pleading," and is a statement of the facts upon which the plaintiff bases his cause of action. Also known as *declaration*.

complementary goods
Two or more commodities that are related because a change in the quantity demanded of one causes a direct change in the quantity demanded of the other, within a consumer's given budget. For example, if a price decrease in bread causes a consumer to increase his quantity demand for bread and this, in turn, raises his quantity demand for butter, then bread and butter are complementary within his budget.

completed date
In manufacturing, the date on which a job order or a specified quantity of a particular end product is completed.

completed operations coverage
See PRODUCTS LIABILITY INSURANCE.

completed quantity
The amount or quantity of an end product that has been completed as a result of a manufacturing process.

completion bond
An obligation under notary seal posted as a guarantee by a contractor of completion of a project according to conditions described in the contract. Also known as *performance bond*.

complex trust
In general, a trust that may accumulate income or make a charitable contribution. See SIMPLE TRUST.

component
A subassembly, piece part, or item of material used in high-level assemblies.

composite index
Published by Standard & Poor as a barometer of performance of the stock market, this is an index of 500 stocks computed by multiplying each stock's price by the number of shares outstanding. Some market analysts contend that the composite index reflects the greater influence of the large companies on the stock market.

composite-life method
A depreciation method that is computed on the depreciation base of a fixed-asset group considered as a whole.

compound
To add interest to principal at periodic intervals, thereby establishing a new basis for subsequent interest calculations.

compound duty
A customs duty consisting of a specific duty to which an ad valorem tax is added.

compound interest
The charges made by a lender or a creditor for the loan of money; calculated by the periodic addition of simple interest to principal. The new base thus established becomes the principal amount for computing the interest for the next accounting period. Individuals or organizations

placing funds on deposit with a bank or other financial institution that offers savings accounts in effect become lenders to or creditors for the financial institution. The moneys placed on deposit thus earn interest on principal, generally calculated at a compound interest rate. See SIMPLE INTEREST.

compound journal entry
A journal entry having three or more elements and often representing several transactions. See SIMPLE JOURNAL.

comprehensive automobile liability policy
Insurance offered to business firms to cover legal liability to the public in connection with the ownership, maintenance, or use of the firm's automobiles.

comprehensive crime insurance
Covers burglary, robbery, and other types of theft-loss, destruction, or disappearance of property. Coverage may be offered on an all-risk basis, including losses from forgery and counterfeiting.

comprehensive general liability insurance
Also known as *CGL*. See LIABILITY INSURANCE.

comprehensive personal liability insurance
Also known as *CPL*. See LIABILITY INSURANCE.

compromiser
In organizational behavior, a manager whose style is to use a high task orientation and a high relationships orientation in a situation that requires a high orientation to only one or to neither. This manager is perceived as being a poor decision maker, as one who allows various pressures to influence him too much, and as avoiding or minimizing immediate pressures and problems rather than maximizing long-term production. See RELATIONSHIPS ORIENTATION and TASK ORIENTATION.

comptroller
See CONTROLLER.

Comptroller General
The head of the General Accounting Office, an arm of the legislative branch of the federal government. The GAO reports directly to the Congress on the financial position and accounting systems of government agencies and, at the request of Congress, provides critiques re-

lated to agency organization and management. See GENERAL AC-COUNTING OFFICE.

Comptroller of the Currency
An officer of the Department of the Treasury, the comptroller oversees the 4,600 national banks and controls a staff of 2,000 bank examiners who are responsible for auditing banks to ensure financial solvency and to protect banks' depositors.

computer-aided design
A technique by which a mechanical design engineer can sketch a mechanical part directly into the central processing unit of a computer. The computer can print out copies of the sketch in the form of a completed drawing or in the form of a punched tape for actuating automated machine shop equipment.

computer-aided mask preparation (CAMP)
A method for creating an automated drafting program for preparing a photolithographic mask set.

computerized relative allocation of facilities program
See CRAFT PROGRAM.

computer method for sequencing operations for assembly lines (COMSOAL)
A work-design methodology based on the rapid generation of feasible solutions by a computer routine. The nature of the computer program biases the generation of feasible solutions toward the better ones in order to save computer time.

computer output microfilm
A technique of producing microfilm directly from magnetic tape.

COMSOAL
See COMPUTER METHOD FOR SEQUENCING OPERATIONS FOR ASSEMBLY LINES.

concealed damage
In transportation, damage that is not evident from viewing an un-opened package.

concentration banking
A means of accelerating the flow of funds of a firm by establishing strategic collection centers. The purpose is to shorten the period be-

tween the time a customer mails in his payment and the time when the company has the use of the funds. The selection of the collection centers is usually based on the geographic areas served and the volume of billings for a given area. When payments are received, they are deposited in the collection center's local bank, eventually reaching the bank or a branch of the bank in which the company maintains its major account. See LOCK-BOX SYSTEM.

concentration ratio
The percentage of an industry's output accounted for by several leading firms.

conceptual skill
Ability to understand the complexities of the overall organization and how one's own operations fit into the organization. This knowledge permits one to act according to the objectives of the total organization rather than only on the basis of the goals and needs of one's own immediate group.

conciliation
See MEDIATION.

condemnation proceedings
An action or proceeding in court authorized by legislation (federal or state) for the purpose of taking private property for public use. It is the exercise by the judiciary of the sovereign power of eminent domain.

condition
A clause in a contract, either expressed or implied, that has the effect of installing or removing the legal rights of the parties to the contract. In a deed, a condition is a qualification or a restriction on the rights to the use of the land that depends on a certain occurrence or set of circumstances. For example, if A allows B to use his land and buildings as a church or for church purposes and if it ceases to be used for such purposes, the title reverts to A, and B may no longer use it for any purpose.

conditional sale contract
A legally enforceable agreement for the purchase of property on an installment payment basis. The buyer does not receive clear title to the property until all payments have been completed. Also known as *installment sale contract*.

condition precedent

In law, a clause in a contract providing that an immediate right shall depend on the happening of a specified event. For example, it may be a condition precedent that a contractor secure an architect's certificate before he is entitled to payment.

In insurance, a requirement that must be performed by the insured, or something that must occur, before an insurance company is obliged to pay a claim. For example, it may be a condition precedent in a casualty policy that specified hazards be removed. Failure to do so removes the obligation on the part of the insurance company to pay a claim.

condition subsequent

In law, a clause in a contract that provides for the happening of an event that divests legal rights and duties. For example, a clause in an insurance policy for fire risk that provides that the policy shall be null and void if combustible material is stored within 12 feet of the building. If a fire should occur and combustible material is found to be within 12 feet of the building, the insurance company is not required to reimburse the insured for the loss.

condition concurrent

A condition that must be fulfilled together with other conditions at the same time by each party to a contract. Payment of money and the delivery of goods in a cash sale are conditions concurrent. Failure to perform by one party permits a cause of action by the other.

condominium

A form of property ownership, usually residential property, in which the owner obtains title through a recordable deed for the specific property plus a proportionate share of the site and of the common areas. The maintenance costs of the site and the common areas is apportioned among all the owners within the tract. Condominium ownership differs from cooperative ownership, which provides that ownership of the entire premises be vested in a corporation created for the purpose, the capital stock of which is held by the tenant-owners who are individually liable for the corporation's tax assessments, interest on mortage loans, and upkeep on all areas not covered by proprietary leases.

confession of judgment

See COGNOVIT.

confidence interval
In statistics, a range of adjacent values used to estimate the true value of a parameter with a specified degree of probability; generally superior to POINT ESTIMATES. The probability associated with a confidence interval is the *confidence level;* it is determined by choice and usually set at 95 percent, 99 percent, or 99.9 percent. The two end points of the interval are the *confidence limits.*

conformity
The yielding of the individual's judgment to group pressure, arising from a conflict between his own opinion and that maintained by the group. See COUNTERCONFORMITY.

conformity, principle of
An appraisal principle in real estate holding that the maximum value is realized when properties in the same area are developed in a similar manner.

conglomerate
A corporation that diversifies its operations by acquiring enterprises in widely varied industries.

Congress of Industrial Organizations
A national organization of trade unions in the United States and Canada created in 1935. Its original name was Committee for Industrial Organization. In 1955, the CIO merged with the AFL to form the American Federation of Labor and Congress of Industrial Organizations (AFL–CIO).

Connolly "Hot Oil" Act
A 1935 act of Congress that prohibited interstate shipments of oil in excess of state production quotas.

consequential-losses insurance
A type of insurance providing coverage for indirect losses. For example, fire insurance policies are intended to provide payment only for losses directly attributable to fire damage; additional insurance may be purchased for indirect or consequential losses, which can be greater than the direct losses. There are several types of consequential-losses insurance, including BUSINESS INTERRUPTION INSURANCE, CONTINGENT BUSINESS-INTERRUPTION INSURANCE, EXTRA-EXPENSE INSURANCE, RENT AND RENTAL VALUE INSURANCE, PROFITS AND COMMISSION INSURANCE, LEASEHOLD INSURANCE, ACCOUNTS RECEIV-

ABLE INSURANCE, and REPLACEMENT COST AND DEPRECIATION INSURANCE.

conservator
A guardian or custodian of property appointed by a court on a temporary basis.

consideration
In law, an essential element in the creation of a contractual obligation; the promise of performance by the other party that the promisor demands as the price of his promise. When one promise is consideration for another promise of performance, a bilateral contract has been created. An act may be performed in expectation of a consideration; this creates a unilateral contract. If A promises B to pay him $1 to chop a cord of wood and B promises to chop the wood, a bilateral contract has been created; each has made a promise to the other.

In behavioral science, a term used to refer to the stage in the development of the relationship between a leader and his work group in which friendship, mutual trust, respect, and warmth are manifest. The concept was identified by the leadership studies initiated in 1945 by the Bureau of Business Research at Ohio State University, which attempted to identify various dimensions of leader behavior.

consignment
Shipping of goods for future sale (or for other purposes) without removal of title or transfer of title from the consignor to the consignee. During the period of consignment the consignee is accountable for the goods, although the goods remain a part of the consignor's inventory until the goods have been sold and title has been transferred to the purchaser. The consignee may become the eventual purchaser or act as an agent in the transaction between the consignor and the buyer of the goods.

consolidated balance sheet
In accounting, a balance sheet in which the assets and liabilities of a controlling company are combined with the corresponding financial data of economic units of the total organization in such a way as to present a combined fiscal report, as though all units of the organization were acting as a single unit. See CONSOLIDATED FINANCIAL STATEMENT.

consolidated financial statement
The statement of the financial condition of two or more economic units of an enterprise, presented in a combined format as though they were

one unit, the specific data for one unit not identified separately from those of any other in the same enterprise.

consolidation
The preparation of a balance sheet or other financial statement into a single format that combines the data of related enterprises, which may be affiliates, divisions, or subsidiaries of a parent or holding company.

Also, the combination of two or more enterprises through the transfer of their net assets to a new corporation formed specifically for this purpose.

consols
Short for *Consolidated Annuities;* perpetual bonds issued by the British government. Consols have no due date. They are a promise to pay interest at stipulated intervals forever, or until the bonds are called for payment by the government.

conspicuous consumption
An expression originated by Thorstein Veblen, meaning that those above the subsistence level—that is, the so-called "leisure class"—are mainly concerned with impressing others through their standard of living, taste, and dress. Also known in the vernacular as *keeping up with the Joneses.*

conspicuous parallel action
Identical price behavior among competing firms. Whether or not it is the result of collusion or prior agreement, it has been held illegal by the courts in tests of the antitrust laws.

constant cost
See FIXED COST.

constant-cost industry
An industry that experiences no increases in resource prices as its production expands, despite new firms entering the market. This happens only when an industry's demand for the resources it employs is an insignificant proportion of the total demand for those resources.

constant-dollar value
A dollar value adjusted for fluctuations in purchasing power in order to make possible meaningful comparisons of physical output volumes in a statistical series. To obtain constant-dollar values, current dollar values may, for example, be divided by the price-index number for that year. See CURRENT DOLLARS and PRICE INDEX.

constituent company
A company that is one of a group of affiliated, merged, or consolidated corporations.

consular invoice
See CUSTOMS INVOICE.

consumer goods
Merchandise, inventory, or real goods bought or used primarily for nonbusiness, personal, family, or household purposes.

Consumer Product Safety Act
A 1972 act of Congress; its express purposes include protecting the public against unreasonable risks of injury associated with products, developing uniform safety standards, and promoting research and investigation into the causes and prevention of product-related injuries.

Consumer Product Safety Commission
An independent regulatory agency, directed by five commissioners who are appointed by the president, CPSC's purpose is to protect the consumer against unreasonable risks associated with consumer products. The commission assists consumers in evaluating the comparative safety of consumer products, develops uniform safety standards for consumer products, attempts to minimize conflicts between state and local regulations, and promotes research and investigation into product-related deaths, illnesses, or injuries.

consumer sovereignty
In economics, the concept of the consumer as "king," in the sense that he registers his preferences for goods by his "dollar votes" in the marketplace. In a highly competitive society or economy, competition among producers will cause them to adjust their production to the changing patterns of consumer demands. In less competitive economies, where monopolistic forces and other imperfections exist, resources will not be allocated entirely in accordance with consumer wishes.

container car
A railroad car specially designed to transport portable freight containers.

content addressable random-access memory (CARAM)
In data processing, a storage device that identifies storage locations by their contents instead of by their names, codes, addresses, or posi-

tions. Also referred to as CAM, acronym for *Content Addressed Memory*.

contingency table
A table designed for the purpose of analyzing, or discovering associations between, qualitative characteristics. It is distinguished from a correlation table, which is restricted to the study of quantitative characteristics.

contingent annuity
A periodic payment that is dependent upon some contingency, such as the death or disablement of a person.

contingent business-interruption insurance
Covers losses to the insured for a loss (such as fire) to the premises of another. Some businesses depend heavily upon other businesses, as in the case of a firm that assembles products entirely from parts supplied by another. Damage to one firm's operations can be quite disastrous to both companies. See CONSEQUENTIAL-LOSSES INSURANCE.

contingent duty
See COUNTERVAILING DUTY.

continuing account
Any asset or liability account that is carried over from one fiscal period to another.

continuing appropriation
In government accounting, an appropriation whose remainder, if any, at the end of a fiscal year is carried over to the next fiscal year and may be expended under the conditions of the original appropriation.

continuity concept
An assumption in accounting that in all ordinary transactions an economic unit of an enterprise will persist indefinitely, or at least long enough for current plans to be implemented. Also known as *going-concern assumption*.

continuous budget
A moving projection of financial operations for a series of accounting periods immediately ahead. At the end of each period, the part of the projection that has just been completed is removed and a new projection for a period of equal length is added to the series. Also known as *rolling forecast, rolling budget,* or *moving projection*.

continuous process
A method of production that enables the uninterrupted flow of materials and parts into a processing operation and of completed end products out of the operation.

continuous production
A production system in which the production units are organized and sequenced according to the essential steps of a manufacturing process. The routing of the jobs is fixed, and changes in setups are seldom required.

contra account
One or more accounts that partially or totally offset other accounts. On financial statements they may be merged or may appear together.

contract
In law, a transaction involving two or more individuals whereby each becomes obligated to the other, with reciprocal rights to demand performance of what is promised. Also, the total legal obligation that results from the parties' agreement as affected by law. A promise or a set of promises that the law recognizes as a duty and that, if breached, has a legal remedy. See BILATERAL CONTRACT, COST-PLUS CONTRACT, ORAL CONTRACT, REQUIREMENTS CONTRACT, UNILATERAL CONTRACT, and QUASI CONTRACT.

contract carrier
Usually refers to a for-hire motor carrier, other than a common carrier, that provides transportation service under contract and in accordance with a permit issued by a government regulatory agency. Unlike common carriers, contract carriers do not have to maintain regular schedules, and their rates may vary with the special circumstances of the contract work for which they have been engaged. Examples of contract carriers include chartered airplanes, buses, and trucks.

contractual liability coverage
Insurance written to cover liability that the insured has voluntarily assumed under a contract with a third party; related to bodily injury and property damage protection. See THIRD PARTY RIGHTS.

contra entry
An item of an account that partially or totally offsets one or more items on the opposite side of the same account.

contributed capital
Payments in cash or property made by stockholders to a corporation in return for capital stock, or in response to an assessment on the capital stock, or as a gift to the corporation.

contribution, principle of
An appraisal principle that holds that maximum real property value is achieved when the improvements on the site produce the highest net return commensurate with the investment.

contribution income
See CONTRIBUTION MARGIN.

contribution margin
In accounting, the excess of sales revenue over variable expenses. The contribution margin ratio is necessary for cost–volume–profit analysis where the information is expressed in terms of dollars instead of units. Sales and expenses may be analyzed as follows:

Unit sales price − unit variable expense = unit contribution margin

Contribution margin percentage is arrived at by dividing the unit contribution margin by the unit sales price, both expressed in dollars. The unit contribution margin may be used to calculate the breakeven point in terms of units sold, as follows:

$$\frac{\text{Fixed expenses + desired net income}}{\text{Unit contribution margin}} = \text{breakeven in units}$$

The breakeven point in dollars may be arrived at in this approach:

$$\frac{\text{Fixed expenses + desired net income}}{\text{Contribution margin percentage}} = \text{breakeven in dollars}$$

Contribution margin is also known as *contribution income, marginal balance,* and *marginal income.*

contribution theory
The doctrine that sales of commodities and services provide a source of funds from which production overhead and other costs are paid. Under systems of direct costing, the excess of selling price over direct costs (marginal income) is the measure of such contribution. The practical effects of this theory are (1) the elimination of any formal distribution of indirect costs and (2) the recognition of the bulk of factory and administrative overhead as joint costs not assigned to a specific process or product.

control account
An account that contains the totals of one or more types of transactions whose details appear in a subsidiary ledger or its equivalent. Its balance equals the sum of the balances of the detail accounts.

control concept of accounting
The recognition by general management that accounting information is an essential tool in the practice of the functions of management.

control data
In data processing, items of data used to identify, select, execute, or modify another routine, record, file, operation, or data value.

controllable cost
In accounting, a cost that varies with changes in production. Also, any cost that may be directly controlled and regulated by the management of the unit of an enterprise to which the cost is allocated. See NONCONTROLLABLE COST.

controlled company
A company that is under the active control of a holding or parent company; a subsidiary.

controller
An accountant whose technical skills and activities are dedicated to a single organization or unit of an organization and who is generally the manager of the bookkeeping and financial recording and reporting functions. Sometimes spelled *comptroller*.

controller's deed
An instrument transferring the title to real estate; issued by the state, usually when property is sold due to tax delinquency.

controlling company
See HOLDING COMPANY and PARENT COMPANY.

convenience goods
Products bought for personal consumption, usually through retail outlets located near the consumer's residence. Such goods are generally staple items of low unit value, purchased frequently and in low volume. Examples are soft drinks, tobacco, newspapers, ice cream. Often such items are bought on impulse and are not "price shopped." See SHOPPING GOODS and SPECIALTY GOODS.

convenience store
A retail sales establishment, generally located away from major shopping centers and open for long hours every day of the year. Usually stocks a limited range of basic grocery items, and prices are often higher than those found in supermarkets. Only national brand items are stocked to assure rapid turnover of inventory, much of which is perishable. Convenience stores depend for their success on their locations and long hours, providing convenience for the shopper.

conventional financing
A loan made without government participation.

convergence hypothesis
In economics, the conjecture that capitalism and communism, driven by the process of industrialization, will eventually merge into a new kind of society in which the personal freedom and profit motive of Western capitalistic democracies will blend with the government controls that exist in communistic economies.

conversion
In data processing, the process of changing information from one form of representation to another. For example, changing from the language of one type of machine to that of another, from one medium to another (such as from magnetic tape to printed page), from one type of machine to another, or from one data processing method to another (such as from punch card equipment to magnetic tape equipment) for information storage and retrieval.

convertible
A bond, debenture, or preferred share that may be exchanged by the owner for common stock or another security, usually of the same company, in accordance with the terms of the issue.

conveyance
The transfer of title to land from one person to another; the instrument that effects and records the transfer.

conveyor
A mechanism that supports and transports moving loads in a fixed path. A conveyor may be designed to operate by hand power, by other power conversion sources, or by gravity.

cooperative
A form of organization whose purpose is to gain for producers or consumers, depending on the type of member organization, the profits or savings that would otherwise accrue to middlemen. Its capital is contributed by the members, who are the stockholders.

cooperative bank
See SAVINGS AND LOAN ASSOCIATION.

cooperative ownership
See CONDOMINIUM.

coordinate of the point
See NUMBER LINE.

coping behavior
The trial-and-error approach to problem solving engaged in by individuals who may be experiencing the tension and anxiety caused by blocked needs satisfaction. If a person continues to strive for something without success, he may substitute goals that can satisfy the need. For example, an engineer who is blocked in his efforts to become chief engineer of a laboratory may settle for the position of project group manager. See BLOCKED NEEDS SATISFACTION.

copyright
A form of protection against the unauthorized use of original literary, dramatic, musical, artistic, and other intellectual material. Formerly, the owner of a copyright was granted by U.S. law for 28 years (renewable for a second 28-year term) exclusive rights in his work, such as: the right to print, reprint, and copy the work; the right to sell or distribute copies; the right to record the work; the right to transform or revise the work by means of dramatization, translation, musical arrangement, or the like; and the right to perform the work publicly, if it is a literary, dramatic, or musical work. Only the author, or those deriving their rights through him, can rightfully claim copyright. See COPYRIGHT ACT.

Copyright Act
A 1976 act of Congress that took effect January 1, 1978, and that modifies the previous regulations. The term of protection for works created after January 1, 1978, is 75 years from the year the work is first published or 100 years from the year it was created, whichever is shorter. If the author has the rights, the term is for the length of his life

plus 50 years. Second term for works copyrighted prior to January 1, 1978, is extended to 47 years. The act also covers photocopying and copyrights for articles published in a magazine or trade journal, and extends copyright protection so that federal statutes supersede state laws.

CORDIPLAN
Acronym for *Central Office of Coordination and Planning*. Established by the government of Venezuela in 1958.

cordoba
Basic unit of currency in Nicaragua.

cordonnier system
See PEEK-A-BOO SYSTEM.

core dump
See STORAGE DUMP.

corner
To buy a stock or commodity on a scale large enough to give the buyer or buying group control over the market price.

corporate veil
Any limitation or means to protect corporate officers from personal liability for debts or actions of the corporation.

corporation
An artificial being created under law; an association of shareholders, or even a single shareholder. Corporations are legal entities entirely different and distinct from the shareholder(s), with the capacity of continuous existence or succession. As legal entities they may take, hold, and convey property, sue and be sued, and exercise such other powers as may be conferred on them by law, just as natural persons may. A corporation's liability is normally limited to its assets, and its stockholders—unlike those of a JOINT-STOCK COMPANY—are protected against personal liability for the affairs of the corporation. See CORPORATION DE FACTO, PUBLIC CORPORATION, PRIVATE CORPORATION, and QUASI CORPORATION.

corporation de facto
Created when a group of persons has attempted in good faith to organize a corporation under a valid statute and has failed in some minor

particular, but has thereafter exercised corporate powers. A minor particular might be the oversight or failure to have the incorporators' signatures notarized on applications for charter.

corporation de jure
A corporation that has been formed by complying with the mandatory requirements of the law that authorizes such a corporation.

Corps of Engineers
A unit of the Department of Defense, the Corps was created in 1824. Under judicial interpretations of the law plus amendments to the Water Pollution Control Act, the Corps of Engineers is empowered to regulate and influence construction along waterways and marshlands and in dredging operations and mine dumping.

corpus
The principal or capital of an estate, fund, or trust, as distinguished from the income received.

correction deed
A document that corrects an error, even if typographical, in a recorded instrument that transfers the title to real estate.

correlation
In statistics, the tendency of certain paired measures to vary in relation to each other. See COEFFICIENT OF CORRELATION.

correlation table
A graphic depiction of the relationships among two or more variable quantities. See CONTINGENCY TABLE.

correspondent
A securities firm, bank, or other financial institution that regularly performs services for clients in a place or market to which the client does not have direct access.

COS
Initials for *cash on shipment.*

cost accountant
A person skilled in the theories and practices of COST ACCOUNTING.

cost accounting
The branch of accounting that deals with the classification, recording, allocation, and summarization of cost factors in the planning or operation of an organization.

Cost Accounting Standards Board
CASB is an organization created by the Congress in 1970 to establish uniform cost-accounting standards for application to negotiated defense contracts and subcontracts exceeding $100,000.

cost and freight
The price quoted for materials delivered to and unloaded at a named location. The buyer assumes responsibility for all insurance coverage. Abbreviated C&F, usually followed by the name of the destination, such as a city.

cost center
A department, division, unit, or other clearly identifiable segment of a business that has no capacity for income, but that for purposes of financial control and analysis is treated budgetarily as an entity. Thus, expenses may be used as a measure of the center's performance. See PROFIT CENTER.

cost-effectiveness
A technique introduced by the U.S. Department of Defense and adopted by management in the private sector for analyzing specific expenditures to determine whether the same expenditure could be used more effectively in another direction, or to ascertain whether the expenditure can be reduced without negatively affecting the expected benefit.

cost improvement proposal
A term applied to employee suggestions for cost reductions or economy measures that are related to their specific areas of activity. For suggestions that are implemented, it is common to offer a cash incentive, bonus, or prize.

costing
The technique of determining the cost of activities, processes, products, or services. See COST ACCOUNTING.

cost, insurance, and freight
The price quoted for materials delivered to and unloaded at a named location. The seller assumes responsibility for securing all insurance coverage. See COST AND FREIGHT.

cost ledger
A subsidiary ledger for the accumulation of accounts used in computing or summarizing the cost of goods manufactured or of services produced.

cost of reproduction
The estimated cost, under present economic conditions, of replacing an asset as it was when it was new.

cost of sales
In manufacturing, cost of sales includes the cost of production of finished goods that have been sold. It excludes overhead, marketing, and selling expense. In retail operations, cost of sales includes the total cost of goods sold during a given accounting period and is based on the invoices and other costs related to the cost of goods purchased.

cost-plus
An expression used to indicate that the eventual purchase price on the completion of delivery of goods or services to the buyer will be determined on the basis of actual costs plus a predetermined and mutually agreed-upon fee, which may be a lump sum or a fixed percentage of total costs.

cost-plus contract
A contract based on a cost-plus purchase price. Used frequently in government procurement or when it is difficult to estimate costs, as in a contract involving a novel product or service. Such a contract has the disadvantage that it gives the seller little incentive to keep costs to a minimum.

cost-push inflation
In economics, the condition of generally rising prices caused by production costs that increase faster than productivity or efficiency. Also known as *price-wage spiral* or *wage-price spiral*.

cost standard
In accounting, a predetermined cost estimate with which actual costs may be compared as a measure of performance. Also known as *standard cost*.

Council of Economic Advisors
See EMPLOYMENT ACT OF 1946.

Council on Wage and Price Stability (COWPS)
An agency within the Executive Office of the President, established in 1974. COWPS monitors the economy of the United States as a whole with respect to such key indicators as wages, costs, productivity, profits, and prices. It also has the responsibility to review and appraise the various programs, policies, and activities of the departments and agencies of the federal government for the purpose of determining the extent to which these programs and activities contribute to inflation.

counterclaim
In a judicial proceeding, a claim of the defendant, by way of cross action, that he or she is entitled to recover damages from the plaintiff. It must arise out of the same transaction set forth in the plaintiff's complaint and be connected with the same subject matter. For example, A sues B for the purchase price of goods that have been delivered by A to B in response to a purchase order. B counterclaims that the goods were defective and that, as a result, damages were suffered.

counterconformity
A form of nonconformity in which a person's judgment and action are impelled by group pressure to deviate even more widely from the group norm than if the pressure had been omitted or relaxed. The counterconformist tends to actively oppose the group and compulsively dissent from it.

countervailing duty
An import charge designed to offset an export subsidy by another country. It may include rebates on exports connected with taxes levied on goods (in particular the value-added tax), and all forms of relief that reduce industrial costs, especially in depressed areas. The term may also be applied to a duty that is levied on imported goods when the country of origin levies duties on similar goods it imports. Also known as a *contingent duty*. See CUSTOMS DUTY.

country bank
The National Banking Act (1863) designated *central reserve city banks, reserve city banks,* and *country banks.* These general classifications were carried over into the Federal Reserve Act (1913). Central reserve city banks were located in a few of the largest cities. Reserve city banks were designated in 47 other cities. The remainder of banks were referred to as country banks.

country club style
A style of leadership wherein thoughtful attention to the needs of people for satisfying relationships leads to a comfortable, friendly organization atmosphere and work tempo. See MANAGERIAL GRID.

county deed
A written legal document used in conveying real property owned by a county.

coupon bond
A bond with interest coupons attached. The coupons are clipped as they come due and are presented by the holder for payment of interest. See BEARER BOND and REGISTERED BOND.

coupon yield
The yield in percentage terms that is stated on the face of a bond. Determined by dividing the annual interest payment in dollars by the par value of the security and converting this figure into percentage terms. See YIELD, CURRENT YIELD, and YIELD TO MATURITY.

Cournot, Antoine Augustin (1801–1877)
Professor of mathematics at Lyons, France, Cournot is recognized as the founder of the mathematical method of classical economics. His *Recherches sur les principes mathématiques de la théorie des richesses* was published in 1838.

covariance
In statistics, the covariance of two random variables is a measure of how they vary together. If two variables are independent of each other, covariance does not exist.

covenant
An agreement that becomes part of a legal document and that promises performance or nonperformance of certain acts or of certain uses of property. Sometimes used as a substitute for the word *contract.*

coverage
In insurance, the face amount of an insurance policy or the amount of compensation provided by the insurer in the event of specified losses on the part of the insured; all the risks and perils covered by an insurance policy. In marketing, the number of persons or the percentage of a demographic entity that is reached by a medium of communications.

covered earnings
That portion of an individual's current income that is recognized in the calculation of a benefit. Some companies calculate pension, profit sharing, and insurance benefits on the basis of salary alone, whereas other companies use both salary and bonus.

covering warrant
In government finance, a document issued by the Secretary of the Treasury and countersigned by the Comptroller General that accompanies a deposit of cash receipts within the federal government.

cowboy
See RATE-BUSTER.

COWPS
See COUNCIL ON WAGE AND PRICE STABILITY.

C/P
Abbreviation for *custom of the port*. Also, see CHARTER PARTY.

CPA
Initials for *critical path analysis;* see CRITICAL PATH METHOD. Also, see CERTIFIED PUBLIC ACCOUNTANT.

CPCU
Initials for *chartered property casualty underwriter*. See AMERICAN INSTITUTE FOR PROPERTY AND LIABILITY UNDERWRITERS.

CPL
Short for *comprehensive personal liability insurance*. See LIABILITY INSURANCE.

CPM
See CRITICAL PATH METHOD.

CPP
Initials for *critical path planning*. See CRITICAL PATH METHOD.

CPS
Initials for *characters per second, cycles per second*, and *critical path series*. See PERT.

CPSA
See CONSUMER PRODUCT SAFETY ACT.

CPSC
See CONSUMER PRODUCT SAFETY COMMISSION.

CPU
See CENTRAL PROCESSING UNIT.

CRAFT program
Acronym for *computerized relative allocation of facilities program*. A computerized technique for evaluating relative savings that might result from the relative physical positioning of major activities as well as from more detailed departmental locations within activities. CRAFT programs are applicable to a wide variety of manufacturing situations and nonmanufacturing activities, such as hospital design and warehouse location.

craft union
A labor union whose membership is limited to people who work at the same craft. See INDUSTRIAL UNION and TRADE UNION.

crawling peg
In economics, a system of foreign exchange rates that permits the par value of a nation's currency to change automatically by small downward or upward increments if, in actual daily trading on the foreign exchange markets, the price in terms of other currencies persists on the "floor" or "ceiling" of the established range for a specified period. Known in some areas outside the United States as *sliding parity*.

CRC
See CIVIL RIGHTS COMMISSION.

CRE
See COEFFICIENT OF RELATIVE EFFECTIVENESS.

credit
The ability to buy or borrow in consideration of a promise to pay within a specified time period following delivery. In accounting, a bookkeeping entry that records the reduction or elimination of an asset or an expense, or the creation of or addition to a liability or item of net worth or revenue. Credit entries are made on the right-hand side of an account. Also, the amount recorded in a credit entry; the balance of a liability, net worth, revenue, or valuation account. As a verb, to record a credit by a bookkeeping entry. In international economics, any transaction that results in a money inflow or receipt from a foreign country. It may be represented on a balance-of-payments statement by a plus sign. See DEBIT.

credit instrument
A written or printed financial document that serves either as a promise or an order to transfer funds from one person to another, or from one firm to another.

credit insurance
Intended to cover losses arising out of credit customers' inability to pay their debts, but only to the extent that losses for the year due to this cause exceed normal losses for the year. Generally written for a 12-month period.

credit life insurance
If a credit purchaser dies, his estate or heirs are subject to the debt. It is customary for commercial banks, finance companies, and credit unions to require borrowers to buy a credit life insurance policy whose face value is at least equal to the amount of the loan. The creditor is named as the beneficiary, and premium payments are included in the borrower's monthly loan payments.

credit line
An agreement by a creditor, lender, or bank to extend credit or to make a loan up to a maximum specified amount, when needed by a customer; usually informal and for an indefinite time period.

credit memorandum
A document notifying a purchaser of goods or services that the supplier has decreased the amount of payment owed. The notice is usually made after an invoice has been rendered and partial payment of the invoice amount has been made. See DEBIT MEMORANDUM.

creditor
One to whom money is owed.

creditors' equity
The total amount of liabilities to outsiders other than stockholders.

credit union
A cooperative whose purpose is to promote thrift and to make small loans to members. A credit union may be federally incorporated and under the jurisdiction and audit of the Federal Deposit Insurance Corporation (FDIC).

creeping inflation
A slow but persistent upward movement in the general level of prices over a long period of years, typically at an average annual rate of up to 3 percent.

cremation certificate
A sworn statement that an agent or other appointee has securities that have been either reacquired and retired or destroyed.

criminal action
See CIVIL ACTION.

criminal-conspiracy doctrine
English common law applied to labor disputes early in the history of the United States. In the first major labor case, 1806, the court held that to combine and concertedly withhold labor in order to exact higher wages was an illegal conspiracy. See ILLEGAL-PURPOSE DOCTRINE.

critical path method (CPM)
A planning method or technique for analysis that shows the interrelationships in sequence of all activities involved in a project. Claimed to have been developed originally as an internal project for the Du Pont Company to plan and control the maintenance of chemical plants, and subsequently applied widely by Du Pont for many engineering functions. Created approximately at the same time the U.S. Navy developed PERT. There are many variations of CPM and PERT in use throughout all industries. Also known as *critical path analysis* (CPA) and *critical path planning* (CPP). See PERT.

crop insurance
Insurance against failure of or damage to a crop. The risk most frequently insured is loss from hail.

crosstalk
In data processing, unwanted signals in a channel that originate from one or more other channels in the same communications system; usually an undesirable effect.

crown agent
A British nonprofit agency that purchases goods on behalf of approximately 80 governments (especially newly independent Commonwealth countries of Great Britain) and more than 160 international and public authorities. Crown agents normally engage in competitive bidding, buying directly from manufacturers for whom they can be active as a channel for export sales.

cruzeiro
Basic unit of currency in Brazil.

CRV
Initials for *certificate of reasonable value*. A document in real estate that contains the Veterans Administration appraisal of a property.

cryogenics
A branch of physics that deals with the production and effects of very low temperatures. At such temperatures, the current-carrying capabilities of some metals, for example, appear to increase significantly and large changes in current flow can be obtained with relatively small changes in magnetic field.

CSC
Initials for *Civil Service Commission*.

CSMFB
Initials for *Central States Motor Freight Bureau*.

CST
See CENTRAL STANDARD TIME.

CT
Initials for *Central time*. See CENTRAL STANDARD TIME.

cubic foot cost
The construction cost of a building per cubic foot of interior space.

Cullom Report
A special committee—known as the Cullom Committee—was established by Congress to investigate and report on needs for regulating railroads. The Committee's report was made in 1886 and, unlike the Windom Report of 1874, placed more emphasis on the evils of discrimination than on the levying of rates. The Committee favored a system of regulation; however, the views of the Senate and the House of Representatives were widely divergent. A compromise was reached by Congress in 1887. See ACT TO REGULATE COMMERCE.

culture lag
The condition that exists when changes in concepts and ideas of political, social, and economic life fail to keep pace with physical changes in the environment that are caused by mechanical invention, technological innovation, depletion of essential natural resources, and similar circumstances.

cumulative dividend
A dividend on cumulative preferred stock that is payable, under the terms of the issue, at stated intervals and before any distribution is made to the holders of common stock.

cumulative preferred stock
Stock having a provision that if one or more dividends are omitted, the omitted dividends must be paid before dividends may be paid on the company's common stock.

cumulative voting
A method of voting for corporate directors that enables a shareholder to multiply the number of his shares by the number of directorships being voted on and cast the total for one director or for a selected group of directors. For example, if a holder of 10 shares normally votes for 12 nominees to the board of directors, he has 120 votes. Under the cumulative voting principle, he may cast 10 votes for each nominee, 120 votes for only one nominee, 60 for two, 40 for three, or any other distribution he chooses. Cumulative voting is required under the laws of some states and is permitted in many others.

curable depreciation
In real estate, deterioration, damage, and wear and tear that are potential causes of equipment or property obsolescence or loss of value, and that are customarily repaired by the owner.

Curb Exchange
Former name of the American Stock Exchange, second largest exchange in the United States. The name comes from the market's origin on a street in downtown New York City.

curing a title
In real estate, the act of removing any defects from a title to make it marketable.

currency
Coins and paper money.

current-asset cycle
The period of time required for sales to equal current assets.

current assets
Those assets of a company that are reasonably convertible to money, that can be sold, or that are consumed in the normal operating cycle of the business. They include cash, U.S. government bonds, receivables, money due from any sources within one year, and inventories with marketable value.

current dollars
A value expressed in dollars and reflecting actual prices of the current year. Economic data are often quoted in current dollars. See CONSTANT-DOLLAR VALUE.

current liabilities
Debts and financial obligations of a company that are due and payable within one year.

current maturity
The portion of a long-term obligation that is to be retired during the next twelve months; usually classified as a CURRENT LIABILITY.

current ratio
One of many ratios used to measure the performance of an enterprise and its management; determined by dividing current assets by current liabilities. See LIQUIDITY RATIOS.

current savings
See SAVINGS.

current yield
The yield of a security determined by dividing its annual interest or dividend payment by the current market price and converting this figure into percentage terms. See YIELD, COUPON YIELD, and YIELD TO MATURITY.

custody
In law, with respect to property, the immediate charge and control exercised by a person under the direction of the true owner, without any interest in the property that might be adverse to the true owner. For example, a servant is in custody of his master's goods.

Customary system
See U.S. CUSTOMARY SYSTEM.

customer's broker
See REGISTERED REPRESENTATIVE.

customer's man
See REGISTERED REPRESENTATIVE.

customhouse
A building where duties on foreign shipments are handled.

customs duty
A tax that is levied on goods transported from one political jurisdiction to another, especially a tax on goods imported from a foreign country. Such a duty is distinguished from a CUSTOMS TARIFF, which is a comprehensive schedule of such duties. See COUNTERVAILING DUTY.

customs invoice
An invoice for goods shipped from one country to another, prepared in a form that provides the information and data required by the country to which the goods are shipped, and sworn to before a consular officer stationed in the country from which the goods are shipped. Also known as *consular invoice*.

Customs Service
An office of the Department of the Treasury. Customs examines all persons and merchandise entering the United States from foreign countries to ensure compliance with documentary and tariff regulations.

customs tariff
A schedule of charges assessed by a government on imported or exported goods.

customs union
A trading alliance of two or more member countries that have no trading or customs barriers between them. Member countries of a customs union may operate a customs barrier or common external tariff applicable to nonmember nations. See EUROPEAN FREE TRADE ASSOCIATION.

CWO
Initials for *cash with order*.

CWT
Hundredweight. In the United States, 100 lbs. In the United Kingdom, 112 lbs.

cybernetics
From the Greek *kybernetes,* "pilot or governor." The science of communications and control theory that is especially concerned with the comparative study of automatic control systems, such as the nervous system and the brain, and electromechanical communication systems. The term is popularly used in connection with experimental systems that attempt to simulate human action and reaction.

cycle count
Regular counting (as often as daily) of items in stores on a rotating basis that assures that each item is counted at least once each year.

cycle inventories
See LOT-SIZE INVENTORIES.

cyclical fluctuations
Variations in business volume; technically described as successive periods of positive and negative percent deviations around the secular trend curve of a time series, with the duration of a complete cycle of fluctuation being more than one year. See SEASONAL FLUCTUATIONS.

cyclical unemployment
Unemployment that results from business recessions or depressions because aggregate demand falls too far below the full employment level of aggregate output and income.

cyclic shift
In data processing, a shift in which the digits dropped off at one end of a word are returned at the other in a circular fashion. For example, if a register holds eight digits, 23456789, the result of a cyclic shift two columns to the right would be to change the contents of the register to 89234567. Also known as *circular shift, end-around shift, logical shift, nonarithmetic shift,* or *ring shift.* See SHIFT REGISTER.

D/A or DAC
See DIGITAL-TO-ANALOG CONVERTER.

dalasi
Basic unit of currency in Gambia.

damages
An amount of money imposed by a court upon a defendant as compensation for the plaintiff. The result of a judicial decision that the defendant has injured the plaintiff by breach of a legal duty or violation of a right guaranteed under law, such as the right to privacy.

data dredging
In statistical analysis, the process of examining data that have been collected for specific purposes but that contain much more information than has been used for the original investigation.

data processing
Synonymous with data handling; in its simplest sense it refers to the production of records and reports. In a broader sense it involves the preparation of source media that contain data or basic elements of information, and the handling of such data according to precise rules of procedure to accomplish such operations as classifying, sorting, calculating, summarizing, and recording. When the processing is performed by electronic equipment it is known as *electronic data processing* (EDP), or *automatic data processing* (ADP).

dated earned surplus
The earned surplus or retained earnings of a corporation accumulated from the date of a reorganization or quasi-reorganization.

date on/off
In manufacturing, the effectivity and ineffectivity dates that indicate when a part is to be added to or deleted from a BILL OF MATERIALS.

dating
See SEASONAL DATING.

Dawes Plan
A plan put into effect in 1924 attempting to fix the reparations amounts owed by Germany to the Allied and associated nations under the terms of the Treaty of Versailles and to facilitate those payments. In 1929 it was superseded by the Young Plan. See YOUNG PLAN.

daybook
In accounting, a diary of business activities; a chronological record of the transactions conducted by an enterprise. Entries in the daybook are subsequently entered in a journal and posted to a ledger. Daybooks have become virtually obsolete.

day order
In the stock market, an order to buy or sell that expires if not executed by the end of the trading day on which it was entered.

DBA
Short for *doing business as*. The legal name under which a person or firm is doing business.
    Also, Doctor of Business Administration.

DCTL

Abbreviation for *direct-coupled transistor logic*. The first logic form that was considered for integrated electronic circuits.

DDR-mark

Basic unit of currency in the German Democratic Republic (East Germany). Also known as *ostmark*.

dead load

The orders ahead of any manufacturing facility that have not yet been released. Sometimes used in dispatching to indicate the orders that a departmental dispatcher has on hand and for which materials and instructions have not yet been received in the department. See LIVE LOAD.

deadweight tonnage

D/W is the number of tons of cargo, stores, and bunker fuel, at 2,240 pounds each, that a vessel can transport. The difference between the number of tons of water a vessel displaces light and the number of tons it displaces when submerged to the load line.

dealer

In the securities business, an individual or a firm acting as a principal rather than as an agent. Typically, a dealer buys for his own account and sells to a customer from his own inventory. The dealer's profit or loss is the difference between the price he pays and the price he receives for the same security. The dealer's confirmation must disclose to his customer that he has acted as principal. The same individual or firm may function at different times either as a broker or as a dealer. See SPECIALIST.

Dean schedule

A system of evaluating relative fire hazards; used as a standard in some states for determining fire-insurance rates for certain types of structures. Also known as *analytic schedule*.

debenture

A promissory note issued by a company and backed by the general credit of the company; usually not secured by a mortgage, lien, or any specific property. A debenture ranks ahead of preferred stock in the event of liquidation of corporate assets.

debenture capital
Proceeds from the sale of debentures.

debit
In accounting, a bookkeeping entry or posting that records the creation of or addition to an asset or expense, or the reduction or elimination of a liability; an entry on the left side of an account. The balance of an asset, expense, or debit valuation account. See CREDIT.

In international economics, any transaction that results in a money outflow or payment to a foreign country. It may be represented on a balance-of-payments statement by a minus sign.

debit memorandum
A document other than an invoice showing the reason and authority for creating a debit. When issued by a bank, it has the effect of reducing the depositor's or customer's account. It may be issued by a customer to his supplier for goods returned to the supplier. See CREDIT MEMORANDUM.

debt discount
The difference between the face value of a loan and the net amount received by the borrower. When the discount relates to a loan, such as a bank loan, that represents a current liability, it is treated as a prepaid expense.

debt-equity ratio
To market analysts, a company's long-term debt divided by the stockholders' equity or net worth. In general, the total amount owed to outsiders divided by the stockholders' equity.

debt limit
In municipal government accounting, the maximum amount of indebtedness that a government unit may incur; established by constitution, statute, or charter.

debt service
The payment of matured interest and principal.

deceit
The conduct in a commercial transaction by which one person, through fraudulent representations, misleads another.

decile
Any of the even tenth percentiles. See PERCENTILE.

decimal coded digit
A digit or character defined by a set of decimal digits, such as a pair of decimal digits specifying a letter or special character in a system of notation.

decimal-to-binary conversion
The process of converting a number written to the base ten (decimal) to the equivalent number written to the base two (binary). See BINARY NOTATION and BINARY-TO-DECIMAL CONVERSION.

decision tree
A method of analysis that evaluates decisions in terms of alternatives, their values, and probabilities of their possible outcomes. The expected value of each alternative is the sum of the various possible outcomes weighted by their probability of occurrence. Also known as *probability tree*.

declaration
In common law, the plaintiff's first pleading, in which the facts on which the cause of action is based are set forth. Synonymous with COMPLAINT.

declaration of restrictions
In real estate, a recorded list of encumbrances imposed by a subdivider that limit the use of a tract. Deeds to individual lots make reference to this document.

declared capital
See STATED CAPITAL.

declared dividend
A dividend that has been authorized by the board of directors to be paid to the stockholders of record on a specified date.

declared value
See STATED VALUE.

declining-balance method
A method of depreciation in which the annual charge for depreciation is arrived at by applying a fixed percentage to the remaining value of the

life of an asset. One of several methods other than the straight-line method for calculating the cost of the lost usefulness or the used-up life of an asset. Usually modified by a quantifier—for example, "double" or "triple" declining-balance method. An illustration of the double-declining-balance method follows for an asset with a useful economic life-span of ten years:

Original cost of asset = $10,000

Year of life	Annual depreciation	Remaining value of asset
1	$2,000	$8,000
2	1,600	6,400
3	1,280	5,120
4	1,024	4,096
5	819.20	3,276.80
6	655.40	2,621.40
7	524.30	2,097.10
8	419.40	1,677.70
9	355.50	1,342.20
10	268.40	1,073.80

Note that the depreciation allowance each year is 20 percent of the remaining value of the asset. The depreciation may be continued beyond the ten-year period or may be written off at the end of that period, but not sooner. In the straight-line method, the allowance each year would have been 10 percent, or one-tenth, of the original cost for an asset with an estimated life of ten years.

decoder
A device that determines the meaning of a set of signals and initiates a computer operation based on the interpreted signals. Also, a matrix of switching elements that selects one or more output channels according to the combinations of input signals.

decoupling inventories
A concept relating to the separation of inventories at various stages, such as on-the-shelf goods in the retail establishment, on-the-floor materials in the manufacturing area, or components in abeyance or holding stages. "Decoupling" these stages removes the immediate performance requirements for inventories.

decreasing variation
In statistical analysis, the principle that the reliability of a sample increases as the square root of the number (n) in the sample increases. A sample of $n = 100$ is twice as reliable as a sample of $n = 25$ because the square root of the former is twice the square root of the latter.

decree
The determination by a court of the rights between parties, in the form of an order to carry out the decree; for example, an order that a contract be specifically enforced.

dedicated manager
A manager who tends to dominate others. He gives many verbal directions to subordinates. His time perspective is immediate. He identifies with superiors and with the technical organizational system. He emphasizes technological rather than human demands. He judges subordinates on quantitative performance and superiors on skill in using power. He believes in punitive corrections. His subordinates often complain about the lack of information. His main weakness is that he argues with others when matters could be solved in other ways. He fears loss of power.

deductible clauses
Insurance clauses that eliminate coverage for minor losses, thereby reducing the relatively high costs of processing and investigating small claims and restraining the growth in premium costs to the insured. There are two forms of deductible clauses found most frequently in property and liability insurance policies: the STRAIGHT DEDUCTIBLE and the FRANCHISE DEDUCTIBLE.

deduction
In logic, the process of reasoning from premises to conclusion. Premises are more general than conclusions, so deduction is a process of reasoning from the general to the specific. See INDUCTION.

deed
A document that, when properly executed and delivered, transfers the title to real estate.

deed, bargain and sale
See BARGAIN AND SALE DEED.

deed, quitclaim
An instrument that transfers the title to real estate and that contains no warranties of any kind. Same as BARGAIN AND SALE DEED.

deed, sheriff's
An instrument that transfers the title to real estate when property is sold by court order in payment of a debt. Also known as *marshal's deed*.

deed, warranty
A deed containing a covenant of guarantee, in which the grantor assures that the title is free from defects, that the property is free of encumbrances other than those listed, and that the grantor agrees to protect the grantee against any loss by reason of the existence of any other title or interest in the property at the time the deed is executed.

deed in lieu of foreclosure
The transfer of a title from a borrower to a lender to avoid foreclosure.

deed of confirmation
A deed used for correction of errors in other deeds.

deed of reconveyance
The transfer of a legal title from a trustee to a trustor after a deed-of-trust debt has been paid. See DEED OF TRUST.

deed of release
A deed used to free land, or a portion thereof, from a mortgage. Also known as *release of mortgage*.

deed of surrender
A deed used to transfer title to an estate for a specific number of years or for life.

deed of trust
A deed to real property held by a trustee to secure the performance by the grantor or another of an obligation owed to the beneficiary of the trust.

de facto corporation
See CORPORATION DE FACTO.

defalcation
A legal term synonymous with *embezzlement* or *misappropriation of funds*. A person in a trust or fiduciary relation who, by reason of his own fault, is unable to account for funds left in his hands has committed a defalcation.

defamation
The use of spoken words that are generally understood to impute some disreputable conduct or moral delinquency to the person about whom they are said. See LIBEL.

defeasance
In real estate, a provision or condition in a deed or other instrument that renders the instrument void under specified conditions.

defendant
A person being sued in a court of law; the person who answers a plaintiff's complaint; the defending party in civil actions. In criminal actions, the defending party is the *accused*.

defensive patent insurance
See PATENT INSURANCE.

deferred compensation
Payment that a corporation is committed to make to an executive at some future date, normally after retirement. The compensation can be in the form of a deferred bonus, a portion of salary, or an additional amount that might have been stipulated in an employment contract. Deferred compensation plans are voluntarily participated in by executives.

deferred revenue
Income or revenue received before it is earned. Examples include rent received in advance, transportation fees paid for in advance, and theater tickets paid for in advance.

deficiency judgment
In law, if mortgaged and foreclosed property does not sell for a sufficient sum to pay the mortgage debt, the difference between the selling price and the mortgage debt is called a deficiency. It is chargeable to the mortgagor or to any person who has purchased the property and assumed and agreed to pay the mortgage.

deflation
A decline in the general price level of all goods and services, equivalent to a rise in the purchasing power of money, as contrasted with INFLATION.

Also, a statistical adjustment of data by which an economic time series expressed in current dollars is converted into a series expressed in constant dollars of a previous period. The purpose of the adjustment is to compensate for the distorting effects of inflation.

deflationary gap
The amount by which the theoretical volume of spending necessary to maintain full employment or to absorb all available goods and services at prevailing prices exceeds actual private spending and government expenses. See INFLATIONARY GAP.

defraud
To cheat another or to withhold wrongfully that which belongs to another; to deprive one of some right by deceitful means. For example, conveying one's property for the purpose of avoiding the payment of a debt is a transfer intended to hinder, delay, or defraud creditors.

del credere agency
From the Italian, "of belief" or "of trust." An agent, factor, or broker is operating under a del credere agency or commission when he undertakes to guarantee to his principal the payment of a debt due from a buyer of goods.

delectus personae
Latin, "choice of person." The selection of a person for a position of responsibility and trust. Delectus personae always exists in a partnership (since the partners choose each other), but not in a joint-stock company.

demand, law of
The principle that the demand for a commodity varies inversely with its price, assuming that all other things affecting demand remain constant. The other influences include income level of buyers, prices of related goods, or preferences of buyers, and the number of buyers in the market. An additional consideration may be the buyer's expectation regarding future prices and income.

demand curve
A curve that relates price per unit of a product to the quantity of the product demanded by consumers. The demand curve is usually drawn between axes with price on the vertical and quantity demanded on the horizontal, and generally slopes downward from left to right.

demand deposit
The promise by a bank to pay immediately an amount specified by the customer who owns the deposit. It is thus checkbook money, permitting transactions to be paid for by check rather than with currency.

de Mandeville, Bernard (1670–1733)
A Dutch physician, de Mandeville spent much of his life in England. He advocated laissez-faire economics and the division of labor. In 1705 he published a satire, *The Grumbling Hive, or Knaves Turned Honest*, which was expanded and republished in 1714 as the *Fable of the Bees; or Private Vices, Public Benefits*. His ideas were later advanced by Adam Smith in his *Wealth of Nations*. See PARADOX OF THRIFT.

demand price
The highest price a buyer is willing to pay for a given quantity of a commodity.

demand schedule
A table showing the number of units of a commodity that buyers would be willing and able to purchase at various possible prices during a given period of time, all other factors remaining the same.

democratic leadership
A style of management in which the leader plays a permissive role, sharing the functions of leadership with the members of the group by encouraging their participation in goal setting and in planning and directing the activities of the group. See LAISSEZ-FAIRE and AUTHORITARIAN LEADERSHIP.

DEMON
Acronym for *decision mapping via optimum networks*. A mathematical network analysis technique for evaluating new product marketing plans. It considers such financial aspects as payback period and breakeven point and assists in decision making relative to the best way to use the marketing budget.

demurrage
A penalty charge against shippers or receivers for delaying carrier equipment beyond allowed free time. The term has been in use since early in the seventeenth century, when it meant the delay of a vessel beyond its scheduled sailing time and the payment for the delay. It was later extended to include rail transport.

demurrer
A procedural method used in a law suit by which the defendant admits all the facts alleged in the plaintiff's complaint, but denies that such facts state a cause for action. It raises a question of law on the facts, which must be decided by the court.

Department of Agriculture (USDA)
A department of the federal government directed by law to acquire and disseminate useful information on agricultural subjects in the broadest sense, including areas of research, education, conservation, marketing, regulatory work, and rural development. USDA is headed by a presidentially appointed secretary, who is a member of the Cabinet.

Department of Commerce (DOC)
A department of the federal government, the DOC encourages, serves, and promotes the nation's economic development and technological advancement. The department offers assistance and information to domestic and international businesses; provides social and economic statistics and analyses for business and government planners; assists in the development and maintenance of the U.S. Merchant Marine; provides research for and promotes the increased use of science and technology in the development of the economy; provides assistance to speed the development of the economically underdeveloped areas of the nation; seeks to improve understanding of the earth's physical environment and oceanic life; promotes travel to the United States by residents of foreign countries; assists in the growth of minority businesses; and seeks to prevent the loss of life and property from fire. The secretary of commerce is appointed by the president and is a member of the Cabinet.

Department of Defense (DOD)
A department of the federal government whose main purpose is to provide the military forces needed to preserve the national security. The main components of DOD are the Army, the Navy (including the Marine Corps), and the Air Force, each of which is headed by a secre-

tary appointed by the president. The secretary of defense is appointed by the president and is a member of the Cabinet.

Department of Energy (DOE)
Established on August 4, 1977, and headed by the energy secretary with Cabinet-level responsibility. The new department's size was projected at the 20,000-employee level with a budget for fiscal 1978 of $10.6 billion. The Energy Department acquired the functions and employees of the Federal Energy Administration, the Energy Research and Development Administration, and the Federal Power Commission. A five-member federal energy regulatory commission, its members appointed to four-year terms by the president and subject to Senate confirmation, was established within the department but is independent of its secretary. The commission sets rates for the transportation and sale of natural gas and electricity and for the transportation of oil by pipeline. The Energy Department has regional marketing authority over electric power, control over the rate of energy production on public lands, and jurisdiction over the naval petroleum and oil shale reserves. It also has authority to set energy conservation standards for buildings and to oversee voluntary industrial conservation programs. Coal development and energy data programs are also housed in the Energy Department. The president is required to perform a comprehensive review of its programs within five years of the Energy Department's startup.

Department of Health, Education, and Welfare (HEW)
The agency is headed by a secretary (a member of the Cabinet) who is appointed by the president. It is the department of government most concerned with people and the nation's human needs. Its major components are the Education Division, Office for Civil Rights, Office of Consumer Affairs, Office of Human Development, Public Health Service, Social and Rehabilitation Service, Social Security Administration, Office of Child Support Enforcement, Health Care Financing Administration, and Office of Special Studies.

Department of Housing and Urban Development (HUD)
HUD is headed by a secretary (a member of the Cabinet) who is appointed by the president. HUD provides assistance for housing and for the development of the nation's communities.

Department of the Interior (DOI)
A federal agency headed by a secretary (a member of the Cabinet) who is appointed by the president. DOI's main functions are to appraise,

manage, conserve, and develop the nation's public land and parks and its mineral, water, wildlife, and energy resources, and to protect the environment. DOI also has major responsibility for American Indian reservation communities and for people living in Island Territories under United States administration.

Department of Justice (DOJ)
A federal agency headed by the U.S. Attorney General (a member of the Cabinet) who is appointed by the president. The department is the principal law enforcement arm of the federal government. Through its prosecuting divisions and the 94 local United States Attorney's offices, it enforces federal statutes through civil and criminal prosecutions in the federal courts. Each U.S. Attorney may designate an Assistant U.S. Attorney to be responsible for all consumer protection matters. The Federal Bureau of Investigation is the department's principal investigating arm.

Department of Labor (DOL)
A federal agency headed by a secretary (a member of the Cabinet) who is appointed by the president. DOL's main purpose is to promote and develop the welfare of wage earners and to improve their opportunities. The position of Special Assistant to the Secretary for Consumer Affairs has been established as liaison with individual consumers, consumer organizations, the Special Assistant to the President for Consumer Affairs, and federal, state, and local consumer units.

Department of State
The U.S. Department of State is headed by a secretary (a member of the Cabinet) who is appointed by the president. The department formulates and executes the foreign policy of the United States. It issues passports to U.S. nationals for use in travel to foreign countries. The Coordinator of Consumer Affairs is responsible for consumer programs and issues, and also serves as the State Department's liaison with consumer groups.

Department of Transportation (DOT)
Created in 1967 and headed by a secretary (a member of the Cabinet) who is appointed by the president. An arm of the executive branch of government, DOT's purpose is to foster the development and maintenance of a safe, efficient, and effective national transportation system. The primary functions of DOT were created through transfers of several activities from the Interstate Commerce Commission, the Federal Maritime Commission, and the Civil Aeronautics Board.

Department of the Treasury
Headed by a secretary (a member of the Cabinet) who is appointed by the president. The Treasury Department is responsible for the fiscal operations of the federal government. The Special Assistant to the Secretary serves as a coordinator of a Treasury-wide consumer representation effort. See ALCOHOL, TOBACCO AND FIREARMS BUREAU, COMPTROLLER OF THE CURRENCY, CUSTOMS SERVICE and INTERNAL REVENUE SERVICE.

department store
A store that carries many kinds of goods, each sold in its own department. Separate departments allow for diversification in promotion and service. See SPECIALTY STORE.

dependent covenant
In law, an understanding that fulfillment of one promise must occur before fulfillment of another promise. For example, in a cash-in-advance sale the buyer must pay the money before the seller is under any obligation or duty to deliver the goods.

dependent demand
In manufacturing, the requirements for parts or assemblies that are generated from high-level subassemblies or assemblies. See INDEPENDENT DEMAND.

depletion
Lessening in value as a result of the using up of an asset; the use of a natural resource at a rate greater than its replacement rate.

depletion allowance
A means of accounting for the depletion of natural resources. It usually consists of charges against earnings based upon the amount of the asset taken out of the total reserves in the period for which the accounting is made. Merely a bookkeeping entry; it does not represent any cash outlay, nor are any funds earmarked for the purpose.

depositary
An institution such as a bank that accepts cash deposits from customers; also, an individual or organization that receives any type of property for safekeeping. "Depositary" and "depository" may be used interchangeably; at one time "depositary" was a person and "depository" a place.

depreciated cost
The cost of an asset less the accumulated depreciation; the book value of a fixed asset.

depreciation
The used-up portion of the life of a fixed asset; expired or lost utility; the process of estimating and recording lost usefulness. According to the AICPA, depreciation is a process of allocation, not of valuation.

depreciation accounting
A branch of accounting that deals with systematically distributing or allocating the cost or other basic value of a fixed asset over its estimated useful economic life by means of periodic charges to expense or against revenue.

depreciation base
The recorded cost of a fixed asset or fixed-asset group that is to be recovered through depreciation, not including the estimated amount that may be recovered from sale or salvage of the asset.

depreciation expense
The portion of the cost of a fixed asset or fixed-asset group that is charged against operations for an accounting period. Also, any provision for depreciation.

depreciation fund
Assets in the form of money or marketable securities that have been set aside or reserved for the purpose of replacement of fixed assets that are depreciating.

depreciation insurance
Insurance that is added to a fire insurance policy by endorsement and that covers the difference between the actual cash value and the replacement cost of the insured property.

depreciation method
In accounting, the mathematical technique employed within Internal Revenue Service guidelines and regulations for the periodic (annual) allocation of depreciation charges to expense or against revenue.

depression
A phase of the business cycle characterized by industrial and commercial stagnation, scarcity of money and goods, low prices, poor expecta-

tions, and mass unemployment. Similar to a recession, but more severe and lengthy in its effects and duration.

depth table
A schedule used by real estate appraisers in determining the relative values of lots of varying depths, or distances from the street.

descent
The disposition by the courts of the real property of a person who has died without leaving a will.

descriptor
A computer word that is used specifically to define characteristics of a program element. For example, descriptors are used for describing a data record, a segment of a program, or an input/output operation.

deserter
In organizational behavior, a manager whose style is to use a low task orientation and a low relationships orientation in a situation where such behavior is inappropriate. He is perceived as uninvolved and passive or negative. See RELATIONSHIPS ORIENTATION and TASK ORIENTATION.

desk jobber
See DROP SHIPPER.

destructive readout (DRO) memory
A computer memory in which reading the contents of a storage location destroys the contents of that location. If the data are to be returned, they must be rewritten after the reading. An example of DRO memory is the common core memory used in some computers. See NONDESTRUCTIVE READOUT MEMORY.

deterministic inventory models
In manufacturing, inventory models used where the actual demand for a time period is known. Such a model may be employed, for example, by a company that produces to a specific backlog. See STOCHASTIC INVENTORY MODELS.

detinue
A common-law action to recover property. It is distinguished from trover, which is an action to recover damages for the property taken rather than the actual property itself. See TROVER.

Deutsche mark
Basic unit of currency in the Federal Republic of Germany (West Germany). Abbreviated DM.

devaluation
An official act that makes a domestic currency cheaper in terms of gold or foreign currencies, generally to increase a nation's exports while reducing its imports.

developer
In organizational behavior, a manager who uses a high relationships orientation and a low task orientation in a situation where such behavior is appropriate. He is perceived as having implicit faith and trust in people and as being primarily concerned with developing them as individuals. See RELATIONSHIPS ORIENTATION and TASK ORIENTATION.

development finance companies
Privately owned or, in some cases, quasi-governmental in structure or controlled by governments, DFCs are a major mechanism for assisting medium-scale productive enterprises, deriving their financial strength from the World Bank. Prior to 1969, the World Bank worked only with DFCs that were privately controlled. Since that time, it has widened its options by agreeing to finance government-controlled DFCs that were, or could be, effective development agents for a nation's economy.

devise
A gift, usually of real property, by a last will and testament.

devisee
A person who receives title to real property by will.

DFC
See DEVELOPMENT FINANCE COMPANIES.

DF car
Abbreviation for *damage-free car*. Railroad term for a boxcar equipped with special bracing material.

diadic product test
In market research, a product test based on consumer reaction to two products submitted simultaneously for comparison and reaction. See MONADIC PRODUCT TEST and TRIADIC PRODUCT TEST.

diagnostic routine
A routine used to locate a malfunction in a computer or to aid in locating mistakes in a computer program. In general, a routine specifically designed to aid in debugging or troubleshooting. See ROUTINE.

dialectical materialism
The logical method of historical analysis used by Karl Marx, based on the concepts of the German philosopher Georg Hegel. The concept that historical change is the result of inherently conflicting or opposing forces in society, forces that are basically economic or materialistic.

DIBA
See DOMESTIC AND INTERNATIONAL BUSINESS ADMINISTRATION.

dictatorship of the proletariat
An expression used by Karl Marx to describe the stage in Marxian socialism when the bourgeoisie or capitalist class is removed from power and, along with its properties, placed under the management of the proletariat or working class, which is also in control of the state.

dictum
An expression of an idea, argument, or rule in the written opinion of a judge that has no bearing on the issues involved and that is not essential for their determination. It lacks the force of a decision in judgment.

DIF
Abbreviation for *direct investment fund*. See OVERSEAS PRIVATE INVESTMENT CORPORATION.

digital
Referring to the use of discrete integral numbers in a given base to represent all the quantities that occur in a problem or calculation.

digital computer
A computer that processes information represented by combinations of discrete or discontinuous data, as compared with an analog computer. A device for performing sequences of arithmetic and logical operations, not only on data but through its own program. See ANALOG COMPUTER.

digital panel meter
In computers, a panel-mounted indicator without mechanically moving parts that displays values directly in digital form. LEDs (light emitting

diodes) and LCDs (liquid crystal diodes) are generally used as the visual elements of the DPM. Prior to the commercial availability of LEDs and LCDs, DPMs used indicators equipped with incandescent or other such elements that glowed when excited by a voltage. See ANALOG PANEL METER.

digital representation
A representation of data by means of digits or discrete values.

digital-to-analog converter
In data processing, circuitry that converts digital signals into a continuous electrical signal suitable for input to an analog computer or to a device that provides analog representation of values.

digit check
One or more redundant digits carried along with a computer word and used in relation to the other digits in the word as a self-checking or error-detecting code to detect malfunctions of equipment in data transfer operations.

digitize
To convert an analog measurement of a physical variable into a numerical value, thereby expressing the quantity in digital form.

dilution
In finance, the weakening of an equity position caused by a reduction in the value of a corporation's stock.

diluvion
The erosion of land through the action of water. The opposite of ALLUVION.

diminishing-provision method
A method of depreciation, more popularly known as DECLINING-BALANCE METHOD.

diminishing returns
The principle that as more of a variable factor is applied to a fixed factor, the output increases less than proportionately. An input whose quantity a business can vary at will is the variable factor of production; an input that cannot be increased is the fixed factor. For example, if it is known that a two-operator machine can produce a certain number of widgets per hour, adding a third operator may not cause a proportion-

ate increase; in fact, the third operator may cause interference, resulting in a negative change in output.

dinar
Basic unit of currency in Algeria, Bahrein, United Arab Emirates, Iraq, Jordan, Kuwait, Libya, People's Democratic Republic of Yemen, Tunisia, and Yugoslavia.

DIP
Acronym for *dual in-line package*. In manufacturing, a container for a solid-state circuit; a package with two parallel rows of lines or leads. Facilitates the automatic insertion of an integrated circuit package on an assembly line.

direct address
In data processing, an address that indicates where the referenced operand is stored, with no reference to an index register or B-box. Also referred to as FIRST-LEVEL ADDRESS.

direct cost
The cost of any good or service that contributes to, and is readily identified with, the processing or manufacturing of a product or the delivery of a specific service. Typical direct costs include the costs of labor, materials, and overhead, costs that vary with the quantity or volume of output. Also known as *variable cost*. See INDIRECT COST.

directed verdict
In a judicial proceeding, when it becomes apparent to reasonable persons and to the court that the plaintiff by his evidence has not made out his case, the court may instruct the jury to bring in a verdict for the defendant, or the judge himself may "direct" a verdict for the defendant. If different inferences may be drawn from the evidence by reasonable men, the court cannot direct a verdict.

direct labor
Labor time that is associated directly with the production cycle of a product and, often, with a specific order.

direct material
In production, the raw materials, parts, or other physical components directly associated with the production of a finished product, including those portions of such materials that are cut away or otherwise lost in processing; often associated with a specific order.

director
A person selected by shareholders to establish company policies. The directors appoint the president, vice presidents, and all other operating officers. They also decide, among other matters, if and when dividends shall be paid.

direct overhead
Factory, selling, or any other expense that may be charged directly to the processing or manufacturing of a specific product or service. See DIRECT COST.

direct reduction loan
A loan repayable in consecutive equal monthly installments, paying interest and principal sufficient to retire the debt within a definite period. "Direct" means that after the monthly interest amount has been deducted from the amount of the payment, the remainder is applied directly to the reduction of the principal of the loan.

direct shipment
See DROP SHIPMENT.

dirham
Basic unit of currency in Morocco.

disability insurance
Protects employees from loss of wages during periods when they are disabled and cannot perform their regular duties or any other type of work for which they are suited through either past experience or education. Sometimes offered as part of a group plan. It may cover all or only part of an employee's regular wages.

disbursement list
A printed list containing the identity and quantity of parts and assemblies to be withdrawn from stock and dispatched to the starting point of manufacture or assembly on a given day.

disbursing officer
In government accounting, a bonded employee who is authorized to pay out cash or to issue checks in settlement of vouchers that have been approved by a certifying officer.

DISC
See DOMESTIC INTERNATIONAL SALES CORPORATION.

discharge
To release from a legal obligation.

disclaimer of opinion
See AUDITORS' REPORT.

discounted cash flow
A method of analyzing investments in which future cash flows are discounted, or converted to their present values. Also known as *time-adjusted return, internal rate of return, project rate of return,* and *investor's method.*

discount rate
The interest rate charged by Federal Reserve Banks on loans to member banks. The interest is discounted when the loan is made, rather than collected when the loan is repaid.

discount store
A store generally featuring a wide variety of goods at prices below the manufacturer's published or suggested user prices. Discount stores appeared shortly after the end of World War II and initially offered few customer services. Today's discount stores offer services comparable to those of department stores and have come to resemble them in physical appearance.

discovery period
The period of time allowed the insured after the expiration date of an insurance contract or bond to discover and report losses that may have occurred while the contract or bond was in force and that would have been covered by the terms of the insurance.

disc pack
A set or stack of discs coated with or manufactured of magnetic material, designed to be placed in an information processing device for reading and writing. Disc packs are mounted on a disc storage drive.

discretionary account
An account in which a client gives his stockbroker or someone else power of attorney as to the purchase and sale of securities and commodities, including selection, timing, amount, and price to be paid or received. This discretionary power may be with or without specific limits.

discretionary income
Income over and above that required for the basic consumer needs of food, clothing, and shelter.

discretionary order
Power given to a stockbroker to act on behalf of a client with respect to the choice of securities to be bought or sold, the total amount to be bought or sold, and whether any transaction shall be for the purpose of buying or selling.

disequilibrium
The state of imbalance in any economic organism or system (such as a household, a firm, a market, or a national economy) wherein the quantities supplied and demanded of a commodity at a given price are unequal, resulting in a tendency for market prices and/or quantities to change.

disguised unemployment
See UNDEREMPLOYMENT.

dishonor
To fail to pay or accept a bill or other negotiable instrument.

disintermediation
In financial economics, the process whereby people withdraw money from interest-bearing thrift accounts in order to purchase higher-return securities, such as Treasury bills. Disintermediation accelerates when interest rates on marketable securities rise above the levels that thrift institutions pay to members and savers.

dispatch earning
An economy or saving in shipping costs as a result of promptly discharging cargo at its destination.

displacement
The weight of a vessel and its contents, in tons of 2,240 pounds.

disposable personal income
Income remaining after payment of personal taxes.

dissaving
Paying for current consumption by drawing on past savings, by borrowing, or by receiving aid from other sources. Spending at a rate that exceeds one's disposable income.

distraint
In law, the seizing of property after the owner has neglected or refused to pay federal income taxes within ten days of notice and demand.

distress merchandise
Merchandise that has been reduced in price to increase the probability of sale; usually the result of a financial difficulty requiring the rapid conversion of inventory to cash. Such merchandise may be sold to consumers or by one dealer to another dealer.

distribution
In marketing and transportation, the movement of products, goods, and materials from manufacturer to user.

distribution expense
The cost of selling a product or service, typically including advertising and delivery expenses.

diurnal
Archaic name for JOURNAL or DAYBOOK.

divided account
In the sale of securities through underwriting syndicates, a divided account is one in which the liability of the members of the syndicates is limited to their percentage participation. If the member sells all the securities alloted him under his participation, he has no liability, regardless of whether or not other members are able to sell their allotments. With an *undivided account,* each member is liable for his percentage participation in the unsold securities of the syndicate, regardless of the number of securities the individual member sells. The principal use of divided accounts is in municipal securities. Virtually all syndicates involved in corporate securities are undivided.

dividend
In finance, the payment designated by a corporation's board of directors to be distributed pro rata among the shares outstanding. On preferred shares it is generally a fixed amount. On common shares the dividend varies with the fortunes of the company and the amount of cash on hand. A dividend may be omitted if business is poor or if the directors decide to withhold earnings to invest in the plant or its equipment. Sometimes a company will pay a dividend out of past earnings if it is not currently operating at a profit.

In insurance, a refund or rebate of a portion of a policyholder's premium that has been paid in anticipation of the insurer's fulfillment of the contract.

dividend in arrears
The amount of undeclared dividends accumulated on cumulative preferred stock, expressed either as dollars per share outstanding or as a total amount.

dividend in kind
See PROPERTY DIVIDEND.

dividend yield
A percentage of the annual return that holders of common or preferred stock derive from their investment. For example, a dividend of $1.50 per share for a stock that costs $30 per share produces a yield of 5 percent:

$$\frac{\$1.50}{\$30.00} \times 100 = 5\%.$$

diversification
Spreading investments among different companies or industries to improve the probability for greater return on investment.

division of labor
See SPECIALIZATION OF LABOR.

D-J
Short for *Dow-Jones*.

DJI
Abbreviation for *Dow Jones index*. See DOW-JONES INDUSTRIAL AVERAGE and SHARE INDEX.

DJIA
See DOW-JONES INDUSTRIAL AVERAGE and SHARE INDEX.

DNR order
Abbreviation for *do-not-reduce order*. A limited order to buy, a stop order to sell, or a stop limit order to sell that is not reduced by the amount of an ordinary cash dividend on the ex-dividend date. Applies only to ordinary cash dividends; it is reduced for other distributions such as a stock dividend or rights.

DOC
See DEPARTMENT OF COMMERCE.

dock
The loading or unloading platform at an industrial location or carrier terminal, on land or water.

dockage
Charges made for the use of a dock.

dock receipt
A document given to a shipper when goods are delivered to a dock.

DOD
See DEPARTMENT OF DEFENSE.

DOI
See DEPARTMENT OF THE INTERIOR.

DOJ
See DEPARTMENT OF JUSTICE.

DOL
See DEPARTMENT OF LABOR.

dollar
Basic unit of currency in Australia, the Bahamas, Barbados, Belize, Bermuda, Brunei, Canada, Montserrat, Pitcairn Island, West Indies, Antigua, Dominica, Grenada, St. Kitts, Ethiopia, Fiji, Guyana, Hong Kong, Jamaica, Liberia, Malaysia, Taiwan, New Zealand, Rhodesia, Singapore, Trinidad and Tobago, and the United States.

dollar cost averaging
A system of buying securities on the stock market at regular intervals with a fixed dollar amount. Under this system, the investor buys by the dollar amount rather than by the number of shares. If each investment is of the same number of dollars, payments may buy more shares when the price is low and fewer when it rises. Thus, temporary downswings in price benefit the investor if he continues periodic purchases in both good times and bad and if the price at which the shares are sold is more than their average cost.

Domestic and International Business Administration (DIBA)
Established on November 17, 1972, by the U.S. Secretary of Commerce to promote the growth of U.S. industry and commerce, foreign and domestic; to stimulate expansion of U.S. exports; and to prepare and execute plans for industrial mobilization readiness through government and business cooperation. Contained within the DIBA are the Bureau of Resources and Trade Assistance (BRTA), the Bureau of International Commerce (BIC), the Bureau of Domestic Commerce (BDC), and the Bureau of East-West Trade (BEWT). DIBA policies and programs are implemented at the local level through 43 district offices and 21 satellite offices located in principal cities throughout the United States and Puerto Rico. The DIBA also publishes the *Commerce Business Daily*.

domestic corporation
A corporation that is created under the laws of a given state or country in which the corporation is officially located. Under the U.S. Internal Revenue Code, a corporation that is established under the laws of the United States or of any of the states or territories. See FOREIGN CORPORATION.

Domestic International Sales Corporation (DISC)
Permitted under the Revenue Act of 1971, DISCs are granted unlimited tax deferral on export profits. To qualify as a DISC, a domestic U.S. corporation must derive 95 percent or more of its gross receipts from exports and related income, and 95 percent or more of its assets must be used in export activities.

domicile
The place a person intends as his fixed and permanent home and establishment and to which, if he is absent, he intends to return. Not synonymous under law with *residence;* a person can have more than one residence, but only one domicile at a time. Also, the state in which a business corporation maintains its headquarters or governing power.

dominant style
In organizational behavior, according to W.J. Reddin, the basic managerial style a manager most frequently uses. See OVERREJECTED STYLE and SUPPORTING STYLE.

dominion
With reference to the delivery of property from one person to another, the removal of all rights to the property, including possession and ownership, from a transferor or donor to a transferee or donee.

DOMSAT
Acronym for *domestic communications satellite*.

dong
Basic unit of currency in Vietnam.

dormant partner
A partner who plays an inactive role in the management of a business and who is not known to the public as having an interest in the enterprise. See SILENT PARTNER and SECRET PARTNER.

DOT
See DEPARTMENT OF TRANSPORTATION.

double-entry bookkeeping
The basis for modern accounting theory, using the principle of balance. "Double entry" means that at least two entries are made in recording each transaction or operation. One entry balances the other and thereby provides a means of proof. If each transaction is recorded so that one entry may be checked against another entry for proof, then the aggregate of all entries may be proved. See SINGLE-ENTRY BOOKKEEPING; also, CREDIT and DEBIT.

double indemnity
A provision in an insurance policy that the insurer will pay twice the face amount of the policy if the insured dies as a result of an accident.

double insurance
Coverage of the same property or risk by two insurance policies.

double option
See STRADDLE.

double taxation
Short for double taxation of dividends. The federal government taxes corporate profits once as corporate income. Any remaining profit distributed as dividends to shareholders is taxed again as income to the receiver–shareholder.

dower
In law, the life estate to which a wife is entitled upon the death of her husband.

Dow-Jones Industrial Average (DJIA)

A quantitative measure of the performance of the stocks of corporations listed on the New York Stock Exchange. The DJIA is based on 30 industrial stocks, which some critics contend are not truly representative of the majority of issues traded daily. The 30 stocks are blue chip stocks that behave differently from the norm. Regardless, the DJIA is often used as a barometer of the performance, rise, and decline of the stock market.

downstairs merger

A merger in which a parent corporation becomes a subisdiary.

down tick

In the stock market, a transaction made at the same price as the preceding sale but lower than the preceding different price. Indicated at each trading post on the floor of the NYSE by a minus sign next to the last price of the stock traded. Also called *minus tick*. See UP TICK.

down time

In manufacturing, the period during which a machine is malfunctioning or not operating due to mechanical, electrical, or electronic failure, as opposed to available time, idle time, or stand-by time, during which the machine is functional but not in actual use.

Dow theory

A theory of stock market analysis based on the performance of the Dow-Jones industrial and transportation stock price averages. The theory says that the market is in a basic upward trend if one of these averages advances beyond a previous important high, accompanied or followed by a similar advance in the other average. When both averages dip below important lows, this is regarded as confirmation of a downward trend. The theory does not attempt to predict the duration of the trend, although it is often misinterpreted as a predictor.

DPM

See DIGITAL PANEL METER.

DPMA

Initials for *Data Processing Management Association*.

drachma

Basic unit of currency in Greece.

draft
A written order drawn by one party, the drawer, that orders a second party, the drawee, to pay a specified amount of money to a third party, the payee.

drawback
A refund of duty paid on imported goods that are subsequently shipped out of the country.

dray
A wheelless and/or sideless vehicle used in local hauling.

drayage
Local hauling by dray or truck.

driving forces
A term used by Kurt Lewin to indicate those forces in an organizational situation that tend to initiate a change and to keep it in motion. For example, in terms of improving productivity in a work group these forces might include pressure from a supervisor, incentive earnings, and competition. See FORCE FIELD ANALYSIS and RESTRAINING FORCES.

DRO memory
See DESTRUCTIVE READOUT MEMORY.

drop rate
The reduction of an interest rate at regular intervals.

drop shipment
A shipment or delivery of goods directly from the manufacturer or supplier to the end user without passing through the physical inventory of the distributor or dealer.

drop shipper
A merchant who takes title to the goods he sells but does not take physical possession. Orders taken from his customers are forwarded directly to the manufacturer of the goods, who then ships the goods directly to the buyer. The recipient of the goods pays the drop shipper for the goods, and he, in turn, pays the manufacturer. The drop shipper usually operates most effectively in the movement of bulky commodities such as lumber, building materials, and fuels, where, because of

the bulk, costs of handling in transportation may be reduced through drop shipment. Also known as a *desk jobber*.

druggists' liability insurance
Issued to druggists to cover claims arising out of the preparation, handling, or sale of drugs, medicines, and other products. A combination of professional liability and products liability insurance.

DS/RO
Initials for *dynamic slack per remaining operation;* a decision-making rule for scheduling used in manufacturing. The next order to be worked on is determined by subtracting the remaining processing time for the order from the total remaining time (due date minus present time) and dividing the result by the number of remaining operations. The order for which this amount is smallest will be processed next. Also known as *minimum slack time per operation*.

DTL
Abbreviation for *diode–transistor logic*. The logic is performed by the diodes; the transistors are used as inverting amplifiers.

dual in-line package
See DIP.

dualism concept
In accounting, the recognition of CREDIT and DEBIT as the two basic elements of transactions both within and outside a business enterprise.

duality theory
See MOTIVATION-HYGIENE THEORY.

dual-purpose fund
A closed-end investment company that sells income shares and capital shares. Owners of income shares receive all the income the company obtains through dividend and interest payments. Owners of capital shares receive the profits the company obtains from capital gains.

due bill
A statement of charges for services rendered, containing details of the services and terms and dates when the amounts due are considered payable. In transportation, a due bill covers additional charges when an original bill for freight charges was too low or in error. Sometimes used

to indicate a receipt signed for ocean bills of lading delivered with specified credit privileges.

due care
The standard of conduct exercised by an ordinary, reasonable, and prudent person. See NEGLIGENCE.

due date
In purchasing, the expected date or receipt for a part; in manufacturing, the expected completion date of a part.

due-date rule
In manufacturing, the sequencing of jobs to be run on the basis of due dates, taking the earliest due date as the first job to be run. See RANDOM DISPATCHING RULE.

dumping
Sale of the same product in different markets at different prices. For example, a monopolist might restrict his output in the domestic market and charge a higher price because demand is relatively inelastic, while "dumping" the rest of his output in a foreign market at a lower price because demand there is relatively elastic. He thereby gains the advantage of lower average total costs on his entire output and earns a larger net profit than if the entire output had been sold on the domestic market.

dunnage
Cushioning and bracing material used to protect goods during shipment.

duopoly
A market situation in which two sellers control the market. It may be either a perfect duopoly or an imperfect one, depending on whether or not there is product differentiation.

duopsony
The condition that exists when two buyers control the demand for goods and services offered by many producers.

duplexing
In data processing, the transmission of two different messages simultaneously over a single circuit.

duress

With respect to property, the seizure by force or the withholding of goods by one not entitled to the goods, and the demand made by such a person who commits the action of something as a condition for the release of the goods.

Dutch auction

A sale in which the price of an article is set rather high and then gradually reduced (often on a daily basis) until the article is sold. Also, a situation in which a vendor takes bids from prospective buyers who do not know each other's identity and who have to rely on the vendor's word as to the amounts bid by the others.

duty

A charge assessed by a government on imported or exported goods.

dystal

Acronym for *Dynamic Storage Allocation,* a computer programming language based on FORTRAN. When using DYSTAL, constructive storage locations are employed to keep the elements of a list so they can be integer-indexed. Programmers can then find the nth item of a list by simple table lookup. DYSTAL frees programmers from some of the constraints of FORTRAN, but it lacks the extensive flexibility in list construction that other list-processing languages contain. The integer-indexing capability is unique.

EAC
See EAST AFRICAN COMMUNITY and ENVIRONMENTAL ADVISORY COMMITTEE.

EAM
Initials for *electrical accounting machine.*

E&OE
Initials for *errors & omissions excepted,* sometimes added at the bottom of an invoice or statement. Its purpose is to reserve for the firm that makes the statement the right to amend or adjust the document if it should later prove to contain inaccuracies.

earned income
As defined by the Internal Revenue Service, income received as payment in connection with one's occupation. Under current regulations, most forms of executive compensation, including salaries, bonuses, and gains from nonqualified stock options, are classified as earned income.

earned surplus
See RETAINED EARNINGS and UNDISTRIBUTED PROFIT.

earning-capacity value
See EARNING POWER.

earning power
The ability of an individual or an organization to make money from its goods or services. Used in the valuation of an enterprise as a whole or in the valuation of a class of securities.

earnings after taxes
See PROFITABILITY RATIOS.

earnings per share
Referring to common stock, the net income over a given period, less preferred stock requirements, divided by the number of shares outstanding at the end of the period. Stated in terms of dollars or cents, whichever is best applied.

earnings report
A statement issued by a company showing its earnings or losses over a given period, usually one fiscal year. It lists the income earned, expenses, and net results. In order to facilitate comparison with the performance of previous years, it is usual practice to display current earnings along with a statistical report of analogous data for the preceding years, often going back as far as ten years. Also known as *income statement* or *profit and loss statement*.

easement
In real estate, an intangible, usually nonprofitable, right of one person to the use or enjoyment of the property of another. *Public easements* deal with the rights of the general public. See RIGHT OF WAY and LICENSE.

East African Community (EAC)
An association of trading countries similar in concept to the European Economic Community (Common Market), formed in 1967 with Burundi, Ethiopia, Kenya, Somalia, Tanzania, Uganda, and Zambia as participating members.

Eastern standard time (EST)
The time of the fifth time zone west of Greenwich that includes the eastern United States. Also known as *Eastern time*.

Eastern time (ET)
See EASTERN STANDARD TIME.

EAT
Initials for *earnings after taxes*. See PROFITABILITY RATIOS.

EBIT
Initials for *earnings before interest and taxes*.

EC
See EXTENDED COVERAGE ENDORSEMENT.

ECA
See ECONOMIC COMMISSION FOR AFRICA.

ECAFE
See ECONOMIC COMMISSION FOR ASIA AND THE FAR EAST.

Eccles-Jordan circuit
See FLIP-FLOP.

Eccles-Jordan trigger
See FLIP-FLOP.

ECE
See ECONOMIC COMMISSION FOR EUROPE.

ECLA
See ECONOMIC COMMISSION FOR LATIN AMERICA.

ECMCA
Initials for *Eastern Central Motor Carriers Association*.

ECMT
See EUROPEAN CONFERENCE OF MINISTERS OF TRANSPORT.

ECN
See ENGINEERING CHANGE NOTICE.

ECO
Initials for *engineering change order*. See ENGINEERING CHANGE
NOTICE.

econometrics
The integration of economic theory, mathematics, and statistics. It
involves expressing economic relationships in the form of mathematical equations and verifying the resulting models by statistical methods.

economic activity
The production and distribution of goods and services. Also, the contribution of persons to the production and distribution of useful goods
and services.

Economic Commission for Africa (ECA)
Based in Addis Ababa, Ethiopia, the ECA is one of four Regional commissions of the United Nations established to stimulate economic activity.

Economic Commission for Asia and the Far East (ECAFE)
Based in Bangkok, Thailand, ECAFE is one of four Regional Commissions of the United Nations established to stimulate economic activity.

Economic Commission for Europe (ECE)
Based in Geneva, Switzerland, ECE is one of four Regional commissions of the United Nations established to stimulate economic activity.

Economic Commission for Latin America (ECLA)
Based in Santiago, Chile, ECLA is one of four Regional commissions of the United Nations established to stimulate economic activity.

Economic Development Administration (EDA)
An agency of the U.S. Department of Commerce, EDA provides funds for public works intended to create employment.

economic entity
A unit of an organization, not necessarily a legal entity; for example, a profit center of a corporation.

economic life
In accounting, the period during which a fixed asset is capable of yielding services that are useful to its owner.

economic lot size
See ECONOMIC ORDER QUANTITY.

economic man
In classical economics, an imaginary individual in a capitalistic society—a worker, entrepreneur, consumer, or invester—conceived of as motivated by economic forces. Thus this individual will always act to obtain the greatest satisfaction for the least sacrifice or cost. Satisfaction may take the form of profits to an entrepreneur or investor, leisure hours to a worker, or pleasure to a consumer from the goods and services purchased.

economic-man theory
The theory that employee motivation depends almost entirely on financial incentives. During the mid-1940s, as the behavioral sciences de-

veloped, the theory was discounted on the basis that there are other kinds of motivation, some of which may be more important to the individual than the financial incentive.

economic model
An abstract framework representing the relationships between the elements of an economic system. Seeks to explain the behavior of persons and institutions in the economy.

Economic Opportunity Loan (EOL)
Operated since the late 1960s in concert with Operation Business Mainstream, this program of the Small Business Administration makes term loans to minority-group, economically disadvantaged, and physically handicapped entrepreneurs who lack the minimum capital needed to obtain a business loan.

economic order quantity (EOQ)
In production, a mathematical computation for determining the lot size with the least total cost. Generally, the EOQ is resolved for the lot size when the ordering cost and the inventory carrying cost are equal. Also known as *economic lot size, standard-run quantity,* and sometimes *optimum order quantity.* The quantity may be calculated from the equation

$$Q = \sqrt{\frac{2AS}{rv}}$$

where Q is quantity to be ordered, A is ordering cost, S is annual sales, r is carrying cost, and v is unit cost.

Economic Research Service (ERS)
An agency of the U.S. Department of Agriculture, ERS develops and carries out programs of research to provide economic intelligence for agriculture, agriculture-related industries, and the public on all aspects of food production, consumption, and prices.

economics
A social science concerned chiefly with the way society chooses to employ its limited resources to produce goods and services for present and future consumption.

economic union
A trade association of two or more countries that permits the free flow of capital, goods, labor, services, and traffic from one member nation to another.

ECSC
See EUROPEAN COAL AND STEEL COMMUNITY.

EDA
See ECONOMIC DEVELOPMENT ADMINISTRATION.

EDF
See EUROPEAN DEVELOPMENT FUND.

EDP
Initials for *electronic data processing*. See DATA PROCESSING.

EEA
See EUROPEAN ECONOMIC ASSOCIATION.

EEC
See EUROPEAN ECONOMIC COMMUNITY.

EEI
Initials for *Edison Electric Institute*.

EEOC
See EQUAL EMPLOYMENT OPPORTUNITY COMMISSION.

Effectivity date
In production scheduling, the date on which a part should be added to or deleted from a list.

Efficiency variance
A variance that results from causes other than a change in the price or direct cost of materials or labor.

EFTA
See EUROPEAN FREE TRADE ASSOCIATION.

EFTS
See ELECTRONIC FUNDS TRANSFER SYSTEM.

EIA
Initials for *Electronic Industries Association*.

eighty-twenty rule
In marketing, an empirical rule reflecting the common experience that a relatively small proportion (20 percent) of items in a company's catalog

generate a large proportion (80 percent) of the company's total activity in sales. The rule also states that approximately 20 percent of the customers are responsible for 80 percent of the sales volume. Some managers claim the same is relatively true of the sales effort, that 20 percent of the sales force produces 80 percent of the orders.

Einfache Gesellschaft
See SOCIÉTÉ SIMPLE.

Einzelfirma
A sole proprietorship, or single-owner firm, under the law of the Federal Republic of Germany.

either-or order
An order to buy or sell a particular stock at a limit price or buy or sell on stop. If the order is for one unit of trading, when one part of the order is executed on the occurrence of one alternative, the order on the other alternative is treated as canceled. If the order is for an amount larger than one unit of trading, the number of units executed determines the amount of the alternative order to be treated as canceled. Also known as an *alternative order*.

ejectment
A statutory action to recover the possession of real property.

elastic demand
See ELASTICITY OF DEMAND.

elasticity of demand
Economists often use a numerical coefficient E to measure elasticity. Demand is defined as elastic when E is greater than 1.0 and as inelastic when E is less than 1.0. It has unitary elasticity when E is exactly equal to 1.0. The formula is:

$$E = \frac{\text{percent change in } Q}{\text{percent change in } P}$$

where E is the elasticity coefficient, Q represents the quantity purchased (equivalent to the change in demand for the item), and P represents the price per unit. Thus if the percent rise in Q is equal to the percent rise in P, the ratio is 1.0, indicating unitary elasticity. If the percent change in Q divided by the percent change in P is greater than 1.0, we have an elastic situation. And so on.

electrical apparatus clause
In insurance, a clause eliminating coverage for damage to electrical appliances, devices, or wiring that is caused by man-made means. However, if fire ensues and damage is caused by the fire, the insurance company is liable.

electronic data processing (EDP)
See DATA PROCESSING.

electronic funds transfer system (EFTS)
A technique using computers to transfer funds between banks.

eleemosynary corporation
A nonprofit corporation organized for charitable purposes.

elevating charge
A charge for services performed in connection with floating or mobile elevators; also, a charge assessed for handling grain through stationary grain elevators.

elevating conveyors
A conveyor intended to provide a means for elevating or lowering materials in a restricted horizontal distance; made in several types. Also manufactured with steps affixed to the conveyor belt for raising or lowering passengers from one level of an operation to another.

Elkins Act
A transportation regulation enacted by Congress in 1903, the act prohibits rebates, concessions, misbillings, and other discriminatory business practices. It also provides specific penalties for violations.

EM
Initials for *engineer of mines.*

EMA
See EUROPEAN MONETARY AGREEMENT.

embargo
A government order prohibiting goods from entering the country. May be placed against a nation, prohibiting any of its products from entering the country, or against a specific product regardless of its national source.

embezzlement
See DEFALCATION.

EMC
See EXPORT MANAGEMENT COMPANY.

Emergency Petroleum Allocation Act
Enacted by Congress in 1973, the act established authority within the Office of the President to allocate oil; this authority was later transferred to the Department of Energy.

Emerson, Harrington (1853–1931)
An early proponent of the principles of scientific management.

eminent domain
The right that resides in a federal, state, county, city, school, or other public body to take private property for public use, on payment of just compensation.

emolument
The return from personal labor received or accrued in the form of compensation, such as a salary, wage, fee, commission, award, price concession, or other personal benefit.

empirical probability
In statistical computations, probability derived from past experience. Used, for example, in preparing insurance mortality tables, which are obviously based on past experience. See A PRIORI PROBABILITY.

employee contribution
The money individual employees pay to participate in company benefit plans, especially common in the areas of insurance, pension, and savings plans. The usual practice is to deduct employee contributions directly from their paychecks.

Employee Retirement Income Security Act (ERISA)
Enacted in 1974 and administered by the Department of Labor and the Internal Revenue Service, ERISA's purpose is to protect the interests of workers and their beneficiaries who depend on benefits from employee pension and welfare plans. The law requires disclosure of plan provisions and financial information; establishes standards of conduct for trustees and administrators of welfare and pension plans; sets up funding, participation, and vesting requirements for pension

plans; and makes termination insurance available for most pension plans. It also provides that an employee not covered by a pension plan (other than Social Security) may put aside a certain amount of his or her income for retirement needs, the money remaining tax-exempt until received as retirement benefits.

employee stock ownership plan (ESOP)

Essentially an incentive-type retirement plan funded with employers' shares of common stock; a hybrid of a stock bonus and a deferred-profit-sharing plan. A corporation establishes an employee benefit trust under the plan in accordance with criteria for tax-exempt plans for retirement. The trust purchases shares of the corporation's stock at fair market value. The plan may borrow money from a lending institution on the corporation's guarantee. The corporation makes annual deductible contributions to the plan in cash or in stock. The cash is used to repay loans. On retirement, a participating employee is paid benefits in company stock that has accrued to his or her account in proportion to salary. The stock in the trust accumulates tax-free until it is distributed. If a participating employee becomes disabled, or terminates his or her services with the corporation, the trust account is paid to the employee in corporation stock.

Employment Act of 1946

An act of Congress designed to maintain high levels of employment and production. It directs the president to make an annual report to Congress on the general economic condition of the nation and to include in this report his recommendations for remedial legislation where the need is indicated. To assist the president in preparing the report and to provide him with expert advice on economic conditions, the act established the Council of Economic Advisors.

Employment and Training Administration (ETA)

A unit of the Department of Labor, it assists the unemployed or those seeking new or improved employment opportunities by providing them with training, placement services, and unemployment compensation through a federal and state system.

Employment Standards Administration (ESA)

A unit of the Department of Labor, it enforces laws and regulations by setting employment standards, providing for compensation payments to workers injured on their jobs, and requiring federal contractors to provide equal opportunity in employment. Also seeks to upgrade the status of working women, members of minority groups, and the handicapped.

encode
In data processing, to apply a code, frequently one consisting of binary numbers, to represent individual characters or groups of characters in a message. The inverse of decode.

encoder
A computer device capable of translating from one method of expression to another, for example, translating a plain-language message into a series of binary digits.

end-around shift
See CYCLIC SHIFT.

end item
See FINISHED GOODS.

end of file (EOF)
Termination or point of completion of a quantity of data entered into a computer. End-of-file marks are used to indicate this point.

endorsement
Insurance companies usually print standard contracts in large quantities. An endorsement is a separate document or additional clause physically attached to the standard policy form for the purpose of amending the standard contract. Also known as a *rider*, especially when the amendment is contained on a separate sheet of paper attached to the original contract.

end product
See FINISHED GOODS.

ENEA
See EUROPEAN NUCLEAR ENERGY AGENCY.

Energy Department
See DEPARTMENT OF ENERGY.

Energy Policy and Conservation Act
A 1975 act of Congress that established oil-pricing policy and set the first major conservation goal for automobiles.

Energy Research and Development Administration (ERDA)
Established in 1974 and activated in 1975 by executive order, ERDA is headed by an administrator appointed by the president. It has the lead

role in conducting national energy research, development, and demonstration programs, including planning, reporting its progress, and working with the private sector to enlist the nation's technological resources in the program's achievement. In 1977, ERDA became part of the Department of Energy.

Engel, Ernst (1821–1896)
German statistician and economist; born in Dresden, studied engineering at Freiburg and Paris, and became head of the statistical department of the government of Saxony and later head of the Prussian Bureau of Statistics. He did research on the cost of rearing children, designed a new measure of consumption, and theorized that the percentage of expenditure on food is a decreasing function of income. His *Die Industrie der Grossen Städte* was published in 1866, and the first volume of *Der Wert des Menschen* appeared in 1883. See ENGEL's LAWS.

Engel's laws
A set of relationships between consumer expenditures and income, derived by the nineteenth-century statistician and economist Ernst Engel, and based on research into workers' purchases in Western Europe during the 1850s. The "laws" state that, as family income increases, (1) the percentage spent on food decreases, (2) the percentage spent on housing and household operations remains about constant, and (3) the percentage spent on all other categories and the amount saved increases. In general, the total amount spent increases as a family's income increases. See ENGEL, ERNST.

engineering change notice (ECN)
A document specifying change or revision to a part or assembly because of considerations of safety, cost reduction, product performance, or modification in design. The document is usually processed by the engineering department and released to the affected departments of purchasing, production, marketing, and finance. Also known as *engineering change order*.

engineering change order (ECO)
See ENGINEERING CHANGE NOTICE.

engineer's chain
A chain 50 or 100 feet long consisting of one-foot links. Used for distance measurements.

enterprise
A business undertaking. Unless otherwise qualified, the entirety of an organization rather than a unit or subdivision. Also, that quality of business management identified with energy, initiative, resourcefulness, and adaptability.

enterprise value
See GOING VALUE.

entity
Existing, in being. For legal purposes, the artificial person created when a corporation is organized is an entity separate from the stockholders. The estate of a deceased person while in administration, a partnership, and the status of marriage are other examples of legal entities.

entry
The notation of a transaction in a journal.

Environmental Advisory Committee (EAC)
A branch of the federal government's Energy Research and Development Administration (ERDA), the EAC is intended to increase the involvement of the public sector in defining the goals and in setting policy for ERDA. The 21 members of the EAC are selected from the fields of science, medicine, industry, state and local government, and environmental protection, as well as from the general public. The committee is scheduled to meet at least four times each year.

Environmental Protection Agency (EPA)
An independent federal agency headed by an administrator appointed by the president, the EPA operates program offices and research laboratories to systematically abate and control pollution. Violations of environmental-control regulations are enforced through the U.S. Department of Justice.

EOF
See END OF FILE.

EOL
See ECONOMIC OPPORTUNITY LOAN.

EOM
Initials for *end of month.*

EONR
See EUROPEAN ORGANIZATION FOR NUCLEAR RESEARCH.

EOQ
See ECONOMIC ORDER QUANTITY.

EOY
Initials for *end of year*.

EPA
See ENVIRONMENTAL PROTECTION AGENCY.

EPS
See EARNINGS PER SHARE.

Equal Employment Opportunity Commission (EEOC)
An independent federal agency headed by five commissioners appointed by the president for five-year terms. The president designates one of the commissioners as chairman. The EEOC is responsible for guaranteeing equal employment opportunities without regard to race, color, sex, religion, or national origin. It has jurisdiction over private employers and unions with 15 or more employees or members, agencies of state and local governments, and public and private educational institutions, but not over federal agencies. It investigates charges of discrimination, attempts conciliation if needed, and files suits in federal courts.

equalizing dividend
A dividend paid to correct inequities caused by changes in established regular dividend dates. As an example, when two companies are merged and each has a different dividend date, an equalizing dividend may be paid.

equation of exchange
An expression of the relation between the quantity of money (M), its velocity of circulation (V), the average price of finished goods and services (P), and the physical quantity of those goods and services (Q):

$$MV = PQ$$

The equation in fact states that the total amount of money spent on goods and services (MV) is equal to the total amount of money received for goods and services (PQ). See QUANTITY THEORY OF MONEY.

equilibrium

In economics, a state in which forces making for change in opposing directions are in perfect balance so that there is no tendency to change. For example, a market will be in equilibrium if the quantity of the product that buyers want to buy at the prevailing price is exactly matched by the amount that sellers wish to sell. If this were not so, the price would be changing as buyers try to buy more of a good than is in fact available, or sellers try to sell more of a good than buyers are prepared to purchase at prevailing prices. In this case, price is the mechanism for creating equilibrium. The concept of equilibrium is a general one that can be applied to any situation that is characterized by a set of interacting forces.

equilibrium income level

The particular level of income in an economy at which aggregate demand and aggregate supply are in balance.

equilibrium level of output

The particular level of output in an economy at which aggregate demand and aggregate supply are equal.

equilibrium price

In economics, a price that equates the quantity demanded with the quantity supplied. It balances the behavior of buyers with that of sellers, thus clearing the market. See EQUILIBRIUM.

equilibrium quantity

The quantity of a good that is bought and sold when a market is in equilibrium. See EQUILIBRIUM.

equipment trust certificate

A type of security issued—generally by a railroad—to pay for new equipment. Title to the equipment, such as a locomotive, is held by a trustee until the notes are paid off. The certificate is usually secured by a first claim to the equipment.

equitable action

Anglo-American law has developed two types of courts and procedures for administering justice: law courts and equity courts. As a remedy, law courts give money damages only. Equity courts may give the plaintiff what his or her complaint asks for. A suit for performance of a specific contract is an equitable action. In many states the two courts are merged into one. See EQUITY.

equitable owner
One who has conveyed the title to property in trust but retains the right to use and enjoy the property.

equitable tax
See PROGRESSIVE TAX.

equity
In finance, a right or claim to an asset. A holder of an equity may be a creditor, part owner, proprietor, or stockholder. Also, an interest in the property or in a business that is subject to claims of creditors. Generally used as a statement of the amount or percentage of ownership interest.

In matters of law, early English courts did not always give an adequate remedy to an aggrieved person; redress was sometimes sought from the king. The appeal having been made to the sovereign's conscience, he therefore referred the case to his spiritual adviser, the chancellor, who was expected to decide the case according to rules of fairness, honesty, right, and natural justice. The rules in equity were developed from this practice. The laws of trusts, divorce, rescission of contracts for fraud, injunction, and specific performance are enforced in courts of equity.

Also, see TOTAL EQUITY.

equity financing
The sale of capital stock by a corporation for cash or other things of value to the operation of the corporation.

equity receiver
A person appointed by a court of equity at the request of the owner, or of creditors, to take control of a property with the intention either to reorganize it and operate it until it can be returned to the owner or to discontinue operations and distribute any remaining assets.

equity security
A transferable certificate of ownership; sometimes used in connection with capital stock, stock warrants, or indebtedness convertible into stock. Also, a controlling company's interest and holding of stocks, bonds, notes, and other formal evidences of ownership or indebtedness of a subsidiary.

equity transaction
Any transaction that has the effect of increasing or decreasing net worth.

ERA
Initials for *Electronics Representatives Association.*

erase
In data processing, to replace all the binary digits in a storage device by binary zeros. Erasing in a binary computer is equivalent to clearing, whereas in a coded decimal computer, where the pulse code for decimal zero may contain binary ones, clearing leaves decimal zero while erasing leaves all-zero pulse codes in storage locations.

ERDA
See ENERGY RESEARCH AND DEVELOPMENT ADMINISTRATION.

erection department
See FINAL ASSEMBLY.

ergonomics
The aspect of technology that is concerned with the application of biological and engineering data to problems related to human beings and the machine. Also known as *biotechnology.*

ERISA
See EMPLOYEE RETIREMENT INCOME SECURITY ACT.

ERP
See EUROPEAN RECOVERY PROGRAM.

error rate
In data processing, the total amount of erroneous information caused by the transmission media, divided by the total amount of information received.

ERS
See ECONOMIC RESEARCH SERVICE.

ES
See EXTENSION SERVICE.

ESA
See EMPLOYMENT STANDARDS ADMINISTRATION.

ESCAP
Initials for *Economic and Social Commission for Asia and the Pacific;* an organization sponsored by the United Nations.

escape clause

A provision in a contractual agreement that allows one or more of the parties to withdraw or to modify promised performance under specified conditions. Also, a clause inserted in tariff agreements under the Trade Agreements Act that allows the U.S. Tariff Commission to recommend that the president withdraw a previously granted concession on the ground that it seriously threatens to injure U.S. suppliers.

escrow agreement

An arrangement that may be made during arbitration of wages in an industrial action between a trade union and management under which an employer delivers to the arbitrator a specified sum of money to be used to pay a wage increase if the arbitrator rules the increase to be warranted.

escudo

The basic unit of currency in Chile, Portugal, Angola, Guinea-Bissau, and Mozambique.

ESOP

See EMPLOYEE STOCK OWNERSHIP PLAN.

EST

See EASTERN STANDARD TIME and EX SHIP'S TACKLE.

estate for life

See FEE SIMPLE ESTATE.

ET

Initials for *Eastern time*. See EASTERN STANDARD TIME.

ETA

See EMPLOYMENT AND TRAINING ADMINISTRATION

et al.

Abbreviation of *et alii,* Latin for "and other persons." Used in pleadings and cases where it is necessary to indicate that persons other than those specifically named are parties to a law suit.

et uxor

Latin for "and wife." Sometimes used in the name of legal cases. For example, "Smith v. Jones et ux." means Smith as an individual versus Jones and his wife.

Euler, Leonhard (1707–1783)
A Swiss mathematician who contributed to the development of the theory of probability.

Euratom
See EUROPEAN ATOMIC ENERGY COMMUNITY.

Eurocrat
A popular term for a member of the staff of the EUROPEAN COMMISSION.

Eurodollar
In international finance, a dollar of U.S. currency held outside the United States, usually on deposit in a bank in Europe but generally in any area outside the United States, as a credit to facilitate commercial transactions. The Eurodollar appeared to a significant extent in the mid-1960s, with the City of London as the major brokering center.

Eurofrancs
The monetary franc dealt in and traded outside France but within the member states of the Common Market.

Euromarks
The monetary mark dealt in and traded outside the Federal Republic of Germany but within member states of the Common Market.

Euromart
See COMMON MARKET.

European Atomic Energy Community (Euratom)
Established by treaty in 1957, Euratom promotes the peaceful purposes and uses of atomic energy among the Common Market member states that have a common market in nuclear materials and equipment, as they have in other goods through the European Economic Community and the European Coal and Steel Community.

European Coal and Steel Community (ECSC)
Established by the Treaty of Paris in 1951, the ECSC operates among the founder members of the Common Market and is financed by a levy on coal and steel production in the member states.

European Commission
A staff of approximately 10,000 civil service employees led by a group of 14 commissioners, responsible under Article 228 of the Treaty of

Rome for negotiating trade agreements with nonmember countries on behalf of the Common Market. The Commission formulates proposals for consideration by the Council of Ministers (the decision-making body of the Common Market) and is responsible for implementing the Council's policies. The Commission may impose fines on firms, individuals, or members of the Common Market that violate the Treaty of Rome or Common Market regulations.

European Communities Act of 1972
Legislation passed by the British Parliament that brought the United Kingdom into the Common Market on January 1, 1973, in accordance with the Treaty of Accession.

European Conference of Ministers of Transport (ECMT)
Established in 1953 to promote the development of inland transport in Europe. The United States acts as an observer.

European Court of Justice
A court that operates or is based in Luxembourg and is responsible for enforcing the Treaty of Rome and the rules and regulations of the European Economic Community. The Court is composed of a judge from each of the member states. Firms, individuals, and member states have the right to appeal to the Court if they believe the terms of the Treaty of Rome have been abused in matters affecting them.

European Development Fund (EDF)
An institution of the Common Market set up by member states under the Yaoundé Convention in 1969. The EDF handles grants and loans to nonmember states under provisions of the Treaty of Rome.

European Economic Association (EEA)
Formed in 1959 to provide advice and encouragement on economic cooperation between the member states of the European Economic Community and the European Free Trade Association.

European Economic Community (EEC)
Operates the Common Market under the Treaty of Rome (1957) and the Treaty of Accession (1972). The founder members were France, West Germany, Italy, the Netherlands, Belgium, and Luxembourg, joined by Denmark, the Irish Republic, and the United Kingdom under the Treaty of Accession. The Common Market/EEC operates a customs union and is working toward economic and monetary union by 1980, with political union possibly to follow later.

European Free Trade Association (EFTA)
Formed in 1959 as a counter to the Common Market. The nine founder members were Denmark, Sweden, Norway, Switzerland, Austria, Portugal, Finland, Iceland, and the United Kingdom. Denmark and the United Kingdom now belong to the European Economic Community. There is no tariff wall between any two member states of EFTA, but, unlike the Common Market, the association is not a customs union and does not have a common external tariff. The purpose of EFTA's remaining seven members is to encourage free trade among themselves.

European Investment Bank
Established by the Common Market and the Treaty of Rome to make grants and loans for regional development, modernization, and projects of common interest to its members. The bank is managed by a board of governors provided by member states that subscribe to its capital in proportions laid down in its statute.

European Monetary Agreement (EMA)
An agreement among states of the Organization for Economic Cooperation and Development, activated in 1958 and replacing the European Payments Union, which set up a fund on which member states could draw for short-term balance-of-payments assistance. EMA provides an arrangement for settling international accounts under which a central bank is assured of payments, in dollars, gold, or equivalent, in clearing credit balances held by it against other member states' central banks.

European Nuclear Energy Agency (ENEA)
Operated by the Organization for Economic Cooperation and Development to promote the peaceful use of nuclear energy.

European Organization for Nuclear Research (EONR)
Established in 1954 for the purpose of nonmilitary nuclear research. Member states are Austria, Belgium, Denmark, France, Greece, Italy, the Netherlands, Norway, Spain, Sweden, Switzerland, West Germany, and the United Kingdom. Observer states are Poland, Turkey, and Yugoslavia.

European Payments Union
Established in 1950 by the 17 members of the Organization for European Economic Cooperation (OEEC), its purpose was to replace the intricate network of restrictive bilateral trade agreements and exchange controls with a payments system that would permit a great expansion of intra-European trade on a multilateral basis. It was replaced in 1958 by the EUROPEAN MONETARY AGREEMENT (EMA).

European Recovery Program (ERP)

Commonly known as the Marshall Plan (for Secretary of State George C. Marshall, who proposed it in 1947), ERP was a comprehensive plan for the recovery of European countries, to be financed by the United States. Its goal was to aid these countries by (1) increasing their productive capacity, (2) stabilizing their financial systems, (3) promoting their mutual economic cooperation, and (4) reducing their dependence on U.S. aid. The ERP was terminated in 1951 and its functions were absorbed by other government agencies and programs.

EWIB

Initials for *Eastern Weighing and Inspection Bureau.*

exact interest

In accounting, simple interest based on a year of 365 days, as compared with ordinary interest and a base of 360 days. The ratio of exact interest to ordinary interest is 0.9863878; the reciprocal is 1.0138. See OR-DINARY INTEREST.

examination of title

See TITLE SEARCH.

ex ante

In economics, intended or planned. Ex ante savings, for example, are planned savings. See EX POST.

Ex. BL

Abbreviation for *exchange bill of lading.*

except gate

An electronic switching circuit in the central processing unit of a computer in which the specified combination of pulses producing an output pulse is the presence of a pulse on one or more input lines and the absence of a pulse on one or more other input lines.

exception principle system

An information or data processing system that reports on situations only when actual results differ from planned results outside the limits of a predetermined range.

exception rates

In transportation, a rate intended to take account of variations in the cost of and demand for the movement of goods by common carriers;

covers items not included in other rate systems. Also referred to as *exception rating*. See CLASS RATES and COMMODITY RATES.

excess deductions account
Generally, an accounting record that taxpayers who claim losses from farming operations are required to keep for federal income-tax purposes.

excess freight
freight in excess of that shown on the original carrier billing.

excess issue
In manufacturing, the quantity of parts issued to a shop order in excess of the quantity required by the bill of material.

excess-line insurance
Insurance obtained by a U.S. firm or individual through a foreign or alien insurance company. Lloyd's of London is well known for writing excess-line insurance coverage.

exchange acquisition
In securities trading, a method of filling an order to buy a large block of stock on the floor of an exchange. Under certain circumstances, a member broker of the exchange can facilitate the purchase of a block of stock by soliciting orders to sell. All orders to sell the security are lumped together and crossed with the buy order in the regular auction market. The price to the buyer may be on a net basis or on a commission basis. See EXCHANGE DISTRIBUTION.

exchange check
A check given in exchange for cash or for another check.

exchange distribution
In securities trading, a method of disposing of large blocks of stock on the floor of an exchange. Under certain circumstances, a member broker can facilitate the sale of a block of stock by soliciting and getting other member brokers to solicit orders to buy. Individual buy orders are lumped together and crossed with the sell order in the regular auction market. A special commission is usually paid by the seller; ordinarily the buyer pays no commission. See EXCHANGE ACQUISITION.

exchange rate
See RATE OF EXCHANGE.

exclusion
A provision in an insurance contract or bond that limits the scope of the coverage offered by the insurer.

ex contractu
See ACTION EX CONTRACTU.

exculpatory clause
A section in a lease that relieves the landlord of liability for personal injury to occupants and for property damage.

ex delicto
See ACTION EX DELICTO.

ex-dividend
In securities transactions, synonym for "without dividend." The buyer of a stock selling ex-dividend does not receive the recently declared dividend.

ex dock
Used principally in U.S. import trade, the term indicates that the freight is "away from the dock."

executed
With reference to contracts and other legal documents, the term means "signed, sealed, and delivered." Legal obligations have thus been created. Also used to signify that the performances required under a contract have been completed; the contract is ended because all promises have been fulfilled.

executive
In organizational behavior, descriptive of a manager who uses a high task orientation and a high relationships orientation in a situation where such behavior is appropriate and who is therefore more effective. Such a manager sets high standards, treats everyone somewhat differently, prefers team management, and is therefore often perceived as a good motivating force. See RELATIONSHIPS ORIENTATION and TASK ORIENTATION.

executive routine
A computer routine that controls the loading and relocation of routines and in some cases makes use of instructions that are unknown to the general programmer. Also known as *supervisory routine*.

exemplary damages
In a tort action, the sum assessed as punishment by the jury, above the compensatory damages, in order to make an example of the wrongdoer as a deterrent to others who might consider similar conduct. Injuries caused by willful, malicious, wanton, and reckless conduct will subject the offender to exemplary damages.

exercise provisions
The clauses in a stock option award governing the timing, amounts, and costs at which the option can be exercised by the recipient.

Eximbank
See EXPORT-IMPORT BANK OF THE UNITED STATES.

expectancy theory
A broad term that encompasses theories on motivation put forth by Vroom, Lawler, and others. The theories hold that an employee's motivation to perform effectively is determined by effort-reward probability and reward-value. The first signifies an individual's subjective view that a given amount of effective effort will result in a given reward. The second refers to the individual's perception of the value of the reward that might be obtained by performing effectively. The concept of reward-value is referred to among behavioral scientists as *valence*.

expected value
The average or mean value in a statistical distribution, represented in formulas by the letter E. It is often used interchangeably with *mathematical expectation*, having at one time been associated with efforts to analyze games of chance.

expediter or **expeditor**
In manufacturing, a person responsible for considering jobs that are late and, after defining the reasons, taking steps to hasten the jobs through the production facility, using such techniques as overtime labor, acquisition of materials that are in short supply, and resequencing of jobs in a queue.

expense bill
The freight bill used to invoice freight charges.

explosion
In manufacturing, an extension of a bill of materials that shows the quantities required to manufacture a given assembly.

exponent

In statistics, an indicated power or self-multiplier of a given number or term. For example, $B^3 = B \times B \times B$.

Export-Import Bank of the United States

An independent agency of the U.S. government founded in 1934 and popularly known as Eximbank. Its function is to assist in financing the export trade of the United States. It is authorized to extend and guarantee credits to overseas buyers of American goods and services; it guarantees medium-term and insures short- and medium-term exporter credits; and it discounts export debt obligations held by commercial banks.

export-import merchant

A merchant who specializes in international trade, selling domestically produced goods in markets overseas, or purchasing goods made overseas and reselling them to customers in the domestic market.

export management company (EMC)

The majority of EMCs work on a buy-and-sell arrangement with manufacturers whom they represent; the rest work on a straight commission basis. The EMC takes orders from foreign buyers and places them with the appropriate manufacturer, paying cash for the shipment and reselling it abroad. Usually, the EMC purchases at distributor-wholesale prices, less a discount in the range of 10 to 20 percent. Under a commission plan, the EMC receives payment ranging from 7½ to 20 percent of the distributor-wholesale price as compensation for sales services. EMCs generally work on biannual contracts and do not work simultaneously with competitive products.

ex post

In economics, actual or existing. Ex post savings, for example, are actual savings. See EX ANTE.

exposure

In insurance coverage, the extent of a risk.

ex-rights

In securities transactions, synonym for "without the rights." Corporations raising additional capital may do so by offering their stockholders the right to subscribe to new or additional stock, usually at a discount from the prevailing market price. The buyer of a stock selling ex-rights is not entitled to the rights.

ex ship's tackle (EST)
Similar to cost, insurance, and freight, but the seller is responsible for loss and damage until the goods are delivered to the dock at the port of destination. Thus, a price quotation that is EST does not include transportation from the dock to the end destination.

extended cost
In accounting, the cost of a unit of material or of a single product multiplied by the quantity of the material or product.

extended coverage (EC) endorsement
Extends a fire insurance policy to cover additional perils. The face amount of the policy is not increased through such endorsements. The aggregate liability of the insurer is not increased.

extension service (ES)
This agency of the Department of Agriculture, in cooperation with state and county governments, conducts continuing education programs for youth and adults in agricultural production, home economics, family life, and related subjects.

externalities
In economics, benefits or costs accruing to some individual or group not involved directly as a buyer or seller in a market transaction. See SPILLOVER EFFECTS.

extra-expense insurance
A business-interruption insurance contract written for an enterprise that must continue to operate regardless of cost. Banks and public utilities are examples of such enterprises. The insurance is meant to cover additional or extra expenses caused by emergency operations. See CONSEQUENTIAL-LOSSES INSURANCE.

extra inventory
See TRANSPORTATION INVENTORY.

extraordinary depreciation
Depreciation caused by unusual wear and tear, obsolescence, unexpected disintegration, or an inadequacy beyond what can be attributed to loss of physical or useful life through ordinary circumstances.

extraordinary expense
Any expense so unusual in nature or amount that it is given special treatment in the accounts or is given separate disclosure in financial statements.

extrapolation
In statistics, the act or process of estimating the direction of trends, based on analysis of historical data combined with deduction from a set of observed values.

ex warehouse
A term indicating that the buyer is responsible for all charges to the destination of the shipment and has to arrange insurance to cover the goods from the time they leave the warehouse at the place of shipment until their arrival at the final destination.

EYCO
In accounting, initials for *Estimated Yearly Cost of Operation.*

F
See FAHRENHEIT.

FAA
See FEDERAL AVIATION ADMINISTRATION.

Fabian socialism
A form of socialism advocated by a group of socialists (the Fabian Society, founded in England in 1884). It emerged as an outgrowth of utopian socialism and advocated gradual, evolutionary reform within a

democratic framework. It is the philosophical basis of the British Labour Party.

FAC
See FEDERAL ADVISORY COUNCIL.

face amount
The maximum loss payment an insurance company will make under the terms of a specific policy.

face value
The value of a bond, which appears on the face of the bond, unless the value is otherwise specified by the issuing company. Face value is ordinarily the amount the issuing company promises to pay at maturity; it is not an indication of market value.

factor
An individual or a firm that buys trade receivables with or without recourse. The profit to the factor as a result of the transaction derives from a commission and from interest payments on advances the factor may make against receivables. As an agent in the sale of merchandise, a factor may hold possession of the goods in his own name or in the name of his principal. He is authorized to sell and to receive payment for the goods. The law concerning factors is codified in some states by legislation, and is called *Factors' Acts*. Also sometimes called *commission merchant*.

factoral income distribution
See FUNCTIONAL INCOME DISTRIBUTION.

Factors' Acts
See FACTOR.

factor's lien
In law, the right of a factor to keep possession of goods consigned to him for the purpose of reimbursing himself for all advances previously made to the consignor of the goods.

factory expense
See MANUFACTURING EXPENSE.

factory ledger
A subsidiary ledger that contains the operating costs of a manufacturing establishment, such as materials, labor, and factory overhead.

factory mutual company
An insurance company that provides coverage exclusively for factory property.

factory overhead
See MANUFACTURING EXPENSE.

Fahrenheit
A thermometric scale so calibrated that the freezing point of water is 32° and the boiling point is 212° as indicated on the graduated scale, at sea level. Body temperature is typically 98.6°F. The zero point approximates the temperature produced by mixing equal quantities by weight of snow and common salt. The scale was invented by the German physicist Gabriel Fahrenheit (1686–1736). To convert from CELSIUS (C) to Fahrenheit, the formula is:

$$F = \frac{9}{5} C + 32$$

Fair Packaging and Labeling Act
A congressional act passed in 1966 for the purposes of (1) helping consumers to become better informed and more able to make valid comparisons by providing them with accurate information on the contents of packages and (2) rewarding efficient producers through encouraged consumer confidence.

FAIR Plan
Short for *Fair Access to Insurance Plan*. A riot-insurance program established by the U.S. Housing and Urban Development Act of 1968. In each state accepting the plan, the state, the insurance industry, and the federal government cooperate to make property insurance available in high-risk areas where a high incidence of vandalism has been recorded. Other insurance plans for such areas carry abnormally high rates for vandalism coverage and are usually too expensive for the small business firm.

fair-trade pricing
Many states within the United States enacted laws that allowed marketers to establish minimum end-user prices for products sold to the consuming public. The first fair-trade laws or regulations were exempted from antitrust statutes by an act of the 1937 Congress whose intent was to protect the small, family-owned, ''mom-and-pop'' stores from large discount houses that might undercut prices and drive the small retail establishments out of business. In December 1975, Presi-

dent Gerald R. Ford signed a bill that closed loopholes in the antitrust laws, thereby voiding state laws that allowed the practice of setting minimum fair-trade prices. The bill became effective in 1976.

fallacy of composition
The erroneous assumption that what is true of one part is necessarily true of the whole. This is a common problem in economics: what is good for a firm or single family may not be good for the aggregate of all firms or families.

family allowance plan
A plan that provides every family, regardless of income, with a certain amount of money based exclusively on the number and age of its children. Families above certain designated income levels return all or a portion of the money with their income taxes, but those below specified income levels keep it. More than 60 countries have family allowance plans.

family partnership
A partnership whose members are all part of a single family.

Fannie Mae
Colloquial expression for FNMA. See FEDERAL NATIONAL MORTGAGE ASSOCIATION.

fan-out
The breakdown of an account into two or more basic accounts.

FAO
See FOOD AND AGRICULTURE ORGANIZATION.

Farmers Home Administration
FmHA, an agency of the Department of Agriculture, provides credit for those in rural America who are unable to get credit from other sources at reasonable rates and terms.

farm mutual company
An insurance company that insures farm property exclusively.

FAS
Abbreviation for *free alongside*. Indicates that the buyer assumes responsibility for materials after they have been delivered to a vessel and are ready for loading.

FASB
See FINANCIAL ACCOUNTING STANDARDS BOARD.

fathom
A unit of measure equivalent to six feet. Used principally to measure the depth of water.

Fayol, Henri (1841–1925)
Managing director of a French industrial and mining firm, Fayol was a theorist in management organization who believed that administrative principles can and should be applied in all forms of human organization, not in business and industry alone. See FAYOL LADDER.

Fayol ladder
Henri Fayol, in his promotion of scientific management methods, emphasized the importance of extensive delegation of authority. He diagramed channels of communications within the hierarchy of an organization. He proposed that direct communications be encouraged horizontally among the branches of an organization tree, and that the procedures and limits for such communications channels should be well defined at the superior levels within the organization. The diagrammatic representation of the organization tree or chart with dotted-line paths to indicate communications channels became known as the *Fayol ladder* or *bridge of Fayol.*

FB
Abbreviation for *freight bill.*

FC&S
Abbreviation for *free of capture and seizure;* a term in ocean marine insurance. Unless otherwise specified, all ocean marine insurance contracts exclude capture and seizure. The same is true of losses resulting from strikes, riots, and civil commotions, known as SR&CC.

FCC
See FEDERAL COMMUNICATIONS COMMISSION.

FCFS
See FIRST COME, FIRST SERVED.

FCIA
See FOREIGN CREDIT INSURANCE ASSOCIATION.

FDA
See FOOD AND DRUG ADMINISTRATION.

FDIC
See FEDERAL DEPOSIT INSURANCE CORPORATION.

FEA
See FEDERAL ENERGY ADMINISTRATION.

featherbedding
Labor union "make work" rules designed to increase the labor or labor time on a particular job. Outlawed by the Taft-Hartley Act of 1947, this practice has the effect of requiring payment of wages for a service that has not actually been given.

Federal Advisory Council (FAC)
A committee within the Federal Reserve system that advises the board of governors on general business conditions and makes recommendations concerning matters within the board's jurisdiction. The council is composed of 12 members, one from each Federal Reserve district being selected annually by the board of directors of the Reserve Bank of the district. The council is required to meet in Washington at least four times each year, and more often if called by the board of governors.

Federal Aviation Act
A 1958 act of Congress that regulates air transportation. Supersedes the Civil Aeronautics Act of 1938.

Federal Aviation Administration
A branch of the U.S. Department of Transportation. Promotes civil aviation generally, including research and promulgation of safety regulations involving all air traffic. Also develops and operates the airways and facilities. Administers the federal airport program.

Federal Communications Commission
An independent agency of seven commissioners appointed by the president. The FCC was created to regulate interstate and foreign communications, including radio and television broadcasting, telephone, telegraph, citizens band radio service and two-way radio operations, cable television operation, and satellite communication. The agency issues construction permits and broadcasting licenses and oversees compliance with fair competition laws. It does not have responsibility for telephone companies operating entirely in one state.

Federal Deposit Insurance Corporation
The Federal Reserve Act of 1933 resulted in the establishment of this agency to provide insurance coverage for bank deposits, to help maintain confidence in the banking system, and to promote sound banking practices. FDIC insures individual deposits up to $40,000 in Federal Reserve member banks and in any state bank that qualifies for this insurance. It also grants financial assistance to insured banks to help effect mergers, and will help a closed bank to reopen or will prevent a bank from failing when the bank is important to the economic well-being of a community. The agency is empowered to institute enforcement proceedings against insured nonmember banks when voluntary compliance with regulations and policy has not been achieved. FDIC is headed by a board of three directors, including the Comptroller of the Currency and two who are appointed for six-year terms by the president.

Federal Energy Administration
An independent agency headed by an administrator appointed by the president. FEA is responsible for ensuring energy conservation and the fair and efficient distribution of energy resources in the United States. FEA sees that the public has access to these energy resources at reasonable prices and in sufficient quantities. It has very limited jurisdiction to deal with individual consumer problems and can do so only when the problem involves a violation of a federal statute. FEA became part of the newly formed Department of Energy in 1977.

Federal Highway Administration
A branch of the U.S. Department of Transportation, this agency is responsible for implementing the federal aid highway program, the National Traffic and Motor Vehicle Safety Act of 1966, and the Highway Safety Act of 1966. It has the responsibility for maintaining reasonable levels for tolls on bridges and navigable waters (previously under the jurisdiction of the Corps of Engineers). The agency also oversees federal highway construction, research planning, safety programs, and federal aid highway funds (formerly under the Bureau of Public Roads), and has jurisdiction over the safety performance of commercial motor carriers engaged in interstate or foreign commerce.

Federal Home Loan Bank Board
An independent agency directed by three presidential appointees, one of whom is designated by the president to be chairman and chief executive officer. FHLBB is responsible for the operation of the Federal Home Loan Bank System and the Federal Savings and Loan Insurance

Corporation (FSLIC). FHLBB protects savers in FSLIC-insured savings and loan associations against a loss up to $40,000 for credit available through Federal Home Loan Banks. Insurance of accounts can be terminated or withheld. Cease-and-desist orders may be issued to stop unsound practices. Association officers may be removed for cause.

Federal Housing Administration (FHA)
A U.S. government agency, established in 1934, that works with private industry to provide good housing. It insures mortgages on private homes, multifamily rental housing projects, cooperative and condominium housing, housing in urban renewal areas, housing for the elderly, and nursing homes. It determines minimum property standards, analyzes local housing markets, makes appraisals, and performs land-planning surveys and technical studies. It also insures loans for property improvement, but does not itself make loans. Such loans are made by banks, building associations, and other approved lending institutions. The borrower applies directly to the lending institution for the needed money. FHA is self-supporting, deriving income from fees, interest on investments, and insurance premiums paid on loans. A commissioner heads the agency, which is now a unit of the Department of Housing and Urban Development.

Federal Information Centers
Operated by the General Services Administration, FIC's provide information to consumers on all aspects of the federal government in 74 cities around the country. FIC's help consumers locate the right agency for assistance with specific problems. Multilingual staff members offer assistance in 46 of the 74 cities served by FIC offices.

Federal Maritime Commission
An independent agency established in 1961, FMC regulates commercial shipping and exercises other regulatory powers as provided in the Shipping Act of 1916 and its amendments. Its major responsibilities are issuing licenses for freight forwarding, approving agreements between common carriers, accepting tariff filings, administering regulations concerning water pollution, and ensuring carrier compliance with the law. Sometimes confused with the MARITIME ADMINISTRATION of the Department of Commerce.

Federal Mediation and Conciliation Service
Established in 1947 as an independent agency by the Taft-Hartley Act. When employers and employees or their representatives cannot reach an agreement in an industrial dispute, FMCS provides experienced

mediators who attempt to narrow the range of differences and assist in reaching agreement. FMCS also maintains a roster of qualified arbitrators available on the request of management or labor. MEDIATION and CONCILIATION have come to mean the same thing.

Federal National Mortgage Association (FNMA)

Nicknamed "Fannie Mae," FNMA is a private corporation chartered by the U.S. government. It helps assure that enough money is available to home buyers. It buys home mortgages from banks, savings and loan associations, and insurance companies. It also sells mortgages to private institutions. These mortgages are insured or guaranteed by government agencies such as the Federal Housing Administration and the Veterans Administration. FNMA was established in 1938 as a government-owned corporation and was placed under the Housing and Home Finance Agency in 1950. In 1954, FNMA was reorganized as a corporation owned jointly by the government and private stockholders. It became a totally private corporation in 1970.

Federal Power Commission (FPC)

A federal agency of five commissioners headed by a chairman who is appointed by the president. FPC is responsible for the regulation of interstate aspects of electric power and natural gas industries. It regulates the wholesale rates and service in interstate commerce of natural gas by natural-gas producers and by interstate pipeline companies, and regulates wholesale sales of electric energy by public utilities, among other complex powers vested in its charter to ensure proper allocation and utilization of resources. FPC became part of the newly formed Department of Energy in 1977.

Federal Railroad Administration

A branch of the U.S. Department of Transportation responsible for the operation of the Alaska Railroad, administration of the High-Speed Ground Transportation Program, and implementation of railroad laws. It advises the Secretary of Transportation on matters pertaining to national railroad policy developments.

Federal Register

Published by the General Services Administration, the *Federal Register* appears five times a week to describe proposed and final regulations and general notice documents significant to the public. The *Register* publishes a notice of intervention when the Regulatory Law Division in the Office of the General Counsel intends to enter a public utility case on behalf of the federal government.

Federal Reserve Bank
See FEDERAL RESERVE SYSTEM.

Federal Reserve Board
See FEDERAL RESERVE SYSTEM.

Federal Reserve System
FRS is composed of a board of governors (also known as "the Fed"), the Federal Open Market Committee, the Federal Advisory Council, 12 Federal Reserve Banks and their 25 branches, and some 5,800 member banks. Membership in the system is optional for state banks but obligatory for all national banks. The seven governors of the board are appointed by the president. The FRS serves as the nation's central bank, whose main purpose and responsibilities are to regulate the flow of money and credit and to perform supervisory services and functions for the public, the U.S. Treasury, and commercial banks.

Federal Savings and Loan Insurance Corporation (FSLIC)
See FEDERAL HOME LOAN BANK BOARD.

Federal Society of Journeymen Cordwainers
One of the first craft labor organizations in the United States, formed in 1794 by shoeworkers in Philadelphia. It was disbanded in 1806, when it was tried and fined for conspiracy.

Federal Trade Commission
The FTC is an independent law enforcement agency. The president appoints its five commissioners, one of whom is designated as chairman. The mission of the FTC is to promote free and fair competition in the American marketplace by enforcing the antitrust laws and similar statutes. Created in 1914, it is charged with the enforcement of the Federal Trade Commission Act and, together with the Justice Department, the enforcement of the Clayton Antitrust Act as amended by the Robinson-Patman Act.

Federal Trade Commission Act
A major antitrust law of the United States enacted in 1914, its chief purpose is to prevent unethical business practices such as unfair, deceptive, dishonest, or injurious methods of competition and, as amended by the Wheeler-Lea Act of 1938, to protect the public against false and misleading advertising of food, drugs, cosmetics, and therapeutic devices. See WHEELER-LEA ACT.

Federal Water Power Act

An act of Congress passed in 1920 that established authority for hydropower development. In 1935 the Federal Power Act greatly expanded government's role in hydropower.

fee simple estate

In law, the complete ownership of land. Such an estate passes upon the death of the owners to the heirs, free from any conditions. Opposed to an *estate for life,* in which all rights to the land cease with the death of the owner. Also known as *estate in fee simple.*

felony

Under common law, a felony was a criminal offense and, upon conviction, the criminal forfeited his lands and goods to the crown and was subject to death. In modern times, by statute, the term covers all criminal offenses that are punishable by death or imprisonment.

Festinger, Leon

A behavioral scientist. See COGNITIVE DISSONANCE.

FHA

See FEDERAL HIGHWAY ADMINISTRATION and FEDERAL HOUSING ADMINISTRATION.

FHLBB

See FEDERAL HOME LOAN BANK BOARD.

FIA clause

Abbreviation for *full interest admitted clause.* See POLICY PROOF OF INTEREST CLAUSE.

fiat

A directive issued by a recognized authority.

FIC

See FEDERAL INFORMATION CENTERS.

fidelity and surety bonding insurance

Fidelity insurance provides coverage against financial, material, or property loss resulting from an employee's dishonesty or treachery. Three kinds of fidelity bonds are available: (1) individual bonds, which name a specific person, (2) schedule bonds, which list all the names or positions covered, and (3) blanket bonds, which cover all employees but do not name them or identify positions within the firm. Surety bonds guarantee that the principal will carry out the terms of an agreement or conditions of a contract.

fiduciary
A person in a position of trust and confidence, as a broker with respect to a principal. The broker as a fiduciary owes a loyalty that cannot be breached under the rules of agency. See AGENCY.

field
In data processing, an assigned area in a record to be marked with information. A set of one or more characters treated as a unit of data. Sometimes referred to as *variable word*.

FIELDCOM
Acronym for *field computer,* a medium-scale, internally stored program processor that is organized into fields instead of words. FIELDCOM storage is 8,000 individual characters. It is left to the resources of the programmer to plan the efficient use of the characters for data items and instructions, consistent with FIELDCOM's engineering design features.

fieri facias
Latin, "you cause it to be made." A writ or order issued by a court that directs the sheriff to levy on the goods or personal property of the defendant in order to satisfy a judgment on behalf of the plaintiff. See LEVY.

FIFO
Acronym for *first in, first out;* in accounting, a method of inventory costing based on the assumption that costs should be charged against revenue in the order in which they are incurred. Thus inventory is valued on the basis of actual cost at the time of acquisition and, as consumed, is charged to cost of sale accordingly. See LIFO and WEIGHTED AVERAGE METHOD.

file
In data processing, an organized collection of information. The records in a file may or may not be sequenced according to a key contained in each record. See RECORD.

fill-or-kill order
A market or limited-price order to a stockbroker that is to be executed in its entirety as soon as it is presented to the exchange. If not so executed, the order is treated as canceled. See STOP ORDER.

final assembly
In manufacturing, the highest-level assembled product, considered a finished good ready for delivery to the customer. Frequently used as the name for the department or section of the manufacturing facility where the product is assembled (also called *erection department*).

final average pay
An individual's earnings during the final period of employment or participation in a compensation plan, typically the last three, five, or ten years' average pay. It is used particularly in the calculation of pension benefits.

Financial Accounting Standards Board
A professional association created in 1973. FASB is governed by seven members who are required to sever all outside financial ties. Four of the members are public accountants, one represents the federal government, and another represents industry. The seventh member represents the public. FASB establishes a "constitution"—rules and regulations governing accounting practices and procedures that are intended to standardize language and data for financial reports and statements. FASB has no explicit power to enforce its recommendations; however, the SECURITIES AND EXCHANGE COMMISSION (SEC) generally adopts FASB standards.

financial risk
In the securities market, the uncertainty of future returns from a security because of changes in the financial capacity of the organization that issued the security. Sometimes called *business risk*. See SECURITY RISK, INTEREST RATE RISK, MARKET RISK, POLITICAL RISK, PURCHASING POWER RISK, and SOCIAL RISK.

finder
A person, acting as an individual or as an enterprise, who brings together a buyer and a seller and earns a fee for the service.

finished goods
Products that are ready for shipment to a customer. Also known as *end item* and *end product*.

fink
A derogatory word, used as either a noun or a verb, to describe a member of a labor union who reports to his employer on the activities of the union and of his fellow employees. It was the practice to expel from the union any person behaving in such a way as to be identified as a fink. The Labor-Management Relations Act (Taft-Hartley Act) of 1947 permits unions to expel a member only for failure to pay union dues or fees.

finnmark
See MARKKA.

fire legal liability
An insurance policy written to cover possible legal liability to others as a result of a fire that develops through the negligence of the insured.

firkin
A capacity measurement used in Great Britain, equivalent to a quarter of a barrel. Approximately equal to 9 imperial gallons or about 56 pounds. The exact amount or capacity of a barrel as a unit of measure for liquids and dry goods is not the same for all commodities, and may be fixed by law in some countries. In the United States, a barrel has 7,056 cubic inches or 115.62 liters for most dry goods; for most liquids, 31½ gallons or 119.24 liters; for petroleum, 42 gallons or 158.98 liters.

first-class mail insurance
This type of coverage is for stock certificates, bonds, coupons, stamps, money orders, and other securities of institutions such as banks, trust companies, insurance companies, stock clearing corporations, and general corporations.

first come, first served
Decision-making rule for scheduling. This rule places orders in line as they arrive at a processing point. The next order to be processed is the one that is first in line.

first in, first out
See FIFO.

first in system, first served
A rule used in decision making for production scheduling that is based on the due dates for orders waiting in line. The order that has the earliest planned due date will be assigned first. Compare FIRST COME, FIRST SERVED.

first-level address
See DIRECT ADDRESS.

first loan
See FIRST MORTGAGE.

first mortgage
A mortgage that has priority as a lien over all other mortgages. Also called *senior mortgage* and *first loan*.

first paramount lien
An encumbrance against property that makes it liable for a debt; this encumbrance has priority over any other lien.

fiscal drag
A large budgetary surplus that might be created by the tax system as the economy approaches full employment. It may act as a brake on the expansion of the economy.

fiscal monopoly
A government monopoly created to generate revenue. Commodities such as salt and tobacco, for example, are sometimes reserved for sale by the government, and their profits are used for public purposes.

fiscal year
Any 12 months in sequence selected as an accounting period, not necessarily corresponding with the calendar year. The fiscal year of the U.S. government, for example, ends September 30 of each year.

FISFS
See FIRST IN SYSTEM, FIRST SERVED.

Fisher, Irving (1867–1947)
An American economist who concentrated on monetary problems with the hope of producing a stabilization of prices and a moderation of the peaks of booms and depressions. See NEOCLASSICAL ECONOMICS.

Fisher equation
See QUANTITY THEORY OF MONEY.

fishyback
The transportation of highway trailers or demountable trailer bodies aboard a ship. This method of shipment permits reduced rates and provides faster service. See also TRAILERS ON FLATCARS.

fixation
In the behavior of an individual, fixation occurs when a person repeats the same negative pattern over and over again, despite experiences that show that it accomplishes nothing. Frustration can freeze old and habitual responses and prevent the use of new and more effectual ones. Common symptoms of fixation in business are the inability to accept change and stubborn refusal to accept new facts when experience shows the old ones to be untenable.

fixed capital
The money invested in fixed assets.

fixed charge
A regularly recurring expense, such as rent or interest, that the company must pay. A fixed expense is deducted from income before earnings on equity capital are computed. See FIXED COST.

fixed cost
An operating expense that does not vary with the volume or activity of business or of production. Also known as *fixed expense,* or *constant cost.*

fixed expense
See FIXED COST.

fixed liability
A long-term liability.

fixed-order quantity
In manufacturing, a system of inventory control in which a reorder point is set to allow the inventory level to be drawn down to the safety stock, or buffer inventory level, assuming average usage is being experienced.

fixed-reorder cycle
In manufacturing, a system of inventory control that operates by placing orders for replenishment of stock at regular intervals. The size of the reorder is varied to absorb the variations in usages, so that the maximum inventory is maintained at a predetermined level.

flag
In data processing, a bit of information attached to a character or word to indicate the boundary of a field. Also known as *sentinel.*

flat
A security market term referring usually to the sale of a bond. A bond is sold "flat" if its trading price includes consideration of all unpaid accruals of interest. This is the common form of trade for bonds that are in default of interest or principal. All other bonds are usually dealt in "and interest," which means that the buyer pays the seller the market price plus interest accrued since the last payment date. When applied to a stock loan, "flat" means without premium or interest.

flatcar
A freight car without ends, sides, or top.

flat lease
See STRAIGHT LEASE.

flexible budget
A budget with alternative provisions that are based on varying rates of activity.

flip-flop
A device in computers that is capable of assuming two stable states; it is used to control the opening and closing of electronic gates. Also known as *Eccles-Jordan circuit* or *Eccles-Jordan trigger*.

float
In finance, moneys, usually in the form of checks, en route to the payee but not yet credited to the payee's account. The payor of the check may have, in the process of effecting payment, deposited the check with a corresponding bank. In effect the deposit may not have yet been made in the payee's bank nor credited to the payee's account. The payee, therefore, may not draw against the deposit that is in "float." However, at its own discretion the payee's bank may waive this restriction. The word "float" is also used to indicate transmittal documents that are en route to a destination wherein they are to be exercised.

floater policy
A type of insurance policy or contract covering property that "floats" or moves about from place to place, or goods of a class in which the particular items change or shift in quantity over relatively short time periods. See ORDINARY POLICY.

floating address

In data processing, an address written in such a way that it can be easily converted to a machine address by indexing, assembly, or some other means.

floating assets

See CURRENT ASSETS.

floating capital

That portion of the capital of a business firm that is not invested in fixed or capital assets but in current and working assets. See WORKING CAPITAL.

floating coverage

A type of insurance coverage common for property that is being transported from one place to another. Such property includes airplanes, boats, and other goods that are of necessity moved from place to place.

floating debt

Current liabilities; short-term obligations. Floating and funded debts represent the total liabilities to outsiders. See FUNDED DEBT.

floating exchange rates

Foreign exchange rates determined in a free market by supply and demand.

floating liability

Current liability. See FLOATING DEBT.

flood insurance

Such insurance is generally difficult to obtain in areas subject to flooding because of the frequency of catastrophic losses. A federal flood insurance program has been authorized to make such protection available at reasonable rates.

floor

Popular term for the trading area, about two-thirds the size of a football field, where stocks and bonds are bought and sold on the New York Stock Exchange. Also used in reference to the trading area of any exchange.

floor broker

A member of a stock exchange who executes orders on the floor of the exchange to buy or sell any listed security.

floor trader
See REGISTERED TRADER.

florin
Basic unit of currency in the Netherlands. Also known as the *Netherlands gulden* or *guilder*.

flowchart
See FLOW DIAGRAM.

flow diagram
In its simplest form, a rough view of the space in which an activity being studied occurs, and the location and extent of the work areas, machines, or desks, with a series of arrows and lines to indicate the route of travel for a given project. Flow diagrams are frequently made up in conjunction with process charts to enable visualizing the process and evaluating the plan. Also known as *flowchart;* used in data processing to visualize the development of a computer program, and in other areas of management to graphically depict any process or procedure within the organization or the hierarchy.

flow process chart
Defined by the American Society of Mechanical Engineers' *Standard 101* as a graphic representation of the sequence of all operations, transportations, inspections, delays, and storages occurring during a manufacture process or procedure. A flow process chart includes information considered desirable for analysis of a procedure, such as time required to perform each activity and distance that materials must be moved. Such charts are of two types: (1) the *materials chart* represents the process in terms of events that occur to the material; (2) the *man chart* presents the process in terms of activities of a given employee.

fluctuation
A security market term. See POINT.

FMC
See FEDERAL MARITIME COMMISSION.

FMCS
See FEDERAL MEDIATION AND CONCILIATION SERVICE.

FmHA
See FARMERS HOME ADMINISTRATION.

FNMA
See FEDERAL NATIONAL MORTGAGE ASSOCIATION.

FNS
See FOOD AND NUTRITION SERVICE.

FOB
Abbreviation for *free on board*. When followed by a modifier, such as "factory," "railroad," or "vessel," FOB indicates the point at which the buyer assumes responsibility for the goods. For example, *FOB factory* means that the buyer assumes responsibility for the goods when they leave the factory. *FOB railroad* means that the buyer assumes responsibility after the goods have been placed on railroad cars.

FOIA
See FREEDOM OF INFORMATION ACT OF 1974.

Follett, Mary Parker (1868–1933)
A writer on the subject of organizational behavior before it was known by that name.

Food and Agriculture Organization (FAO)
A United Nations agency that develops programs intended to cope with poverty, hunger, and malnutrition throughout the world.

Food and Drug Administration
FDA is a unit of the Department of Health, Education, and Welfare. Originally created in 1931, it now has a staff of 7,000 and is responsible for the safety and efficacy of drugs and medical devices and the safety and purity of food. It also regulates labeling, overseeing approximately $200 billion worth of industrial output.

Food and Nutrition Service
FNS, an agency of the Department of Agriculture, administers USDA's various food-assistance programs, such as food stamps and child nutrition.

forbearance
The act of giving up the right to enforce a valid debt, right, or obligation. The act of forbearance is treated as sufficient consideration to make a new promise given by the debtor legally binding.

forced-sale value
The amount derived from a sale of assets or goods on an urgent basis, usually where the seller is under legal or economic compulsion to sell. See LIQUIDATION VALUE.

force field analysis
A technique for diagnosing organizational situations and leader effectiveness, developed by Kurt Lewin. He assumes that there are "driving" and "restraining" forces in any situation that influence any change that may occur. Equilibrium, representing an existing level of productivity, is reached when the sum of the driving forces equals the sum of the restraining forces. The level of productivity can be changed—raised or lowered—by changes in the relationship between driving and restraining forces. See DRIVING FORCES and RESTRAINING FORCES.

forcible entry and detainer
In law, the violent taking and keeping possession by one of any lands and tenements occupied by another, by means of threats, force, or arms, and without authority of law. After a forcible entry and detainer has occurred, the aggrieved party is entitled to seek legal aid in restoring possession to the one who has been wrongfully deprived of the possession. The question of title is not tried, but only the right to possession.

foreign car
A car owned by one railroad but operating on the rails of another.

foreign corporation
In state corporation laws, a corporation that has been created under the laws of a state or country other than the one in which the corporation is officially located. In federal law, a corporation established under the laws of another country.

Foreign Credit Insurance Association
Approximately 50 leading insurance companies participate in this association, whose purpose is to provide insurance policies for the protection of American exporters against such political risks as inconvertibility, cancellation of an import license, war, and expropriation, and against such commercial risks as the buyer's insolvency or protracted default in the payment of principal and interest. The EXPORT-IMPORT BANK OF THE UNITED STATES together with the FCIA covers the aforementioned risk situations.

foreign exchange rate
Price of one currency in terms of the currency of another country.

foreign trade zone
See FREE PORT.

foreshore
Land between the high and low water marks of a stream, lake, or ocean.

Forest Service
An agency of the U.S. Department of Agriculture, FS provides for the conservation and wise use of the nation's forest and land resources, including recreational uses.

forfeitures
Funds relinquished by a terminating employee in a qualified profit-sharing or thrift plan. These funds are sometimes used by the company to reduce future company contributions to the plan, or they may be allocated to current participants to increase their shares.

forgery
The alteration or false writing of an instrument with the intent of deceiving and injuring another person; for example, signing someone's name to a check without his or her consent.

forint
Basic unit of currency in Hungary.

form stop
In computers, the automatic device on a printer that stops the machine when the paper has run out.

formula pension
The category of pension covering most salaried employees, under which a rate formula is applied to individual earnings to calculate the employee's pension

Formula Translation
See FORTRAN.

FORTRAN
Acronym for *Formula Translation;* a computer programing language designed for problems that can be expressed in algebraic notation. The

FORTRAN compiler is a routine for a given machine that accepts a program written in FORTRAN source language and produces a machine-language routine object program. Later improvements in the program added the ability to use Boolean expressions, and some capabilities for inserting symbolic machine language sequences within a source program. See OBJECT PROGRAM and SOURCE PROGRAM.

forwarding fee
A charge made by a lender for sending a beneficiary's statement to a title company.

FOSDIC
Acronym for *Film Optic Sensing Device for Input to Computers.*

foundation exclusion clause
This clause in a disaster or general insurance policy excludes coverage for the costs of excavations, underground flues, pipes, underground wiring, and drains below the undersurface of the lowest basement floor.

founders' stock
Stock in a new venture issued to the founders and, in some cases, to key executives. Typically, the stock of this category is priced below the amount paid by other investors.

Fourier, Charles (1772–1837)
A French theorist who believed in communal life as a cure to economic and social ills and claimed that the world was about to enter a millennium. He succeeded in establishing a few small cooperative communities. None survived, however, despite the fact that some noted Americans, such as Nathaniel Hawthorne, Bronson Alcott, and Margaret Fuller, became converts to Fourier's socialistic ideas. See UTOPIAN SOCIALISM.

FPA
Abbreviation for *free of particular average.* In ocean marine insurance, "particular average" means partial loss. Thus "free of particular average" means excluding partial loss.

FPC
See FEDERAL POWER COMMISSION.

FRA
See FEDERAL RAILROAD ADMINISTRATION.

franc
Basic unit of currency in Belgium, Burundi, France, Guinea, Luxembourg, Malagasy Republic, Mali, Rwanda, and Switzerland.

franc CFA
Abbreviation for *franc de la Communauté Financière Africaine;* basic unit of currency in Cameroon, Central African Republic, Chad, Congo, Dahomey, Gabon, Ivory Coast, Mauritania, Niger, Senegal, Togo, Upper Volta.

franchise
An agreement whereby one enterprise, the franchisor, extends to another, the franchisee, the right to conduct a certain type of business operation in accordance with policies, practices, procedures, and merchandise created and owned by the franchisor.

franchise deductible
A clause found most frequently in ocean marine insurance policies for property and liability coverage. It provides that if losses are less than a specified amount, such as a percentage of the value of the property, nothing will be paid. If the loss exceeds the percentage, the insurance company pays the full amount of the loss. See DEDUCTIBLE CLAUSES.

franchise tax
A tax on the right of a corporation to do business under its corporate name.

franken
The term for the Swiss franc.

fraud
Under the law, an intentional misrepresentation of the truth for the purpose of deceiving another person. The elements of fraud are: (1) the intentional misrepresentation of a material fact, not opinion, (2) the intent that the deceived person should act on the representation, (3) the knowledge that the false statement would cause a deception, and (4) a loss of property or of a legal right by the deceived person as a result of his acting on the misrepresentation of the fact.

fraudulent conveyance
Under the law, a conveyance of property by a debtor for the intent and purpose of defrauding his creditors. Such a conveyance has no legal effect, and the property which has been fraudulently conveyed may be reached by the creditors through legal proceedings.

free alongside
See FAS.

free astray
Designation for a shipment that is lost but subsequently found. Such a shipment is usually sent to its proper destination without additional charges.

free currency
Money that may be exchanged for the money of another country without legal restrictions. See BLOCKED CURRENCY.

Freedom of Information Act of 1974
FOIA and the Privacy Act of 1974 permit individuals to write for copies of personal records collected by federal agencies, to correct any inadequacies in those records and, within limits, to control disclosure of them to other agencies.

freehold estate
An interest in real estate that continues forever, or for the life of an individual, or for the lives of more than one individual. An estate-less-than-freehold is one that lasts for a certain or uncertain number of years; for example, a commercial lease is an estate that continues for a fixed term, while a tenancy-at-will is an estate that continues at the will of either the landlord or the tenant.

free of capture and seizure
See FC&S.

free of particular average
See FPA.

free on board
See FOB.

free port
A restricted area at a seaport for the handling of duty-exempted import goods. Also known as *foreign trade zone*.

free-rein leadership
A name given by Auren Uris to the style of leadership better known as LAISSEZ-FAIRE.

free-trade area
An association of trading nations whose participants agree to impose no restrictive devices such as tariffs or quotas on one another, but are free to impose whatever restrictive devices they wish on nonparticipants. See EUROPEAN FREE TRADE ASSOCIATION.

freight allowed
This expression means that shipments will move freight-collect and, unless otherwise specified, that an amount equal to the charges paid by the buyer to the carrier will be deducted from the total cost of the goods when the seller's invoice is paid. See FREIGHT PREPAID.

freight consolidator
An independent contractor who receives many small shipments for the account of one industrial company and combines them into one carload or truckload.

freight forwarder
An individual or company accepting less-than-carload (LCL) shipments from shippers and combining or forwarding them in carload (CL) lots. A foreign freight forwarder handles customs procedures and documents on export shipments.

freight-in
Freight paid on an incoming shipment. An element of cost of the goods or materials received.

freight-out
Freight charges paid or allowed by the seller on goods or materials shipped out.

freight prepaid
This expression means the seller will pay transportation charges to the carrier and the buyer will remit the full amount of the invoice without deduction for freight charges. See FREIGHT ALLOWED.

frequency polygon
A method of graphically depicting statistical information. The x or horizontal axis represents the class of data, the y or vertical axis represents units of time, dollars, or other reference information. The frequency polygon appears as a broken-line graph showing the frequency of the data with respect to the variable represented by the y axis. See OGIVE.

frequency shift keying (FSK)
In data processing, a method of data transmission. A binary *1* shifts the frequency above the center carrier frequency; a binary *0* shifts the frequency below the center carrier frequency.

Friedman, Milton
Professor of economics at the University of Chicago, born 1912. Friedman was awarded the Nobel Prize in Economics by the Swedish Royal Academy of Science in 1976 and is recognized as the leader of the so-called Chicago school of monetarist economics. In his book *A Monetary History of the United States, 1867–1960,* coauthored with Anna Schwartz in 1963, he argues that to bring about stability and steady expansion in jobs without flaring inflation, government policy makers need only maintain a gradual, controlled growth in the money supplied by the Federal Reserve. By reducing the nation's money supply in the 1930s, Friedman contends, the Federal Reserve Board caused a recession to turn into the Great Depression.

friendly fire
See HOSTILE FIRE.

FRS
See FEDERAL RESERVE SYSTEM.

frustration
In human behavior, the blocking or thwarting of goal attainment, defined in terms of the condition of the individual rather than in terms of the external environment. Frustration may take different forms of expression, including aggression against unrelated persons or objects. If a person cannot attack the cause of his frustration directly, he may search for and find a scapegoat on which to vent his hostility. For other expressions caused by frustration, see RATIONALIZATION, REGRESSION, FIXATION, and RESIGNATION.

FS
See FOREST SERVICE.

FSK
See FREQUENCY SHIFT KEYING.

FSLIC
Initials for *Federal Savings and Loan Insurance Corporation.* See FEDERAL HOME LOAN BANK BOARD.

FTC
See FEDERAL TRADE COMMISSION.

full-faith-and-credit debt
In municipal accounting, the debt of a municipality or municipal enterprise, the repayment of which is a direct obligation of the municipality.

full interest admitted clause
See POLICY PROOF OF INTEREST CLAUSE.

full liability
A liability of a sole person or company, not shared with others.

functional finance
The doctrine in economics that the government should pursue whatever fiscal measures are necessary to achieve noninflationary full employment and economic growth, without regard to budget balancing. The federal budget is viewed as a functional and flexible tool for achieving economic objectives, rather than as an accounting statement to be balanced periodically.

functional income distribution
The allocation of the national income to the owners of the economic resources—land, labor, and capital—that contributed to its production. Also known as *factoral income distribution.*

functionalism
See FUNCTIONAL ORGANIZATION STRUCTURE.

functional organization structure
A hierarchal arrangement of an organization that is based on the concepts of division of labor and specialization—the assignment of subtasks to units of people who are skilled in performing narrow, highly specialized functions. Thus, in forming functional departments, people of similar skill, training, and occupational specialization are brought together. For example, the functional organization structure groups engineers into an engineering organization or department, production people into a production department, financial people into the finance department, and so on, where each group is charged with the specific responsibilities related to its own area of specialization.

funded debt
Outstanding bonds or notes that are evidence of a debt. See BONDED DEBT and FLOATING DEBT.

funded pension plan
A pension plan that has a fund specifically set aside for the payment of promised funds to retirees. The fund consists of company contributions, employee contributions (where they are part of the plan), and the income from investments of the fund.

funded reserve
Any of several types of reserves for pensions, bonuses, the retirement of preferred stock, or any other prospective liability against which certain assets have been accumulated, set aside, or earmarked.

funding bonds
Bonds that are issued for the purpose of retiring current or long-term indebtedness or to finance current expenditures.

funding company
The name given to a type of financial company that offers investors a package of mutual fund shares and life insurance.

fund obligation
A liability or encumbrance of a particular fund.

fund surplus
The excess of the amount accumulated in a specific fund over its obligations.

FUTA
Acronym for *Federal Unemployment Taxes*.

futures
The term for contracts to buy and sell commodities, usually traded on a commodities exchange. The contracts or futures deal in the deliveries of commodities at some specified date in the future. For example, a trader who speculates that the price for a certain commodity will decline next April will sell contracts for the delivery of the commodity at that time; however, the price is based on the current market position. On the other hand, the trader who believes the price will rise next April will buy contracts or futures.

GAAP
See GENERALLY ACCEPTED ACCOUNTING PRINCIPLES.

gain
The excess of revenues over related costs; a profit or advantage.

Galbraith, John Kenneth
Born in 1908 at Ontario, Canada, Galbraith became a U.S. citizen in 1937 and a professor of economics at Harvard University in 1949. From 1961 to 1963 he served as ambassador to India. Galbraith's many books on economics and its numerous aspects have stimulated widespread interest in economic issues. He is known as a historian of economics, having written and lectured widely about the evolution of economic thinking and practice.

galloping inflation
See HYPERINFLATION.

GAMA
Initials for *Gas Appliance Manufacturers Association.*

game theory
A mathematical theory concerned with the process of selecting an optimum strategy in the face of an opponent who has a strategy of his own.

Gantt, Henry Laurence (1861–1919)
A close associate of Frederick W. Taylor, Gantt later became an independent consultant. He supported incentive systems for production workers. See GANTT CHART.

Gantt chart
A pictorial method for displaying and monitoring a process, project, or production schedule so as to evaluate performance against a timetable. Gantt charts, if properly maintained, can serve as valuable tools for planning, scheduling, and controlling the various aspects of a production situation.

GAO
See GENERAL ACCOUNTING OFFICE.

gapped schedule
In manufacturing, the finishing of every piece in a lot at one work center before any piece in the lot can be processed at the succeeding work center. The movement of material in complete lots may cause gaps between the end of one operation and the beginning of the next. Also known as *straight-line scheduling* and *gap phasing*. See OVERLAPPED SCHEDULE.

gap phasing
See GAPPED SCHEDULE.

garage keepers' legal liability insurance
An insurance policy written to cover a single hazard: the liability of a garage keeper for automobiles left in his care. Sold to garages, parking lots, and other firms that have temporary custody of automobiles owned by other persons. Payment is made only if the garage keeper is judged legally liable.

garage liability policy
Basically an owners', landlords', and tenants' (OL&T) contract tailored to the needs of automobile dealers, garages, repair shops, and service stations.

garnishee
A person upon whom a garnishment is served. He is the debtor or a defendant and has money or property that the plaintiff is trying to reach in order to satisfy a debt from the defendant. See GARNISHMENT.

garnishment
A legal proceeding by which a plaintiff seeks to reach the money or property of the defendant that is in the hands of a third party. A gar-

nishment differs from an attachment in that by an attachment an officer of the court takes actual possession of property through a writ. In a garnishment, the money or property is retained by the plaintiff until final adjudication.

gate
In data processing, an electronic switching circuit yielding an output signal that is dependent on some function of an input signal. See AND GATE, EXCEPT GATE, and OR GATE.

gateway
A freight interchange point between territories.

GATT
See GENERAL AGREEMENTS ON TARIFFS AND TRADE.

Gaussian distribution
A symmetrical, bell-shaped curve representing the normal frequency distribution in statistical analysis. See NORMAL DISTRIBUTION.

GBL
Initials for *government bill of lading.*

GCT
Initials for *Greenwich civil time.* See GREENWICH MEAN TIME.

GEICO
Acronym for *Government Employees Insurance Company.*

general accountant
An accountant who is competent by education or experience, or both, to deal with any type of accounting situation in the organization.

General Accounting Office (GAO)
An agency of the federal government responsible for auditing the operations of other government agencies. The GAO is responsible to the Congress of the United States. It is directed by a comptroller general, who is appointed by the president of the United States, subject to Senate confirmation, for a 15-year term, and who may not be reappointed. He retires at full salary and may be removed only upon a majority vote of both houses after an inquiry similar to an impeachment procedure. See COMPTROLLER GENERAL.

General Agreements on Tariffs and Trade (GATT)
An international commercial agreement signed in 1947 by the United States and many other countries for the purpose of achieving four basic long-range objectives: (1) nondiscrimination in trade through adherence to unconditional most-favored-nation treatment, (2) reduction of tariffs by negotiations, (3) elimination of import quotas (with some exceptions), and (4) resolution of economic differences through consultation.

general average loss
Dating back many centuries, it applies to ocean marine cargoes, regardless of whether or not insurance is carried. It is one of the perils covered by modern ocean marine insurance policies. A general average loss is incurred in time of emergency for the common welfare of the vessel, and involves sacrificing a part of the cargo or the hull in order to save the entire ship. The expenses of the loss are shared proportionally by all parties involved.

general contingency reserve
In accounting procedures, a reserve for contingencies that is not identified with any specific future need; as contrasted with SPECIAL CONTINGENCY RESERVE.

general contractor
A person or firm whose contracts include several types of skilled work in the construction field. See INDEPENDENT CONTRACTOR.

general expense
An administrative expense, not identified with a specific process, product, or service generated by the operation of the facility. Also known as *burden*.

general fund
In finance, moneys available for expenditure that are not earmarked for any specific program or project.

general land office
See BUREAU OF LAND MANAGEMENT.

generally accepted accounting principles (GAAP)
In 1959 the Association of Independent Certified Public Accountants organized the Accounting Principles Board (APB), which reviewed

accounting practices, with special notice given to the preparation of financial statements for corporations, in accordance with requirements of the law. From 1959 to 1973 the APB issued 31 major opinions on financial accounting principles and practices. In 1973 the APB was replaced by the Financial Accounting Standards Board (FASB). As with the APB, opinions published by the FASB become required positions for certified public accountants to take in the practice of the profession. See ACCOUNTING PRINCIPLES BOARD and FINANCIAL ACCOUNTING STANDARDS BOARD.

general merchandise store
See GENERAL STORE.

general merchandise warehouse
This operation stores and ships a great variety of merchandise rather than specializing in one type, provided that controlled environmental conditions are not required.

general mortgage
A mortgage that involves all the properties of a mortgagor.

general mortgage bond
A bond that is secured by a blanket mortgage on the company's property, but that is often outranked by one or more other mortgages.

general overhead
In accounting procedures, the expense of administration and selling.

general partner
An active member of a partnership who has unlimited liability for the actions of the partners. An enterprise formed as a partnership with one or more partners is required by law to have at least one general partner for liability purposes. See LIMITED PARTNER and PARTNERSHIP.

General Services Administration (GSA)
A non-Cabinet agency directed by an administrator who is appointed by the president. The GSA is the centralized purchasing and real estate agency for the federal government. It stockpiles strategic and critical materials for use in national emergencies; disposes of surplus land and personal property to organizations and consumers; coordinates the federal government's civil emergency preparedness program; runs the federal data processing and telecommunications programs; publishes the *Federal Register,* a compilation of proposed and final regulations;

and distributes federal information for consumers. See FEDERAL REG-
ISTER and FEDERAL INFORMATION CENTERS.

general store
A type of retailing institution that usually sells a limited selection of a
wide range of goods. The general store is distinguished from the DE-
PARTMENT STORE in that its limited selections of goods in each line are
not departmentalized. Also called *general merchandise store*.

general warranty
In real estate, a covenant in a deed whereby the grantor agrees to
protect the grantee against any claimant.

genetic industry
In economics, an industry engaged directly in increasing the supply of
some form of plant or animal life. Farming and cattle raising are examples.

geometric mean
See MEAN.

geometric progression
In statistics, a numerical progression or series whose values increase at
a constant ratio. Also known as *geometric series*.

geometric series
See GEOMETRIC PROGRESSION.

George, Henry (1839–1897)
Born in Philadelphia, died during a second attempt to win an election as
mayor of New York. He was noted for his study of the problems of
poverty and his attempts at remedy, and famous for his theory of the
single tax, or a tax on land, as set forth in 1879 in his book *Progress and
Poverty,* which created a stir but did not have a long-lasting effect on
economic policy. See SINGLE TAX.

Gesellschaft mit beschränkter Haftung (GmbH)
A limited-liability company under Austrian, German, and Swiss law.
Also known in Switzerland as *SARL*.

Gestalt psychology
A school of psychology sometimes considered useful in personnel
selection and testing, the Gestalt movement was begun in 1912 by Max

Wertheimer (1880–1943), a professor of psychology at the University of Berlin. A basic idea of Gestalt psychology is that human beings do not perceive an object as a collection of its parts, but rather as a unified whole. Its basic thesis is that the complete personality of the individual must be considered along with the way particular characteristics interrelate, or a misleading view of the mental processes of the individual will be obtained. Gestalt psychology became established in the United States during the 1930s, after many leading German psychologists had come to America. Several who followed Wertheimer's concept extended Gestalt principles to the study of human relations and made important contributions to theories of personality and social psychology. The word "Gestalt" is German for "form," "figure," or "pattern." It is sometimes translated as "configuration."

GFTC–ERR
Initials for *General Freight Traffic Committee—Eastern Railroads*.

ghetto
Historically, a section of a city in which people of specific races or religious beliefs were required to live and to earn their livelihoods. Currently, an economically depressed urban area in which members of minorities live.

GIDEP
See GOVERNMENT-INDUSTRY DATA EXCHANGE PROGRAM.

gift causa mortis
In law, a gift made by a donor in anticipation of death. In order for the gift to be legally valid as a gift causa mortis, the donor must have been in sickness at the time of proclaiming the gift and must later die as anticipated. If the donor survives the sickness, the gift is revocable. See GIFT INTER VIVOS.

gift deed
An instrument that transfers the title to real estate for which the consideration is love and affection, rather than material consideration.

gift inter vivos
In law, the delivery of a gift during the life of the donor. A *gift inter vivos* causes the gift to be effective immediately at the time of delivery, unlike a *gift causa mortis* made in contemplation or anticipation of death due to sickness, wherein the gift is effective only upon the death of the donor. See GIFT CAUSA MORTIS.

gigacycle
Same as GIGAHERTZ.

gigahertz
A unit of frequency equal to 10^9 hertz, or one billion cycles per second.

Gilbreth, Frank Bunker (1868–1924)
The most prominent figure in the history of operation analysis or motion study. Assisted by his wife, Lillian, a professional psychologist, Gilbreth developed motion-time-study techniques through the use of motion pictures that have become standards in production practice and in the field of industrial engineering. Together the Gilbreths developed a system of basic elements of motion known as *therbligs* and performed many historic studies on worker fatigue. They had 12 children who, as a family unit, served as subjects for many of their time motion studies. Two of the children wrote the book *Cheaper by the Dozen*. See THERBLIG CHART.

Gilbreth, Lillian Moller (1878–1972)
See GILBRETH, FRANK BUNKER.

gilt-edged bond
A high-grade bond issued by a company that has demonstrated its ability to earn profits over a period of years and pay its bondholders their interest without interruption.

Ginnie Mae
A colloquial expression for GNMA. See GOVERNMENT NATIONAL MORTGAGE ASSOCIATION.

give-up
The splitting of a stockbroker's commission with participating brokers following a large trade; now forbidden by the stock exchanges.

giving-effect statement
See PROJECTED FINANCIAL STATEMENT.

glass insurance
Property insurance coverage including plate glass windows, glass signs, motion picture screens, glass bricks, glass doors, showcases, countertops, and insulated glass panels. The comprehensive policy is generally used to provide all-risk coverage, excluding damage due to

fire, war, and nuclear destruction. It is assumed the firm's fire insurance contract will cover damages and losses due to fire.

glued load
In this type of goods handling, an adhesive with a high shear strength but a low tensile strength (to prevent dislodging through a laterally oriented force yet permitting relatively easy separation in the vertical direction) is applied in two narrow strips near the edge of each box of goods. The boxes are then handled as a unit during shipping or warehousing. As many as 20 boxes are connected together in this manner to facilitate handling operations.

GmbH
See GESELLSCHAFT MIT BESCHRÄNKTER HAFTUNG.

GMT
See GREENWICH MEAN TIME.

GND
See GROSS NATIONAL DISPRODUCT and GROSS NATIONAL DEBT.

GNE
See GROSS NATIONAL EXPENDITURE.

GNMA
See GOVERNMENT NATIONAL MORTGAGE ASSOCIATION.

GNP
See GROSS NATIONAL PRODUCT.

going-concern assumption
See CONTINUITY CONCEPT.

going value
An owner's equity in a business enterprise, as established by accounting records and reports; equivalent to net worth.

gold certificate
In the United States, a form of paper money in circulation from 1865 to 1933. The certificate represented gold bullion that fully secured the certificate. From 1933 to 1955, gold certificates were issued, in a revised form, only to Federal Reserve Banks for reserve purposes. Since 1955, the reserves have been indicated only by bookkeeping entries in a record known as the Interdistrict Settlement Fund.

gold standard
See BIMETALLIC STANDARD.

Gompers, Samuel (1850–1924)
Born in London, moved to the United States at age 13. One year later he became the first member of the Cigar-Makers' International Union, which became one of the most successful of trade unions. Elected as the first president of the American Federation of Labor and considered the most important among those who influenced the shaping of that organization, from 1886 until his death in 1924, Gompers missed only one year (1895) as president. He insisted that unions rely on bargaining with employers and avoid ties with government officials and political parties.

gondola car
A freight car with low sides and low ends. Usually it has no top but some cars are equipped with removable covers.

go no-go gage or go not-go gage
In manufacturing, a type of limit gage utilized to measure the dimensions of a mechanical part to determine whether or not the part is within allowable limits. Not necessarily intended for use in determining the exact variance or departure from the mean dimensional tolerance, it is used to sort defective and nondefective parts with respect to tolerances or limits.

good
In economics, a single element of wealth; a commodity; an item of merchandise, raw material, or finished goods.

good-faith bargaining
Criteria for good-faith bargaining in labor-management disputes are described in the Wagner Act and the Taft-Hartley Act. They require that all parties in a collective bargaining situation genuinely try to achieve agreement and develop a system of communication that will prevent disputes or solve them where they already exist. The National Labor Relations Board is responsible for interpreting individual situations to ensure that bargaining is being conducted in *good faith*.

goods in process
See WORK IN PROCESS.

good-till-canceled (GTC) order
See OPEN ORDER.

good title
A title to land or property that is free from encumbrance, such as mortgages and liens, as disclosed by a complete abstract of the title taken from the records in the recorder's office.

goodwill
One of the intangible values of a business beyond its net worth. Goodwill may include such assets as general reputation, brand name recognition, technical know-how, location, and the historic ability of the company to retain its accounts on the basis, for example, of services. The value of goodwill in establishing the marketable worth of a company is difficult to establish and depends on subjective judgment and negotiation, but it can have a considerable effect on the gross value of the company in a merger or sale-of-assets situation.

goon squad
A strong-arm gang used either by a trade union or by management during contract negotiations or a strike to influence the outcome through physical force.

Gopertz curve
A curve that graphically displays the actual or potential sales of a new product against a time base. Typically it shows three key stages in the life cycle: (1) growth, (2) plateau, and (3) decay or decline. See PRODUCT LIFE CYCLE.

Gossen, Herman Heinrich (1810–1858)
A German public official noted for his mathematical statement of economic theories, *Die Entwickelung der Gesetze des Menschlichen Verkehrs* (1854). Disgusted because no one would buy his book, he destroyed the entire edition save one copy, which reached England, where it was finally brought to public attention.

Gosset, William S. (1876–1937)
An Irish statistician employed by a brewery that did not allow its employees to publish their research, Gosset used the pen name *Student*. His research on t-distribution was published in 1908 and is often referred to as *Student's t-distribution*. See t-DISTRIBUTION.

gourde
The basic unit of currency in Haiti.

government bond
A financial obligation of a government. In the United States, U.S. government bonds are regarded as the highest-grade issues in existence.

Government-Industry Data Exchange Program (GIDEP)
A data bank for parts buyers that contains test information on 80 broad categories of parts, components, materials, and supplies such as adhesives, alarms, aluminum, batteries, printed circuit boards, cleaning fluids, audio devices, and so on. The information includes test reports, data on demonstrated failure and replacement rates, and other similar facts. Procedures for the recalibration of test equipment are also provided. There is no charge for the information, but to obtain it a company must agree to contribute regularly to the program on performance information related to the parts it purchases and uses.

government monopoly
A monopoly both owned and operated by a federal or local government. Examples include the central banks of most countries and water and waste disposal systems.

Government National Mortgage Association (GNMA)
Popularly referred to as "Ginnie Mae," an office of the Department of Housing and Urban Development (HUD). Under the direct leadership of a president, the association carries out the following HUD programs: the giving of special assistance in financing eligible types of federally underwritten mortgages; the mortgage-backed security program; the management and liquidation of the portfolio of mortgages held by GNMA; the management of the government mortgage liquidation trust, federal assets liquidation trust, and federal assets financing trust; and the guarantee of timely payments of principal and interest on such trust certificates or other securities backed by trusts or pools composed of mortgages insured by HUD or guaranteed by the Veterans Administration.

Government Printing Office (GPO)
Part of the legislative branch of the federal government and headed by the public printer, who is appointed by the president. The GPO's purpose is to print and bind publications for the Congress and other federal government departments and agencies. It sells 24,000 books and pamphlets through the superintendent of documents, operates 24 bookstores throughout the country, and supplies 1,183 depository libraries with copies of federal government publications for public use.

gozinto chart
From the words "goes into." Used as a vernacular for *assembly chart*, which details the step-by-step procedure for defining what goes into the manufacturing of a product or a component of the product and in which order the elements are assembled. See ASSEMBLY CHART.

GPO
See GOVERNMENT PRINTING OFFICE.

Gracchus, Gaius
An idealistic leader of the Roman proletariat during the second century B.C. The name *Gracchus* was often adopted by the economist François Émile Babeuf, an active socialist and economic theorist who died on the guillotine in France. See BABEUF, FRANÇOIS ÉMILE.

graduated lease
A lease of property that provides for a variable rental rate, often based on future determination such as a periodic appraisal. A feature primarily of long-term leases.

graduated life table
In insurance calculations, the tabular counterpart of a mortality curve or of a survivor-life curve.

grant
A transfer of real or personal property or goods by deed or writing. Also, the instrument by which such a transfer is made. Also, the property so transferred.

grant, bargain, and sell
In real estate, a phrase sometimes used in a deed to pass title, meaning the grantor promises that he or she has good title to transfer, free from encumbrances, and warrants it to be such.

grant deed
In real estate, the instrument used most often in California to transfer the title to property. The deed carries implied warranties.

grantee
One who acquires the title to property or goods by deed.

grantor
One who conveys the title to property or goods by deed.

grant-in-aid
See SUBSIDY and SUBVENTION.

graph of the number
See NUMBER LINE.

graveyard shift
In an enterprise operating three 8-hour shifts, the shift that extends from 12 midnight to 8 A.M.

gray market
A market in which scarce commodities are purchased and sold using business methods that are generally disapproved of even though they are not strictly illegal. See BLACK MARKET.

Great Leap Forward
An ambitious economic plan undertaken by The People's Republic of China during the years 1958–1960 to significantly accelerate its rate of economic growth. The plan was unrealistic and forced the country into a major economic crisis.

greenback
A form of paper money issued by the U.S. Treasury in 1862. Eventually the total issue was $450 million. Some greenbacks were retired under the Resumption Act of 1875, but more than $346 million were left in circulation, and subsequent legislation provided for a constant reissue of the currency. In 1900, under the Gold Standard Act, a gold reserve of approximately $150 million was established to ensure the redeemability of the greenbacks. It is estimated that about $300 million worth of greenbacks are still in circulation.

green revolution
A term descriptive of the development of high-yielding varieties of seed grains, which has had a dramatic impact on the agricultural output of developing nations.

Greenwich civil time (GCT)
See GREENWICH MEAN TIME.

Greenwich mean time
Mean solar time, based on the longitude of 0° at Greenwich, England, which is at the center of a standard time zone with a width of 15° longitude. Each successive zone of 15° longitude to the east or west

represents one hour of time difference. Also known as *Greenwich time* and *Greenwich civil time*.

Greenwich standard time (GST)
Local time at Greenwich, in southeast England, on the zero meridian. It is often used as a world-time reference for international air travel and simultaneous meteorological reports. See GREENWICH MEAN TIME.

Greenwich time (GT)
See GREENWICH MEAN TIME.

Gresham's law
The principle that cheap money tends to drive dear money out of circulation. Thus, if two kinds of metal circulate with equal legal-tender powers (as happened in the United States with gold and silver under the bimetallic standard during the nineteenth century), the cheaper metal will become the chief circulating medium while the dearer metal will be hoarded, melted down, or exported, thereby disappearing from circulation. The *law* is named after Sir Thomas Gresham, Master of the Mint under Queen Elizabeth I in the sixteenth century. See MINT RATIO and BIMETALLIC STANDARD.

gross
In accounting procedures, an amount or quantity that is not yet reduced by related deductions or expenses. As an adjective, the term may be applied to income, sales, expenses, and similar items of accounting. See NET.

In retail marketing, a *gross* is 12 dozen of an item of merchandise.

gross domestic product (GDP)
Calculated by subtracting payments of wages, interest, rent, profits, and other items paid abroad as income from gross national product (GNP). Nations in which foreigners have a heavy investment or whose citizens have extensive holdings abroad usually find the GDP concept a more revealing gauge of economic activity than the GNP.

gross earnings
See GROSS INCOME.

gross income
The total of revenues before deductions are taken for any items of expense. Also known as *gross revenue, gross earnings,* and *gross sales* when the reference is to the total of goods or services sold.

gross loss
The excess of the cost of goods or services sold over the amount of sales; opposite of GROSS PROFIT. Also known as *loss*.

gross margin
The excess of sales revenues over the direct costs of the products sold. Also known as *price margin*. Also, see GROSS PROFIT.

gross merchandise margin
In retail accounting, net sales less the cost of merchandise.

gross national debt (GND)
The total national debt outstanding. It includes that part of the debt held by government units in trust, in investment, or in sinking funds.

gross national disproduct (GND)
The sum of all the social costs or reductions in benefits to society that result from producing the gross national product. For example, pollution of air and water is part of the gross national disproduct, to the extent that it is caused by production of the GROSS NATIONAL PRODUCT.

gross national expenditure (GNE)
The total amount spent by the four sectors of the economy—household, government, private business, and international—on the nation's output of goods and services. It is equal, by definition, to the GROSS NATIONAL PRODUCT.

gross national product (GNP)
The value in current prices of all final goods and services produced by the economic system over a time period, usually one calendar year. It is the best known and most widely used single measure of the performance of a nation's economy. It includes personal consumption expenditures for goods and services, gross private domestic investment, government purchases of goods and services, and the net export of goods and services. Depreciation is not considered in calculating the GNP. See NET NATIONAL PRODUCT.

gross negligence
See NEGLIGENCE and DUE CARE.

gross operating spread
In retail accounting, gross merchandise margin minus the cost of merchandise procurement.

gross profit
Net sales less the cost of goods sold before considering selling and general expenses, incidental income, and income deductions. In an enterprise engaged in manufacturing, gross profit is the excess of net sales over direct costs and factory overhead, and is to be distinguished from marginal income, which is the excess of net sales over direct costs only.

gross-profit ratio
A ratio by which performance of a product or of its management may be measured; it is computed by the formula: gross profit divided by net sales.

gross requirements
In production procedures, the total requirements for a part or assembly; quantity on hand is not considered.

gross revenue
See GROSS INCOME and GROSS SALES.

gross sales
The total amount of sales revenue, before deductions are taken for returns and allowances but after deducting trade discounts, sales taxes, excise taxes based on sales, and cash discounts. Also known as *gross revenue*.

gross ton
2,240 pounds. Same as LONG TON.

gross tonnage
Generally applies to vessels, not to cargo. It is determined by dividing 100 into the contents, in cubic feet, of the vessel's closed-in spaces. A vessel ton is 100 cubic feet.

gross weight
The combined weight of goods and their container. Also, the total weight of a freight vehicle and its cargo.

ground rent
See CAPITAL RENT.

group account
A British accounting term for a consolidated statement.

group dynamics
The study of the behavior of groups and of the interacting behavior of individuals as members of the group.

group insurance
Offered to employers to cover groups of workers. To get maximum insurance protection for their employees at minimum cost, employers usually buy term insurance in a group plan. The employer is generally considered to be the agent of the employee in making payments; therefore, if the employer fails to pay the group premiums, the insurance will lapse and the insurer is not held liable to the employees or the beneficiaries. Employment by the firm is usually the only requirement for eligibility in the group plan. On leaving the group, an employee loses his or her eligibility to participate in the plan.

group structure
The differentiated system of positions and roles of a group. The structure of most groups is hierarchical; the positions within the group are ordered in status and power from high to low.

growth stock
Stock of a company with prospects for future growth. Also, a company whose earnings are expected to increase at a relatively rapid rate, with anticipation that the market value of the stock will also increase.

GSA
See GENERAL SERVICES ADMINISTRATION.

GST
See GREENWICH STANDARD TIME.

GT
Initials for *Greenwich time*. See GREENWICH MEAN TIME.

GTC order
Initials stand for *good till canceled*. See OPEN ORDER.

guarani
The basic unit of currency in Paraguay.

guarantee
One to whom a guaranty is given. A promise by one person to make good for the failure of another who is liable for a debt or the perfor-

mance of a contract or duty. The obligation involved in a guaranty. Also, an alternative spelling for GUARANTY.

guaranteed bond

A bond whose interest, principal, or both are guaranteed by a company other than the issuer. Usually found in the railroad industry when a large company, leasing a section of trackage owned by a small company, may guarantee the bonds of the smaller company. See GUARANTEED STOCK.

guaranteed stock

Usually preferred stock on which dividends are guaranteed by another company, under much the same circumstances as a bond is guaranteed. See GUARANTEED BOND.

guaranteed-wage plan

That part of a labor contract in which employees are guaranteed either employment or a stated amount of wages during a specific time period.

guarantor

A person who promises to make good if another fails to fulfill an obligation that has been specified in the guaranty.

guaranty

See GUARANTEE and WARRANTY.

guardian

A person appointed by the court to supervise the property rights of a minor, an insane person, or a person legally defined as incapacitated or incompetent.

guardian ad litem

A special guardian appointed by the court for the sole purpose of carrying on litigation for and preserving the interests of a ward. He or she exercises no control or power over property.

guide meridians

Survey lines running north and south. Used in government surveys.

guild

Historically, an association of tradesmen or artisans that controlled the production or output of a particular commodity or service and regulated the admission of members. Currently, a labor union or a professional association.

guilder
See FLORIN.

gulden
See FLORIN.

habeas corpus
Latin, "You should have the body." A writ issued to a sheriff, warden, or official who has custody of a person. It directs that the person, alleged to be unlawfully held, is to be brought before a court in order to determine the legality of the imprisonment.

haggling
Colloquial expression for the process of bargaining or negotiating the price of a sale or purchase. The buyer attempts to buy at as low a price as possible, while the seller attempts to sell at as high a price as possible. If the sale and purchase are eventually consummated, a market price is established for the specific good or service. Also called *higgling*.

halo effect
A tendency toward distortion in an appraisal or performance rating of an individual caused by the reaction of the person doing the appraisal or conducting the interview. A high rating on one factor tends to result in a high rating on all other factors. In effect, a *halo* surrounds the person being appraised. The halo effect may also act negatively; a

characteristic that displeases or disturbs the appraiser may result in a poor rating on other characteristics. The appraiser is not always aware of being affected by the halo, and that he or she may be reacting entirely subjectively, to the good or bad fortune of the interviewee.

hang-up
In data processing, a nonprogramed stop in a routine. It is usually an unforeseen or unwanted halt in a machine pass. It is most often caused by improper coding of a machine instruction or by the attempted use of a nonexistent or improper operation code.

harbor line
On navigable rivers, a line specified by authorities beyond which wharves and other structures may not be built.

hard-core unemployed
People who are unemployed because they lack the education or skills required by a complex economy. Discrimination may be a contributing factor. The ranks of the hard-core unemployed consist mainly of members of certain minority groups such as blacks and Mexicans, persons who are "too young" or "too old," high-school dropouts, and those who are permanently displaced because of technological change.

hardware
In data processing, the physical equipment or devices that constitute a computer and its peripherals.

harmonic mean
See MEAN.

Harris, F. W.
A mathematician who, in 1915, developed the first mathematical model of an economic lot size for a simple situation in manufacturers' inventory control. Comprehensive mathematical solutions to inventory control problems required the use of so much time that it would have required human lifetimes of calculations to arrive at them manually. It was not until the 1950s that high-speed computers and programs enabled the rapid development of solutions to complex inventory control problems.

hash total
In data processing, a sum of numbers in a specified field of a record or of a batch of records used for checking purposes.

Hawthorne studies
Begun in 1924 at the Chicago Hawthorne Works of the Western Electric Company—with the participation of Harvard University researchers—and designed to determine the effects of lighting on worker productivity. Two groups of workers were selected for comparison and control. The performance of both groups improved with each increase or decrease in lighting. It became evident that the unusual attention being given to their activities, their knowledge of being tested, their social affiliation as a group, and their interest in the results had a greater effect on their performance than did the environmental conditions. This controlled experiment is considered by many to be the beginning of behavioral science as a profession. The Hawthorne studies were concluded in 1932.

hazard
The various factors or the primary factor contributing to uncertainty in a given insurance situation. The risk of loss to any particular person or company may be calculated as the total of all hazards present. A hazard may be anything that may conceivably bring about a loss, whereas the word *peril* is used to denote the factor that actually caused the loss. See PERIL.

head
An electromagnetic component of a data processing device that reads, records, or erases information in a storage medium such as a magnetic tape, a disk, or a drum.

head-end business
The transportation of property such as mail, baggage, and express in the cars immediately behind the locomotive of a passenger train.

Head Start Bureau
See OFFICE OF CHILD DEVELOPMENT.

head tax
A tax that may be levied on immigrant aliens entering at any port of the United States.

Health Insurance Association of America (HIAA)
An association of leading writers of accident, health, and sickness insurance contracts, formed as a self-regulating agency to furnish a high standard for both policy wording and advertising.

Health Resources Administration (HRA)
A unit of the Public Health Service, the HRA identifies, develops, and makes use of the nation's health resources.

Health Services Administration (HSA)
A unit of the Public Health Service, the HSA works to reach underserved populations, to improve quality of health care, to foster effective and efficient health service delivery, and to provide services to certain defined populations.

Health Systems Agencies (HSA)
A federally sponsored group organized on the community level under a 1974 act of Congress. The function of HSAs is planning, primarily for the purpose of advising state health agencies that set standards and allocate resources for hospitals and health facilities. The agencies advise their respective state regulators on how to organize better healthcare delivery, and make recommendations on whether hospitals should be permitted to expand or to purchase expensive new equipment.

hearsay evidence
In legal procedures, evidence that is obtained from someone else. Its value does not derive from the credit or credibility of the witness giving the testimony, but rests on the truthfulness of the person from whom the evidence was first heard. It is not considered good evidence because there is no opportunity to cross-examine the person who is the source of the information.

heater car
An insulated boxcar equipped with heating apparatus for the protection of perishables.

hectare
A metric unit of area equal to 100 ares, 10,000 square meters, or 2.471 acres.

hedge fund
A type of mutual fund whose investment policy is to seek profit through the purchase of relatively high risk investments, often using borrowed capital to increase profit potential.

Hegel, Georg Wilhelm Friedrich (1770–1831)
A German philosopher who studied theology at Tübingen and taught at Jena and Heidelberg. His metaphysical theories were the dominant system of thought throughout Europe during the second quarter of the

nineteenth century. He developed the dialectic method of progression from thesis and antithesis to synthesis, which proved to be crucial in the development of the economic theories of Karl Marx.

HEMA
Initials for *Health Education Media Association.*

Herzberg, Frederick
A behavioral scientist, born 1923. See MOTIVATION-HYGIENE THEORY.

Herzberg theory
See MOTIVATION-HYGIENE THEORY.

heuristic routine
In data processing, a routine in which the computer attacks a problem, not by a direct algorithmic procedure, but by a trial-and-error approach frequently involving the act of learning.

HEW
See DEPARTMENT OF HEALTH, EDUCATION AND WELFARE.

hexadecimal
Of or relating to a computing system that uses the equivalent of the number 16 as a base. Same as *sexadecimal.*

HIAA
See HEALTH INSURANCE ASSOCIATION OF AMERICA.

hidden amenities
Conditions of agreeable living or beneficial influence arising from the location of or improvements to property, which are not noticed at once but which enhance property value; such conditions include superior materials and workmanship.

hidden reserve
The amount of the understatement of net worth that may result from a variety of accounting practices, for example, classifying additions to fixed and other assets as expense. Disclosure of hidden reserves is required for any substantial amounts that may be so classified. Also known as *secret reserve.*

hierarchy of needs
In the psychological system developed by Abraham Maslow, the ascending order of needs that affect the behavior of the individual:

physiological (food, clothing, shelter), safety (security), social (affiliation), esteem (self-esteem and recognition from others), and self-actualization (desire to become what one is capable of becoming). Maslow argues that the behavior of an individual at a particular moment is determined by his or her strongest need. As each need is satisfied, another need increases in strength and determines the individual's behavior. Maslow contends that once the physiological and security needs have been met, other needs in the hierarchy seek satisfaction, but not necessarily in the order stated.

higgling
See HAGGLING.

high-flier or high-flyer
See RATE-BUSTER.

highland
A region that is higher and hillier than the neighboring countryside.

hire purchase
The equivalent of installment buying in the United Kingdom. The buyer pays an initial deposit, takes possession of the goods or receives the benefits of the services, and then makes regular payments that cover the remainder of the purchase price plus interest or carrying charges. The buyer does not take title to the goods until the last periodic payment or installment is paid in full.

histogram
In statistical analysis, a graphic representation of a frequency distribution by means of a vertical bar graph with no space between the bars. The class boundaries are of equal size and are depicted on the horizontal axis, while the frequencies are depicted on the vertical axis. Thus each bar is equal in width to all others; height varies in accordance with the reference data.

historical cost
The cost of a fixed asset at the time of acquisition by the present owner.

Hobbs Act
Its main provision is that anyone who "obstructs, delays, or affects commerce or the movement of any article or commodity in commerce, by robbery or extortion" is guilty of a felony. Also known as the *Anti-Racketeering Law, 1934.*

Hobson, John A. (1858–1940)

A British economist and reformer. In his *Work and Wealth* (1914) he argued that accepted theory and practice laid too much emphasis on the mere quantity of production without sufficient consideration for the welfare of the consumer.

Hoffman-Neill rule

A method for appraising property, no longer in use.

hold-back pay

Wages withheld by an employer for the purpose of calculating payroll periods. For example, employees may be paid on Friday for all work up to the previous Tuesday of a given weekly period, the difference between the wages earned between Tuesday and Friday being "held back" but owed to the employee.

hold-harmless agreement

A contract whose terms assure one party to the contract that the liability described in the contract will be assumed by another party in the event of loss or legal action.

holding company

A company that owns the securities of one or more other companies, in most cases with voting control. Also known as *controlling company*. See PARENT COMPANY.

hold order

In manufacturing, a written order directing that certain operations or work activities be interrupted or canceled, pending a change in design or material.

hold point

A stock storage point for semifinished inventory.

hold track

A railroad track where cars are placed while awaiting disposition orders from shippers or receivers.

Hollerith code

In data processing, a widely used system of encoding alphanumeric information onto cards that are punched. Such cards were first used in 1890 for the U.S. census and were named after Herman Hollerith, their originator. They are often popularly, but incorrectly, called *IBM cards*.

Homans, George C.
A behavioral scientist, born 1910. See HUMAN GROUP.

home car
A freight car on the tracks of the railroad company that owns it. As distinguished from FOREIGN CAR.

Hopf, Harry Arthur (1882–1949)
A pioneer and advocate of scientific management and long-range corporate planning.

hopper car
A railroad car designed to carry bulk dry cargo that unloads, usually by gravity, through openings in the underside of the car. May or may not have a top.

horizontal merger
A merger involving firms that produce closely related products and sell them in the same market. The usual objective is to round out a product line that is sold through the same distribution channels, thereby offering joint economies in sales and distribution.

hospital professional liability insurance
Offered to hospitals, infirmaries, clinics, nursing homes, and similar institutions. Similar to DRUGGISTS' LIABILITY INSURANCE.

hostile fire
One of two types of fire distinguished by law for insurance purposes. A hostile fire is one that is out of control. Only loss or damage resulting from a hostile fire is covered by the fire policy. The other type is *friendly fire,* exemplified by a fire in a fireplace that is under control. Should valuable property be thrown into the fireplace and be destroyed it might not be covered by the insurance policy. A friendly fire may spread and become a hostile fire.

hotchpot
In accounting, a combining of the properties of two or more persons to enable an equal redistribution of the properties.

household goods warehouse
A warehouse that specializes in storing household articles and furniture. Such enterprises often operate fleets of moving vans and offer the service of moving the goods of entire households to any point in the

United States. Some such warehouses offer delivery service to virtually any point in the world.

housekeeping
In data processing, the setting up of constants and variables to be used in preparing a computer program.

HRA
See HEALTH RESOURCES ADMINISTRATION.

HSA
See HEALTH SERVICES ADMINISTRATION and HEALTH SYSTEMS AGENCY.

HSP
Initials for *high-speed printer*.

HSR
Initials for *high-speed reader*.

HUD
See DEPARTMENT OF HOUSING AND URBAN DEVELOPMENT.

human group
A model of social systems introduced in 1950 by George C. Homans for use in determining where and how informal work groups gain their power to control the behavior and productivity of their members. The social system of Homans's *human group* contains three elements: (1) activities, the tasks people perform; (2) interactions, the behavior that occurs between people in performing these tasks; and (3) sentiments, the attitudes that develop between individuals and within groups. Homans argues that the elements, although separate, are closely related and are mutually dependent on each other. A change in any of the three will produce a change in the other two.

human relations movement
Originating in the early 1900s, the body of thought of such theorists as Elton Mayo of Harvard University and his contemporaries, who argue that, in addition to finding the best technological methods to improve output, as was done by Frederick Taylor in his writings on scientific management and the division or specialization of labor, it will benefit management to look into human affairs; that the real power within an organization is centered in the interpersonal relationships that develop

within a working unit. The human relations movement stresses a concern for people rather than for the task per se. See HAWTHORNE STUDIES, RABBLE HYPOTHESIS, and MAYO, ELTON.

human skill
In management activities, ability and judgment in working with and through people, including understanding of motivation and application of effective leadership.

hump
In railroad yards, a high track from which uncoupled cars roll by gravity to desired tracks.

hundred percent location
A retail business location considered optimum for attracting business.

hygiene factors
See MOTIVATION-HYGIENE THEORY.

hyperinflation
An economic situation in which prices are rising with little or no increase in output. Also known as *runaway inflation* and *galloping inflation*.

hypothecated asset
See PLEDGED ASSET.

hypothecation
The pledging of securities as collateral for a loan. The security is then said to be hypothecated.

hypothesis
A working guess or an assumption about the behavior of persons or things in the real world. It applies to many areas of business and is used there in analyzing quantitative variables. In economics, the *things* may be the number of consumers, business firms, homeowners, and so on, and the *variables* may include prices, wages, consumption, production, and other factors and economic quantities essential to a statistical analysis.

IAA
See INTERNATIONAL ADVERTISING ASSOCIATION, INC.

IAEA
See INTERNATIONAL ATOMIC ENERGY AGENCY.

IAL
See INTERNATIONAL ALGEBRAIC LANGUAGE. Also, see ALGOL.

IAMAW
See INTERNATIONAL ASSOCIATION OF MACHINISTS AND AEROSPACE WORKERS.

IANEC
See INTER-AMERICAN NUCLEAR ENERGY COMMISSION.

IAS
See INTERNATIONAL ACCOUNTANTS' SOCIETY, INC.

IASC
See INTERNATIONAL ACCOUNTING STANDARDS COMMITTEE.

IATA
See INTERNATIONAL AIR TRANSPORT ASSOCIATION.

IBM card
See HOLLERITH CODE.

IBRD
Initials for *International Bank for Reconstruction and Development.*
See WORLD BANK.

IC
See INTEGRATED CIRCUIT.

ICAO
See INTERNATIONAL CIVIL AVIATION ORGANIZATION.

ICC
See INTERNATIONAL CHAMBER OF COMMERCE and INTERSTATE
COMMERCE COMMISSION.

ICCAP
Initials for *International Coordination Committee of the Accounting
Profession.* See INTERNATIONAL ACCOUNTING STANDARDS COMMIT-
TEE.

ICFTU
Initials for *International Confederation of Free Trade Unions.* See
WORLD FEDERATION OF TRADE UNIONS.

IDA
See INTERNATIONAL DEVELOPMENT ASSOCIATION.

IDB
See INTER-AMERICAN DEVELOPMENT BANK.

IDDD
Initials for *international direct distance dialing.*

ideal assumptions
In statistics, many possible sets of assumptions could be formulated
about the distribution of the variables in the population regression
model. One particular group of assumptions has become known as the
ideal assumptions, in that they yield relatively simple estimators that
possess many desirable properties, and they result in test statistics that
possess commonly known distributions.

idem sonans
Latin for "the same sound." A doctrine holding that absolute accuracy
in the spelling of names in legal documents is not required. A mis-
spelled name, although technically different from its actual spelling,

does not diminish the legal effectiveness of the documents. This holds when the pronunciation of the name sounds the same for various spellings; examples are Smythe and Smith, Johnes and Jones, Parkes and Parks.

identity equation
An equation stating an equality that is true by definition. For example, the total output of an economy (its gross national product or GNP) is equal to the sum of consumption, investment, and government expenditures in a closed economic system; that is, $GNP = C + I + G$.

idle capacity
In manufacturing, unused productive potential, in reference to machinery, operations, or a factory's facilities that are not in use or are used only partially. Idle capacity may be expressed in units of output capability that could be realized through full usage, or in hours available for use.

idle-capacity cost
In accounting, the variance that can be attributed to the failure to use facilities at projected rates.

IEEE
Often spoken as "I-triple-E," the initials for *Institute of Electrical and Electronics Engineers*. Formerly the Institute of Radio Engineers (IRE).

IFA
Initials for *Illinois Freight Association*.

IFC
See INTERNATIONAL FINANCE CORPORATION.

IHF
Initials for *Institute of High Fidelity*.

ILA
Initials for *International Longshoremen's Association*.

illegal-purpose doctrine
The use of the criminal-conspiracy doctrine was discouraged by a Massachusetts labor case in 1842. The court ruled that the legality of a concerted action on the part of employees depended on the purpose or

the objective sought, not on the mere fact of withdrawal of labor. See CRIMINAL-CONSPIRACY DOCTRINE.

illuviation
See ALLUVION.

ILO
See INTERNATIONAL LABOR ORGANIZATION.

ILWU
Initials for *International Longshoremen's & Warehousemen's Union*.

IMA
See INTERNATIONAL MANAGEMENT ASSOCIATION, INC.

IMC
See INSTITUTE OF MANAGEMENT CONSULTANTS.

IMF
See INTERNATIONAL MONETARY FUND.

IMI
See INLAND MARINE INSURANCE.

IMIB
See INLAND MARINE ISURANCE BUREAU.

immaturity-maturity theory
Chris Argyris, while at Yale University, examined industrial organizations to determine what effect management practices have had on individual behavior and personal growth within the work environment. He concluded that seven changes should take place in the personality of an individual if he or she is to develop into a mature person. These changes range from the immature state of passiveness as a child to the mature state of self-awareness and control over self. Argyris argues that keeping people immature is built into the very nature of formal organizations, since these are created to achieve goals that can best be met collectively. Also, see LIFE-CYLE THEORY.

imperfect competition
A classification of market structures that falls between the two extremes of PERFECT COMPETITION and MONOPOLY. It consists of MONOPOLISTIC COMPETITION and OLIGOPOLY.

imperfect oligopoly
See OLIGOPOLY.

implicit costs
The costs of self-owned or self-employed resources that are not entered in a company's account books. Rental receipts and wages that a self-employed proprietor forgoes by owning and operating his or her own business are examples.

implied contract
A contract that is inferred from actions of the parties who fulfill promises without the existence of an expressed contract.

implied easement
In real estate, an easement that is not recorded but is apparent through continued use.

implied warranty
Ocean marine insurance policies contain three implied warranties: (1) seaworthiness of the vessel, (2) no deviation from the prescribed course, and (3) the legality of the enterprise.

In business transactions, an implied warranty is a guarantee assumed by law to exist although it is not specifically stated in a document.

impound
In government accounting, to reduce authority to incur obligations by withholding all or any portion of a Congressional appropriation. Also, any action by the Office of Management and Budget that has the effect of modifying the character of an agency's operations is an impounding action.

In law, to seize and possess property, cash, or other assets in protective custody by means of a legal process, such as a court order.

In real estate transactions, an impound is a trust account established by lenders with respect to mortgages, for the accumulation of funds to meet taxes, FHA mortgage insurance premiums, and future insurance policy premiums required to protect their security. Impounds are usually collected with note payments.

impoverished style
A style of managerial leadership that exerts a minimum effort to get the required work done with the minimum of control considered to be appropriate to sustain organization membership. See MANAGERIAL GRID.

imputed cost
In accounting, a cost that is indirectly estimated and that is attributed rather than directly measured.

IMUA
Initials for *Inland Marine Underwriters Association*. See INLAND MARINE INSURANCE BUREAU.

inactive post
A trading post on the floor of the New York Stock Exchange where inactive securities are traded in units of ten shares instead of the usual 100-share lots. Known among professionals as *post 30*.

inactive stock
An issue traded in relatively low volumes on an exchange or in the over-the-counter (OTC) market. Volumes may be no more than a few hundred shares a week and are sometimes even less. On the New York Stock Exchange many inactive stocks are traded in 10-share units rather than the customary 100. See ROUND LOT.

inadmitted asset
See UNADMITTED ASSET.

inalienable
In legal proceedings, unassignable, not capable of transfer or sale. For example, the right to sue for a tort is inalienable; contracts for personal services are inalienable choses in action.

in-and-out trade
A security market expression for the purchase and sale of the same security within a short time period, a day, a week, or a month. An in-and-out trader is generally more interested in day-to-day price fluctuations than in dividends or long-term growth.

Inchmaree clause
May be made part of hull insurance to protect the shipowner against damage to the machinery of the vessel caused by breakdowns or accidents in loading, discharging or handling cargo, bunkering, and entering dry docks. Protection is also afforded against contact with any land or conveyance as well as against negligence of the master, charterer, mariners, engineers, or pilots. Coverage assumes that due diligence will be exercised by the insured owners or managers. The master, engineers, pilots, or crew are not considered part owners. Formulated

as a result of the sinking of the *Inchmaree* in Liverpool harbor in March 1884.

inchoate
In law, incomplete, not yet perfect, situations out of which rights and duties may later arise. For example, a wife's dower is inchoate until the death of her husband.

income bond
Generally, an income bond promises to repay principal as stipulated but to pay interest only when earned. In some cases unpaid interest on an income bond may accumulate as a claim against the corporation when the bond becomes due. An income bond may also be issued in lieu of preferred stock.

income-consumption curve
In indifference-curve analysis, a line showing the amounts of two commodities that will be purchased by a consumer whose income changes while the prices of the commodities remain the same. Geometrically, it is a line connecting the tangency points of price lines and indifference curves as income changes while prices remain constant. See INDIFFERENCE CURVE.

income elasticity of demand
In economics, this measures the percentage change in quantity demanded as a result of a given percentage change in income. If consumption increases proportionately with income, the income elasticity is one. If consumption increases more than proportionately, income elasticity is greater than one, and we call the consumed item a *luxury*. If the income elasticity is less than one, the item is a *necessity*.

income fund
A type of investment company whose main investment goal is to obtain liberal current income for shareholders of the fund.

income statement
See EARNINGS REPORT.

income velocity of money
The average number of times per year that a dollar is spent on purchasing the national economy's annual flow of goods and services, the GNP. It equals the ratio of GNP to the quantity of money. See EQUATION OF EXCHANGE.

incontestable clause
A clause in an insurance policy stating that after a certain period of time the policy may not be contested except for the nonpayment of premiums.

inconvertible paper standard
A monetary system by which a nation's unit of currency cannot be converted into any metal or other precious substance in terms of which it may or may not be defined. Historically, this standard has existed on a domestic basis in all countries since the worldwide abandonment of the gold standard in the 1930s.

incorporated pocketbook
See PERSONAL HOLDING COMPANY.

increasing returns
A phase in a production process, where when the variable input increases, output expands more than proportionately to the increase in the input.

in-cycle work
Work performed by an operator while a machine is in its operational cycle. See OUT-CYCLE WORK.

indemnity
The legal protection or security whereby a person or an organization is obligated to make good a loss or damage another has suffered. The compensation for that loss or damage. Also, legal exemption incurred by one's actions.

indemnity, principle of
The purpose of insurance is not to allow the insured to make a profit, but to indemnify the party or the firm for a loss that has been suffered. To avoid a moral hazard, insurance companies sometimes contract to pay less than the full amount of the loss. In calculating market or replacement value of the loss, this takes into account downward fluctuation, in the case of property, and the fact that many insurance compensations are tax-exempt.

indented bill of material
In manufacturing, a bill of material that has the highest-level assemblies positioned on the left-hand margin of the reporting document and subsequent lower levels indented sequentially to the right. Also referred to as an *indenture*.

indenture

In financial transactions, a written agreement under which debentures are issued, setting forth maturity date, interest rate, and other terms.

In real estate proceedings, a deed executed by both parties to the transfer of title to land or property. Also, see INDENTED BILL OF MATERIAL.

independent contractor

A person or firm whose time and efforts in fulfillment of a contract are not regulated by others. See GENERAL CONTRACTOR.

independent demand

The requirements for goods and materials that are directly related to customer demand and must therefore be forecast. The demand made on finished-goods inventories is usually an independent variable, while the demand for components and subassemblies of the finished goods is dependent and may be calculated. See DEPENDENT DEMAND.

independent union

A labor union that is not affiliated with any federation of labor organizations. It may be national or international, and not limited to workers in any one firm.

index numbers

A statistical measure used by economists and business managers to gain an overall view of such areas as prices, volumes, and rates of change. Econometricians develop and use index numbers to establish a reference base for depicting growth or decline in a condition of microeconomics. An index number may be a ratio or other number derived from a series of observations and used as an indicator or measure of a condition or a phenomenon. Index numbers are a composite made up of many parts. In economics, they measure an average, or a consensus, of elements whose behavior may differ widely from the group as a whole. In the use of time, a sequence of years for example, a single year is selected as the *base* and is assigned a value of 100. The phenomenon or condition to be observed is then referenced to the base year and increments or decrements in the condition being observed are related to the quantity of 100.

index register

In data processing, a register containing a quantity that may be used to modify addresses. Also referred to as *B box*.

indictment
A grand jury's determination that there is sufficient reason to believe the accused is guilty as charged, and the delivery of this information to the accused so that he or she may prepare a defense.

indifference curve
In economics, a graph of an indifference schedule. Every point along the curve represents a different combination of two commodities, each combination being equally satisfactory to a recipient because each yields the same total utility. See INDIFFERENCE SCHEDULE and PRICE-CONSUMPTION CURVE.

indifference schedule
A table showing the various combinations of two commodities that would be equally satisfactory or yield the same total utility to a recipient at a given time.

indirect cost
In accounting, a cost or expense attributable not directly to the processing or manufacturing of a specific product or service but indirectly to a more general activity of the enterprise, and a cost or expense that also does not necessarily vary with the quantity or volume of output. Indirect costs generally include a variety of factory operating costs, such as supervision, building depreciation, maintenance, utilities, general administration, and marketing expenses. The British term for indirect cost is *oncost*. See OVERHEAD and DIRECT COST.

indirect expense
See MANUFACTURING EXPENSE.

indirect labor
Factory and office labor time that cannot be classified as direct or cannot be charged to a specific order. Formerly called *nonproductive labor*. See DIRECT LABOR.

indirect material
A material consumed in the operations of a factory or an office that cannot be classified as direct or cannot be charged to a specific order. See DIRECT MATERIAL.

indirect tax
A tax that can be shifted either partially or entirely to someone other than the individual or firm responsible for paying the tax. Examples are sales taxes, excise taxes, and taxes on business or rental properties.

indivisibility of public goods
A characteristic of public goods is that the benefits received by one person are received by all persons. National defense and police and fire protection are examples.

induction
The process of reasoning from particular observations or cases to general laws or principles. Most human knowledge is inductive or empirical since it is based on the experience of our senses. See DEDUCTION.

industrial broker
A natural or legal person who acts for another in a transaction and who specializes in industrial real estate.

industrial goods
Various kinds of materials used or consumed by a business, and those that are used in the production of other goods.

industrial life insurance
Designed for individuals who are financially unable to buy ordinary life insurance. The face amount of the policy issued may be for amounts less than $1,000. As with ordinary insurance, industrial life insurance may be whole life, limited-payment life, or endowment. See GROUP INSURANCE.

industrial park
A real estate area zoned and used for industrial purposes.

industrial property
Property zoned or used for industrial purposes.

industrial relations
Rules and regulations governing the relations between a labor union and management. They often deal with such matters as contract negotiation, the type of recognition accorded the union, the financial arrangement for collecting membership dues from employees, the methods of controlling the quantity and kind of union membership through apprenticeship requirements, licensing provisions, initiation fees, seniority rules, and the handling of grievances.

industrial union
A labor union that admits to membership people who work within an industry, irrespective of their occupation or craft. See CRAFT UNION and TRADE UNION.

Industrial Union Department
A group of 58 AFL–CIO unions with a combined membership of approximately 6 million workers. It aids member unions in organizing, bargaining, and similar activities.

industrywide bargaining
See MULTIUNIT BARGAINING.

inelastic demand
See ELASTICITY OF DEMAND.

inferior good
A commodity whose purchase and consumption decrease relative to other commodities as the incomes of consumers rise. Examples of inferior goods are potatoes, used clothing, and other commodities sometimes referred to as *poor man's goods*.

inflation
Any increase in the general price level that is sustained and non-seasonal in character. The effect is to decrease the consumers' purchasing power.

inflationary gap
The amount by which actual private spending and government expenses exceed the theoretical amount of spending necessary to maintain full employment or to exceed the theoretical amount of spending that is adequate to absorb all available goods and services without appreciably raising the price level. See DEFLATIONARY GAP.

informal organization
The patterns of interpersonal and intergroup relations that develop within the formal organization of an enterprise. The informal organization includes cliques and friendship groups. An informal organization may develop when the formal organization proves to be inefficient or when it fails to satisfy important needs of the members.

information theory
In data processing, the mathematical theory that deals with information rate, channels, channel width, noise, and other factors affecting information transmission. Originally developed for electrical communications, it is applied to business systems and other techniques that handle information units and the flow of information in networks.

inherent vice
In insurance, this refers to a characteristic of an article that makes it tend to destroy itself. An improperly constructed machine or a precious stone with imperfections that could cause it to break apart under normal handling is said to have an inherent vice; it would therefore not be covered by insurance. See INLAND MARINE INSURANCE.

injunction
A writ of judicial process issued by a court of equity according to which a person or organization is required to do or refrain from doing a particular thing.

inland marine insurance (IMI)
Often representing a combination of different kinds of insurance, it is intended to provide coverage for goods in process of being transported on other than ocean-going vessels, or in process of being transported to or from an ocean-going vessel. It developed out of the need for broader coverage than was historically provided by *ocean marine insurance* contracts and is therefore referred to as *marine insurance* with the modifier *inland*. See OCEAN MARINE INSURANCE.

Inland Marine Insurance Bureau (IMIB)
Formed in 1931 by a large number of stock companies under the name of the *Inland Marine Underwriters Association*. The bureau prepares standard policies and forms for its members, collects statistics, and establishes rates in those lines where it is practical to do so.

Inland Marine Underwriters Association (IMUA)
See INLAND MARINE INSURANCE BUREAU.

innovation theory
Put forth by Joseph Alois Schumpeter, this theory attributes business cycles and economic development to innovations that forward-looking entrepreneurs adopt in order to reduce costs and increase profits. Once an innovation proves to be successful, other entrepreneurs follow with the same or similar techniques and methods, and these innovations cause fluctuations in investment that in turn cause business cycles. The innovation theory has also been used as a partial explanation of how profits arise in a competitive capitalistic system. See SCHUMPETER, JOSEPH ALOIS.

in personam
A legal proceeding whose judgment binds the defeated party to a personal liability.

in-process inventory
See WORK IN PROCESS and PIPELINE INVENTORY.

input device
The mechanical unit designed to bring ·data to be processed into a computer, for example, a card reader, tape reader, or keyboard.

input-output analysis
In economics, a tabular display of data that serves the major purpose of emphasizing the intricate relationships among the various sectors or industries of the economy and how each affects the others. Wassily W. Leontief is largely responsible for input-output analysis, which he presented in a simplified version in his article "Input-Output Economics" (*Scientific American,* October 1951).

inquiry station
A computer terminal, usually with a keyboard, where inquiries may be entered directly into a computer. The inquiry terminal is usually geographically separated from the computer, at a remote location or at the computer console.

in rem
A legal proceeding whose judgment binds, affects, or determines the status of property.

insolvent
In law, an insolvent debtor is one whose property and other assets are insufficient to pay all his or her debts.

inspection ticket
In manufacturing, a sheet, card, or other document used to report that an inspection function has been performed.

installment sale contract
See CONDITIONAL SALE CONTRACT.

in statu quo
The conditions that exist at the start of a legal action, or, in the case of a rescission of a contract, the position of the parties immediately prior to the creation of the contract.

Institute of Management Consultants (IMC)
An accrediting agency for individual consultants, founded in 1970.

Institute of Radio Engineers
See IEEE.

instruction
In data processing, a set of characters, together with one or more addresses or without an address, that defines an operation and, as a unit, causes the computer to perform the operation on the indicated quantities. *Instruction* is preferable to *command* or *order*. *Command* is reserved for a specific portion of the instruction word; *order* is reserved for the sequential arrangement of the characters.

insurable interest
An interest of such a nature that the insured party would be financially injured by the occurrence of the event insured against. An insurable interest is required in all lines of insurance before a contract is legally valid.

insurable value
Generally, a calculation for the face value of an insurance contract based on the current replacement cost of the insured item if materials of like kind and quality are used, less a reasonable deduction for depreciation.

insurance broker
A person engaged in obtaining insurance for those who apply to him or her for this service. It is usual for individual brokers to represent several insurance companies so that they are in a position to obtain the best insurance to suit the needs of their clients.

insurance underwriter
A member of a syndicate or an individual firm concerned with assessing and arranging insurance coverage.

insured deposit
A deposit in a bank or other financial institution that is insured by the Federal Deposit Insurance Corporation or any other federal- or state-sponsored insuring agency. If the institution fails, deposits are insured against loss up to specified maximum limits per account. See FEDERAL DEPOSIT INSURANCE CORPORATION.

insuring clause
In an insurance policy, a description of the risk assumed by the insurer.

intangible asset
In accounting procedures, any asset having no physical existence; examples are goodwill, patents, trademarks, formulas, licenses, franchises, and research-and-development costs. Some tax authorities define intangible assets as any asset other than cash or real estate.

intangible choses
See ASSIGNMENT.

integer
Any digit or group of digits expressing a whole number, as contrasted with a number containing a fraction.

integrated circuit (IC)
A self-contained module of electronic components that is manufactured as a single and solid unit. Integrated circuits have replaced discrete components such as transistors, diodes, capacitors, and resistors and have thus eliminated the need to assemble and interwire them in numerous electronics applications. The integrated circuit is directly and indirectly responsible for the rapidly decreasing physical size of computers and calculators and for the simultaneous increase in their powers and capabilities.

integrated manager
A term describing the manager who likes to become part of the people, things, and processes he or she manages. Such managers are joiners and take pains to get involved with individuals and groups about their work. They like to communicate in group settings and therefore use frequent meetings. They are oriented to the future, identify with co-workers, and emphasize teamwork. They judge subordinates on their willingness to join the team and judge their superiors on their skill in teamwork. In stressful situations they tend to postpone making decisions and are willing to compromise. The integrated style of such managers and their emphasis on the group may cause their subordinates to suffer loss of feelings of independence. Integrated managers themselves fear loss of involvement and fear that others might become dissatisfied.

integrated pension plan
A pension plan that adjusts the employee's pension benefits downward to reflect the company's contribution to social security.

intelligence quotient
See IQ.

Inter-American Development Bank (IDB)

Formed in 1959, the IDB promotes economic and social development partly through the provision of technical assistance among its member nations: Argentina, Barbados, Bolivia, Brazil, Chile, Colombia, Costa Rica, Dominican Republic, Ecuador, El Salvador, Guatemala, Haiti, Honduras, Jamaica, Mexico, Nicaragua, Panama, Paraguay, Peru, Trinidad and Tobago, United States of America, Uruguay, and Venezuela.

Inter-American Nuclear Energy Commission (IANEC)

Established in 1959 as an agency of the Organization of American States (OAS), it has the same member countries as the OAS. The purpose of IANEC is to develop and promote peaceful uses of nuclear power as a source of energy. See ORGANIZATION OF AMERICAN STATES.

interchange point

A location where one carrier delivers freight in transit to another carrier.

interchange track

A specific railroad track location where one carrier delivers freight in transit to another carrier or to an industrial switch.

intercoastal

Extending or operating between sea coasts, usually referring to points between the Atlantic coast and the Pacific coast.

Interdistrict Settlement Fund

See GOLD CERTIFICATE.

interest

In financial transactions, the price a borrower pays to a lender for the use of the latter's money. It is calculated as a periodic percentage of the principal amount of the loan; however, payments of interest do not alter the principal amount of the loan.

interest, theory of

See LIQUIDITY PREFERENCE.

interest rate risk

In the securities market, the uncertainty of future returns or security prices resulting from changes in market rates of interest. Also, see

SECURITY RISK, FINANCIAL RISK, MARKET RISK, POLITICAL RISK, PUR-
CHASING POWER RISK, and SOCIAL RISK.

interline waybill
In transportation, carriers' waybill used whenever more than one carrier is involved in a single shipment of goods.

interlocking directorate
A situation in which an individual serves on the boards of directors of
two or more competing corporations. This tends to create a monopoly
by bringing the management of these corporations under a single control. Outlawed by the Clayton Antitrust Act of 1914.

interlocutory decree
A decree by a court of equity that does not finally settle a complete
issue, but provisionally settles some intervening aspect of the issue
while a final decree is awaited.

internal rate of return
See DISCOUNTED CASH FLOW.

Internal Revenue Service (IRS)
A unit of the Department of the Treasury, the IRS offers assistance in
filling out tax forms and provides education courses and bilingual assistance. Problems related to business taxes are assigned to district and
regional directors of the IRS or directly to the IRS office in Washington,
D.C. The IRS is responsible for all the audit and tax collection procedures of the federal government.

International Accountants' Society, Inc. (IAS)
A professional association of accountants in the United States.

International Accounting Standards Committee (IASC)
Established in 1973 by the Association of Independent Certified Public
Accountants (AICPA) and professional accounting associations in
other countries. Its purpose is to establish standards for the presenta-
tion of audited financial statements; affiliated with the International
Coordination Committee of the Accounting Profession (ICCAP).

International Advertising Association, Inc. (IAA)
Set up in 1938 to promote advertising standards and the free market
concept at the international level.

International Air Transport Association (IATA)
Formed in 1945, IATA works toward the development of safer and more economical air transportation services among nations. Approximately 90 international carriers are full members and 20 domestic airlines are associate members.

International Algebraic Language (IAL)
The forerunner of ALGOL.

International Association of Machinists and Aerospace Workers (IAMAW)
A trade union in the United States and Canada with more than 900,000 members; established in 1889 as International Association of Machinists (IAM).

International Atomic Energy Agency (IAEA)
An agency of the United Nations that seeks to promote the peaceful uses of atomic energy.

International Bank for Reconstruction and Development (IBRD)
See WORLD BANK.

International Brotherhood of Teamsters, Chauffeurs, Warehousemen and Helpers of America
See TEAMSTERS UNION.

International Chamber of Commerce (ICC)
Set up in 1919 as the international focal point for chambers of commerce.

International Civil Aviation Organization (ICAO)
An agency of the United Nations that works with civil aviation authorities worldwide for international cooperation on matters related to air transportation and navigation.

International Confederation of Free Trade Unions (ICFTU)
See WORLD FEDERATION OF TRADE UNIONS.

International Coordination Committee of the Accounting Profession (ICCAP)
See INTERNATIONAL ACCOUNTING STANDARDS COMMITTEE.

International Development Association (IDA)

Established in 1960 as an institution of the World Bank, the IDA's purpose is to provide financial assistance to developing countries on terms that would not bear heavily on the balance of payments of the borrowing countries. The IDA concentrates on giving assistance to countries that have an annual per capita gross national product of $375 or less. In 1975 more than 40 countries met this criterion. See WORLD BANK.

International Finance Corporation (IFC)

An agency of the United Nations in affiliation with the World Bank and the International Development Association (IDA), the IFC has been given the role of stimulating private investment and enterprise in the developing countries.

International Labor Organization (ILO)

An organization created by the Treaty of Versailles in 1919 as part of the League of Nations and designed as a forum for governments, employers, and workers to develop conventions on working conditions, such as health and safety, and to urge member nations to adopt these conventions as standards in national laws. The United States became a member in 1934. The AFL–CIO and the U.S. Chamber of Commerce are the U.S. delegations to the ILO, which in 1946 became an agency of the United Nations.

International Management Association (IMA)

See AMA/INTERNATIONAL.

International Monetary Fund (IMF)

The IMF was established by the United Nations in 1944 for the purpose of (1) eliminating exchange restrictions and providing for worldwide convertibility of currencies so as to encourage multilateral trade based on international specialization; (2) stabilizing exchange rates to reduce or eliminate short-term fluctuations in a nation's economy that result from changes in its exports, imports, or speculative capital movements; and (3) assuring that changes in a country's exchange rate shall occur only with the Fund's approval, and only after the country has experienced a prolonged deficit or surplus in its balance of payments. More than 100 nations belong to the Fund.

international monopoly

See CARTEL.

International Organization for Standards (IOS)
Formed in 1946, the IOS attempts to bring about international agreement on industrial, technical, and commercial standards. The national standards institutions of approximately 50 countries are members, including the AMERICAN NATIONAL STANDARDS INSTITUTE (ANSI).

international system
SI units, or Système International d'Unités; a system of metric units of measurement that has gained widespread acceptance as a means of handling all forms of measurements. The International Organization for Standards (IOS) developed a wide range of recommendations based on SI units including the meter (length), the kilogram (mass or weight force), the second (time), and the ampere (electric current). The international system (popularly known as the *metric system*) is superseding the U.S. customary system and the British imperial system.

International Telecommunications Union (ITU)
A United Nations agency dedicated to encouraging international cooperation in the use and technical development of telecommunications. The ITU was formed in 1934, predating the United Nations.

International Trade Commission (ITC)
An independent agency of the U.S. government, created in 1916 by an act of Congress as the United States Tariff Commission. The name was changed to the United States International Trade Commission by section 171 of the Trade Act of 1974. The Commission's powers and duties are provided for largely by the Tariff Act of 1930, the Antidumping Act of 1921, the Agricultural Act, the Trade Expansion Act of 1962, and the Trade Act of 1974. The ITC furnishes studies, reports, and recommendations involving international trade and tariffs to the President, the Congress, and other government agencies. In this capacity, the ITC conducts a variety of investigations, public hearings, and research projects pertaining to the international trade policies of the United States.

Interstate Commerce Commission (ICC)
Established in 1887, one of the oldest of the administrative federal agencies. The ICC is an arm of the legislative branch of the U.S. government and thus reports directly to Congress. It has 11 commissioners appointed by the president who designates one member as chairman. The Commission regulates operating certification, rates, finance, and control of interstate railroads, trucks, buses, barges,

ships, oil pipelines, express delivery companies, and freight forward-
ers.

in toto
In law, all together; the whole amount. Used in the context of "the
persons liable in toto."

intrinsic forecast
In marketing, a forecast based on past history, possibly developed
from a moving average set of data.

inventory
The stock of goods that a business firm has on hand, including raw
materials, supplies, work in process, and finished goods.

inventory control
The control of merchandise, materials, work in process, finished
goods, and supplies on hand by means of accounting and physical
methods.

inventory pricing
See LIFO, FIFO, and WEIGHTED AVERAGE METHOD.

inventory shrinkage
Losses that result from such nonproductive processes and actions as
deterioration, disposal as scrap, and pilferage.

inventory turnover
In accounting, the number of times inventory is cycled annually. A
ratio of the performance of a company, inventory turnover is calculated by dividing the material cost of annual sales by the average inventory level.

investment adviser
A person who on a professional service basis gives advice to another
person on investment situations. Investment advisers are required to
register with and report their activities to the U.S. Securities and Exchange Commission.

Investment Advisers Act of 1940
An act of Congress designed to protect the public in its dealings with
those who sell investment advice. The act calls for registration of advisers and stipulates against certain practices.

investment bank
In the United States, a term for a bank that specializes in the acquisition of new issues and their resale in small batches to investors. In the United Kingdom, these functions are handled by a *merchant bank* or *issuing house*. See UNDERWRITER.

investment company
A generic term that describes a company handling mutual funds or closed-end funds, or any of several other types of companies engaged in the business of investing the money of their shareholders in securities and in other organizations. See INVESTMENT TRUST.

Investment Company Act of 1940
Provides for the registration with the Securities and Exchange Commission (SEC) of investment companies and subjects their activities to regulation to protect investors.

investment trust
A company that uses its capital to invest in other companies. There are two principal types: the closed-end and the open-end, or mutual fund. Shares in closed-end investment trusts (some of which are listed on the New York Stock Exchange) are readily transferable in the open market and are bought and sold like other shares. Capitalization of these companies remains the same unless action is taken to change it, which is a rarity. Open-end funds sell their own new shares to investors. They stand ready to buy back their old shares, and are not listed. Open-end funds are so called because their capitalization is not fixed (open maximum, open minimum); they issue more shares as people want them.

investor's method
See DISCOUNTED CASH FLOW.

invisible hand
An expression used by Adam Smith in his book *The Wealth of Nations* (published in 1776) in which he contends that the desire for personal profit within the framework of a competitive economic system works like an *invisible hand* to guide the system toward the greatest welfare for all.

invoice
A document that shows the quantity, price, terms, character, nature of delivery, and other related details for goods sold or services rendered.

I/O
Input/output. An expression and an abbreviation used in many disciplines of management. In data processing it is a general term for the equipment used to communicate with a computer and the data involved in the communication.

IOS
See INTERNATIONAL ORGANIZATION FOR STANDARDS.

IOU
An informal document that serves as evidence of a debt of cash.

IQ
Initials for *intelligence quotient*. A measurement of intelligence expressed as a ratio of mental age to chronological age. Thus an IQ of 100 is the average for a particular age and an IQ of 125 is 25 percent above average. The validity of IQ tests is challenged on the basis that they ignore certain important qualities such as creative skills and abilities and cultural and ethnic backgrounds and influences.

IRE
Initials for *Institute of Radio Engineers*. See IEEE.

IRI
See ISTITUTO PER LA RICOSTRUZIONE INDUSTRIALE.

irrational number
A number that has an infinite extension, such as $\sqrt{2} = 1.41421356237$ . . . to infinity.

irrevocable trust
In law, a trust that cannot be set aside by its creator.

IRS
See INTERNAL REVENUE SERVICE.

issuing house
See INVESTMENT BANK.

Istituto per la Ricostruzione Industriale (IRI)
The Italian state company under which major parts of Italian industry have been nationalized.

ITA
Initials for *Industrial Truck Association* and *International Tape Association*.

ITC
See INTERNATIONAL TRADE COMMISSION.

itemized appropriation
In finance, an appropriation of funds with detailed specifics for the disposition or application of the funds. See LUMP-SUM APPROPRIATION.

item number
In manufacturing procedures, a number assigned to each line item, part, or assembly in a bill of material for purposes of identification. Item numbers are normally assigned sequentially for each bill of material.

ITU
See INTERNATIONAL TELECOMMUNICATIONS UNION.

ITVA
Initials for *Industrial Television Association*.

IUD
See INDUSTRIAL UNION DEPARTMENT.

jawboning
The use of exhortation and persuasion by the government (sometimes in the person of the president) to affect wage and price decisions.

Jenning's corollary
A satirical principle holding that the chance of bread falling with the buttered side down is directly proportional to the cost of the carpet on which it lands.

jerry-build
To build a thing inexpensively and quickly of low-grade or out-of-the-ordinary materials.

jet lag
The physical and mental effects experienced by a person who completes a flight on a jet aircraft involving the crossing of a number of time zones in a short period; the person is thus required to adjust to a new biological rhythm.

Jevons, William Stanley (1835–1882)
British pioneer in the mathematical school of classical economics; known for having discovered the works of earlier economists who might otherwise have gone unnoticed, and for the suggestion that periodic crises may be due to sunspots acting by way of the weather on crop yields. See CLASSICAL ECONOMICS and NEOCLASSICAL ECONOMICS.

JFMIP
See JOINT FINANCIAL MANAGEMENT IMPROVEMENT PROGRAM.

jobber

In the distribution of goods, an individual or a firm that intervenes between a wholesaler–distributor and the retailer. Jobbers may act exclusively as brokers or sales agents, carrying no inventory of the goods purveyed, or they may so organize and finance their activities as to provide warehousing facilities for the goods. The arrangement between the wholesaler and the jobber with respect to commission varies according to the extent of the services provided by one to the other.

job classification

The process of describing the duties, responsibilities, and characteristics of a job, point-rating it (sometimes through the use of formulas based on time studies of workers already in such jobs), and then grouping the jobs into graduated classifications with corresponding wage rates and wage ranges.

job description

A document that outlines in broad terms the purpose, scope, duties, and responsibilities of a job for which a person is hired. Also known as *position guide*.

job number

In manufacturing processes, a number assigned to each job or kit for purposes of identification, the number traveling with the job or kit throughout the plant.

job order

A document that authorizes the production of a specified number of units, or the delivery of specified services. The job order may serve as a basis for the costing of a particular process, production, or sale. Also known as *special order*.

job price

The price quoted or paid for completing a specified task without regard to time required for completion.

job shop

A functional organization whose departments or work centers are organized around particular types of equipment or operations, such as drilling, forging, wave soldering, and assembly. Products flow through departments in batches corresponding to individual orders, which may be either stock orders or individual customer orders.

Also, a company that supplies skilled labor, such as draftsmen, technicians, and engineers, on a temporary basis.

job shortage
The total quantity of items or parts that is short or lacking for work in process.

job ticket
See TIME TICKET.

Joint Financial Management Improvement Program (JFMIP)
Authorized by the Budget and Accounting Procedures Act of 1950, the JFMIP is a joint and cooperative undertaking of the Office of Management and Budget (OMB), the General Accounting Office (GAO), the Treasury Department, the General Services Administration (GSA), and the Civil Service Commission. The overall objective of the JFMIP is to improve and coordinate financial management policies and practices throughout the government so that they will contribute significantly to the effective and efficient planning and operation of government programs.

joint-stock association
See JOINT-STOCK COMPANY.

joint-stock company
An organization established by a group of individuals who act jointly to operate a business firm under an artificial name, with invested capital divided into transferable shares, an elected board of directors, and other characteristics similar to those of a corporation. In most states, joint-stock companies operate without formal government authority. The shareholders have unlimited liability for the debts and obligations of the company, which is taxed as a corporation. Joint-stock companies, also known as *joint-stock associations,* have become rare as a result of the ease with which a corporation may be formed under law. In British usage, a joint-stock association is a corporation. See CORPORATION.

joint tenancy
In law, a single estate in property, whether real or personal, owned by two or more persons under one instrument or act of the parties, with an equal right of all to share in the enjoyment of the property during their lives. On the death of a joint tenant, the property descends to the survivor or survivors and at length to the last survivor.

joint tenancy deed
An instrument that transfers the title to real estate and names the grantees as joint tenants.

joint tortfeasors
In law, when two persons commit an injury with a common intent, they are joint tortfeasers.

Jorgenson, Dale
An economist teaching at Harvard University, Jorgenson argued in 1977 that the explosive rise in world oil prices has brought about a fundamental change in the U.S. economy through a change in the relationship between the cost of capital and the cost of labor, the former having risen at a higher rate than the latter. As a consequence, Jorgenson contends, more new jobs are created and fewer are wiped out by technological change, and there will be a more rapid return to full employment than people expect, identified by an unemployment rate of 4.5 to 5 percent. However, continues Jorgenson, the greater use of labor and the decreased use of more productive capital will, by the end of the century, cause a reduction in gross national product.

journal
In accounting, a book of original entry.

journeyman
A skilled worker who has completed an apprenticeship and is an employee, not an employer and not self-employed. In medieval times, descriptive of the practice of skilled artisans who journeyed from place to place in pursuit of work.

journeywoman
A female journeyman.

JP
Initials for *justice of the peace*.

judgment in personam
A legal judgment against a person, directing that person to do or not do something as sentence for an offense.

judgment in rem
A legal judgment against a thing, as distinguished from a judgment in personam. Its object is the disposition of the property, without reference to the title of individual claimants. A judgment in rem is conclusive upon all who may have, or claim to have, any interest in the subject matter of the litigation.

junior financing
See JUNIOR MORTGAGE.

junior mortgage
A mortgage second in lien to a previous mortgage; a subordinate mortgage. Also known as *junior financing*.

junior security
See SENIOR SECURITY.

jurisdictional strike
A strike caused by a dispute among craft unions over which shall have jurisdiction over a specific job; outlawed by the Taft-Hartley Act. See TAFT-HARTLEY ACT.

kame
A narrow ridge of gravel and sand left by a glacier.

Kartell
The German term for CARTEL.

KD
See KNOCKED-DOWN.

Kennedy round
Agreements on general tariff reductions negotiated among member states of the General Agreement on Tariffs and Trade (GATT) organization between 1964 and 1967; originally initiated by John F. Kennedy during his presidency.

key lot
A marketable parcel of land one of whose sides adjoins the rear of other lots. Usually one of the least desirable lots in a subdivision because it does not offer optimum access or privacy.

key-man insurance
Provides temporary protection to ensure financial solvency in the event of loss through death of a key executive. The business firm pays the premium and is the beneficiary. Premium costs are not tax-deductible; however, proceeds from the policy are not subject to federal income taxation.

Keynes, John Maynard (1883–1946)
A British economist for whom a school of economic theories and principles is named; considered one of the most influential economists of all time. Keynes's *General Theory of Employment, Interest, and Money* (1936) ranks among the most important books on economics. In this book he analyzed economic processes that lead to depressions, and described policies that could be used to avoid depressions. His ideas helped shift emphasis away from LAISSEZ-FAIRE, the economic theory whose basic premise is that governments should not interfere in economic affairs. Keynes was born in Cambridge, England, and studied at Cambridge University to which he later returned as a lecturer (1908–1915). At age 28 he became editor of the *Economic Journal*. Keynes served on the Indian Currency Commission and, from 1915–1919, at the British Treasury, which he represented at the Versailles peace conference. He held advisory positions in British finance, industry, and government, and was appointed a director of the Bank of England. In 1942 he was made Lord Keynes of Tilton. In 1944 he led the British delegation at the monetary conference at Bretton Woods, New Hampshire, taking an active part in the establishment of the International Monetary Fund and the International Bank for Reconstruction and Development.

Keynesian economics
The economic theories and principles advanced by or attributed to the British economist John Maynard Keynes and his followers.

Keynes's law of consumption
A principle of Keynesian economics that at every level of income a certain proportion of that income is spent for consumption goods, the proportion decreasing as the income increases. See PROPENSITY TO CONSUME and LIQUIDITY PREFERENCE.

keypunch
In data processing, a mechanical device that punches holes in cards or tape to represent letters, digits, and special characters as a medium for storing information.

keystone
A wedge-shaped stone at the crown of an arch, which keeps the other stones in position; hence a part or a force on which associated parts or forces depend for support.

kg
See KILOGRAM.

KG
See KOMMANDITGESELLSCHAFT.

KGaA
See KOMMANDITGESELLSCHAFT AUF AKTIEN.

kilogram (kg)
A metric measure of weight equal to 2.2 pounds.

kilomegacycle
1,000 megacycles; a billion cycles; 10^9 cycles; a GIGACYCLE.

kilometer (km)
A metric measure of distance equal to 1,000 meters or 3,280.8 feet, approximately ⅝ mile.

kilowatt
A unit of power equal to 1,000 watts or about 1.34 horsepower.

kilowatt-hour (kwh)
A unit of work or energy expended in one hour at a steady rate of one kilowatt; generally used as the base for determining costs of electricity delivered to the consumer.

kinked demand curve
In economic analysis, a bend in the demand curve of an oligopoly that occurs at the existing market price, suggesting the possible behavior of the oligopolist when confronted with the possibility of a changing price. If the company raises its price above the *kink*, its sales will fall off rapidly because other sellers are not likely to follow its lead as the price

moves upward; if it drops its price below the kink, its sales will expand relatively little because other sellers are likely to follow its price downward. Therefore, the market price tends to stabilize at the kink.

kip
The basic unit of currency in Laos.

kiting
An unauthorized *borrowing* or theft of money through the continuing action of drawing and cashing a check on one bank, following that shortly by a covering deposit in the form of an unrecorded check on another bank, that check, in its turn, being covered by a check drawn on a third bank, the process possibly continuing undetected through several banks. The success of the act depends on the time it takes for checks to clear through the banking system. The growing use of electronics in expediting and automating the transfer of funds from one bank to another is expected to have a significant impact on transactions that have depended on clearance-time delays.

kit list
In manufacturing, a list of items that are needed to fill requisitions and that are to be taken from inventory and delivered to the production area.

km
See KILOMETER.

Knights of Labor
The first nationwide labor association in the United States. Originated in Philadelphia in 1869, it developed a membership of about three-quarters of a million workers by the year 1886. After 1893 it declined, being replaced by unions affiliated with the AFL.

knocked down
Descriptive of articles that have been taken apart to reduce the cubic foot displacement or to improve the unit as a shipping format. Also, consisting of parts that can be assembled (*knocked-down* furniture).

knot
A unit of speed of one nautical mile per hour. See NAUTICAL MILE.

Kollektivgesellschaft
A general partnership under Swiss law. Also known as *société en nom collectif.*

Kommanditgesellschaft (KG)
A limited partnership under Austrian, German, and Swiss business law. An alternative name in Switzerland is *société en commandité*.

Kommanditgesellschaft auf Aktien (KGaA)
A limited partnership under German law.

Kondatrieff cycle
In economic analysis, a 40-to-60-year wavelike movement in economic activity that is approximately divided between good and bad times. A theory of business cycles proposed by the Russian economist Nikolai D. Kondatrieff, born in 1892. Also known as the *wave theory*.

Korman, A. K.
See LIFE-CYCLE THEORY.

koruna
The basic unit of currency in Czechoslovakia.

krona
The basic unit of currency in Sweden. The plural form is *kronor*.

krone
The basic unit of currency in Denmark and Norway. The plural form is *kroner*.

kurtosis
In statistical analysis, the state or quality of the shape of a distribution, related to its flatness or peakedness. The term given to this characteristic of shape is *kurtosis*. See LEPTOKURTIC DISTRIBUTION and PLATYKURTIC DISTRIBUTION.

Kuznets, Simon
An American economist noted for his factual studies of national income, economic growth, and business cycles; winner of the 1971 Nobel prize in economics. His pioneering study of national income, *National Income and Its Composition, 1919–1938* (1941), helped economists develop accounting methods for national income. Kuznets was born in Kharkov, Russia, in 1901, but spent all his adult life in the United States. He taught at the University of Pennsylvania, Johns Hopkins University, and Harvard University.

Kuznets cycle
In economic analysis, a 15-to-25-year wavelike movement in rates of economic growth that appears to be associated with changes in population growth.

kw
See KILOWATT.

kwacha
The basic unit of currency in Malawi and Zambia.

kwh
See KILOWATT-HOUR.

kyat
The basic unit of currency in Burma.

labor
The element of production represented by those hired workers whose efforts or activities are directed toward making the product; also, all personal services including the activities of wageworkers, professional people, and independent businessmen. *Laborers* may thus receive compensation in the form of wages, salaries, bonuses, commissions, and so on.

labor-cost ratio
The standard cost of direct labor divided by its actual cost.

labor efficiency
The relationship between the planned labor requirements for a task and the actual labor time charged to the task.

labor force
All employed people 16 years of age or older, plus all those currently unemployed but actively seeking work.

labor injunction
A court order requiring an individual or a group to perform or cease to perform certain actions that have been deemed injurious and for which money damages are not a suitable remedy under law.

labor-intensive
A process or product is called labor-intensive if it uses proportionately more labor than other elements in its production. Hand-made goods with a low materials content are produced by a labor-intensive process. Service industries are usually labor-intensive. See CAPITAL-INTENSIVE.

Labor-Management Reform Act, 1959
See LANDRUM-GRIFFIN ACT.

Labor-Management Relations Act, 1947
Also known as the *Taft-Hartley Act,* this lengthy, controversial legislation made significant alterations in the Wagner Act. It expanded the National Labor Relations Board from three to five members and extended the area of government intervention into labor relations considerably further than did the Wagner Act. See TAFT-HARTLEY ACT.

Labor-Management Reporting and Disclosure Act, 1959
Also known as the *Labor-Management Reform Act,* or more popularly as the *Landrum-Griffin Act.* See LANDRUM-GRIFFIN ACT

Labor-Management Services Administration
This unit of the Department of Labor enforces laws affecting certain activities of unions, private pension funds, and welfare benefit plans as well as veterans' reemployment rights. Also works to improve labor and management relations.

labor relations
Similar in concept to industrial relations; however, the term generally refers to employer–employee relations, whereas *industrial relations* refers to union–management relationships. See INDUSTRIAL RELATIONS.

labor-standard rolled-up cost
The total labor cost required to build an assembly. This figure includes the labor cost of both the assembly and its subassemblies.

labor theory of value
The doctrine that all exchange value in economic transactions is created by labor. It is the basis of Marxian economic theory.

labor union
An organization of workers created for the purpose of advancing its members' interests with respect to wages and working conditions. See CRAFT UNION, INDUSTRIAL UNION, and TRADE UNION.

laches
In law, negligence or undue delay in asserting one's rights or in doing what by law a person should have done and did not do. Such behavior gives an equitable defense to another party.

lading
The contents of a freight shipment. See BILL OF LADING.

LAFTA
See LATIN AMERICAN FREE TRADE ASSOCIATION.

lagging indicators
In economic analysis, those time series that tend to follow or trail behind aggregate economic activity. See LEADING INDICATORS.

laissez-faire
The doctrine that government should *let things alone* and allow economic activity to go forward in response to individual and private objectives.

In the management of a particular enterprise, a style directly opposite to that of authoritarianism. The manager gives minimum direction and exercises little direct or obvious control over employees or subordinates, but rather *leaves them alone* to do their jobs as they think best. While this does not necessarily mean the total absence of direction or control, skillful laissez-faire managers provide it so subtly that their people are or may become highly motivated through personal commitment to responsibility. Perhaps the true skill of an effective laissez-faire manager is in selecting employees or subordinates who respond positively to this unencumbered style. See AUTHORITARIAN LEADERSHIP, DEMOCRATIC LEADERSHIP, and PARTICIPATORY LEADERSHIP.

laity
Persons in a profession who are not skilled with respect to that profession. In accounting, for example, the laity includes those who are not

skilled in accounting but who might need auditors' reports in the completion of their own tasks.

land
An element of production that includes land itself in the form of real estate as well as mineral deposits, timber, water, and other nonhuman or *natural* resources.

landed price
The quoted or invoiced price of a commodity, including costs of loading, shipping, and unloading at its destination.

land improvement
Improvement in the utility, and generally in the value, of land through the addition of paving and sidewalks, sewers, water, gas, and electric power lines, clearing, grading, and spur-railway tracks.

landlocked
A lot or acreage surrounded by private lands, without ingress or egress.

landlord's warrant
A legal recourse for obtaining payments for rent upon default in a lease, giving the landlord the right to possess the tenant's personal property as security until the debt is paid.

land office
A government office that records sales or transfers of public land.

land patent
See PATENTED LAND.

Landrum-Griffin Act
Popular term for the *Labor-Management Reform Act, 1959,* named after its chief sponsors. Enacted in response to public concern over abuses revealed by congressional hearings on the internal affairs of some unions. Those sections of the act regulating in detail the internal management of labor organizations are considered almost unique in federal labor law and are viewed by many as excessive intervention by a federal act. Also known as the *Labor-Management Reporting and Disclosure Act.*

land trust
The title to land held in trust by a trustee.

land warrant
An instrument given by the government to a purchaser of public land to show that the purchaser is in fact the owner.

language sheet
A term used by federal government agencies, in their accounting practice, to denote the narrative portion of an appropriation bill that accompanies an agency's submission of its budget to Congress.

lap phasing
See OVERLAPPED SCHEDULE.

lapse
Expire, or be forfeited, as in the case of an insurance policy that is canceled or lapses on its expiration date or for nonpayment of the premium. In government accounting, the unexpended balance of an ordinary appropriation is said to lapse at the end of the fiscal year.

larboard
See PORT.

large-scale integration (LSI)
A large number of interconnected integrated circuits manufactured simultaneously on a single slice of semiconductor material and usually containing more than 100 gates or basic circuits with at least 500 circuit elements. Compare with MEDIUM-SCALE INTEGRATION (MSI).

laser
Acronym for *light amplification by stimulated emission of radiation,* a device that produces a very narrow and intense beam of light of only one wavelength going in only one direction. Also known as *optical maser.*

last change date
In manufacturing, the last date on which a part was changed in a specific bill of material.

last cycle count date
In manufacturing, the date on which a particular part was counted in an inventory. This date is used to determine when the next physical inventory should be taken.

last in, first out
See LIFO.

last material standard cost
In accounting, the standard cost of the material prior to the last change in its cost.

last material standard cost date
In accounting, the last date on which the material standard cost was changed.

last transaction date
The last date on which a transfer of a particular material was transacted.

Latin American Free Trade Association (LAFTA)
An organization that regulates the import-export activities among eleven countries: Argentina, Bolivia, Brazil, Chile, Colombia, Ecuador, Mexico, Paraguay, Peru, Uruguay, and Venezuela. Founded in 1960 by ten countries, it took in Bolivia as its eleventh member in 1967.

law of averages
See LAW OF LARGE NUMBERS.

law of comparative advantage
See COMPARATIVE ADVANTAGE, LAW OF.

law of demand
The principle that the quantity of a commodity or service demanded is inversely proportional to the price of the commodity or service. That is, the consumer will buy more of a product or service when its price is low and less when its price is high.

law of improbable events
See POISSON PROBABILITY DISTRIBUTION.

law of large numbers
A law of probability, commonly but incorrectly called the *law of averages*. This law states that if we increase the number of trials, if we repeat whatever we are doing a great number of times, it is practically certain that the relative actual frequency of successes will come close to the assumed probability of success. Our ability to accurately predict

the probability of an occurrence improves as we increase the number of trials. We are then dealing in *large numbers* rather than any so-called *law of averages*.

law of selective gravity
A satirical principle holding that an object will fall so as to do the most damage.

law of supply
The principle that the quantity of a commodity producers are willing to supply varies directly with the price of the commodity. At higher prices, therefore, the quantity supplied will be greater than at lower prices. This "law" ignores the short-term effect of demand or non-demand.

lay days
The agreed-upon number of days that a marine vessel may remain in port for loading and unloading without penalty.

LC
See LETTER OF CREDIT.

LCD
Initials for *liquid crystal diode*.

LCL
See LESS THAN CARLOAD.

Lda
See LTDA.

LDC
See LOCAL DEVELOPMENT CORPORATION.

LDR
See LINEAR DECISION RULE.

Lea Act
Makes it unlawful to force a radio station to hire or pay for more employees than are actually required. Also forbids forcing a station to pay more than once for work performed only once. Other similar devices to extort pay for work not needed or never performed are banned.

leader effectiveness
The extent to which a leader influences his co-workers in the achievement of group objectives.

leading indicators
In economic analysis, those time series that tend to move ahead of aggregate economic activity, reaching peaks and troughs before the economy as a whole does. See LAGGING INDICATORS.

lead time
In materials control, the time it takes to replenish an item in inventory; this includes the total time taken from decisión to reorder to actual time of receipt of goods into inventory. Also see SETUP TIME and MAKEREADY TIME.

lease
A contractual agreement that transfers possession and use of property for a limited period under specified terms and conditions. A lease is an encumbrance against the title, since the rights it grants to the lessee are likewise binding on the successor or successors to the title.

lease assignment
A written legal document that generally conveys all rights of the assignor for the remaining term of the lease.

leaseback
A long-term lease of real estate or equipment that has been sold to an independent agent and is then taken back under the lease agreement by the original seller.

leasehold
An interest in land under the terms of a lease; normally classified as a tangible, fixed asset.

leasehold insurance
This type of policy may be written for a tenant who has an unusually favorable lease, lower in cost than could be obtained at current market prices. It provides a measure of financial protection in the event the premises are rendered uninhabitable because of fire. See CONSEQUENTIAL-LOSSES INSURANCE.

lease purchase agreement
An instrument whereby it is agreed that a portion of the note payments will be applied to the purchase price. The title is transferred on completion of the agreement.

least processing time
Generally known by the initials *LPT.* See SMALLEST PROCESSING TIME RULE.

least-squares method
The statistical process for determining the relationship between two or more variables, so that, when expressed as a curve, the sum of the distance (deviations) of the plotted available data (observations) from the curve is zero.

LED
Initials for *light-emitting diode.* Often used as an acronym and pronounced as a word.

ledger
A book of accounts; any book of final entry.

ledger clerk
An employee who is assigned the task of posting and balancing a ledger.

ledger journal
A book with multicolumned pages, used as a record of transactions, functioning as both a journal and a ledger. Usually the record contains debit or credit columns or both, and is used only when the number of accounts is few and transactions are relatively few and simple. See CASH JOURNAL.

legal capital
The part of a corporation's paid-in capital that becomes the par or stated value of the capital stock, as determined by law, agreement, or resolution of the board of directors. Also, the portion of net assets that is restricted from withdrawal, under corporation law.

legal debt margin
In municipal accounting, the excess of authorized debt over outstanding debt.

legal entity
Any individual, partnership, corporation, or organization empowered by law or custom to own property or engage in business transactions.

legal liability
An obligation that is enforceable by law, as distinguished from a moral responsibility.

legal-liability risk
See LIABILITY RISK.

legal list
A list of investments selected by various state governments in which certain institutions and fiduciaries such as insurance companies and banks may invest. Legal lists are often restricted to high-quality securities that meet defined specifications. See PRUDENT MAN RULE.

legal monopoly
See NATURAL MONOPOLY.

legal reserve
The minimum proportion of its demand deposits that a bank is required by law to keep in the form of cash in the vault or as a deposit at the Federal Reserve Bank. A decrease in the legal reserve requirement is expansionary because it enables banks to increase their loans; an increase in the legal reserve requirement is contractionary because it forces banks to reduce their loans.

legal tender
A currency that a creditor must by law accept in payment of a debt.

legatee
A person to whom a legacy or bequest is given by the terms of a will.

lek
The basic unit of currency in Albania.

lempira
The basic unit of currency in Honduras.

leone
The basic unit of currency in Sierra Leone.

Leontief, Wassily W.

Born in Russia in 1906, studied economics in Leningrad and Berlin, and came to the United States in 1931 to begin an academic career at Harvard University, where he remained until 1975. Leontief was awarded the Nobel prize in economic science in 1973 for his development of input-output analysis. See INPUT-OUTPUT ANALYSIS.

leptokurtic distribution

A statistical distribution that is relatively peaked, not flat. See KURTOSIS and PLATYKURTIC DISTRIBUTION.

less developed country

See UNDERDEVELOPED NATION.

less than carload (LCL)

Low-volume shipments generally require higher freight rates than high-volume shipments. It is not unusual for an LCL rate to be as much as 50 percent higher than the carload (CL) rate.

less than truckload (LTL)

The same cost conditions apply for shipments by truck as for shipments by railway. See LESS THAN CARLOAD.

letter of credit (LC)

A document issued by a bank or similar institution allowing a borrower to draw a bill of exchange on it for specified purposes. In the case of international trade, an overseas buyer may arrange for a bank in the country of the supplier to issue a letter of credit to the supplier accepting a bill of exchange drawn on it upon delivery of the relevant export shipping documents. Normally, the overseas buyer opens an irrevocable letter of credit with the vendor's bank in the vendor's country.

letters close

Letters issued by a government or a sovereign to a private person concerning a private matter. Distinguished from LETTERS PATENT.

letters patent

A writing from an official person or organization that confers on a designated person a grant (such as a right, title, status, property, authority, privilege, monopoly, franchise, immunity, or exemption) in a form readily open for inspection by all. Distinguished from LETTERS CLOSE.

letter stock
Stock issued to founders, early executives, and investors that is not registered with the Securities and Exchange Commission and thus is not subject to restrictions on sale and disposition. It is called letter stock because a letter of intent to invest, not to trade, must be filed with the appropriate regulatory body. Also known as *unregistered stock* or *founder's stock*.

level
A term used in manufacturing to denote the structure of a product and its documentation. Level 0 might represent the final assembled product; level 1 might represent all the components that comprise this final assembly; and level 2 might denote those components or subassemblies that form level 1.

leveling
In time studies, the use of the best judgment of the persons engaged in the study to adjust the performance of an observed worker to the level that is considered average or normal. This takes into account superior or inferior manual dexterity or other skills that may be unique to the observed worker. Without this leveling, erroneous conclusions might be reached with respect to the typical time a worker with average skill requires to complete a job.

leveling effect
In a management meeting, the effect created by a dominant person who, by force of personality or rank and title, causes others in his group or among his peers to tend to agree with his views, that is, come to his level.

leverage
The extent to which the money capital of a firm is divided between fixed interest or fixed dividend capital (debentures, preference shares, loan capital) and equity or ordinary shares that are not entitled to a guaranteed or minimum return. A company with a high proportion of fixed interest capital is referred to as *highly leveraged* while one with a high proportion of equity capital has *low leverage*.

leverage ratios
A set of financial ratios intended to display the nature of the methods and sources of financing used in acquiring the corporation's assets and to indicate their impact on the earnings available to common stockholders. Such ratios include debt to total assets, defined as total debt

divided by total assets; fixed charge coverage, defined as income available for fixed charges divided by fixed charges; and times interest earned, defined as earnings before taxes plus interest charges divided by interest charges.

levy
A tax assessment. In management, a request made on members of an organization for contributions of capital.

In law, a writ of levy refers to the seizure of a defendant's property by the sheriff to satisfy the plaintiff's judgment. The word sometimes is used to indicate that a lien has been attached to land and other property owned by the defendant by virtue of a judgment. See FIERI FACIAS.

liability
An amount owed by one person (debtor) to another (creditor). The debtors or the creditor may also be an organization, enterprise, or business firm.

liability dividend
See SCRIP.

liability insurance
Insurance basically intended to cover the insured party's responsibility for payment obligations to others as a result of bodily injury or property damage. In order to qualify for protection by an insurer, such a liability must have been incurred as a matter of legal judgment or through voluntary or contractual agreement. Also known as *third-party liability insurance; public liability insurance; liability, other than automobile, insurance;* and *owners', landlords', and tenants' (OL&T) public liability insurance.*

liability, other than automobile, insurance
See LIABILITY INSURANCE.

liability risk
Sometimes called *third-party risk* or *legal-liability risk,* this involves the possibility that the insured party may become legally obligated to pay money to a third party.

libel
The malicious publication of a defamatory statement about a person by printing, writing, signs, or pictures, for the purpose of injuring the

reputation and good name of the person; the act of exposing a person to public hatred, contempt or ridicule. See DEFAMATION.

libel liability insurance
Available to publishers of books and magazines to cover written defamation of character. Usually written with deductible clauses of high dollar value. The insured party is required to conduct his or her own defense.

library
In data processing, a file or collection of magnetic tapes containing information for use with a computer.

Library of Congress
Part of the legislative branch, a research arm for Congress. It has become recognized as a national library because its services have been extended to other branches of the federal government, to other libraries here and abroad, to the scholarly world, and to the public. The Librarian of Congress is appointed by the president. The Copyright Office, where creative works may be registered, is operated by the library. Established in Washington, D.C., in 1830.

license
As distinguished from easement and right of way, a license in real estate transactions is a revocable permission to use a piece of land given by the owner to another. It does not represent an interest in the real property, and it may be created orally. See EASEMENT and RIGHT OF WAY.

licensed public accountant
A person who has registered under state law to practice as a public accountant. In many states, the licensee must be a certified public accountant.

lie detector
See PSYCHOGALVANOMETER.

lien
A right one person has to keep possession or control of the property of another in satisfaction of a debt. Among the many kinds of liens are the artisan's lien, the attorney's lien, the innkeeper's lien, the mechanic's lien, and the vendor's lien.

life annuity
An annuity whose payments terminate on the death of the beneficiary. In the business world, it may be an annuity derived from the purchase of an insurance policy of a special type, or the result of a special perquisite provided as part of an employment contract.

life-cycle theory
A theory of business leadership, considered to be an outgrowth of the tridimensional theory and model of leadership effectiveness developed by Reddin and consistent with Argyris's immaturity-maturity concept, which holds that as the maturity level of a leader's followers continues to increase, appropriate leader behavior requires a decreasing structure or task orientation and may also entail a decrease in socioemotional or relationships support. The life-cycle theory of leadership was developed by A. K. Korman, a social scientist. Also, see REDDIN, WILLIAM J., and IMMATURITY-MATURITY THEORY.

Life Insurance Medical Research Fund (LIMRF)
Established by life insurance companies, the fund attempts to stimulate research that places a special emphasis on longevity.

life tenant
A person entitled to the use of or income from property during his or her lifetime. Also applies to organizations.

LIFO
Acronym for *last in, first out*. A method of inventory valuation developed in response to the claim that it more nearly reflects the operating point of view than other methods do. Under LIFO, the total inventory of a material is valued at the cost of the most recently paid purchase price, which, theoretically, is most nearly related to the prices at which sales are made. See FIFO and WEIGHTED AVERAGE METHOD.

lift trucks
Handling equipment used in warehouses and storerooms. Among the most common types are the rider, standup, walk, conventional counterbalance, narrow-aisle, straddle-arm narrow-aisle, straddle-arm telescopic, four-directional, straddle, side-load, fork carrier, platform carrier, manual power, battery power, gasoline power, gasoline-electric power, compressed-gas power, diesel power, hydraulic-lift, chain-drive-lift, telescopic mast, nontelescopic mast, high-lift, low-lift, direct-operator control, and remote-control lift trucks.

lighter
An open or covered barge towed by a tugboat and used in harbors or inland waterways.

lighterage
The charge billed for freight carried by a lighter.

Likert, Rensis
Born in 1903; professor of sociology and psychology at the University of Michigan until his retirement in 1970. Likert's writings on industrial psychology and on human behavior in the industrial environment earned international fame. In his *New Patterns of Management* (McGraw-Hill, 1961), Likert holds that the leadership and other processes of the organization must be such as to ensure maximum probability that in all interactions and all relationships with the organization each member will, in light of his or her background, values, and expectations, view the experience as supportive and one that builds and maintains the individual employee's sense of personal worth and importance. See LINKING-PIN CONCEPT.

limit
See LIMITED PRICE ORDER.

limited access land
Real property that is difficult to reach or is partially inaccessible.

limited audit
See SPECIAL AUDIT.

limited liability
A liability that is restricted by law or valid contract. Examples include the liability of a stockholder of a corporation or of an inactive, limited partner in a firm.

limited order
See LIMITED PRICE ORDER.

limited partner
A member of a partnership whose liability to creditors of the partnership is limited to the amount of his or her investment. A limited partner may not participate in management. Also known as *special partner*.

limited price order
In securities trading, an order to buy or sell a stated amount of a security at a specified price, or better price, if obtainable after the order is presented on the floor.

limited SBIC
See LIMITED SMALL BUSINESS INVESTMENT COMPANY.

Limited Small Business Investment Company
Formerly known as *Minority Enterprise Small Business Investment Company* (MESBIC), given statutory recognition by amendments in 1972 to the Small Business Investment Act. See SMALL BUSINESS INVESTMENT COMPANY and MINORITY ENTERPRISE SMALL BUSINESS INVESTMENT COMPANY.

LIMRF
See LIFE INSURANCE MEDICAL RESEARCH FUND.

linear decision rule (LDR)
Developed in 1955 by C. C. Holt, F. Modigliani, J. F. Muth, and H. A. Simon as a quadratic programming approach for making aggregate employment and production rate decisions. The quadratures are (1) regular payroll, (2) hiring and layoff, (3) overtime, and (4) inventory holding, back-ordering, and machine setup costs.

linear programming
A mathematical technique for the simulation of business situations, especially in manufacturing, intended to provide a means for problem solving; an aspect of operations research. Also known as *mathematical programming*.

linear service
Vessels that operate as common carriers serving particular trade routes and carrying a wide variety of packaged goods for many shippers. They adhere to published schedules. See TRAMP SERVICE.

linear tariff cut
A reduction in all tariffs by the same percentage.

linear trend
In statistical analysis, a trend that, when portrayed on a graph, appears as a straight line.

line layout
See PRODUCT LAYOUT.

line printer
In data processing, a unit of equipment that is capable of printing an entire line of characters at once across a page; that is, 100 or more characters are printed simultaneously as continuous paper advances line by line in one direction past type bars or a type cylinder containing all characters fixed in all positions.

link
A unit of land measurement equal to 0.01 surveyor's (or Gunter's) chain or 0.66 foot.

linking-pin concept
The interlinking relationships of supervisors or managers within their organizational hierarchies. Essentially, the concept developed by Rensis Likert holds that every superior is a member of two work groups— the one for which he or she has responsibility and the one to which he or she is responsible. Likert contends that the capacity to exert influence upward is essential if supervisors or managers are to perform their supervisory functions successfully. To be effective in leading his or her own work group, a superior must be skilled both as a supervisor and as a subordinate.

Lipsey equation
Developed by R. G. Lipsey in the United Kingdom in 1960; adds a level of sophistication to the Phillips curve by taking into account changes in retail prices during the preceding 12 months. See PHILLIPS CURVE.

liquid asset
Cash in banks and on hand, and other cash assets not set aside for specific purposes besides the payment of current liabilities. A marketable security that is readily converted to cash may also be considered a liquid asset. Also known as *quick asset*.

liquidating dividend
A pro rata distribution to stockholders or owners by an organization in liquidation. Also, a pro rata distribution to the stockholders of a company having *wasting assets,* such as mines, oil wells, and timber, representing a return of paid-in capital; a return of capital to the investors.

liquidation
The payment of a debt. The conversion of accounts receivable, investments, or inventory to cash. The settlement of an organization's debts through the sale of assets as a result of voluntary or involuntary termination of the enterprise.

liquidation value
The price that can be obtained from the sale of assets in a liquidation proceeding. Also known as *forced-sale value*. In the event of the liquidation of a corporation, liquidation value is the agreed-upon amount per share to be paid to preferred shareholders.

liquidity
A general term used to describe the ability of a business enterprise to convert noncash assets into a resource that enables the enterprise to meet its short-term obligations.

liquidity preference
The theory that people prefer to hold assets in the form of money because it is more readily convertible into other forms. Money flows or can be made to flow quite readily, thus money is liquid. Also known as the *theory of interest*, formulated by John Maynard Keynes. See KEYNES, JOHN MAYNARD, and KEYNES'S LAW OF CONSUMPTION.

liquidity ratios
Ratios of financial data used as indicators of an enterprise's ability to meet its current obligations in the event of stress. The best known of these ratios are the *current ratio* and the *quick ratio*. The latter is also known as the *acid test*. See ACID TEST and CURRENT RATIO.

lira
The basic unit of currency in Italy, Syria, and Turkey. The lira in Syria and Turkey is also known as a *pound*.

lis pendens
A court that has control of property involved in a suit issues a *lis pendens* notice that translates into: "Pending the suit, nothing should be changed." This means that persons dealing with the defendant regarding the subject matter of the suit do so subject to the final determination of the court.

List, Friedrich (1789–1846)

Followed the lead of Adam Müller in arguing against the classical economists. Appointed professor of economics and political science in 1817 at the University of Tübingen, he advocated abolition of import duties between the separate German states and establishment of a customs union within Germany. As a result he lost his university position and was later forced to emigrate. He took up residence in the United States, traveling around the country with Lafayette. In 1832 he returned to Germany, where, in 1841, he published his doctrine in the book *The National System of Political Economy*. His idea for a customs union was put into effect and served to unify Germany. Also, see MÜLLER, ADAM.

listed

A term used to describe a security that has been granted the trading privileges of an exchange.

listed stock

A company's stock that is traded on a securities exchange, and for which a listing application and a registered statement giving detailed information about the company and its operations have been filed both with the Securities and Exchange Commission (SEC)—unless the stock is otherwise exempted—and with the exchange itself. The various stock exchanges have different standards for listing.

list price

A published price, intended to be the price paid by the ultimate consumer. Any trade or other discounts are calculated from the list price.

liter

1.06 liquid quarts.

live load

The orders or the load of manufacturing orders that are actually available to be worked on by a manufacturing facility. See DEAD LOAD.

livestock insurance

Intended to provide coverage for groups of animals, or for individual animals such as a valuable racing horse. Insurance is available to those who professionally raise or breed game or fur-bearing animals for profit.

Lloyds Associations
An association of individual insurance underwriters, with each company assuming such risks or portions thereof as it feels are within its scope. Lloyds Associations are divided into Lloyd's of London and American Lloyds Associations.

Lloyd's of London
Originally composed of a small group of ocean marine underwriters who met at Lloyd's Coffee Shop in London to exchange information about shipping and risks. Lloyd's of London per se does not write insurance contracts. Its members are carefully screened and audited for financial solvency and dependability in the payment of claims, and they cooperate in underwriting high-risk high-value policies. The underwriters are well known for their ability to insure unusual risks. Policies issued to cover American risks contain clauses that provide that Lloyd's of London may be sued in any court having jurisdiction in the United States. Also see AMERICAN LLOYDS ASSOCIATIONS.

Lloyd's Register of British and Foreign Shipping
A compilation of technical information on ships that may be used as a reference document for establishing insurance rates for specific ocean marine vessels. Similar to the *Record*. See AMERICAN BUREAU OF SHIPPING.

load
In data processing, to put data into a register or into storage; to put magnetic tape onto a tape drive or put cards into a reader.

In production, the amount of work a manufacturing facility has scheduled ahead, usually expressed in hours of work.

In finance, the portion of the offering price of shares of open-end investment companies that covers sales commissions and all other costs of distribution. The load is incurred only at the time of purchase. In most cases there is no charge when the shares are sold (redeemed). See LOADING.

load center
A group of similar machines or work stations that can all be considered simultaneously for planning the workload. Also known as *work center* and *machine center*.

loading
In finance, the amount sometimes added to an installment contract to cover selling and administrative costs, interest, risk, and other factors

related to the contract. In an investment trust or mutual fund, it is the amount added to the market price of securities, representing administrative and selling costs, trustee's fees, and brokerage and management fees. In cost accounting, it is the addition of overhead to prime cost. See LOAD and MACHINE LOADING.

load leveling
The planning of work orders so that the work is spread over a period of time and tends to be distributed evenly.

load point
In data processing, a preset point at which magnetic tape is initially positioned under the read-write head to start reading or writing.

loanable funds theory of interest
A theory that the interest rate is determined by the demand for and the supply of loanable funds only, as distinguished from the total supply of money. The sources of demand for loanable funds are businesses, households that want to finance consumer purchases, and government agencies that want to finance deficits. The sources of supply are the central banking system that influences the supply of money (and hence loanable funds) in the economy, and households and businesses that make loanable funds available out of their past and present savings.

loan value
In insurance, an amount of money available to the owner of the policy and which the owner may borrow from the insurer. The insurance policy serves as collateral for the loan repayment.

loan-value ratio
In real estate, the ratio of the appraised real property value to the total mortgage loan.

Local Development Corporation (LDC)
To assist small business at the grass-roots level, the federal government encourages community residents to form LDCs. Resident-organized and -capitalized, LDCs solicit Small Business Administration (SBA) and bank loans to buy or build facilities for local small businesses. They raise their capital by selling shares to 25 or more local residents. After identifying small businesses in need, an LDC is eligible for one SBA loan or guarantee up to a specified maximum dollar level per year and unlimited bank loans for each small business it assists.

Local-Improvement Fund
See SPECIAL ASSESSMENT.

location
In data processing, a storage position in the main internal storage that can store one computer word and that is usually identified by an address.

location code
In production, a code used to indicate an item's stocking location.

lock-box system
A means of accelerating the flow of funds from the time of customer payment to the time of deposit in the company's bank account. A lock-box arrangement usually is on a regional basis, with the company choosing regional banks according to its billing patterns. The company rents a local post office box and authorizes its bank in each of the cities in which a box is rented to pick up the remittances in the box. The bank picks up the mail several times a day and deposits the checks in the company's account. Compare CONCENTRATION BANKING.

Locke, John (1632–1704)
English philosopher who emphasized the natural rights of life, liberty, and property that should accrue to those who labored. His work strongly influenced Thomas Jefferson in writing the Declaration of Independence.

locked in
A security trading term. An investor is said to be *locked in* when a security he owns shows a profit but he refrains from selling the security because the profit would immediately become subject to the capital gains tax.

lockout
The act of an employer in closing down a facility to keep workers out of their jobs.

log
See LOGARITHM.

logarithm
The power, known also as the *index* or *exponent*, to which one number, called the base, is raised to make it equal to another number. For

example, the logarithm (log) of 1,000 to the base 10 is 3, or 10 × 10 × 10 = 1,000; expressed as $10^3 = 1,000$.

logarithmic coordinates
The graduations on a logarithmic scale are located along the axes according to measurements from the origin that are proportional to the logarithms of the scale values. The scale is cyclic, one log cycle representing a change in the scale value by a factor of 10 if based on common logarithms, or e if based on natural logarithms. It is characteristic of such a scale that the increments of length corresponding to successive multiplications of the scale value by a constant—from 2 to 4, 4 to 8, 8 to 16, and so forth—are equal.

logger
An item of data processing equipment that automatically records physical processes and events, usually in chronological order.

logic
A science that deals with the canons and criteria of the validity of inference and demonstration; the science of normative formal principles of reasoning.

In data processing, the interrelation or sequence of signals and elements in the architecture of a computer or calculator that produces inevitable or predictable results.

logical shift
See CYCLIC SHIFT.

long
In securities trading terms, this signifies ownership of securities. "I am long 100 U.S. Steel" means the speaker owns 100 shares of that company's stock.

long term
A general expression for a period of time that extends through one or more fiscal years.

long-term contract
Any contract for goods or services that extends beyond one year.

long-term debt
An obligation or liability that is due after one year, as contrasted with short-term debts or liabilities that are current and due within the next 12 months. Also known as *long-term liability*.

long-term lease
An obligation for rental payments on real or personal property over an extended period, in excess of one year.

long-term liability
See LONG-TERM DEBT.

long ton
2,240 pounds. Same as GROSS TON.

Loop
The central business district of Chicago, Illinois.

loose rein
A term for a style of management also known as *laissez-faire*. See LAISSEZ-FAIRE.

Lorenz curve
An array, using the x–y axes of a chart, that depicts the percentage of an economy's spending units—normally taken to be family units—and the percentage of income received by these spending units. The Lorenz curve is used to show the distribution of wealth in the economy in the context of property and other privately held claims on the assets of the society. It is an aid in understanding the impact of public policy on the distribution of income.

loss
The excess of costs over related revenues; a disadvantage. Also known as *gross loss*.

loss ratio
A term used to express the ratio between the total of premiums paid to an insurance company and the total value of claims paid out by the company.

lost usefulness
In accounting, the gradual dissipation from any cause or for any reason of the service life or usefulness of an asset.

lot book
See PLAT BOOK.

lot-book report
In real estate transactions, a nonliability letter issued by a title company showing the last owner of record and any encumbrances thereafter. Such a letter is not a title report.

lot-size inventories
The quantity of supplies or materials required to support production for a specific time period, usually expressed in weeks. Also known as *cycle inventories*.

lottery
In business transactions, any scheme for the distribution of goods that involves the three elements of payment of consideration: (1) a return promise, (2) an act performed, and (3) a forbearance. This involves a prize to some but not all of those who give consideration, and also involves chance. The use of lotteries to market goods is considered unfair competition. The U.S. postal laws and regulations prohibit the sending of any matter through the U.S. mails that is in the nature of a lottery.

lot tolerance percent defective (LTPD)
Applied to a component, process, or finished product, the dividing line between good and bad lots, below which the quality is regarded as poor and not acceptable. Also known as *rejectable quality level*. See ACCEPTABLE QUALITY LEVEL.

low-level code
A data processing technique applied to materials planning to identify the lowest level at which requirements for a particular component may appear to ensure that all gross requirements have been accumulated before net requirements are calculated.

LPM
Initials for *lines per minute*, the printing speed of a computer printer terminal.

LPT
Initials for *least processing time*. See SMALLEST PROCESSING TIME RULE.

LS
The letters LS appear on legal documents and are the initials for the Latin phrase *locus sigilli*, meaning "place for the seal."

LSI
See LARGE-SCALE INTEGRATION.

Ltd.
Abbreviation for *Limited,* a British term equivalent to "incorporated" in the United States, indicating the limited liability of stockholders. See also LTDA.

Ltda
Sociedade anonima de responsabilidade limitada, a joint stock company under Portuguese law, formed either by public or private subscription. Also written as *Lda* or *Ltd.*

LTL
See LESS THAN TRUCKLOAD.

LTPD
See LOT TOLERANCE PERCENT DEFECTIVE.

Luddite
One of a group of early nineteenth-century workers in England who destroyed labor-saving machinery as a protest. Named after Ned Ludd, an eighteenth-century half-witted Leicestershire worker.

lump-sum appropriation
An allotment of funds for a specific purpose or for the operation of an economic unit without a statement of the details applicable to individual items of proposed expenditure.

lump-sum purchase
The purchase of a group of assets without requiring a detailed listing of individual items. The acquisition price of the assets is stated as a single sum. Also known as *basket purchase.*

Lutine bell
A bell taken from the ship *Lutine* that sank in the North Sea in 1799 with a cargo of bullion. It is sounded at Lloyd's in London to signal the announcement of important news, twice for good news, once for bad news.

MAC
Initials for *Middle Atlantic Conference*. Also, see MILITARY AIRLIFT COMMAND.

Machiavelli, Niccolò (1469–1527)
A leading Italian statesman and political writer. His ideas, expressed in *The Prince* (1513), had a significant influence on political and economic thought. He contended that politics should be free from ethical or theological influences; that although morality should be the guide for private conduct, the strong leader is justified in using any means necessary to keep his government in a sound condition—a state must expand or perish. In modern usage, *Machiavellian* has come to suggest the idea "the end justifies the means, however ruthless."

machine address
In data processing, an absolute, direct, unindexed address expressed as such or resulting after indexing and other processing has been completed.

machine center
See LOAD CENTER.

machine-hour rate
A rate of the cost per hour of work performed by a machine applied to work in process. The cost being calculated includes direct and indirect expenses: labor, depreciation, power, maintenance, supplies, and a portion of prorated factory overhead. The machine-hour rate may be based on estimates or actual costs.

machine loading
In manufacturing, the process of compiling the *load* or quantity of work assigned to each machine for a given period. Every job allotted to a

machine decreases its capacity for additional work for the period. It is important to know how long the work already assigned will occupy the machines.

machinery and equipment
The category of industrial goods that includes all machines of all sizes used in production and office work, not intended for resale.

macro accounting
A composite of accounts maintained by members of an industry or for the whole of an economic activity within a region or a country. See MICRO ACCOUNTING.

macroeconomics
Study of the issues that pertain to the economy as a whole, to aggregates of individuals, or to groups of commodities. Examples would be total employment without regard to type of employment or skill, the income derived from such employment, or the total consumption of goods as contrasted with the consumption of a specific consumable item. See MICROECONOMICS.

macro instruction
In data processing, an instruction to a computer consisting of a sequence of micro instructions; the more powerful instructions that combine several operations in one instruction. See MICRO INSTRUCTION.

magnetic core storage
In data processing, a storage device in which binary data are represented by the direction of magnetization in each unit of an array of magnetic material, usually in the shape of toroidal rings.

magnetic disk
In data processing, storage device on which information is recorded on the magnetizable surface of a rotating disk.

magnetic drum
In data processing, a cylinder having a surface coating of magnetic material, which stores binary information. The drum is rotated at a uniform rate.

magnetic ink character recognition (MICR)
A means for reading data that have been imprinted with magnetic ink on a document for entry into an automatic data processing system.

magnetic shift register

In data processing, a register that makes use of magnetic cores as binary storage elements, and in which the pattern of binary digital information can be shifted from one position to the next leftward or rightward position.

MAIA

Initials designating a member of the American Institute of Appraisers of the National Association of Real Estate Boards.

Maier's law

A satirical principle holding that, when the facts are not in conformity with the theory, the facts must be disposed of because they're obviously in error.

mail-order wholesaler

Serving as a middleman in the distribution of goods, this merchant substitutes mail-order catalogs and order forms for a personal sales force. Such a wholesaler meets the needs of retailers who are located at great distances from regular merchant wholesalers.

mainframe

See CENTRAL PROCESSING UNIT.

main storage

See PRIMARY STORAGE.

maintenance

In a lawsuit, the act of assisting either party to a lawsuit by a person who has no interest therein; an officious intermeddling in a lawsuit.

maintenance, repair, and operation (MRO)

Usually applied to a type of goods or a requisition for such goods used in routine support of a business property's facilities.

makeready time

In manufacturing procedures, the time required to prepare machines and other facilities prior to the start of a process or of production. Also known as *lead time* and *setup time*.

malice

In legal proceedings, a wrongful act that is done with intent to injure and that is reckless concerning the law and the rights of others.

Malthus, Thomas Robert (1776–1834)

The Malthusian doctrine contends that unchecked human breeding causes the population to grow by a geometrical progression, whereas the food supply can grow only in an arithmetical ratio. Credited with the "law" of diminishing returns in relation to land: There comes a point beyond which it does not pay to add to the effort to improve the yield of the land. His thesis *An Essay on the Principle of Population* was published anonymously in 1798. It was enlarged and published again in 1803 under his own name.

Malthusian doctrine

See MALTHUS, THOMAS ROBERT.

Malthusian theory of population

See MALTHUS, THOMAS ROBERT.

malum in se

Latin for "offense in itself"; an act that is evil or wrong by its own nature or by inherent natural law but is void of any legal penalty. A contract to do immoral acts is held to be illegal and void because of malum in se. Such acts are to be distinguished from acts *mala prohibita*, illegal because they are prohibited by statute. See MALUM PROHIBITUM.

malum prohibitum

Latin for "prohibited offense"; an act not inherently evil or wrong but declared to be so by statute. See MALUM IN SE.

MANA

Initials for *Manufacturers' Agents National Association.*

management by exception (MBE)

A management method under which subordinates handle normal details of their assignments and are sensitive to exceptional events that they then bring to the attention of their supervisors. Also abbreviated as *MBX*.

management by objectives (MBO)

A management technique for achieving performance goals. Generally, the technique is based on the development of an informal *contract* between a supervisor and his or her subordinates under which specific targets are agreed upon, actual performance toward the objectives is monitored and measured, and, if indicated, corrective action is taken.

management control system (MCS)
The scientific method by which managers set goals, measure performance in terms of results, and take appropriate action in the form of rewards, penalties, or additional training for employees.

management information system (MIS)
A system or program, usually making use of the capabilities of electronic data processing, designed to provide management with information for decision making.

manager
In the most fundamental interpretation of the word, a person who occupies a formal position in a formal organization, is responsible for the work of at least one other person, and has formal authority over that person. It is policy among some companies to set the minimum number of persons or subordinates in a group as the determining factor, or one of the determining factors, in the application of the title *manager*.

managerial effectiveness
The extent to which a manager achieves the productivity or output requirements of his or her position.

managerial grid
A concept of leadership styles concerned with relationships and task orientations, developed by Robert R. Blake and Jane S. Moulton. In the managerial grid, five different types of leadership based on concern for production (task) and people (relationships) are depicted in four quadrants of a square. The square is calibrated in gradients from 0 to 9, both vertically and horizontally. A leader rated 9 on the horizontal axis has a maximum concern for the task; a rating of 9 on the vertical axis indicates a maximum concern for people. See IMPOVERISHED STYLE, COUNTRY CLUB STYLE, TASK STYLE, MIDDLE-OF-THE-ROAD STYLE, and TEAM STYLE.

managing director
The chief executive of·a company. The title is generally preferred in areas outside the North American continent. Broadly equivalent to president of a company, the title preferred in the United States.

mandamus
A writ issued by a court of law, in the name of the state, directed to some inferior court, officer, corporation, or person, commanding that

party to do a particular thing that appertains to his, her, or its office or duty.

M&C
See MANUFACTURERS' AND CONTRACTORS' LIABILITY INSURANCE.

manifest
A listing of all shipments loaded in a vehicle or vessel. Usually used in reference to ship's cargo.

mantissa
The decimal portion of a common logarithm.

manual rate
In insurance policies, an established premium rate, usually stated in dollars cost per thousand dollars of protection or risk.

manufacturers' and contractors' (M&C) liability insurance
Generally covers claims by the public against the insured party because of accidents to such persons as job applicants visiting the premises, people touring the facilities, vendors, and even trespassers if the insured party is judged legally liable.

manufacturer's part number
A number that is used generally to indicate a part's source. It may also be used as an additional descriptor for the part.

manufacturing cost
Any item of expense that occurs during a processing operation. Also, the collective fixed and variable costs of a manufacturing process or operation, including raw materials, parts, direct labor, and manufacturing overhead.

manufacturing expense
The cost of manufacturing, other than the cost of raw materials consumed and direct labor. Also known as *factory expense, indirect expense*, and *factory overhead*.

MAPI
Initials for *Machinery and Allied Products Institute*.

margin
In securities trading, the amount paid by the customer when using his or her broker's credit to buy a security. Under Federal Reserve regula-

tions during the past 20 years, the initial margin required has ranged from 40 percent of the purchase price all the way to 100 percent. A stockbroker or brokerage firm may set margin limits that are below the maximum allowed by the Federal Reserve. See REGULATION T.

marginal balance
See CONTRIBUTION MARGIN.

marginal cost
The increase or decrease in total cost that occurs with a small variation in output (such as a unit), measured by the equation

$$\text{Marginal cost} = \frac{\text{change in total cost}}{\text{change in quantity}}$$

Ascertaining marginal cost is of importance in determining whether to vary the rate of production.

marginal cost pricing
A method of setting prices in which price is made equal to marginal cost. Since price must be set in such a way that all output is sold, and since marginal cost varies with output, marginal cost pricing implies that the price should be set at the point at which the demand curve cuts the marginal cost curve. Marginal cost pricing is considered an appropriate policy for nationalized industries on the grounds that it maximizes economic welfare. See MARGINAL COST.

marginal desirability
See MARGINAL UTILITY.

marginal income
See CONTRIBUTION MARGIN.

marginal land
Land that barely pays the cost of working or using it.

marginal propensity to consume
In economic theory, the principle that with every increase in income, part is used to increase consumption and the rest to increase savings. The marginal propensity to consume tells what proportion of each additional dollar of income will be used for consumption. For example, if a household increases its consumption from $9,600 to $11,200 as its income rises from $10,000 to $12,000, its marginal propensity to consume is the ratio of $1,600 to $2,000, or 0.8, even though its average propensity to consume is the ratio of $11,200 to $12,000, or 0.93. The

marginal propensity to save is the proportion of additional income used for saving. In this example the marginal propensity to save is 0.2, which is 1.0 minus the marginal propensity to consume.

marginal propensity to save
See PROPENSITY TO CONSUME, PROPENSITY TO SAVE, and MARGINAL PROPENSITY TO CONSUME.

marginal rate of substitution
In economic demand theory, the rate at which a consumer is willing to substitute one commodity for another along an indifference curve. It is the amount of change in the holdings of one commodity that will just offset a unit change in the holdings of another commodity, so that the consumer's total utility remains the same. Thus, along an indifference curve:

$$\text{Marginal rate of substitution} = \frac{\text{change in commodity Y}}{\text{change in commodity X}}$$

marginal revenue
The increase (or loss) in total revenue resulting from selling an additional unit of output. It is measured by the equation:

$$\text{Marginal revenue} = \frac{\text{change in total revenue}}{\text{change in quantity}}$$

marginal revenue product
The gain (or loss) in total revenue resulting from adding an extra unit of a variable factor of production, such as labor cost. It is measured by the equation:

$$\text{Marginal revenue product} = \frac{\text{change in total revenue}}{\text{change in variable input}}$$

marginal tax rate
A ratio, expressed as a percentage, obtained by dividing the change in total tax by the change in the base on which it is imposed; for example:

$$\text{Marginal personal income tax rate} = \frac{\text{change in total personal income tax}}{\text{change in total taxable income}}$$

marginal utility
In a supply of various goods, the least utility attributed to any one item. The extent to which the marginal utility of an item diminishes depends

on the individual concerned and the objects desired. If, for example, an individual desires to own a home, a boat, a car, and a private airplane, the item to which that individual attributes the lowest priority becomes identified with marginal utility. Also called *marginal desirability*. See MENGER, KARL.

margin call
A demand on a customer to put up money or securities with his or her broker. The call is made at the time of a purchase, or if a customer's equity in a margin account declines below the minimum standard set by the Exchange or by the firm. See MARGIN.

margin regulations
The authority for setting the percentage down payment required of a borrower to finance the purchase of stock. The rate is set by the Federal Reserve System's Board of Governors. An increase in margin requirements is intended to dampen security purchases; a decrease in margin requirements is intended to encourage such purchases. See MARGIN REQUIREMENT.

margin requirement
The Federal Reserve Board of Governors has authority to set the margin requirements for the purchase of securities and for member bank loans on securities. The margin requirement specifies the amount of down payment required on credit purchases of securities. For example, a margin requirement of 20 percent would obligate the purchaser to pay at least $20 on a purchase of $100 worth of stock or other securities and forbid that party to borrow more than $80 from a member bank on the purchase. The objective is to provide the Federal Reserve Board with the power needed to control or stabilize the securities market.

marine insurance
Perhaps the oldest type of insurance, dating from ancient times, marine insurance indemnifies for loss or damage to vessels, cargo, or other property exposed to the perils of the sea. See NATIONAL BOARD OF MARINE UNDERWRITERS.

marine perils
See PERILS OF THE SEA.

Maritime Administration
Established in 1950 as an office of the Department of Commerce to administer programs intended to aid in the development, promotion,

and operation of the U.S. Merchant Marine. It is also charged with organizing and directing emergency merchant ship operations. The Administration administers a War Risk Insurance program that insures operators and seamen against losses caused by hostile action if domestic commercial insurance is not available. Through the Maritime Subsidy Board, the Administration administers subsidy programs under which the federal government, subject to statutory limitations, pays the difference between certain costs of operating ships under the U.S. flag and under foreign competitive flags on essential services, and the difference between the costs of constructing ships in U.S. and in foreign shipyards. It also disposes of government-owned ships considered not essential to national defense.

markdown
In retail merchandising, the amount by which an original selling price is reduced.

marked capacity
The weight limits of cargo loaded into a railroad car as stenciled on the side of the car.

market
In economics, any area, place, or location without geographic limits, local or worldwide, with the essential feature that buyers and sellers are free to interact so that a price is established for the commodity or service being exchanged. See PRICE.

marketable securities
A balance-sheet classification for negotiable stocks, bonds, and Treasury securities carried as a current asset in the form of investments.

market economy
An economic system in which the questions of what to produce, how much to produce, and for whom to produce are decided in an open market through the free operation of supply and demand. There are no *pure* market economies, but several specialized markets such as the organized commodity exchanges closely approximate some of the properties of a pure market system.

market equilibrium
The economic state in which the supply of goods is limited to the quantity already produced and placed on the market.

market letter
A general term for short publications or newsletters issued by broker-age firms and investment advisory services to provide investors with recommendations to buy or sell securities and with other pertinent investment information.

market order
An instruction to a broker to buy or sell shares, stocks, or commodities at the prevailing market price.

market penetration
See MARKET SHARE.

market price
In securities trading, market price is the last reported price at which a security has been sold. Generally, the actual price prevailing in a marketplace at any particular moment.

market risk
In the securities market, the condition of uncertainty about future prices because of changes in investor attitudes. Also, see SECURITY RISK, FINANCIAL RISK, INTEREST RATE RISK, POLITICAL RISK, PURCHASING POWER RISK, and SOCIAL RISK.

market saturation
The theoretical point at which, because of decreased consumer need or disappearance of prospective buyers, few or no additional sales are likely in a marketplace.

market segmentation
The analytical procedure whereby elements of a total market are divided into segments according to some reference, such as buying behavior of the consumer, need patterns, socioeconomic status, age, or sex.

market share
Sales of a product in a particular market segment as a proportion of the total sales in that segment. Also known as *market penetration.*

market theory
A wage theory whose basic tenet is that wage levels are determined by the supply of and demand for labor. Thus, if there is a shortage of qualified workers with a particular skill, those who possess that skill should be paid higher wages than workers possessing skills that are not

in short supply. To some extent, this theory treats labor as a commodity, since commodity prices are determined largely by supply and demand factors.

markka
The basic monetary unit of Finland. Also known as *finnmark*.

markon
See MARKUP.

markup
The total amount by which established selling prices are increased during a given period in setting new selling prices. Also, an amount that is added to the purchase price of merchandise to arrive at a selling price; also known as *markon*.

Marshall, Alfred (1842–1924)
The son of a cashier of the Bank of England, he wrote a highly technical but influential book, *Principles of Economics*. He thought of economics as a science useful in the service of humanity rather than as a description or defense of the status quo. See NEOCLASSICAL ECONOMICS.

Marshall Plan
See EUROPEAN RECOVERY PROGRAM.

marshal's deed
See DEED, SHERIFF'S.

Marsto-Chron
A timing device used in time studies. When it is necessary to record time intervals that are too short to be measured with a stopwatch, a Marsto-Chron may be used to register times in the order of 0.01 minute. The device consists of a small box through which a scaled paper tape is drawn at a uniform speed by means of an electric motor. The principal advantage is that the observer's attention need not be diverted from the activities of the worker to record time intervals or to make notes. Time intervals are marked on the paper tape and can be read at any convenient time.

Marx, Karl Heinrich (1818–1883)
The son of a well-established lawyer, Marx studied law, philosophy, and history. Considered a radical thinker from his early student days, his writings caused him to be banished from Germany, France, and

Belgium. He settled in London, living in near poverty for the rest of his life. Marx's *Das Kapital,* published in 1867, became the "bible" of socialism and communism. Marx described a new social system and was convinced that capitalism was doomed to failure. Volumes 2 and 3 of *Das Kapital* were published in 1885 and 1894, and were intended to show the self-destructive tendencies of capitalism. See MARXISM.

Marxism
The theories of Karl Marx, characterized by the central claims that the ruling middle class (bourgeoisie) will be overthrown by the working class (proletariat) through revolutionary action, and that a classless society will emerge in which the principal means of production will be publicly owned. Marx did not present a clear strategy for revolution; his theory is vague as a political guide, and as a result, Marx's followers have continuously quarreled among themselves over interpretations of his speeches, writings, and scattered notes. Many still read Marx in search of an explanation of current social, economic, and political events. See MARX, KARL HEINRICH.

maser
Acronym for *microwave amplification by stimulated emission of radiation,* a device that utilizes the natural oscillations of atoms or molecules between energy levels for generating electromagnetic radiation in the microwave region of the spectrum.

Maslow, Abraham H. (1908–1970)
A behavioral scientist who described his theory of a *hierarchy of needs* in *Motivation and Personality* (1954), a work that has found wide practical application outside the field of behavioral science. See HIERARCHY OF NEEDS.

Massachusetts trust
See BUSINESS TRUST.

master file
In data processing, a file containing relatively permanent information.

master in chancery
An officer appointed by a court of equity to assist it in taking testimony, computing interest, auditing accounts, estimating damages, ascertaining liens, and doing tasks that are incidental to the suit and that the court may require to be performed. The power of a master in chancery is advisory and fact-finding.

master instruction tape (MIT)
In data processing, a tape on which all the programs for a system of runs are recorded.

master schedule
A schedule that designates the total number of items to be produced without providing details relative to subassemblies or components. Also, see EXPLOSION and REGENERATION.

master tariff
A tariff filed with the Interstate Commerce Commission applying to a large number of applicable tariffs.

matched and lost
In securities trading, when two bids to buy the same stock are made on the trading floor simultaneously and each bid is equal in price or larger than the quantity of stock offered, both bids are considered to be on an equal basis. The two bidders flip a coin to decide who buys the stock. Also applies to offers to sell.

material current cost
Each time a purchase order is issued, the cost data for the relevant material are updated. The latest purchase cost becomes the current cost for the material.

Material Handling Institute (MHI)
A national trade association of U.S. manufacturers of materials-handling equipment, systems, components, and normally user-specified essential parts. Founded in 1945.

material requirements planning (MRP)
A relatively new technique for scheduling and ordering materials for manufacturing processes. MRP makes use of computer programs to explode materials requirements with reference to time phasing, netting gross requirements against on-hand and in-process inventory. This enables replenishment orders to be generated on a timely basis, and permits open orders for materials to be rescheduled to conform with changing requirements.

materials control
The process of providing the required quantity and quality of material needed in a manufacturing process at the required time and place and with the lowest practicable investment.

materials explosion
See EXPLOSION.

materials handling
The industrial science of developing the most efficient unit loads, improving the use of floor and cubic space, and selecting handling equipment.

materials in process
See WORK IN PROCESS.

materials management
A concept of organization that places under a single manager all functions concerned with the movement of materials, production control, inventory control, traffic, storage, materials handling, purchasing, and other similarly related activities.

mathematical expectation
See EXPECTED VALUE.

mathematical programming
See LINEAR PROGRAMMING.

matured liability
Generally refers to bonds; an obligation that is due or past due.

maturing liability
Generally refers to bonds; an obligation that is about to reach maturity.

maturity
The date on which a loan, bond, or debenture falls due and is to be paid off.

maturity basis
The method for calculating the values of bonds and their rates of return, based on the assumption that the bonds will be held until maturity.

maturity yield
See YIELD TO MATURITY.

max/min
An inventory control system under which materials are reordered up to predetermined maximum levels whenever stocks drop to a predetermined minimum level.

Mayo, Elton (1880–1949)
Leader of the research team from Harvard University that conducted the famous Hawthorne Studies. He also developed the *rabble hypothesis* and deplored the authoritarian, task-oriented management practices it created. See HAWTHORNE STUDIES, RABBLE HYPOTHESIS, and HUMAN RELATIONS MOVEMENT.

M.B.A.
Initials for *Master of Business Administration.*

MBE
See MANAGEMENT BY EXCEPTION.

MBK
See MR. BUSINESSMAN'S KIT.

MBO
See MANAGEMENT BY OBJECTIVES.

MBX
See MANAGEMENT BY EXCEPTION.

McGregor, Douglas (1906–1964)
A behavioral scientist who, in *The Human Side of Enterprise* (1960), postulated two theories of human behavior: Theory X and Theory Y. These theories are essentially a set of assumptions that McGregor believed managers have about people. Theory X and Theory Y are not of themselves management styles, although they are often misunderstood to be specific *styles.* They are intended to assist managers in understanding human needs so that they can develop appropriate styles in dealing with their subordinates. See THEORY X and THEORY Y. Also see THEORY Z.

MCM
See MERGED CHARGE MEMORY.

MCS
See MANAGEMENT CONTROL SYSTEM.

MCTA
Initials for *Motor Carriers Traffic Association*.

mean
In statistical analysis, the *arithmetic mean* (sometimes called the *average*) is the sum of the values of the items divided by the number of items. The *geometric mean* is a term between the first and last terms of a geometric progression; it is applied to data for which the ratio of any two consecutive numbers is either constant or nearly constant. This occurs in such data as those that represent the size of a population at consecutive time intervals or the value of a sum of money that is increasing at a compound interest rate. The *harmonic mean* is used most frequently in averaging speeds where the distances traveled are the same for each speed calculation.

mean absolute deviation
In statistical analysis, the arithmetic mean of the absolute values of the deviations from the mean of a distribution. For a normal distribution, the mean absolute deviation is equal to 0.8 of the standard deviation. See TRACKING SIGNAL and SIGMA (the Greek letter σ).

mean time between failures (MTBF)
A quantitative expression of the reliability of a manufactured product or component.

mechanic's lien
A lien that has been created by statute to assist laborers in collecting their wages. Its purpose is to subject the land of an owner to a lien for materials and labor expended in the construction of buildings. Having been placed on the land, the buildings become a part of the land by the law of accession.

median
In statistical analysis, a method for finding the average of a group of numbers arranged in either ascending or descending order of magnitude; the median of a set of N numbers is the middle number of the set if N is odd, and is the mean of the two middle numbers if N is even.

mediation
In industrial relations, a method of settling differences between two parties, such as a labor union and management, by the use of an impartial third party, called a mediator, who is acceptable to both sides. The

mediator's decisions are not binding on either party. The mediator works by encouraging constructive discussions, searching for common areas of agreement, and suggesting compromises. Federal, state, and many local governments provide mediation services for labor-management disputes. Mediation is sometimes referred to as *conciliation*.

Medicaid
A medical aid program operated by individual states and designed to supplement the federal Medicare program.

Medical Services Administration (MSA)
A unit of the Social and Rehabilitation Service of the Department of Health, Education and Welfare, MSA supervises the expenditure of federal funds in joint federal and state programs (Medicaid) of medical assistance to welfare recipients of Supplemental Security Income and, at a state's option, other low-income people.

Medicare
A federal medical aid program designed particularly for the aged, operated by the U.S. Social Security Administration.

medium-scale integration (MSI)
A number of interconnected integrated circuits manufactured simultaneously on a single slice of semiconductor material and having at least 12 gates or basic circuits with at least 100 circuit elements. Compare with LARGE-SCALE INTEGRATION (LSI).

megabit
In data processing, one million binary bits.

megacycle
See MEGAHERTZ.

megahertz
A million hertz. Equal to a million cycles per second.

member bank
A bank that belongs to the Federal Reserve System. All national banks chartered by the federal government must be members of the Reserve System. State banks may join if they meet specific requirements established by the Federal Reserve Board.

member corporation
A securities brokerage firm organized as a corporation and having at least one member of the New York Stock Exchange as a director and a holder of voting stock in the corporation. See MEMBER FIRM.

member firm
A securities brokerage firm organized as a partnership and having at least one general partner who is a member of the New York Stock Exchange. See MEMBER CORPORATION.

memomotion
The name given in 1950 by Marvin E. Mundel to the application of time-lapse photography to work-study procedures.

memorandum bill of lading
The third copy of a bill of lading. See BILL OF LADING.

memory
See STORAGE.

memory capacity
See STORAGE CAPACITY.

memory dump
See STORAGE DUMP.

Menger, Karl (1840–1921)
An Austrian economist; from 1873–1903, professor of economics at Vienna University. He developed his marginal utility theory in his major work, *Grundsätze der Volkswirtschaftslehre* (1871). Exchange takes place, he argued, because individuals have different subjective valuations of the same commodity. See NEOCLASSICAL ECONOMICS.

mens rea
Latin for "guilty mind"; criminal as distinguished from innocent intent. An element that has to be proven to sustain a verdict of guilty for a criminal offense. It is generally presumed from the proven facts.

mercantilism
A set of economic principles and practices intended to build national prosperity and government power by (1) accumulating precious metals through maintaining a favorable trade balance, (2) achieving economic independence through imperialism, and (3) exploiting colonies by

monopolizing their raw materials and precious metals while reserving them as exclusive markets for exports.

merchandise
Goods that have been purchased or manufactured for purposes of commercial sale. Also, the inventory of a merchant.

merchant
A buyer or seller of goods who does not add to, subtract from, or in any way alter or modify the form of the goods.

merchant bank
In the United Kingdom, a bank that provides long-term venture capital or risk capital rather than the short-term loans handled by a commercial or clearing bank. See INVESTMENT BANK.

merchant marine
Designates oceangoing, privately owned freight and passenger ships, generally over 1,000 gross tons, documented under the U.S. flag.

merchant's rule
See UNITED STATES RULE.

merchant wholesaler
A general term for a trader who takes title to goods for sale to retailers who in turn resell them to end users. Other names for a merchant wholesaler include *distributor,* JOBBER, MERCHANT, and *wholesaler.*

merged charge memory (MCM)
A solid-state device developed by IBM at its System Products Division, Essex Junction, Vermont. The device approaches the conceptual limit of the intersection of two conductors and is a benchmark in microminiaturization—a 64-bit MCM is smaller than the printed dot on a magazine page.

merger
Amalgamation of two or more firms under one ownership. The three common forms of merger are (1) horizontal, uniting similar plants and products; (2) vertical, uniting dissimilar plants in various stages of production; and (3) conglomerate, uniting dissimilar plants and products.

merger treaty
Formalized in 1967, this treaty united the European Economic Community (EEC), the European Atomic Energy Community (EURATOM), and the European Coal and Steel Community (ECSC) under the Council of Ministers and the European Commission.

meridian line
In land surveying, the principal north–south line in a township or range system. Generally, a north–south line running through any point on the earth's surface.

merit salary increase
The increase in base pay granted a salaried employee, theoretically intended to reward increased job competence and good performance. However, merit increases are also used to adjust salaries for increases in costs of living, to keep salaries on a scale approximating those of organized (unionized) employees, to maintain a level of compensation comparable to the level that prevails in an industry or a geographic region for a specific job function, and to maintain a degree of internal equity in salary relationships.

MESA
See MINING ENFORCEMENT & SAFETY ADMINISTRATION.

MESBIC
See MINORITY ENTERPRISE SMALL BUSINESS INVESTMENT COMPANY.

mesne profits
Mesne (pronounced *mean*) is the archaic French word for intermediate. Mesne profits are those that accrue from a property during a period when a rightful owner is wrongfully deprived of the earnings.

messenger insurance
See ARMORED CAR INSURANCE.

metal-oxide semiconductor (MOS)
One of the solid-state technologies used for fabricating large, low-cost computer memories with very high input impedance.

Metcalfe, Henry (1847–1917)
A career army captain, assigned to the management of several arsenals. Pioneered systems for cost and materials control that served to advance scientific management of inventories and related costs.

meter
A unit of length in the metric system, equal to 39.37 inches or 3.28083 feet.

metes and bounds
The boundaries of a tract of land established by reference to natural or artificial signposts along it, such as a stream, ditch, fence or road; distinguished from those boundaries established by beginning at a fixed starting point and running therefrom by established compass courses and distances.

methods analysis
See MOTION STUDY.

methods engineering
See MOTION STUDY.

methods manual
Detailed information developed as sets of instructions for the routing and operations to be performed in the processing or manufacture of a part or a product. See ROUTE SHEETS and OPERATION SHEETS.

methods research
See MOTION STUDY.

methods study
A systematic procedure for the analysis of work designed to (1) eliminate unnecessary work, (2) arrange the remaining work in the best order possible, and (3) standardize the use of proper work methods.

methods-time measurement (MTM)
In manufacturing procedures, a methods engineering technique for acquiring data that may apply to all classes of work involving manual motions.

metrication
The process of transferring from a local nonmetric system to an international metric system. See INTERNATIONAL SYSTEM.

Metric Conversion Act of 1975
Established a U.S. policy in support of metric measurement, coordinating the increasing use of metric standards on a voluntary basis. The act supplements the Treaty of the Meter (1875) in which the United States

committed itself to the metric standard by signing the international agreement.

metric system
See INTERNATIONAL SYSTEM.

metric ton
2,204.6 pounds.

MHI
See MATERIAL HANDLING INSTITUTE.

MICR
See MAGNETIC INK CHARACTER RECOGNITION.

micro accounting
Accounting for individual, business, nonprofit, or government organizations, or for any department or other subdivision thereof. See MACRO ACCOUNTING.

microchronometer
A specially designed clock driven by a synchronous motor, calibrated to measure units of 0.001 minute. The clock has two hands, one making 10 revolutions per minute and a small one making 1 revolution per minute. It is adapted for use with motion pictures in analyzing time and motion studies.

microeconomics
Studies or statistics that depict the behavior of individual issues, groups, or commodities in the economy. Examples would be an analysis of the employment data for those engaged in the manufacture of aircraft or automobiles, or of the demand for a specific commodity or consumable item. See MACROECONOMICS.

microfiche
Microfilm photocopies of the equivalent of several pages of text, drawings, or other documents assembled onto a small and transparent sheet of film.

micro instruction
A small, single, short, add, shift, or delete type of instruction to a computer. See MACRO INSTRUCTION.

micro-PERT
See PERT.

micromotion study
A work analysis method that uses motion pictures with a timing device to obtain times for each motion.

microsecond
One millionth of a second; 10^{-6} cycles per second.

middle-of-the-road style
A style of managerial leadership based on the belief that adequate organization performance is possible through balancing the need to get out the work with the need to maintain the morale of people at a satisfactory level. See MANAGERIAL GRID.

Midwest Stock Exchange (MSE)
One of the major U.S. stock exchanges, based in Chicago.

mile
A measure of length equal to a distance of 5,280 feet or 1.609 kilometers.

Military Airlift Command (MAC)
Under the Secretary of the Air Force, MAC is responsible for military air cargo shipments and personnel movements overseas.

Military Sealift Command (MSC)
Under the Secretary of the Navy, the MSC is responsible for military ocean cargo shipments and personnel movements overseas.

Military Traffic Management and Terminal Service (MTMTS)
Under the Secretary of the Army, the MTMTS is responsible for the procurement and use of all modes of transportation in the United States for military purposes. The agency manages surface transportation of military cargo and military personnel within the United States, including operations at all military ocean terminals except those used by the Navy in support of fleet activities.

mill
One-tenth of a U.S. penny.

Mill, John Stuart (1806–1873)

Precocious eldest son of the Scottish philosopher, historian, and economist James Mill. He exemplified British liberalism in the nineteenth century, voting with the advanced Radical party and advocating women's suffrage. A spokesman for the philosophy of UTILITARIANISM, famous throughout the world for his treatise *On Liberty* (1859), he also wrote about and broadened Adam Smith's classical theories of economics. See WAGE-FUND THEORY.

millimicrosecond

See NANOSECOND.

millisecond

One thousandth of a second; 10^{-3} second.

mineral lease

A legal contract that permits the lessee to explore for and extract minerals from the leased property under prescribed conditions as to time, price, rental, or royalties. Also known as *mining lease.*

minimum planned start date per operation (MINSD)

In this rule for production scheduling, the order assigned next is the one with the earliest planned start date for the current operation. This is the theoretical operation start date that has been calculated previously by the scheduling procedure.

minimum processing time per operation

See SMALLEST PROCESSING TIME RULE.

minimum rate

See CLASS RATES.

minimum slack time per operation

See DS/RO.

Mining Enforcement & Safety Administration (MESA)

An agency of the Interior Department, MESA was created in 1973 to remove regulation of mine safety from the industry-dominated Bureau of Mines. MESA enforces all mine safety regulations, including air quality and equipment standards.

mining lease

See MINERAL LEASE.

min/max system
An industrial procedure for stock replenishment that establishes points at which the minimum quantity on hand indicates the need to reorder so as to return the quantity to the maximum level.

Minority Enterprise Small Business Investment Company (MESBIC)
Inspired by the racial unrest of the 1960s, MESBICs were introduced in 1969 to serve only those small businesses that are owned by a minority group, a minority-group individual, or other socially and economically disadvantaged Americans. See SMALL BUSINESS INVESTMENT COMPANY and LIMITED SMALL BUSINESS INVESTMENT COMPANY.

MINSD
See MINIMUM PLANNED START DATE PER OPERATION.

mint ratio
Under a bimetallic standard, the ratio of the weight of one metal to another, determined by the equivalent value of those quantities of metal in terms of the national unit of currency (such as the dollar) as defined by the government. During the nineteenth century when the United States was on a bimetallic standard, the government defined the mint ratio for many years as

$$15 \text{ grains silver} = 1 \text{ grain gold} = 1 \text{ dollar}$$

The mint ratio was therefore 15 to 1. Since the ratio remained fixed by law, it resulted in either gold or silver being driven out of circulation, depending on the relative international market values of the two metals. See GRESHAM'S LAW and BIMETALLIC STANDARD.

minus tick
See DOWN TICK.

MIP
Initials for *marine insurance policy*. Also, see MONTHLY INVESTMENT PLAN.

MIS
See MANAGEMENT INFORMATION SYSTEM.

misappropriation of funds
See DEFALCATION.

miscellaneous asset
An asset of minor significance that cannot be classified under any other heading or subheading of a balance sheet.

miscellaneous expense
In accounting procedures, an incidental expense, not classifiable as manufacturing, selling, general, or administrative expense. It appears as an item on an income statement below operating income or as a subdivision of income deductions.

miscellaneous revenue
Minor, incidental revenues such as interest on bank balances and occasional rent on unused facilities.

misdemeanor
A criminal offense, less than a felony, that is not punishable by death or imprisonment in a state penitentiary.

misfeasance
The improper performance of a duty that has been imposed by law or contract and that injures another person. As distinguished from *nonfeasance,* the failure to perform an imposed duty.

missionary
In the organizational setting, a manager whose style is to use a high relationships orientation and a low task orientation in situations where such behavior is inappropriate and therefore less effective. Such a manager is perceived as being primarily interested in harmony. See RELATIONSHIPS ORIENTATION and TASK ORIENTATION.

MIT
See MASTER INSTRUCTION TAPE.

Mitchell, Wesley Clair (1874–1948)
An American economist who used the scientific method, which depended on data and statistics, for developing an analytical approach to conclusions in economics. He was concerned with economic research and the investigative school for the development of theories. During World War I he was an adviser to the government on mobilization of the economy and the control of prices. He organized and became the research director of the National Bureau of Economic Research, now a function of the U.S. Department of Commerce.

mixed economy
An economic system in which the questions of what and for whom to produce are decided partially by the free market and partially by a central government authority. There are varying forms and degrees of mixed economies.

mixed estate
A ground rent for 99 years, renewable forever.

mixed inventory
An inventory of a class of goods whose individual items are not or cannot be identified with a particular lot.

MMFB
Initials for *Middlewest Motor Freight Bureau.*

mnemonic system
In accounting, an indexing of accounts or groups of accounts by means of letters that suggest their name or nature.

mode
In data processing, a computer system of data presentation, for example, the binary mode. Also used to refer to any selected mode of computer operation.
   In statistical analysis, another type of average—the number or class (or classes) for which the frequency of occurrence is greatest when the group of numbers is arranged in ascending or descending order.

modem
Acronym for *modulator/demodulator.* In data processing, a modem performs modulation in the form of signal conversion, interfacing computers or computer peripheral equipment to a telephone line. The modem converts logic data into pulsed audio tones that travel over the telephone line and enter a companion modem at the end of the line. There the audio tones are converted back into logic, interfacing and communicating with a computer or computer peripheral equipment. The logic is in the form of zeros and ones.

modulator/demodulator
See MODEM.

module
In data processing, an interchangeable, usually plug-in, assembly or subassembly of components.

monadic product test
A market research term for a consumer test of a single product. See DIADIC PRODUCT TEST and TRIADIC PRODUCT TEST.

monetarists
Economists who view the money supply as the single most important determinant of the price level and the general level of economic activity, including the level of employment.

monetary policy
Measures taken by the central bank and the national treasury to manipulate the money supply with the intent to influence the output of goods and services, employment, the price level, the rate of economic growth, or the balance of international payments.

monetary theory of business cycles
A theory that attributes business cycles to monetary factors, such as changes in the quantity of money and credit and changes in interest rates. Upswings occur when credit and borrowing conditions become favorable enough for business firms to borrow money; downswings occur when the banking system begins to restrict its expansion of money and credit.

monetary union
A situation in which two or more countries share a common currency and common financial policies and institutions.

money
Anything that serves as a medium of exchange and thus facilitates the economic process of production, distribution, and consumption. Econometricians define money as currency and checking accounts. Superficially, credit cards appear to be money; however, credit cards do not immediately demand the movement of currency, and they may be paid for by check from the credit card holder's checking account at some time later than the delivery of the goods or services received by the consumer.

money market
In the field of finance, a center where short-term credit instruments are bought and sold.

money supply
Currency and demand deposits in use as money in an economy.

money supply rule
A guide for the expansion of the economy advanced by the monetarist school of thought, especially by Milton Friedman. The rule states that the Federal Reserve should expand the nation's money supply at a steady rate in accordance with the economy's growth and capacity to produce, approximating 3 to 5 percent a year for the United States. More than this would lead to strong inflationary pressures; less would tend to have a stagnating if not deflationary effect.

monomial expression
An algebraic expression that consists of only one term, such as 7bx. See BINOMIAL EXPRESSION, TRINOMIAL EXPRESSION, and POLYNOMIAL EXPRESSION.

monopolistic competition
A type of market structure in which a relatively large number of the sellers of products that are similar but not identical possess some degree of control over their selling price. Product differentiation and advertising are usually characteristic of this type of competition, without emphasis on price differences. Compare with NONPRICE COMPETITION.

monopoly
A market situation in which there is a single producer or seller of a commodity or service with few, if any, substitutes. By definition the firm constitutes the industry. See NATURAL MONOPOLY.

monopsonistic competition
An economic situation in which a fairly large number of buyers exist for the consumption of a good or service.

monopsony
A market situation in which a single firm is the only buyer of a product, although there may be more than one seller; also known as a *buyer's monopoly*. Monopsonies occur most frequently in labor markets, when a single firm is the only important employer in a locality. The early textile-mill towns of New England and the coal-mining towns of Pennsylvania were examples of labor monopsony. The improvements in and the increased availability of transportation have enabled laborers to expand their reach beyond the town in which they live or domicile, thus lessening monopsony power.

Monte Carlo method
A trial-and-error method of repeated calculations to discover the best solution to a problem. This method is often used when a great number

of variables are present with interrelationships so complex as to preclude the practicability of doing a direct analysis of the data.

Monthly Investment Plan (MIP)

A pay-as-you-go method of buying New York Stock Exchange listed shares on a regular payment basis for a minimum of either $40 per month or $40 every three months. Under MIP the investor buys stock by the dollars' worth rather than by the unit. If the price advances for a specific stock being accumulated, the investor acquires fewer shares, and if the price declines, the investor gets more shares with each purchase. The investor may discontinue purchases at any time without penalty. The amount of commission charged varies with the amount invested periodically in the plan.

monthly usage
In production procedures, the use of a part number on a monthly basis.

moral hazard
The possibility that the insured party may bring about a loss to the insurance company, either deliberately or through carelessness. Companies are obviously not anxious to insure individuals or firms with a record of or reputation for carelessness, since excessive losses must be anticipated from insuring such persons or firms.

moral suasion
In the field of finance, oral or written appeals by the Federal Reserve Board to member banks urging them to expand or restrict credit but not requiring them to comply.

more or less
In documents dealing with a conveyance of land, these words following a statement of the number of acres therein are intended to cover a reasonable excess or deficit that might be revealed through a land survey.

mortality chart
A group of data on life expectancy commonly used by life insurance companies in the United States for calculating insurability and premium rates.

mortality curve
In management procedures, a curve that displays the estimated life spans of persons or things. It may also be used to display the history of actual life spans. See SURVIVOR-LIFE CURVE.

mortgage
A conditional conveyance of property that operates as a lien on land, buildings, and other property, fixed or movable, given by a borrower to the lender as security for his or her loan.

mortgage bond
A bond secured by a mortgage against specific property or properties of the issuer of the bond.

mortgagee
A lender of money who accepts a property mortgage as security.

mortgage guaranty insurance
Insurance available to mortgagees to protect them against financial loss.

mortgage insurance policy
A policy that protects the mortgagee against loss in the event that title should prove defective.

mortgaged material
See RESERVED MATERIAL.

mortgagee's statement
A summary by the holder of a mortgage note indicating the present status of payments and the remainder owed.

mortgagor
One who borrows money or makes a loan, using property to which he or she has title as security for the loan.

MOS
See METAL-OXIDE SEMICONDUCTOR.

most-favored-nation clause
A clause in a treaty by which each signatory nation agrees to extend to the other the same preferential tariff and trade concessions it may in the future extend to nonsignatories, that is, the same treatment each gives to its most favored nation.

MOT
Initials for *military ocean terminal*.

motion study

This area of motion and methods study has many names. It is known as *methods analysis, methods engineering, methods research, work study,* and *work analysis.* F. B. and L. M. GILBRETH define motion study as the science of eliminating wastefulness resulting from using unnecessary, ill-directed, and inefficient motions. The aim of motion study is to find and perpetuate the scheme of least-waste methods of labor. Also, see TIME AND MOTION STUDY.

motivational research

An expression used in marketing for investigations of the reasons why consumers may choose one product in favor of another.

motivation-hygiene theory

Also known as the *duality theory,* proposed in 1959 by Frederick Herzberg of Case-Western University and expanded to include a theory of work motivation. Herzberg argues that when people feel dissatisfied with their jobs they become concerned about the work environment, or about *hygiene factors.* When people feel good about their jobs, it may be due to the work itself, the *motivators.* From another perspective, the hygiene factors are not necessarily motivators. The job itself, according to Herzberg, is effective in motivating people to superior performance.

Motor Carrier Act, 1935

An act of Congress placing motor carriers under federal regulation.

motor carrier's cargo liability policy

Coverage is for cargo only and insures the policyholder for legal liability to others resulting from specific perils.

Moulton, Jane S.

See MANAGERIAL GRID.

Mountain standard time (MST)

Local time of the seventh time zone west of Greenwich. This zone includes the Rocky Mountain states of the United States.

Mountain time (MT)

See MOUNTAIN STANDARD TIME.

movable-aisle system
A filing system of modular units of conventional shelves mounted on tracks directly embedded in the floor. The shelf units are compacted together and move from side to side to create an aisle between any two.

movement inventory
See TRANSPORTATION INVENTORY.

moving average
A technique for studying the behavior of a time series in problems in which the trend of the series is obviously not a straight line and in problems in which the analysts are interested only in the general motion of the series, be it a trend, cycle, or both. A moving average is an artificially constructed time series in which the figure for each time interval is replaced by the average (mean of the value) of the data for the time interval and for those of the preceding and succeeding periods. The advantage of this moving average presentation is that it tends to eliminate the ragged appearance of the time series and emphasize the general picture of its development.

moving budget
See MOVING PROJECTION.

moving projection
The continuous forecasting and reforecasting, on a periodic basis, usually monthly or quarterly, of budgets for expenses, sales, revenues, and other operational factors. Each new forecast considers an additional accounting period; for example, an annual forecast divided into quarterly periods might be updated or moved forward at the end of each quarter, the quarter just completed being discarded and a new quarter added.

MPA
Initials for *Master of Public Accounting* and for *Master of Public Administration*.

M-Q register
In data processing, a *multiplier-quotient* register used for performing arithmetical operations.

Mr. Businessman's Kit (MBK)
A portfolio of tax information for the small business owner offered by the Internal Revenue Service as an aid to record keeping and the preparation of tax returns.

MRP
See MATERIAL REQUIREMENTS PLANNING.

MSA
See MEDICAL SERVICES ADMINISTRATION.

MSC
See MILITARY SEALIFT COMMAND.

MSE
See MIDWEST STOCK EXCHANGE.

MSI
See MEDIUM-SCALE INTEGRATION.

MST
See MOUNTAIN STANDARD TIME.

MT
Initials for *Mountain time*. See MOUNTAIN STANDARD TIME.

MTBF
See MEAN TIME BETWEEN FAILURES.

MTM
See METHODS-TIME MEASUREMENT.

MTMTS
See MILITARY TRAFFIC MANAGEMENT AND TERMINAL SERVICE.

mu
The Greek letter μ, pronounced *myew*. In statistical analysis, stands for the population mean in a probability distribution.

Mullen test
Procedure, using a Mullen tester, to test the bursting strength of fiberboard shipping containers or other paper. Also known as *Cady test*.

Müller, Adam (1779–1829)
A German economist who attacked the economic theories of the classicists, in that he believed money not only had materialistic value in furthering individual well-being, but also fulfilled a social function. Money is money "insofar as it is not private property but is the common property of as many people as possible, and, indeed of all . . .

only at the moment of exchange or of the circulation of the substances of money, are these latter really money." Although they were influential, his thoughts lacked precision.

multinational company
A commercial firm with a financial or managerial interest in companies, affiliates, or subsidiaries in a variety of countries.

multiple-choice questions
See OSGOOD SCALES.

multiple-maturity time deposit
A type of savings deposit that has limited withdrawal privileges and pays a higher-than-normal interest rate.

multiplexing
The transmission of a number of different messages simultaneously over a single circuit (as in telephony and telegraphy) or over a single channel (as in radio, television, and computers).

multiunit bargaining
Collective bargaining arrangement that covers more than one plant. It may occur between one or more firms in an industry and one or more unions, and it may take place on a national, local, or regional level. It is sometimes inaccurately called *industrywide bargaining,* although it is rarely completely industrywide.

Mun, Thomas (1571–1641)
Well-educated son of a London merchant and member of the East India Company beginning in 1615. Contributed to the theory of foreign trade in a publication entitled *England's Treasure by Foreign Trade,* in which he discussed the importance of exporting more than one imports in order to bring money into the country and so achieve a favorable international balance of payments.

municipal bond
A bond issued by a state or by a political subdivision such as a county, city, town, or village. The term also designates bonds issued by state agencies and authorities. Generally, interest paid on municipal bonds is exempt from federal income taxes.

municipal corporation
The structural form under which a county, city, town, village, school district, or other territorial division of a state transacts its business.

Murphy's law
The satirical assumption that if it is possible for something to go wrong, it will go wrong. The statement is sometimes ironically extended to include the comment "and all efforts to set it right will only make matters worse."

mutual fund
See INVESTMENT TRUST.

mutual insurance company
An association of persons organized under the insurance code of each state as a nonprofit corporation. Each policyholder is legally a part owner of the company, and in theory is therefore both the insurer and the insured. Excess income is returned to policyholders in the form of dividends or reductions in premiums. Policyholders elect a board of directors responsible for company operations. Also, see STOCK COMPANY.

mutual investment company
A financial investment company that has a variable number of shares outstanding and that is ready at any time to issue or redeem shares at or near the current liquidating value. Also known as *mutual investment trust*.

mutual investment trust
See MUTUAL INVESTMENT COMPANY.

mutual savings bank
A bank that receives savings deposits and that is organized without stock, whose earnings accrue entirely to the benefit of the depositors.

mutual water company
A company organized by or for water users in a given district, with the object of obtaining an ample water supply at a reasonable rate. Stock is issued to users of the water supply.

NAA
See NATIONAL ASSOCIATION OF ACCOUNTANTS.

NAB
Initials for *National Association of Broadcasters.*

NAC
See NATIONAL ADVISORY COMMITTEE.

NACMAC
See NORTH AMERICAN CONFERENCE OF MANAGEMENT CONSULTANTS.

NAEB
Initials for *National Association of Educational Broadcasters.*

NAIA
See NATIONAL ASSOCIATION OF INSURANCE AGENTS.

NAM
See NATIONAL ASSOCIATION OF MANUFACTURERS.

nanosecond
A billionth of a second; 10^{-9} second; a millimicrosecond. Abbreviations are *nanosec* and *nsec.*

NAPM
See NATIONAL ASSOCIATION OF PURCHASING MANAGERS.

NARDA
Initials for *National Appliance and Radio–TV Dealers Association.*

NAREB
See NATIONAL ASSOCIATION OF REAL ESTATE BOARDS.

NARI
Initials for *National Association of Recyclying Industries.*

narr
See COGNOVIT.

NAS
Initials for *National Academy of Sciences.*

NASA
See NATIONAL AERONAUTICS AND SPACE ADMINISTRATION.

NASBIC
Initials for *National Association of Small Business Investment Companies.*

NASD
See NATIONAL ASSOCIATION OF SECURITIES DEALERS, INC.

NASDAQ
Initials for *National Association of Securities Dealers Automated Quotations.* See SHARE INDEX.

NASPO
See NATIONAL ASSOCIATION OF STATE PURCHASING OFFICIALS.

NATESA
Initials for *National Alliance of Television & Electronic Service Associations.*

National Advisory Committee (NAC)
A private-sector group that reviews the policies of the Occupational Safety and Health Administration (OSHA). See OCCUPATIONAL SAFETY AND HEALTH ADMINISTRATION.

National Aeronautics and Space Administration (NASA)
A federal agency responsible for research and development in aerospace flight and exploration of outer space.

National Association of Accountants (NAA)
A professional association established in 1919, based in the United States, with approximately 65,000 members worldwide.

National Association of Insurance Agents (NAIA)
Establishes codes of ethics that define members' responsibilities to the public, to the companies, and to other members of the association.

National Association of Manufacturers (NAM)
An association of major manufacturers in the United States, established in 1895.

National Association of Purchasing Managers (NAPM)
A professional association with approximately 20,000 members, established in 1915.

National Association of Real Estate Boards (NAREB)
This organization endeavors to promote high professional standards of practice, provide educational facilities and publications, administer a code of ethics, and regulate relationships between realtors and the public.

National Association of Securities Dealers, Inc. (NASD)
An association of brokers and dealers in the over-the-counter securities business. The Association has the power to expel members who have been declared guilty of unethical practices. Among NASD's objectives is to "adopt, administer, and enforce rules of fair practice and rules to prevent fraudulent and manipulative acts and practices, and in general to promote just and equitable principles of trade for the protection of investors."

National Association of State Purchasing Officials (NASPO)
Established in 1945 to encourage improved purchasing practices among the central purchasing officers in state governments, NASPO is an affiliate of the Council of State Governments, which is financed by the states.

National Board of Fire Underwriters (NBFU)
Maintained by a large group of the leading stock fire insurance companies. It has set up recommended standards for building construction with a special view to fire prevention, has engaged in extensive public education, and is of major importance in investigations and suppressions of arson, for which a core of trained investigators is maintained.

National Board of Marine Underwriters (NBMU)
Protects wrecked and damaged property abroad and develops rules for the safe loading of oceangoing vessels. See MARINE INSURANCE.

National Bureau of Standards (NBS)
Established by an act of Congress in 1901, the Bureau provides the basis for the nation's measurement standards. These standards are the means through which people and nations buy and sell goods, develop products, judge the quality of their environments, and provide guidelines for the protection of health and safety. The Bureau's overall goal is to strengthen and advance the nation's science and technology and facilitate their effective application for the public benefit. NBS is an office of the Department of Commerce.

National Credit Union Administration (NCUA)
An independent regulatory agency headed by an administrator who is appointed by the president, the NCUA serves as the governing agency for all federal-chartered credit unions, which are privately owned, cooperative associations organized for the purpose of promoting thrift among their members and creating a source of credit. The NCUA is empowered to grant federal charters to qualified groups and to supervise and examine federal credit unions throughout the country. It may insure accounts of federal credit unions and of those state-chartered credit unions that request such coverage.

National Federation of Independent Business (NFIB)
An association of small business enterprises founded in 1943 and growing to a membership of 500,000 by mid-1977.

National Fire Protection Association (NFPA)
A voluntary group of organizations and individuals interested in controlling fire damage. Serves as a clearing house for technical information on methods of controlling fires. The Underwriters Laboratory (UL) is maintained by the Association. See UNDERWRITERS LABORATORY.

National Highway Traffic Safety Administration (NHTSA)
A unit of the U.S. Department of Transportation, the NHTSA works to reduce highway deaths, injuries, and property losses through enforcement of federal performance standards for cars, motorcycles, small trucks, and vehicle equipment, through investigation of reported safety-related defects and enforcement of laws requiring the recall and free remedy of such defects, and through the development of various

highway safety standards that are designated by the NHTSA for each state's adoption and enforcement.

national income
Not to be confused with the total income received by people from all sources (that is, personal income), national income is the total of all net incomes earned by or attributed to the factors of production: the sum of wages, rent, interest, and profits that accrue to the suppliers of labor, land, capital, and entrepreneurship. Generally and in theoretical discussions, *national income* is often used simply to represent the income or output of an economy.

National Industrial Traffic League (NITL)
Organized in 1907 as a professional association of industrial traffic executives.

National Institute for Occupational Safety and Health (NIOSH)
An office of the Department of Health, Education and Welfare, operated under the Center for Disease Control to ensure safe and healthful working conditions for all working people. NIOSH develops safety and health standards and conducts special research activities related to its objectives. It is distinct from the Occupational Safety and Health Administration (OSHA), which is an agency of the Department of Labor.

National Institutes of Health (NIH)
An office of the Department of Health, Education and Welfare, its mission is to improve the health of the American people. To carry out this mission, it conducts and supports biomedical research into the causes, prevention, and cure of diseases; supports research training and the development of research resources; and makes use of modern methods to communicate biomedical information.

nationalization
The action of a government in assuming ownership of an industry; usually used in reference to an industry that was formerly privately held or operated within the private sector.

National Labor Relations Act, 1935
Also known as the Wagner Act, this legislation extended government protection to the right of workers to organize and bargain collectively. It also created the National Labor Relations Board (NLRB) to deal with employer practices that interfered with these rights and to provide machinery for determining the proper bargaining unit and representatives. See NATIONAL LABOR RELATIONS BOARD.

National Labor Relations Board (NLRB)
A five-member group appointed by the president to hear labor complaints and to determine whether or not any U.S. labor laws have been violated. See NATIONAL LABOR RELATIONS ACT.

National Marine Fisheries Service (NMFS)
An agency of the U.S. Department of Commerce, NMFS is responsible for developing standards and specifications for quality, conditions, quantity, grade, and packing of fish, fishery plants, and fishery products and for inspecting and grading such products and plants.

National Retail Dry Goods Association (NRDGA)
See NATIONAL RETAIL MERCHANTS ASSOCIATION.

National Retail Merchants Association (NRMA)
An association of department, chain, and mass merchandise and specialty stores, retailing men's, women's, and children's wearing apparel and home furnishings. Before 1958 known as the *National Retail Dry Goods Association* (NRDGA).

National Safety Council (NSC)
Supported in large part by insurance companies, the Council collects statistics on many types of accidents.

National Service Life Insurance (NSLI)
Created in 1940 by the National Service Life Insurance Act to provide coverage for servicemen and servicewomen during World War II. See UNITED STATES GOVERNMENT LIFE INSURANCE.

National Small Business Association (NSBA)
Founded in 1937, the oldest organization in the United States representing independent business firms.

National Technical Information Service (NTIS)
An arm of the U.S. Department of Commerce, the NTIS is the central source for the public sale of government-sponsored research, development, and engineering reports and other analyses prepared by federal agencies, by their contractors or grantees, or by special technology groups. The NTIS is also a central source for federally generated machine-processable data files. The agency is located in Springfield, Virginia.

National Trades' Union (NTU)
Formed in New York City in 1834, the NTU was the first attempt to found a national labor federation in the United States. It failed to survive the financial panic of 1837.

NATO
See NORTH ATLANTIC TREATY ORGANIZATION.

natural business year
A fiscal year that ends at the annual low point of business activity or at the conclusion of a business season.

natural financing
A sale or exchange of real property that requires no outside financing or mortgages, as when properties are traded and each party assumes the other's mortgages, or as in an all-cash sale.

Natural Gas Act, 1938
An act of Congress that established federal authority over interstate pipelines.

natural monopoly
A form of business organization that occurs in a market situation in which monopoly rather than competition appears to be the most feasible and efficient arrangement for the production and distribution of a commodity or service. Public utilities are natural monopolies. Such monopolies are established by a state or federal government and are also called *legal* or *virtual* monopolies.

natural person
In law, an individual human being. See ARTIFICIAL PERSON and PERSONA FICTA.

natural resources
These comprise both the raw materials and the conditions of nature that are required in production. They include mineral wealth, soil, climate, waterways, and topography. By means of foreign trade, domestic natural resources may be exchanged for those of another country or for finished products, so that productive labor therefore becomes part of the trade.

nautical mile
A unit of distance officially fixed in the United States at 6,080.20 feet, in Great Britain at 6,080 feet, and internationally at 6,076.11549 feet, or

1,852 meters. The United States has officially used the international standard since July 1, 1959. See KNOT.

NAVA
Initials for *National Audio-Visual Association*.

navigational change principle
A principle of management decision making that holds that a decision maker should consider the ability he or she will have to change a decision once it is made.

NBFU
See NATIONAL BOARD OF FIRE UNDERWRITERS.

NBMU
See NATIONAL BOARD OF MARINE UNDERWRITERS.

NBS
See NATIONAL BUREAU OF STANDARDS.

NCITD
Initials for the *National Committee on International Trade Documentation*.

NCTA
Initials for *National Cable Television Association*.

NCUA
See NATIONAL CREDIT UNION ADMINISTRATION.

NDR
See NONDESTRUCTIVE READ.

NDRO memory
See NONDESTRUCTIVE READOUT (NDRO) MEMORY.

near-money
A financial instrument with some of the qualities of money. Savings deposits, shares in savings and loan associations, U.S. Treasury bills, and the cash value of personally held life insurance policies are examples of such an instrument. Also known as *liquid asset*.

NEDA
Initials for *National Electronic Distributors Association*.

need

A concept taken from behavioral science, assumed by many industrial psychologists to be the initiating and sustaining force of behavior. A positive need or desire is defined as a force that impels a person toward the achievement of a goal. A negative need is an anxiety, a force that repels a person away from certain objects or conditions, often through fear of failure. Common synonyms for need are *drive* and *want,* when positive; *fear* and *aversion,* when negative.

needs satisfaction

Fulfillment of a want. When a need is satisfied, it may no longer serve as a motivator. For example, a hungry person is highly motivated to acquire food and will perform a difficult task in moving toward that objective. However, once the desired amount of food has been eaten, hunger is removed as a motivator and promises of more food at that moment may not produce additional work motivation. Other needs or wants now become more important. See BLOCKED NEEDS SATISFAC-TION, HIERARCHY OF NEEDS, and MOTIVATION-HYGIENE THEORY.

negative asset

A liability.

negative income tax

Proposed government payments to a family to equalize the difference between income earned and a minimum guaranteed income level.

negligence

In legal procedures, the failure to do what an ordinary, reasonable, prudent person would do, or the act of doing what an ordinary, reasonable, prudent person would not do. *Ordinary negligence* arises from errors in judgment, not from willful deceit. *Gross negligence* is attributable to recklessness and an extreme disregard for common standards. See DUE CARE.

NEMRB

Initials for *New England Motor Rate Bureau.*

neoclassical economics

An approach to economics that flourished in Europe and the United States between 1870 and World War I. Among its leaders were William Stanley Jevons, Carl Menger, Leon Walras, Vilfredo Pareto, Alfred Marshall, John Bates Clark, and Irving Fisher. The neoclassicists were primarily concerned with refining principles of price and allocation theory, the theory of capital, and related aspects of economics. In developing their analyses and models, they made early and extensive use of mathematics, especially differential and integral calculus. Much of the structure of modern economic science is built on their pioneering work.

NESDA
Initials for *National Electronic Service Dealers Association.*

net
In accounting procedures, the amount remaining after diminution of an item by its related and associated deductions of charges, outlays, and losses. As distinguished from GROSS.

net assets
See NET WORTH.

net asset value
A term usually used in connection with investment trusts, meaning net asset value per share. It is common practice for an investment trust to compute its assets daily, or even twice daily, by totaling the market value of all securities owned. All liabilities are deducted, and the remainder is divided by the number of shares outstanding. The resulting figure is the net asset value per share.

net avails
The net proceeds of a discounted note.

net cash generation
See CASH FLOW.

net cash income
See CASH FLOW.

net change
The change in the price of a security from the closing price on one day to the closing price on the following day on which the stock is traded. In the case of a stock that is entitled to a dividend one day, but is traded *ex-dividend* the next, the dividend is considered in computing the change. For example, if the closing market price of a stock on the last day it was entitled to receive a 50-cent dividend was $45 a share, and if it sold for $44.50 at the close of the next day when it was ex-dividend, the price would be considered unchanged. The same applies to a split-up of shares. A stock selling at $100 the day before a 2-for-1 split and on trading day selling at $50 would be considered unchanged.

net current assets
See WORKING CAPITAL.

net income
See NET PROFIT.

net lease
A lease on real property requiring the lessee to assume all operating expenses, such as maintenance, insurance, and taxes, in addition to the payment of rent.

net loss
The opposite of net income or net profit. See NET PROFIT.

net national product (NNP)
Gross national product (GNP) less capital consumption allowances, such as depreciation, accidental damage to fixed capital, and capital outlays charged to current expense. See GROSS NATIONAL PRODUCT.

net operating loss (NOL)
See OPERATING LOSS.

net operating profit (NOP)
See OPERATING INCOME.

net proceeds
Proceeds from the sale or disposition of property or the marketing of an issue of securities less directly related costs.

net profit
The profit that remains after all related costs from sales revenue have been deducted. Also known as *net income*.

net profit on sales
The balance that remains after selling and other expenses that vary directly with sales have been deducted from gross profit on sales. Also known as *net trading profit*.

net profit ratio
The ratio of a firm's net profit after taxes to its net sales. One of several general measures of a company's performance.

net purchases
The cost of purchases of goods and services plus freight charges less returns and allowances and usually less cash discounts taken.

net requirements
In manufacturing procedures, the actual production or purchasing requirements for a particular item, part, subassembly, or assembly.

net sales
The dollar amount of gross sales less returns and allowances, freight charges, and cash discounts allowed. The general practice is to treat net sales as the net amount received from the customer after discount.

net ton
2,000 pounds.

net tonnage
A vessel's gross tonnage minus deductions for space occupied by crew, machinery, navigation equipment, the engine room, and fuel storage. The net tonnage is the capacity or space available for passengers and cargo.

net trading profit
See NET PROFIT ON SALES.

net weight
The weight of goods without their shipping containers. Also the weight of the contents of a freight car.

network analysis
See PERT.

net working capital
See WORKING CAPITAL.

network planning
See PERT.

net worth
The aggregate dollar amount that appears on the accounting records of the equities that represent the organization's proprietary interests; the excess of assets over liabilities to outsiders. In a corporation, net worth is the total of paid-in capital, retained earnings, and appropriated

surplus. In a sole proprietorship, it is the proprietor's account. In a partnership, it is the sum of the accounts of the partners. Also known as *net assets*.

net-worth turnover
A ratio for determining an aspect of the financial worth of an enterprise, calculated by dividing net sales by stockholders' equity.

new economics
A body of economic thought that originated with the British economist John Maynard Keynes in the 1930s and has since been modified and extended to the point where its basic analytical tools and methods are now used by practically all economists. Whereas classical economics emphasized the automatic tendency of an economy to achieve full employment equilibrium under a government policy of laissez-faire, the new economics demonstrates that an economy may be in equilibrium at any level of employment. It therefore concludes that appropriate government fiscal and monetary policies are needed to maintain full employment and steady economic growth with a minimum of inflation.

new issue
A stock or bond sold by a corporation for the first time. Proceeds may be used to retire outstanding securities of the company, to build a new plant, to purchase new equipment, or as additional working capital. Also known as *primary distribution* and *primary offering*. See SECONDARY OFFERING.

New York Clearing House Association (NYCHA)
Established in 1853 as a central clearing house for U.S. commercial banks.

New York form
See STANDARD FIRE INSURANCE POLICY.

New York Stock Exchange (NYSE)
Located on Wall Street in New York City, it provides a marketplace for the buying and selling of ownership shares of publicly held companies. Formed in 1792 by a group of merchants and auctioneers who decided to meet daily under an old buttonwood tree on Wall Street. The 24 men who were the original members of the Exchange handled the public's buy and sell orders in the new government's issues of stock and in the shares of insurance companies, Alexander Hamilton's First United

States Bank, the Bank of North America, and the Bank of New York. In 1793 they moved indoors to a newly completed coffee house at the corner of Wall Street and William Street.

New York Stock Exchange (NYSE) Index
This compilation covers the price movements of all common stocks listed on the big board. It is based on the close of the market on December 31, 1965, as 50.00 and is weighted according to the number of shares listed for each issue. The index is computed continuously by the exchange's market data system and is printed on the ticker tape each half hour of the working day. Point changes in the index are converted to dollars and cents so as to provide a meaningful measure of changes in the average price of listed stocks. The composite index is supplemented by separate indexes for four industry groups: industrials, transportation, utilities, and financials. See SHARE INDEX.

NFIB
See NATIONAL FEDERATION OF INDEPENDENT BUSINESS.

NFPA
See NATIONAL FIRE PROTECTION ASSOCIATION.

NFPCA
Initials for *National Fire Prevention and Control Administration,* an agency of the U.S. Department of Commerce.

NFTA
Initials for *National Freight Traffic Association.*

NHTSA
See NATIONAL HIGHWAY TRAFFIC SAFETY ADMINISTRATION.

NICB
Initials for *National Industrial Conference Board;* now the Conference Board.

NIDA
Initials for *National Industrial Distributors Association.*

NIH
See NATIONAL INSTITUTES OF HEALTH.

NIOSH
See NATIONAL INSTITUTE FOR OCCUPATIONAL SAFETY AND HEALTH.

NITL
See NATIONAL INDUSTRIAL TRAFFIC LEAGUE.

NLRB
See NATIONAL LABOR RELATIONS BOARD.

NMFC
Initials for *National Motor Freight Classification.*

NMFS
See NATIONAL MARINE FISHERIES SERVICE.

NNP
See NET NATIONAL PRODUCT.

no-benefit-to-payee clause
A clause added to their bills of lading by many transportation companies and agencies such as railroads and motor carrier lines. It provides that any insurance payable in connection with the property being transported shall be payable to the transporting company.

no-fault insurance
In theory, replaces the traditional method of compensating automobile accident injuries, in which the victim makes a claim directly against an individual wrongdoer or, in reality, against the wrongdoer's insurance company. Under no-fault, a claim for damages is made to the victim's own company instead of to his or her opponent's. The question of who is negligent or at fault is dropped from the legal dialog.

NOI
Initials for *not otherwise indexed,* with reference to tariff classification.

NOIBN
Initials for *not otherwise indexed by name,* with reference to tariff classification.

NOL
Initials for *net operating loss.* See OPERATING LOSS.

nolle prosequi
The discharge of a particular indictment against the accused by the court upon request of the prosecuting officer. It is neither an acquittal nor a pardon, and the accused may be indicted again and tried for the same offense.

no-load mutual fund
A type of mutual fund that does not charge sales commissions. These funds are readily identified in the lists of mutual fund quotations appearing in the press because bid and asked prices are identical.

nolo contendere
A plea of no contest or no challenge made by the accused in a criminal action. It is an implied confession of the offense as charged, virtually equivalent to a plea of guilty, and a judgment of conviction follows such a plea.

NOMA
See AMS.

nominal capital
The amount of capital represented by the par or stated value of a corporation's issued stock.

nominal partner
An individual who lends his or her name to a partnership but is not actually a partner. The value to the partnership is in the promotional value of the nominal partner's name and reputation for which the nominal partner receives a fee in payment.

nominal wage
A token wage, paid in money, for services rendered by an individual.

nomographic chart
The term *nomograph* is derived from the Greek *nomos*, law, and *grapho*, to write. The term has come to be associated with one particular type of chart that uses functional scales for the solution of numerical problems.

nonadmitted asset
See UNADMITTED ASSET.

nonarithmetic shift
See CYCLIC SHIFT.

nonassessable capital stock
Capital stock that is fully paid for by the stockholder who is not normally accountable for the liabilities of the corporation. This is the common stock ordinarily issued by U.S. corporations.

non compos mentis
Latin phrase meaning "not having mastery of one's own mind"; a person who lacks the capacity to comprehend the nature, extent, and meaning of his or her contracts or other legal obligations.

noncontrollable cost
In accounting, a cost that does not fluctuate with changes in volume of production. Also, any cost that is allocated to a unit of an enterprise but is not actually incurred by that unit. See CONTROLLABLE COST.

noncumulative dividend
A dividend on preferred stock that does not become cumulative or need not be made up at a later date, if passed (not distributed to stockholders). This may not hold in all jurisdictions, since some courts have declared that such dividends are cumulative.

noncumulative stock
A preferred stock on which the unpaid dividends do not accrue. Omitted dividends, as a rule, are gone forever. See CUMULATIVE PREFERRED STOCK and NONCUMULATIVE DIVIDEND.

nondestructive read (NDR)
In data processing, a reading of the information in a register without changing the information.

nondestructive readout (NDRO) memory
In data processing, a procedure in which the read operation does not cause the storage device to lose the stored information. Semiconductor memories are of this type. See DESTRUCTIVE READOUT (DRO) MEMORY and NONDESTRUCTIVE READ.

nonfeasance
The failure to perform an imposed duty. As distinguished from *misfeasance*, the improper performance of a duty that has been imposed by law or contract and that injures another person.

nonoperating revenue
The revenue of an enterprise that is received from sources not classified as being within the firm's regular activities.

nonprice competition
The market situation that occurs among rival sellers whose goods or services are priced comparably or identically, and whose competition

in the marketplace is generally concerned with claims of superiority in quality or service. Compare with MONOPOLISTIC COMPETITION.

nonproductive labor
An obsolete term for INDIRECT LABOR.

nonprofit corporation
See ELEEMOSYNARY CORPORATION.

nonqualified stock option
A stock option that is not eligible for capital gains tax treatment; also known as *unqualified stock option.*

nonrecurring charge
In accounting procedures, an expense or involuntary loss not likely to reoccur. If the loss is in material, it may be stated on an income statement as an income deduction.

nonrevenue receipts
In government accounting, collections that are other than earned income during a given accounting period. Examples are recovered expenditures and receipts from loans.

nonstandard material
Raw material or other goods whose quality standard differs from that appearing in a standard engineering specification.

nonstock corporation
A corporation without issued capital shares. Examples include mutual savings banks, savings and loan associations, credit unions, and religious or charitable organizations.

nonsuit
A judgment given against a plaintiff who is unable to prove his or her case or who fails to proceed with the trial after the case is at issue.

nontariff barrier
Trade-restrictive practices other than customs tariffs employed either by governments or by private firms.

NOP
Initials for *net operating profit.* See OPERATING INCOME.

no-par-value capital stock
Capital stock that does not have a specified par or nominal value.

normal curve
See NORMAL DISTRIBUTION.

normal curve of error
See NORMAL DISTRIBUTION.

normal distribution
For rapid calculation of a probability distribution, if one were to draw a histogram with all deviations from the mean depicted of equal value with positive and negative respect to the mean and then draw a curve from the lowest value through the central tendency to the highest value, the resultant curve would be symmetrical and bell-shaped. The mean value then becomes the zero reference for statistical analysis. Also known as *normal curve, normal curve of error, normal function, normal probability distribution,* and *Gaussian distribution.*

normal function
See NORMAL DISTRIBUTION.

normal probability distribution
See NORMAL DISTRIBUTION.

normal table
In statistical analysis, a tabular presentation of selected values calculated from a normal curve.

normative economics
The part of economics that is concerned with values, ethics, and opinions of what ought to be rather than of what is. Normative propositions would be: Sin is bad, unemployment is too high, inflation ought to be stopped, and other similar generalities about the economy. See POSITIVE ECONOMICS.

Norris–La Guardia Act, 1932
The act strictly limited the power of federal courts to issue a restraining order or a temporary or permanent injunction in cases involving labor disputes. It recognized the legitimate interest of a labor union and its members beyond the direct employment relationship, so that many union self-help activities became privileged activities under the law. It

outlawed the yellow-dog contract. Also known as the *anti-injunction act*. See YELLOW-DOG CONTRACT.

North American Conference of Management Consultants (NACMAC)

An association of U.S. and Canadian consultants who hold a group conference once each year for the purpose of sharing knowledge related to the functions and operations of a management consulting enterprise.

North Atlantic Treaty Organization (NATO)

A defense agreement established in 1949 among Belgium, Canada, Denmark, France, Iceland, Italy, Luxembourg, the Netherlands, Norway, Portugal, the United States, and the United Kingdom. Later joined by West Germany, Greece, and Turkey. Headquarters, originally in Paris, moved to Brussels in March 1966.

NOS

Initials for *not otherwise specified*.

notation

In data processing, the act, process, or method of representing facts or quantities by a system or set of marks, signs, figures, or characters.

note payable

A promissory note of the maker held by the payor as a liability. See NOTES PAYABLE.

note receivable

A promissory note held by the payee as an asset. See NOTES RECEIVABLE.

note register

A book in which notes receivable are recorded in chronologic order in accordance with the date received or issued.

notes payable

An account showing details of notes owed to creditors. See NOTE PAYABLE.

notes receivable

An account showing details of notes due from debtors. See NOTE RECEIVABLE.

notice account
A type of savings account that requires the depositor to give notice of his or her intent to withdraw funds. Such accounts usually receive a premium rate of interest.

notice of default
A notice filed by the owner of a trust deed with the county recorder informing that official that a borrower has defaulted and foreclosure proceedings or repossession may be started.

notice of loss
Insurance policies usually require that the insured party give written *notice of loss* to the insurance company either "immediately" or "as soon as practicable." Oral notice may not be considered legally adequate.

NPCFB
Initials for *North Pacific Coast Freight Bureau.*

NRBA
Initials for *National Radio Broadcasters Association.*

NRC
Initials for *National Research Council.* Also, see NUCLEAR REGULATORY COMMISSION.

NRDGA
See NATIONAL RETAIL MERCHANTS ASSOCIATION.

NRMA
See NATIONAL RETAIL MERCHANTS ASSOCIATION.

NSBA
See NATIONAL SMALL BUSINESS ASSOCIATION.

NSC
Initials for *navy supply center.* Also, see NATIONAL SAFETY COUNCIL.

NSLI
See NATIONAL SERVICE LIFE INSURANCE.

NTIS
See NATIONAL TECHNICAL INFORMATION SERVICE.

NTU
See NATIONAL TRADES' UNION.

Nuclear Regulatory Commission (NRC)
Created in 1973 as a spin-off of the Atomic Energy Commission, its mission is to regulate civilian nuclear safety, which basically involves the licensing of atomic power plants.

nuisance
In legal proceedings, any continuing conduct that causes annoyance, inconvenience, or damage to a person or to property. The word usually applies to any unreasonable and wrongful use of property that produces material discomfort, harm, or damage to the person or property of another. Examples are noxious fumes from a factory and noise from aircraft taking off from and approaching an airport.

null hypothesis
The assumption that any observed difference between two samples of a statistical population is purely accidental and not due to a systematic cause.

number line
In mathematics and in the preparation of graphs, a horizontal line whose points are associated with numbers. To represent whole numbers on the number line, choose two distinct points on the line. Label the point on the left *0* and that on the right *1*. Using the interval between these points as a unit of measure and beginning at the point associated with *1*, locate points equally spaced along the line. Label each point from left to right with successive whole numbers. The number associated with a point is called the *coordinate of the point*. The point associated with a number is called a *graph of the number*. The number line may be used to visualize the addition of whole numbers. For example, to add *3* to *4*, start at *0* and move to the right 4 units and then move to the right 3 more units, which locates the point whose coordinate is *4 + 3*.

NWPMA
Initials for *National Wooden Pallet Manufacturers Association*.

NYCHA
See NEW YORK CLEARING HOUSE ASSOCIATION.

NYSE
See NEW YORK STOCK EXCHANGE.

NYSE Index
See NEW YORK STOCK EXCHANGE (NYSE) INDEX.

OAPEC
See ORGANIZATION OF ARAB PETROLEUM EXPORTING COUNTRIES.

OAS
See ORGANIZATION OF AMERICAN STATES.

OASDI
Initials for *old-age, survivors, and disability insurance.* See SOCIAL SECURITY ACT.

OASI
Initials for *old-age and survivors insurance.*

objection to title
In legal proceedings, a disapproval or opposition to a title; a fault or flaw in a title requiring correction or clarification.

objective function
In manufacturing procedures, the function that is to be optimized in a linear or nonlinear programming problem.

objective value
In accounting procedures, a value for an asset established by an independent appraisal made by an agent deemed to be free of bias or

prejudice, or established by market quotation for a similar quantity, quality, condition, and usefulness.

object program
In data processing, the output of an automatic coding system. Often the object program is a machine language program ready for execution, but it may well be in an intermediate language. Also known as *target program* and *object routine*.

object routine
See OBJECT PROGRAM.

obligated material
See RESERVED MATERIAL.

OBM
See OPERATION BUSINESS MAINSTREAM.

OCA
See OFFICE OF CONSUMER AFFAIRS and OFFICE OF THE CONSUMER AVOCATE.

OCAS
See ORGANIZATION OF CENTRAL AMERICAN STATES.

OCAWI
Initials for *Oil, Chemical & Atomic Workers International*. A labor union affiliated with the AFL-CIO.

Occam's razor
A principle in argumentation developed by William of Occam, a fourteenth-century English monk, and used by economists; popularized by Sir John Hicks of Oxford University in the 1940s. The principle says that *entia non sunt multiplicanda* ("entities are not to be multiplied"); that is, when there is more than one possible explanation of a phenomenon, the simplest is usually to be preferred to those that are more complex. William of Occam dissected every question *as with a razor;* his philosophy prepared the way for the scientific method of Francis Bacon. Also spelled *Ockham's razor*.

occupancy rate
The ratio of apartment units or offices rented as compared with the total number contained within the building, or the ratio of leased to total space, expressed as a percentage.

Occupational Safety and Health Administration (OSHA)
An agency of the Department of Labor that sets and enforces job safety and health standards for workers, trains employers and employees in proper occupational safety and health practices, and continuously conducts regional and field investigations.

Occupational Safety and Health Review Commission (OSHRC)
Although the commission is not an integral part of the Occupational Safety and Health Administration (OSHA), the three OSHRC commissioners are appointed by the president and have the authority to review OSHA decisions when these are challenged by businesses affected by them.

OCD
See OFFICE OF CHILD DEVELOPMENT.

ocean bill of lading
See AFFREIGHTMENT.

ocean marine insurance
The oldest form of commercial insurance; it may be obtained in either domestic or foreign ports. Lloyd's of London has gained fame as an ocean marine insurer. See INLAND MARINE INSURANCE.

Ockham's razor
See OCCAM'S RAZOR.

OCP
See OWNERS' OR CONTRACTORS' PROTECTIVE LIABILITY INSURANCE.

OCR
See OPTICAL CHARACTER READING. Also, see OFFICE OF CIVIL RIGHTS.

OCTV
See OPEN-CIRCUIT TELEVISION.

OD
See ORGANIZATIONAL DEVELOPMENT.

ODD
See OFFICE FOR DEVELOPMENTAL DISABILITIES.

odd-even check
See PARITY CHECK.

odd lot
In the securities market, an amount of stock that is less than the established 100-share or 10-share unit of trading; from one to 99 shares for the great majority of issues, from one to 9 for the so-called inactive stocks. See ROUND LOT.

odd-lot dealer
A member firm of the New York Stock Exchange that buys and sells odd lots of stocks: one to 9 shares in the case of those traded in 10-share units, and one to 99 shares for those traded in 100-share units. The odd-lot dealer's customers are commission brokers acting on behalf of their customers.

odd parity system
See PARITY BIT.

ODECA
Initials for *Organización de Estados Centrales Americanos*. See ORGANIZATION OF CENTRAL AMERICAN STATES.

OECD
See ORGANIZATION FOR ECONOMIC COOPERATION AND DEVELOPMENT.

OEEC
See ORGANIZATION FOR EUROPEAN ECONOMIC COOPERATION.

OEM
Abbreviation for *original equipment manufacturer*.

OEO
See OFFICE OF ECONOMIC OPPORTUNITY.

OFCCP
See OFFICE OF FEDERAL CONTRACT COMPLIANCE PROGRAMS.

off-board transaction
An over-the-counter transaction in unlisted securities, or a transaction involving listed shares that was not executed on a national securities exchange. See OVER-THE-COUNTER MARKET.

offene Handelsgesellschaft (OHG)
A general partnership under the law of the Federal Republic of Germany.

offer
The price named for services, goods, or securities that are ready to be sold. The price named by one proposing to buy services, goods, or securities. See BID.

Office and Professional Employees International Union
A white-collar trade union in the United States and Canada.

Office for Developmental Disabilities (ODD)
A unit of the Office of Human Development of HEW, ODD assists state and local public agencies and private nonprofit organizations serving persons who have a disability resulting from mental retardation, cerebral palsy, epilepsy, autism, or severe dyslexia that originates before age 18 and is a substantial handicap.

Office of Child Development (OCD)
A unit of the Office of Human Development of the Department of Health, Education and Welfare, OCD operates programs such as Head Start and the National Center on Child Abuse. It serves as a point of coordination for federal programs for children and families and acts as an advocate for the children of the nation.

Office of Civil Rights (OCR)
An agency of the Department of Health, Education and Welfare, OCR is responsible for administering and enforcing departmental policies that prohibit discrimination with regard to race, color, national origin, religion, mental and physical handicap, and sex under Title VI of the Civil Rights Act, 1964; Executive Order 11246, as amended; Title IX of the Education Amendments of 1972; Sections 799A and 845 of the Public Health Service Act; Section 504 of the Rehabilitation Act of 1973; Section 407 of the Drug Abuse Office and Treatment Act of 1972; and Section 321 of the Comprehensive Alcohol Abuse and Alcoholism Prevention, Treatment and Rehabilitation Act of 1970.

Office of Consumer Affairs (OCA)
An agency of the Department of Health, Education and Welfare (HEW), OCA is headed by a director who is also the special assistant to the president for consumer affairs, advises the president and the secretary of HEW on matters of consumer interest, coordinates all

federal activities in the consumer field, and seeks ways to aid and protect the consumer.

Also, a unit of the U.S. Department of Transportation (DOT). Its function is to determine consumer needs and concerns for all forms of transportation, to inject these findings into the policy-making and decision-making processes throughout DOT, and to provide information to consumers that will enable them to become more knowledgeable buyers and users of transportation.

Office of Economic Opportunity (OEO)

Established within the Executive Office of the President by an act promulgated on August 20, 1964. On July 6, 1973, all OEO programs except three were transferred by administrative action to the Department of Health, Education and Welfare, the Department of Labor, and the Department of Housing and Urban Development. The three remaining programs—the Community Action Program, the Economic Development Program, and the Legal Services Program—were transferred to the Community Services Administration (CSA) by an act promulgated on January 4, 1975. The CSA was renamed the Public Services Administration on November 3, 1976, and was transferred to the Office of the Assistant Secretary for Human Development of the Department of Health, Education and Welfare by the secretary's reorganization of March 8, 1977.

Office of Federal Contract Compliance Programs (OFCCP)

Created in 1962 as a unit of the Department of Labor, this office administers prohibitions against discrimination by race or sex on the part of employers holding federal contracts.

Office of Human Development (OHD)

An agency of the Department of Health, Education and Welfare (HEW), OHD organizes HEW's planning and resources for certain groups of "vulnerable" Americans with special needs: children and youth, the aged, physically and mentally disabled persons, Native Americans, and persons living in rural areas. Programs serving these groups have been consolidated into 13 OHD units, six of which are chartered to grant funds to assist certain groups of Americans.

Office of Management and Budget (OMB)

An executive agency of the federal government responsible for collating and preparing the federal budget and for advising on the budgetary management of federal programs.

Office of Minority Business Enterprise (OMBE)

An agency of the Department of Commerce, OMBE provides funds for local business development organizations (BDOs) to help small businesses iron out operating problems and find outside money when they need it. OMBE was established in 1969. See BUSINESS DEVELOPMENT ORGANIZATIONS.

Office of Native American Programs (ONAP)

A unit of the Office of Human Development of the Department of Health, Education and Welfare (HEW), ONAP assists American Indians, Alaskan Natives, and Native Hawaiians to attain social and economic self-sufficiency through a policy of self-determination. It also serves as the principal adviser to the secretary of HEW on matters relating to departmental programs and activities concerning Native Americans.

Office of the Consumer Advocate (OCA)

A unit of the Civil Aeronautics Board (CAB), OCA handles consumer complaints against airlines, attempts to resolve consumer problems by contact with the companies involved, publishes monthly statistical reports detailing complaints received by the office, and participates in selected CAB proceedings as an advocate of air transportation consumers.

Office of Youth Development (OYD)

A unit of the Office of Human Development of the Department of Health, Education and Welfare, OYD assists states, localities, and private nonprofit organizations that are providing temporary shelter care and counseling services to youth under age 18.

officer

In business management, any principal executive of a corporation to whom authority has been delegated by the board of directors or by the bylaws of a corporation.

off-license shop

See PACKAGE STORE.

off-line system

In data processing, a system and its peripheral devices in which operation of the peripheral equipment is not under the control of the central processing unit but requires human operation. See ON-LINE SYSTEM.

offset statement
A report by the owner of a property or the owner of a lien against a property, which sets forth the present status of liens against that property.

offsetting error
An error in bookkeeping that eliminates or reduces the effect of another erroneous entry.

off the books
The payment of wages for services performed but not recorded in the *books* or on the payroll records of the employer. Paying an employee *off the books* may be illegal, depending on rules and regulations pertaining to the number of employees actually working for the employer. The practice is sometimes followed by a company to reduce its costs for fringe benefits, such as Social Security, unemployment insurance, and medical and other types of insurance that may be required by local, state, and federal regulations. Benefits to the employee are evasion of income taxes and increased purchasing power or disposable income; but the practice is clearly illegal for the employee.

ogive
In statistical analysis, a cumulative frequency polygon, with the cumulative frequencies shown on the vertical axis. See FREQUENCY POLYGON.

OHD
See OFFICE OF HUMAN DEVELOPMENT.

OHG
See OFFENE HANDELSGESELLSCHAFT.

oil and gas lease
A deed by which a landowner grants another party the right to extract oil and gas from the leased property.

OJT
See ON-THE-JOB TRAINING.

OL&T
Initials for *owners, landlords, and tenants.* See LIABILITY INSURANCE.

old-age, survivors, and disability insurance (OASDI)
See SOCIAL SECURITY ACT.

oligopoly
A market situation in which sellers are so few that the supply offered by any one of them materially affects the market price. Thus, each company is able to measure with a high degree of accuracy the effect its price and production decisions will have on the courses of action its competitors might follow. A *perfect* or *pure* oligopoly is one in which the products of the sellers are homogeneous or undifferentiated, such as the output of copper, cement, and steel producers. Differentiated products such as automobiles, soap, detergents, and household appliances are part of an *imperfect* oligopoly. See OLIGOPSONY.

oligopsony
A market condition wherein there are few buyers for the output of several sellers. See OLIGOPOLY.

OMB
See OFFICE OF MANAGEMENT AND BUDGET.

OMBE
See OFFICE OF MINORITY BUSINESS ENTERPRISE.

ombudsman
An official of a government who is responsible for receiving and answering complaints and queries related to administrative practices and for making recommendations for corrective measures where indicated. In the U.S. government, this function is filled to some degree by the comptroller general.

OMR
See OPTICAL MARK RECOGNITION.

ON
See ORDER-NOTIFY.

on account
Partial clearing of a monetary obligation, as in *payment on account*. Also, in credit terminology, the expectation that payment is to be made at a date later than the delivery date, as in *purchased on account*.

ONAP
See OFFICE OF NATIVE AMERICAN PROGRAMS.

on consignment
Transmitted to another for the purpose of sale, display, demonstration, or similar use without actual transfer of title, as in merchandise delivered on consignment.

oncost
British term for INDIRECT COST or OVERHEAD.

on hand
Owned or possessed. For example, with reference to a balance-sheet item such as inventory on hand, the value listed is for items owned by and in possession of the entrepreneur.

on-hand quantity
The quantity in stock and available for use in production.

on-line system
In data processing, a system and its peripheral devices in which operation of the peripheral equipment is under the control of the central processing unit. See OFF-LINE SYSTEM.

on order
In manufacturing, the total of all outstanding replenishment orders. For example, the on-order balance increases whenever a new order is released and decreases whenever an order is canceled. The releases and cancellations may be for the full quantity ordered or for partial quantities. Also, there may be receipts that do not affect the on-order balance, such as customer returns, adjustments after physical inventory counts, and production surpluses.

on-the-job training (OJT)
The training of employees in skills by the process of actually assigning them the task or job. During OJT, the trainee is usually under the guidance and instruction of an experienced worker, a supervisor, or a foreman.

OPEC
See ORGANIZATION OF PETROLEUM EXPORTING COUNTRIES.

OPEIU
See OFFICE AND PROFESSIONAL EMPLOYEES INTERNATIONAL UNION.

open account
An account covering the unsecured amount owed by a debtor to a creditor who has delivered services or goods without requiring payment either in advance or on delivery. Also, any account that has not been closed out.

open-circuit television (OCTV)
The technique of transmitting television signals to an unrestricted audience. Typical home TV sets and TV stations that broadcast regularly scheduled programs constitute open-circuit television. See CLOSED-CIRCUIT TELEVISION.

open-end fund
See INVESTMENT TRUST.

open-end investment company
An investment company that can increase its size through the sale of additional stock. See INVESTMENT TRUST.

open-end investment trust
See INVESTMENT TRUST.

open-end mortgage
A mortgage agreement that permits the mortgagor to borrow additional money after the loan has been reduced, without requiring that the mortgage agreement be rewritten. Opposite of CLOSED-END MORTGAGE.

opening balance
The balance of an account at the beginning of a specific accounting period, usually a month or a year.

open-market operations
An activity of the Federal Reserve intended to provide a basis for maintaining geographic equilibrium in the interest rate and control of the money supply. Through its Open Market Committee the Federal Reserve purchases government securities from and sells them to member banks. The open-market operations enable Federal Reserve banks in one part of the country to buy and sell eligible paper securities in other sections of the country. Thus money may be transferred from areas of plenty to areas of scarcity, which results in a national equilibrium of the interest rate. Open-market operations are used extensively by the Federal Reserve to control the money supply and, thereby, the availability of credit.

open mortgage
A mortgage that can be paid off before maturity without penalty or payment of a surcharge.

open order
In securities trading, an order to buy or sell that remains in effect until it is either executed or canceled. Also known as a *good-till-canceled* or *GTC* order.

open policy
In the insurance of property, a policy in which the amount recoverable, up to the face value of the policy contract, is ascertained after a loss has occurred. Fire insurance is the most common example of an *open policy*. A fire insurance contract may be written for a maximum amount of $25,000, for example, but the specific amount recovered as a result of loss through fire and paid to the insured party can be determined only after the loss has occurred.

open shop
In data processing, a computer facility in which computer programming, coding, and operating may be performed by any qualified employee of the organization, not merely by the personnel of the computer center, and in which the programmer may assist in, or oversee, the running of his or her program on the computer.

Also, in industrial relations, a business firm in which the employees are not required to belong to a union. The employer is free to hire either union or nonunion members. See CLOSED SHOP.

open-to-buy
In retailing operations, the amount of money or the quantity of goods to which a firm is limited in its purchases from vendors; the portion of a budgetary allotment remaining available for such purchases.

open-to-buy reports
A report of relationships between inventory and sales, used to calculate open-to-buy amounts or quantities.

operand
In data processing, a quantity entering or arising in an instruction. It may be an argument, a result, a parameter, or an indication of the location of the next instruction, as opposed to the operation code or symbol itself. It may be the address portion of an instruction.

operating account
A revenue and expense account.

operating budget
A budget that applies to recurrent revenue and expense items. See CAPITAL BUDGET.

operating company
A business firm that is actively conducting transactions with individuals or outside firms.

operating cost
An expense incurred in the conduct of the principal activities of the enterprise. Also known as *operating expense*.

operating cycle
The period of time between the purchase of inventory and its conversion to cash receipts.

operating expense
See OPERATING COST.

operating income
The excess of the revenues of a business firm over the expenses incurred in producing the revenue. Income derived from sources other than those that pertain to the regular activities of the firm is excluded, and the calculation is made before income deductions. Also known as *operating profit*. See OPERATING RESULTS.

operating loss
The difference between revenues derived from regular sources and the costs incurred in generating such revenue, when the costs exceed the revenues received. See OPERATING INCOME.

operating profit
See OPERATING INCOME.

operating profit ratio
Ratio of a firm's operating profit to its net sales.

operating ratio
Any comparison of an item from a financial statement with net sales; in calculations, the dollar value for net sales is placed in the denominator.

operating results
Net income or net loss. See OPERATING INCOME.

operating revenue
The gross sales of goods and services, less returns and allowances and cash discounts, together with gross amounts received from any other regular source of income; net revenue from sales.

operating statement
A detailed income statement that displays financial operations over a stated accounting period.

operational research
See OPERATIONS RESEARCH.

Operation Business Mainstream (OBM)
Operated since the late 1960s in concert with Economic Opportunity Loan, this program of the Small Business Administration makes term loans available to minority groups and to economically disadvantaged and physically handicapped entrepreneurs who lack the minimum capital needed to obtain business loads.

operation process chart
A chart presented by the American Society of Mechanical Engineers' Standard 101 as a graphic representation of the points at which materials are introduced into the process, and of the sequence of all operations and inspections except those involved in materials handling. It includes information considered desirable for analysis, such as time required and location.

operation sheets
Precise specifications and descriptions of manufacturing methods telling in detail how an operation is to be performed. Compared with drawings that specify what part or product is to be manufactured, route and operation sheets specify how to manufacture it. See ROUTE SHEETS and METHODS MANUAL.

operations research (OR)
Developed during World War II, the application of scientific methods of analysis, including mathematical models, to process complex information and arrive at decisions that offer a maximum probability for achieving organizational objectives. The British term for the procedure is OPERATIONAL RESEARCH.

operations sequence
The sequential steps a given assembly or part should follow as it flows through the plant, as recommended by manufacturing engineering.

OPIC
See OVERSEAS PRIVATE INVESTMENT CORPORATION.

opinion
In accounting procedures, the written statement of an auditor with respect to the fairness of the data presented by a corporation in its report of financial results, and with respect to the corporation's use of generally accepted accounting principles in recording transactions and preparing the report.

Opitz classification
In manufacturing, a German classification and coding system for tools and components based on shapes and significant features. A 5-digit code is used. A 4-digit supplementary code provides information on dimensions, material, form, and accuracy.

opportunity cost
The return on capital that might have resulted if the capital had been used for some purpose other than the one to which it had actually been put. The term is used to indicate the best alternative use of capital.

optical character reading or **optical character recognition (OCR)**
A system for optically reading data for entry into an automatic data processing system.

optical mark recognition (OMR)
Same as OPTICAL CHARACTER RECOGNITION.

optical maser
See LASER and MASER.

optimize
To rearrange the instructions of data stored in a computer so that a minimum number of time-consuming jumps or transfers are required to run a program.

optimum order quantity
See ECONOMIC ORDER QUANTITY.

option
In securities trading, the right to buy or sell specific securities or properties at a specified price within a specified time. In business transactions, the legal right to buy or sell goods, property, or services at a specified price within an agreed-on period of time.

optional dividend
A dividend payable in more than one form, such as cash and capital stock, at the election of the individual shareholder.

option financing
The arrangement under which an individual with a stock option pays for the shares over a period of time. Financing provisions may range from a personal bank loan negotiated by the individual, at times with the unofficial assistance of the company, to low- or no-interest loans made available or cosigned by the company.

OR
See OPERATIONS RESEARCH.

oral contract
A contract that is not in writing or that is not signed by the parties; within the statute of frauds, an oral contract is a real and existing contract that lacks only the formal requirement of a memorandum to render it enforceable in litigation.

order
See INSTRUCTION.

order-notify (ON)
A bill of lading term; to request surrender of the original bill of lading before the freight is delivered. Order-notify documents are usually handled through a bank.

order point
A level of inventory for a specific item at which it must be reordered. The order point is calculated on the basis of estimated demand, replenishment lead time, and a safety stock to cover forecast errors.

ordinal number
A number designating the place occupied by an item in an ordered series of units, such as first, second, third, and so on.

ordinance
The legislative act of a municipality; a law of a city; an authoritative decree or direction promulgated by a government.

ordinary annuity
An annuity that is payable at the end of each period of specified time.

ordinary depreciation
Decrease in or loss of the usefulness of a fixed asset as a result of normal wear, tear, and aging and the normal action of the elements.

ordinary interest
Simple interest that is based on a year of 360 days, as distinguished from exact interest and a base of 365 days. The ratio of ordinary interest to exact interest is 1.0138; the reciprocal is 0.9863878. See EXACT INTEREST.

ordinary life insurance
A contract between an individual and an insurer, usually a company regulated by state law. The insurance is usually offered in units of $1,000. The four most common types of ordinary life insurance are (1) whole life, or straight life, (2) limited payment, (3) endowment life, and (4) term life.

ordinary negligence
See NEGLIGENCE and DUE CARE.

ordinary policy
A type of insurance policy or contract that covers property only while the property remains at the place or location mentioned in the contract. See FLOATER POLICY.

ordinary shares
British term for COMMON STOCK.

organizational development (OD)
A planned process for changing a business system. Its two essential phases are diagnosis and intervention. Diagnosis begins with a comprehensive description of the organization as it presently exists; the procedures, structures, attitudes, and values of individual and group members; and the elements of interpersonal and intergroup behavior. Interventions are then designed and undertaken to facilitate the efforts

of members of the organization in solving problems. OD does not provide solutions but works to increase the capacity of members of the organization to solve their problems and bring about the dynamics of the organization.

organization expense
A liability incurred in establishing an organization, such as the legal and accounting fees for incorporation and promotional costs created by the issuance of capital stock.

Organization for Economic Cooperation and Development (OECD)
Set up in 1961 as successor to the Organization for European Economic Cooperation to promote economic cooperation and development and world trade. The founder member states were Austria, Belgium, Canada, Denmark, France, the Federal Republic of Germany, Greece, Iceland, Ireland, Italy, Luxembourg, the Netherlands, Norway, Portugal, Spain, Sweden, Switzerland, Turkey, the United Kingdom, and the United States.

Organization for European Economic Cooperation (OEEC)
Established in 1948 under the Marshall Plan and operated until it was succeeded by the Organization for Economic Cooperation and Development in 1961.

Organization of American States (OAS)
Set up in 1948 to promote cooperation among member states. OAS members include Argentina, Barbados, Bolivia, Brazil, Chile, Colombia, Costa Rica, Dominican Republic, Ecuador, El Salvador, Guatemala, Haiti, Honduras, Jamaica, Mexico, Nicaragua, Panama, Paraguay, Peru, Trinidad and Tobago, Uruguay, the United States, and Venezuela. Canada participates as an observer.

Organization of Arab Petroleum Exporting Countries (OAPEC)
Formed in 1968 to promote the joint interests of its members, Abu Dhabi, Algeria, Bahrein, Dubai, Egypt, Kuwait, Libyan Arab Republic, Qatar, Saudi Arabia, and Syria.

Organization of Central American States (OCAS or ODECA)
Set up in 1951 to promote cooperation and economic development among its member states, which include Costa Rica, El Salvador, Guatemala, Honduras, and Nicaragua.

Organization of Petroleum Exporting Countries (OPEC)
Set up in 1960; a union of countries in the Mideast, Africa, and South America who are leading exporters of petroleum. OPEC members are Algeria, Ecuador, Gabon, Indonesia, Iran, Iraq, Kuwait, Libyan Arab Republic, Nigeria, Qatar, Saudi Arabia, United Arab Emirates, and Venezuela.

organization theory
Studies of group and individual behavior, motivations, influences, and conflicts to determine more effective means of organization management and control.

or gate
In data processing, an electronic gate or mechanical device that implements the logical OR operator. An output signal occurs whenever there are one or more inputs on a multichannel input.

original capital
The amount of capital paid into an enterprise at the time of organization or incorporation.

original entry
An accounting entry that records a transaction in a book of original entry. It may include full information concerning the transaction or refer to supporting vouchers or memoranda that contain the data on which the entry is based.

origin period
In statistical analysis, the period of time within a time series selected as the base period.

Osgood scales
A system of multiple-choice or precoded questions developed in the United States by William F. Osgood (1864–1943), originally for use in market research interviews. The subject chooses an answer to a question from among a group of prepared answers.

OSHA
See OCCUPATIONAL SAFETY AND HEALTH ADMINISTRATION.

OSHRC
See OCCUPATIONAL SAFETY AND HEALTH REVIEW COMMISSION.

Ostmark
See DDR-MARK.

OTC market
See OVER-THE-COUNTER MARKET.

other assets
On a balance sheet, minor assets not classifiable under other usual headings; generally a small part of the total assets.

other deductions
In accounting procedures, a grouping of minor costs shown as a single total in order to minimize the presentation of unimportant detail.

other liabilities
On a balance sheet, minor liabilities not classifiable under other usual headings; generally a small part of total liabilities.

other revenue
In accounting, income from minor sources or sources that are not the principal activity of the business. Examples include interest on customers' notes, installment accounts, and overdue accounts; dividends and interest from minor investments; and incidental profits from the disposal of assets other than inventory.

O'Toole's commentary on Murphy's law
A satirical principle holding that Murphy was an optimist. See MURPHY'S LAW.

out-cycle work
Work performed by an operator while a machine is at rest. See IN-CYCLE WORK.

Outer Continental Shelf Lands Act (1953)
An act of Congress that covers oil and gas leasing in federal offshore waters.

outlay cost
The cost represented by an expenditure of cash or a transfer of property.

out-of-pocket cost
An expense incurred by an individual, paid for in cash not charged to the individual's personal account, for which reimbursements may be sought.

output device
The part of a data processing machine that translates the electrical impulses representing data processed by the machine into permanent results, such as printed forms, punched cards, and magnetic writing on tape.

outstanding
Uncollected or unpaid, as applied to an account or a note receivable. Also, publicly issued and sold, as applied to certificates representing shares of capital stock in the hands of the public.

overbought
Characterized by prices considered too high, as in reference to a security that has had a sharp rise or to the securities market as a whole after a period of vigorous buying. See OVERSOLD.

overcharge
A charge on a freight bill based on an error in rate, weight, or rating, resulting in excessive freight charges.

overdraft
The amount by which any type of demand payment exceeds the amount of credit against which it is drawn.

overflowed land
In real estate, land that is flooded from time to time and hence needs special improvements in order to be utilized.

over freight
Freight in possession of a carrier, without waybill or identifying markings.

overhead
In doing business, the cost that cannot be identified as a direct cost of providing a product or a service. See DIRECT COST and INDIRECT COST.

overhead rate
In accounting procedures, a standard rate at which overhead is allocated.

overinvestment theory
A theory of business cycles holding that economic fluctuations are caused by too much investment in the economy as business firms try to anticipate the rise in demands during an upswing, and by sharp cutbacks in investment during a downswing when business firms realize they expanded too much in the preceding prosperity.

overlapped schedule
In manufacturing, the overlapping of several successive operations, whereby completed units of a job at a work center are forwarded to and processed at one or more succeeding work centers before the remaining pieces are finished and forwarded for further processing. Also known as *lap phasing* and *telescoping*. See GAPPED SCHEDULE.

overrejected style
In organizational behavior, the basic style a manager uses far less frequently than the average manager. See DOMINANT STYLE and SUPPORTING STYLE.

overrun
The quantity manufactured or received from a manufacturer that is in excess of the quantity ordered.

Overseas Private Investment Corporation (OPIC)
Formally organized in 1971 as an arm of the Agency for International Development (AID), whose purpose is to stimulate private capital investment in the developing nations. The corporation offers investors insurance against currency inconvertibility, expropriation, and damage from war, insurrection, and revolution. It also makes direct loans through its Direct Investment Fund for projects too small to interest large institutional lenders, or makes loans too short for institutional lending but too long for commercial banks. It offers other incentives to U.S. investors and construction firms to stimulate aid to developing nations.

oversold
Characterized by prices considered too low, as when a single security or a securities market has declined to an unreasonable level. See OVERBOUGHT.

overt act
In legal procedures, any conduct openly manifested as an intention to perform in a manner that will lead to a desired result.

over-the-counter (OTC) market
A market for securities made up of securities dealers who may or may not be members of a securities exchange. It is a market mainly made over the telephone. Thousands of companies have insufficient shares outstanding, stockholders, or earnings to enable successful application for listing on the New York Stock Exchange. Securities of these companies are traded in the OTC market between dealers who act either as principals or as brokers for customers. It is the principal market for U.S. government and municipal bonds and stocks of banks and insurance companies. See NATIONAL ASSOCIATION OF SECURITIES DEALERS, INC. and OFF-BOARD TRANSACTION.

Owen, Robert (1771–1858)
A highly successful Welsh manufacturer credited with having given significant inspiration to the British socialist movement. He reduced hours and raised wages among his thousands of employees, built model housing, installed free education, and placed in the schools all children under ten, whom he would no longer employ. He opened a company store to make food and clothing available at low prices. Fines for spoiled work were abandoned. Recreation was provided and insurance funds were established. Despite the worldwide attention his practices gained, industry as a whole did not follow his example. The most famous of the ''Owenite'' communities he founded was the one at New Harmony, Indiana (1825–1828). See UTOPIAN SOCIALISM.

owners', landlords', and tenants' (OL&T) public liability insurance
See LIABILITY INSURANCE.

owners' or contractors' protective (OCP) liability insurance
Not a direct coverage for the acts of the insured party, but a contingent coverage for the acts of others. Sometimes referred to as a *defense coverage*, it is often purchased because of the insurance company's promise to defend the insured party in court against lawsuits. OCP insurance may be written in connection with an owners', landlords', and tenants' (OL&T) or a manufacturers' and contractors' (M&C) policy.

OYD
See OFFICE OF YOUTH DEVELOPMENT.

paanga
The basic unit of currency in Tonga.

PABST
Acronym for *primary adhesively bonded structure technology,* a bonding method used in the manufacture of aluminum panels.

pacer
A fast worker sometimes used by management to set the pace for other workers in a factory, or to establish piecework rates. See WHIP.

Pacific standard time (PST)
Local time of the seventh time zone west of Greenwich. This zone extends from the panhandle of Alaska southward and includes the Pacific coastal region of the United States. Also known as *Pacific time.*

Pacific Stock Exchange
A major U.S. stock exchange based in San Francisco and Los Angeles, California.

Pacific time (PT)
See PACIFIC STANDARD TIME.

package car
A freight car containing two or more less-than-carload shipments that a railroad dispatches from an original point to a principal break-bulk point to improve service.

package freight
Freight shipped in less-than-carload lots and billed by the piece.

package mortgage
A popular form of mortgage used with new residential sales in which the debt includes the cost of certain mechanical or electrical equipment.

package store
In the United States, a store that sells sealed bottles of alcoholic beverages for consumption off the premises. In the United Kingdom, such a store is called an *off-license shop*.

packing density
In data processing, the number of units of useful information contained within a given linear dimension, usually expressed in units per inch; for example, the number of binary digit magnetic pulses or number of characters stored on magnetic tape or a drum, per linear inch, per track.

packing list
A statement prepared by the shipper and generally not required by the carrier to show particulars about the merchandise in the shipment. Generally, the packing list is affixed to the exterior of the shipping container to aid handlers and consignees to identify packages and verify the contents.

paid-in capital
The total amount of cash, property, and services contributed to a corporation by its stockholders.

paid-in surplus
See CAPITAL SURPLUS.

pair-or-set clause
In insurance coverage, applicable to items used in pairs or sets. The purpose is to make it clear that, even though the pair or set may be relatively valueless if one of the articles in it is lost, the company will not pay for a total loss.

P&I policy
See PROTECTION AND INDEMNITY POLICY.

P&L statement
See PROFIT-AND-LOSS STATEMENT.

panic
In economics, a widespread fear, uncertainty, and insecurity concerning the financial stability of a country. Historically, a panic results in efforts by large segments of the populace to quickly convert assets, especially securities, into cash, in runs on banks by depositors, and in the unwillingness of investors to engage in new enterprises. In the United States, federal insurance of deposits and stringent regulation of the securities markets have placed controls on the elements that have contributed to business panics in the past.

paper
In accounting procedures, a written or printed piece of evidence of short-term indebtedness.

paper gold
See SPECIAL DRAWING RIGHTS.

paper money
Paper currency in the form of Federal Reserve notes, issued by Federal Reserve Banks with the authorization of Congress. There are a few minor types of paper money in existence in the United States, most of which are being retired from use in the interest of a more uniform currency. These minor types of paper money are collectively called Treasury currency, since, at one time or another, they were directly issued by the Treasury. The coin and paper money components of the U.S. money supply are frequently lumped together and simply labeled currency.

paper profit
An unrealized profit on a security that has not been sold by its owner. Although the market value of a security may have increased over the purchase price, such paper profits become realized profits only when the security is sold.

paper tape
A method of data storage in the form of a continuous strip of paper in which holes are punched to represent the data.

par
In the case of common stock, the dollar value assigned to a share by the company's charter. Par may also be used to compute the dollar amount of the common shares on the balance sheet. It has little significance as far as market value of common stock is concerned; many companies

issue no-par stock but give a stated per share value on the balance sheet. At one time, par was intended to represent the value of the original investment behind each share in cash, goods, or services. In the case of preferred shares and bonds, however, par is important. It often signifies the dollar value on which dividends on preferred stock and interest on bonds are calculated.

paradox of thrift
The demonstrated proposition that an increase in saving may be desirable for an individual family, but for an entire economy it will lead to a reduction in income, employment, and output if it is not offset by an increase in investment. The concept was introduced by Bernard de Mandeville in *Fable of the Bees* (1714) and was later applied in the writings of the classical economists.

paradox of value
The phenomenon that a good having utility does not necessarily have economic value, and a good having economic value is not necessarily useful. The crucial factor in determining value is scarcity of a good relative to the desire for it; this is the basis of economic value.

parallel access
In computers, the means of obtaining information from or placing information into storage where the time required for such access depends on the simultaneous transfer of all elements of a word from a given storage location. Also known as *simultaneous access*. See RANDOM ACCESS and SERIAL ACCESS.

parallel computer
A computer in which the digits or data lines are handled concurrently by separate units of the computer. See SERIAL COMPUTER.

parallel transfer
In data processing, a method of data transfer in which the characters of an element of information are transferred simultaneously over a set of paths. See SERIAL TRANSFER.

paramount title
A title to real property that is superior to all others.

parcel post insurance
Most insurance policies exclude coverage for parcel post shipments because the post office is not a common carrier and cannot be sued for

loss of a parcel post package. Parcel post insurance may be obtained from the post office on an all-risk basis with protection against all external causes of loss, including nondelivery.

parent company
A company that controls the finances and operations of subsidiary companies. If the controlling company does not have a trade or business of its own, it is known as a *holding company* or *controlling company*.

Pareto, Vilfredo (1848–1923)
Engineer and economist. Studied mathematics and physics at the University of Turin and became an engineer. He subsequently taught applied economics and sociology at the University of Lausanne, Switzerland. After mathematically analyzing income data from many countries, he formulated *Pareto's law,* which states that, regardless of social or political institutions, income distribution trends have been and will remain the same; not generally accepted as a "law." Pareto also expanded the theory of general equilibrium and developed the indifference curve through which he tried to determine consumer demand. See NEOCLASSICAL ECONOMICS.

pari materia
Latin for "related to the same matter." Statutes and convenants concerned with the same subject matter are said to be in *pari materia*.

Paris Treaty
See TREATY OF PARIS.

parity
A ratio between prices received by farmers and prices paid to them in some prior, base period. The Agricultural Adjustment Act of 1933 established the concept of parity as a cornerstone of the agricultural policy of the United States. The rationale of the parity concept can be envisioned in both real and money terms. In real terms, parity conveys the concept that year after year for a given output of farm products a farmer should be able to acquire a given total amount of goods and services. A given real output should always result in the same disposable income. In money terms, the relationship between the prices received by farmers for their output and the prices they must pay for goods and services should remain constant.

parity bit
In data processing, a check bit that indicates whether the total number of binary 1 digits in a character or word is odd or even. If a 1 parity bit indicates an odd number of 1 digits, then a 0 bit indicates an even number of them. If the total number of 1 bits, including the parity bit, is always even, the system is called an *even parity system*. In an *odd parity system* the total number of 1 bits, including the parity bit, is always odd.

parity check
In data processing, a summation check in which the binary digits in a character or word are added and the sum checked against a single, previously computed parity digit. Also known as *odd-even check*. See DIGIT CHECK.

parity digit
See PARITY CHECK.

parity of authority
The management principle holding that a superior within an organization has the legal and moral right to issue orders to his or her subordinates. See UNITY OF COMMAND and PARITY OF RESPONSIBILITY.

parity of responsibility
The management principle holding that a subordinate within an organization has the obligation to be responsive to orders from a higher authority. The principle also holds that the degree of authority and responsibility must be equal if a manager is to be effective. See UNITY OF COMMAND and PARITY OF AUTHORITY.

parity price
The price that yields an equivalence to some defined standard. For example, in agriculture, a price of an agricultural commodity that provides purchasing power, in terms of the goods farmers buy, equivalent to its purchasing power in a previous base period; in international economics, the price or exchange rate between the currencies of two countries that makes the purchasing power of one currency substantially equivalent to the purchasing power of the other.

parity ratio
In agriculture, the prices farmers currently receive divided by the prices they pay. It is used to measure the economic status of agriculture.

Parkinson's law
Cyril Northcote Parkinson's satirical view of the effectiveness of human beings and their organizations; the law holds that "work expands so as to fill the time available for its completion." It was formulated to apply to government red tape and bureaucratic inefficiency in Britain, but it now is seen to apply to all organizations.

par of exchange
The ratio of one country's unit of currency to that of another country, as defined by the official rates between the two countries.

parole evidence rule
A legal rule stating that, once parties have entered into a written agreement in writing, they are bound thereby and cannot offer proof of an oral agreement that contradicts the terms that have been written into the agreement.

part
An item used as material for producing an assembly, or an assembled item used to complete a product or a higher-level assembly.

part description
The definition of a part, usually accompanied by its part number.

partial equilibrium theory
An economic theory or model of a particular market that assumes other markets are in balance and will remain so. It ignores the interrelationships of prices and quantities that may exist between markets. For example, ordinary supply and demand analysis is normally of a partial equilibrium nature since it usually focuses on a single market while neglecting others.

partial reconveyance deed
An instrument for transferring a title, used to reconvey a portion of land encumbered by a blanket mortgage or a trust deed.

partial release clause
A part of a mortgage or trust deed that provides for removal of certain property from the effect of the lien on payment of an agreed-on sum. A subdivider must have such a clause in his mortgage if his tract is subject to a blanket lien.

participating preferred stock
A security in a company, entitled to its stated dividend as well as to additional dividends on a specified basis at the time of dividend payment on common stock. See COMMON STOCK and PREFERRED STOCK.

participatory leadership
A style of management in which the leader plays an active consulting and advising role but gives subordinates a considerable amount of independence in making final decisions. See LAISSEZ-FAIRE, AUTHORITARIAN LEADERSHIP, and DEMOCRATIC LEADERSHIP.

particular average loss
In marine insurance, an unavoidable partial loss borne by only one of the several interests in a ship and its cargo, arising from damage caused to that interest's goods by perils of the sea. See GENERAL AVERAGE LOSS.

partition deed
A deed used when tenants in common, joint tenants, or co-owners divide their land into individual ownerships.

partnership
A business structure with two or more owners whose relationship is determined by mutual agreement. The partners are free to establish among themselves the features or conditions of the partnership, the contribution of each partner to the business, the divisions of authority and profits, and to some extent the limits of each partner's liabilities. There are several types of partners. See GENERAL PARTNER, LIMITED PARTNER, SILENT PARTNER, SECRET PARTNER, DORMANT PARTNER, NOMINAL PARTNER, and SPECIAL PARTNER.

partnership life insurance
When a partner dies, the partnership is dissolved. Partnership life insurance is supported by a buy-and-sell agreement that assures that authority is given to use the proceeds of the policy to purchase the partnership interest from the estate of the deceased partner. The agreement establishes the value of the partnership for tax purposes, assures funds to pay the heirs the established value of the deceased share, may eliminate the need for forced liquidation of the business, and preserves the business for the surviving partners. Also known as BUSINESS LIFE INSURANCE.

parts
Manufactured items that will become components of larger articles such as radios, bearings for machinery, wheels for automobiles, and elements of computer hardware. See INDUSTRIAL GOODS, SEMIMANUFACTURED GOODS, and RAW MATERIALS.

parts clause
When written into an insurance contract, its intention is to make clear that, even though the article may not be usable following loss of or damage to a part, the insurer cannot consider that a total loss has occurred merely because a part has been lost or damaged.

parts consolidation
In manufacturing, a report showing the gross requirements, without relation to time, for a build plan, specified as a series of part numbers and quantities.

parts list
A basic list of parts or components that are used in an assembled product.

par-value capital stock
Capital stock each share of which has been assigned a fixed nominal or face value by the terms of a corporate charter.

passed dividend
Omission of a regular or scheduled dividend.

past due
In accounting, descriptive of a delay in payment of an obligation beyond the time agreed on for payment.

pataca
The basic unit of currency in Macao.

PATCA
Initials for *Professional and Technical Consultants Association*.

patent
An exclusive right conferred by a government on an inventor for a limited time. It authorizes the inventor to make, use, sell, transfer, or withhold the invention—which he or she is free to do even without a

patent—but it also gives the inventor the right to exclude others or to admit them on his or her own terms, which is possible only with a patent. Thus, patents are a method of promoting invention by granting temporary monopolies to inventors. Patents are granted only in the name(s) of the inventor(s) but may be assigned to another individual, group, organization, or firm. See PATENT COOPERATION TREATY.

A patent is also an original conveyance of lands in which the title is granted by letters patent. See PATENTED LAND.

Patent Cooperation Treaty
An international agreement, effective January 24, 1978, that provides a system whereby one application covers all the signatory nations in which the prospective patentee desires to obtain patent protection. Previously, applicants had to file simultaneously and separately in each of the different countries. The new system provides international patent-search reports. The objectives of the treaty include savings of both time and money in providing appropriate patent protection on an international scale. Signatories to the treaty as of January 1978 were the United States, Great Britain, France, Switzerland, West Germany, and nine African nations.

patented land
Land formerly owned by a state or national government as part of the public domain and voluntarily conveyed to a private owner, the transfer of title being evidenced by an instrument referred to as a *land patent.*

patent insurance
The protective type of this insurance covers expenses a patentee might incur in legal actions to protect the patent against infringement by others. The defensive type of this insurance provides coverage against legal actions alleging that the insured has infringed on the patent of another.

patent monopoly
The monopoly power a firm exercises because the government has conferred upon it the exclusive right, through issuance of a patent, to make, use, or market its own invention or discovery.

patronage dividend
A distribution by a cooperative to its members, in the form of a rebate on purchases made by the individual member.

payable
In accounting, an unpaid obligation, a liability, a debt owing to another. See ACCOUNTS PAYABLE.

payback
Financial return usually related to the time required for a project, product, or other investment with measurable return in revenue to reach the dollar level of the original investment.

payback period
The time required to achieve PAYBACK.

payroll
A record that shows the wages or salaries earned by employees for a specific period, and the deductions for various purposes or requirements.

PBGC
See PENSION BENEFIT GUARANTY CORPORATION.

PCB
Initials for *printed-circuit board.* See PRINTED CIRCUIT.

PD
Initials for *property damage;* covered by liability insurance.

Pearson, Karl (1857–1936)
An English mathematician who first popularized the coefficient r, which indicates in a single figure the degree of relationship or predictability that exists between two sets of data. Also known as the *Pearsonian product moment* r. See COEFFICIENT OF CORRELATION.

Pearsonian coefficient
See COEFFICIENT OF CORRELATION.

Pearsonian product moment *r*
See PEARSON, KARL.

peek-a-boo system
An information retrieval system that uses a so-called *peek-a-boo* into which small holes are drilled at the intersections of coordinates (column and row designations) to represent document numbers. Also known as *batten system, cordonnier system,* and *aspect cards.*

pegging
The act of fixing a price during the initial distribution of a security. Also, the act of fixing the rate of exchange of one currency as against another.

pegging requirements
In manufacturing, a statement of the relationship between the requirements for end products and the requirements these end products generate for lower-level parts or components.

pendente lite
Latin for "during the progress of a suit at law."

penetration pricing
A pricing policy intended to capture as large a share of the market for a product or service as early in the life of the product or service as possible. This may be done by offering the product or service at an unusually low price.

penny
A measure of the length of a nail, abbreviated as D. Originally, referring to the price per hundred nails of a particular length: fourpenny nails (four pennies per hundred), sixpenny nails, tenpenny nails, and so on. Typically, a fourpenny nail is 1⅜ inches long; a sixpenny nail, 2 inches; an eightpenny nail, 2½ inches; and a tenpenny nail, 3 inches.

penny stocks
In securities trading, a low-priced issue that is often highly speculative and sells for less than a dollar a share. Although some penny stocks have developed into investment-caliber issues, the term is sometimes used to disparage a stock considered to be of low value and to offer little promise of growth.

pension
A benefit plan that provides for payment of income to an individual who retires. Qualified pension plans are funded and must meet all IRS nondiscrimination tests. The recipient of the pension is not taxed until payment actually starts.

Pension Benefit Guaranty Corporation (PBGC)
A federal corporation governed by a board of directors consisting of the secretary of Labor (the chairman), the secretary of Commerce, and the secretary of the Treasury, and guided by a committee appointed by

the president. The committee advises the corporation on policies and procedures related to the appointment of trustees, the investment of moneys, and whether pension plans that are terminating should be continued or liquidated. This advisory committee is composed of two labor, two business, and three public members. The PBGC can seek the appointment of a trustee for a plan that appears financially unsound.

pension reserve
A fund established by an employer in recognition of a future obligation to pay annuities or pensions to employees.

PEP
Initials for *Programmed Emulation Partition.* See PERT.

P/E ratio
See PRICE-EARNINGS RATIO.

per capita
Latin for "by heads"; for each individual.

percentage order
A market or limited price order to buy or sell a stated amount of a specified stock after a fixed number of shares of such stock have been traded.

percentile
In statistics, the position of a score or other measure of quantity in a frequency distribution derived on a percentage basis. Below this point or value in the distribution lies the percentage of the group indicated by the number. See DECILE and QUARTILE.

per curiam
In legal proceedings, a decision by the full court given without the expression of opinion.

per diem
Latin for "by the day."

peremptory challenge
An objection made by a party to a law suit against a person proposed as a juror, and for which objection no reason need be given.

perfect competition
Descriptive of a market structure or an industry that is characterized by a large number of buyers and sellers all engaged in the purchase and sale of homogeneous commodities, with all the participants having perfect knowledge of market prices and quantities, with no discrimination in buying or selling, and with perfect mobility of resources. *Perfect competition* is often used synonymously with *pure competition*, although there is a technical distinction: pure competition does not require perfect knowledge or perfect resource mobility, and hence does not produce as smooth or rapid an adjustment to equilibrium as perfect competition does. In economic theory, both types of competition lead to essentially the same results.

perfection standard cost
A standard cost based on the best possible productivity obtained under the most favorable conditions.

perfect oligopoly
See OLIGOPOLY.

perforation rate
In data processing, the rate at which characters, rows, or words are punched into a paper tape.

performance bond
See COMPLETION BOND.

performance evaluation and review technique
See PERT.

performance rating
See LEVELING.

performance share
A long-term stock bonus with vesting and payout terms that depend on certain corporate performance conditions such as earnings-per-share growth; a form of long-term incentive and a capital accumulation vehicle.

peril
Within the terms of an insurance policy; the actual cause of a given loss. The specific loss-producing agency, such as fire, theft,

windstorm, explosion, riot, and so forth. The specific peril involved in an actual loss may be defined as covered or not covered within the language of the insurance policy. See HAZARD.

perils of the sea
Perils associated with natural hazards of a voyage; covered by ocean marine insurance. The perils include risks of sinking, stranding, overturning, and colliding with other vessels. Losses due to negligence are not covered by the insurance. Also known as *marine perils*.

period cost
An expenditure charged to an expense account on a time basis rather than on the basis of use or yield. In many instances the factors of time and use coincide; for example, rent, interest, real estate taxes. Straight-line depreciation may be considered a period cost.

periodic audit
An audit that covers an intermediate accounting period such as a month.

periodic income
Income that is accounted for in periods of time, such as bond interest, rent paid in advance, and profit from an installment sale.

peripheral equipment
Auxiliary machines that may be placed under the control of a central computer. Examples are card readers, card punches, magnetic-tape feeds, and high-speed printers. Peripheral equipment may be used on-line or off-line, depending on computer design, job requirements, and economics.

perk
See PERQUISITE.

permanent asset
See CAPITAL ASSET.

permanent residence
Broadly interpreted in law as any place of abode that is more than temporary. The term is often used as being synonymous with domicile, since a person's residence is usually also his or her domicile and since the two terms have been held equivalent in the judicial construction of some statutes. However, in a strict sense, residence applies to the mere

fact of a person dwelling in a particular abode, while domicile is a person's legal home, or the place the law presumes is his or her permanent residence, regardless of temporary absence. See DOMICILE.

permutation
In statistics, an arrangement of a set of objects in which there is a first, second, and third order through n. If, for example, we are given a set of objects a, b, c, d, e, f (a total of $n = 6$), they may be arranged in a different number of permutations calculated as $6 \times 5 \times 4 \times 3 \times 2 \times 1 = 720$. Note that a, b, c, d, e, f is one permutation of the group while a, c, b, d, f, e is a different permutation. The number of different arrangements is 720.

perpetual inventory system
In manufacturing, a system of inventory control or measurement in which each transaction in and out is recorded and a new balance is calculated.

perquisite
A special benefit or privilege provided as an additional, indirect form of compensation. It may take such forms as a company car, club memberships, or special entertainment allowances. Colloquially known as *perk*.

persona ficta
Latin for "fictitious person." Used in reference to a corporate entity or an artificial legal person. See NATURAL PERSON and ARTIFICIAL PERSON.

personal effects floater
An all-risk insurance policy intended to cover the personal property generally carried by travelers. Written for a single face amount with specific limitations on payments of claims.

personal holding company
A corporation the majority of whose outstanding capital stock is owned by a small group of individuals. Also known as an *incorporated pocketbook*.

personal income
With respect to individuals, PI includes moneys and taxable benefits received prior to legally authorized deductions, and includes wages, salaries, commissions, bonuses, interest and dividend payments re-

ceived, and other moneys received that may be determined from time to time by the regulations of the Internal Revenue Service as subject to declarations as taxable income.

personality
In industrial psychology, the image others have of the sum of the habit patterns or conditioned responses to various stimuli that an individual develops as he or she matures. As an individual's behavior repeats itself under similar conditions, others learn to recognize that behavior of that person as his or her personality. They expect and may attempt to predict certain kinds of behavior under a set of assumptions with respect to the environment.

personal liability
An amount owed by a natural person, as contrasted with the liability of a business firm.

personal power
Within an organization, an individual who is able to induce or influence the behavior of others through his or her personality and behavior is said to have *personal power*. See POSITION POWER.

personal property
Temporary or removable assets, as contrasted with *real property*.

personal property floater
An all-risk insurance contract intended to offer personal rather than business protection, it covers all perils except those specifically excluded. Unscheduled, or unspecified, property that is related to the insured's business is not covered, with the exception of personally owned professional books, instruments, and equipment at the insured's residence. The insurance covers only direct losses, and excludes property normally covered by other policies, such as automobiles, aircraft, and boats.

personal property tax
See PROPERTY TAX.

personal risk
The possibility of death or injury to an individual; covered by such classes of insurance as life, accident, and sickness.

personal sector
See PRIVATE SECTOR.

personal service
In law, service of a process actually delivered in person to the defendant or to an agent of the defendent authorized by statute to receive service in the case at issue.

PERT
Acronym for *performance evaluation and review technique.* Also known as *network planning* and *network analysis,* PERT was originated by the U.S. Navy to pictorially plot and monitor exceptionally complex construction projects, the first of which was the Polaris missile program. The PERT technique was widely credited with helping to shorten by two years the time originally estimated for the completion of the engineering and development program for the Polaris missile involving approximately 3,000 separate contracting organizations. In nonmilitary contexts, the term *critical path method (CPM)* is more commonly used. Other network planning programs include those designated as *CPS, Micro-PERT, 1-time PERT, PERT/COST,* and *PEP.*

PERT/COST
See PERT.

peseta
The basic unit of currency in Equatorial Guinea and in Spain.

peso
The basic unit of currency in Argentina, Bolivia (called peso boliviano), the Central American Common Market, Colombia, Cuba, Dominican Republic, Mexico, the Philippines, and Uruguay.

Peter principle
Described by Dr. Laurence J. Peter and Raymond Hull in their book *The Peter Principle,* it holds that every employee in a hierarchy tends to rise to his or her level of incompetence. The subtitle of the book is *Why Things Always Go Wrong.*

petty cash fund
In business accounting, a small amount of cash kept either on hand or on deposit and made immediately available for minor disbursements.

phantom freight
A transportation charge included in the delivery price of a commodity that is in excess of the charge for service actually performed.

phantom stock option
A form of stock that simulates an option on paper. Under a phantom stock plan, a grant of stock units is made and the executive receives the appreciation in market price, and sometimes the dividends, over a period of time. Also known as *shadow option*.

Phillips curve
Named for the British economist A. W. H. Phillips; a graphic technique, first published in 1958, for demonstrating the relationship between employment and changes in the price level. Its main implication is that, since a particular level of unemployment in the economy will imply a particular rate of wage increase, the aims of low unemployment and a low rate of inflation may be inconsistent. Among the other choices available to it for maintaining economic stability, the government might then have to choose between the feasible combinations of unemployment and inflation, as shown by the Phillips curve.

PHS
See PUBLIC HEALTH SERVICE.

physical asset
See TANGIBLE ASSET.

physical budget
A budget expressed in units other than dollars, such as number of employees, number of worker-hours, and units of material.

physical inventory
An inventory determined by actual measurement of weight, or by unit count. See BOOK INVENTORY.

physical life
In accounting, the total potential operating life of a machine, without recognition of obsolescence or useful economic life. See SERVICE LIFE.

physicians', surgeons', and dentists' liability insurance
May be written for an individual practice or a medical partnership; affords broad coverage for claims, including negligence, assault, slander, incompetence, or error on the part of the insured. To avoid the interpretation that settlement is an admission of guilt, the insurer agrees not to make any settlement of a claim without the written consent of the professional practitioner.

physiocrats
Name given to followers of the economic school of physiocracy founded by François Quesnay (1694–1774). The physiocrats are notable for several reasons. One is their invention of the term and the policy of LAISSEZ-FAIRE, which has lingered ever since as a subject of economic discussion. Another is their ground-breaking analysis of the circulation of wealth, which purported to show how national income originates and is distributed. Physiocrats believed in the doctrine that all wealth was derived from the land. Without food, fibers, wood, minerals, and stone, human beings could not exist or accumulate possessions. The physiocrats contended that everything representing a departure from the natural order was the cause of dissatisfaction and should be done away with.

pi
Pronounced *pie,* the symbol π or Π, the sixteenth letter of the Greek alphabet. Used to signify the ratio of the circumference of a circle to its diameter; its value is 3.141592653589+.

PI
Initials for *programmed instruction.* Also, see PERSONAL INCOME.

picking
In manufacturing, the act of pulling or withdrawing materials from a storeroom in order to create a kit of parts that are to be delivered to the production line for processing. Also known as *pulling.*

In wholesale marketing operations, the withdrawal of merchandise from the shelves of a stockroom in accordance with the requirements of a purchase order prior to packing and shipping.

picosecond
A trillionth of a second; a thousandth of a nanosecond; 10^{-12} second.

pictograph
See PICTORIAL CHART.

pictorial chart
A chart readily understood and enjoying widespread use by all management disciplines in charting statistics. Graphic symbols represent numerical magnitudes; quantities are compared or evaluated by means of lengths, heights, or areas of the symbols. Pictorial charts are not usually studied critically but are intended to convey an instant impression of relative values.

piece rate
A plan under which employees are paid on the basis of a predetermined monetary amount for each acceptable unit produced. Also known as *piece work*.

piecework
See PIECE RATE.

pie charts
Sometimes called circle charts, used to show the relative sizes of components in a group of statistics of the same class. The form is visually similar to a round pie that is sliced into a multiple number of sections, each related to its numerical quantity as a part of the whole pie.

piggyback
See TRAILERS ON FLATCARS.

pilot
An experimental model used in marketing to test the feasibility or acceptance of a product.

pilot interview
A dynamic testing program intended to check the validity of a full-scale market research program involving interview techniques before the program is actually undertaken.

pilot production
An initial production run of a new product, in relatively small lots, partly to test the validity of the product's design and documentation, partly to evaluate production methods, and partly to provide marketing people with an advance or early sample for market tests and customer reactions.

pinboard
A type of control panel that uses pins instead of wires to control the operation of a computer. On certain small computers using pinboards, a program is changed by the simple removal of one pinboard and the insertion of another.

ping-pong
In data processing, the programming technique of using two magnetic-tape units for multiple-reel files and switching automatically between the two units until the complete file is processed.

pink-tea picketing
Picketing that involves a small number of pickets who behave peacefully and discreetly.

pipeline inventory
The aggregate inventory of materials, including items that may be in transit to the warehouse from a supplier and those already received and on the floor or in an abeyance area. Also known as *in-process inventory*.

PITB
Initials for *Pacific Inland Tariff Bureau*.

PITI
Initials for *principal, interest, taxes, and insurance*. Generally used to indicate that these separate accounts are included in the final settlement of a debt that has been repaid in equal installments.

plaintiff
In a legal action, the complainant, the party who commences the action and seeks a remedy in court.

planned economy
An economic system in which the government, according to a preconceived plan, plays a primary role in directing economic resources for the purpose of deciding what to produce, how much, and possibly for whom. A planned economy may or may not be a command economy, depending on whether the government operates within a substantially authoritarian or a substantially democratic framework. See COMMAND ECONOMY.

planned obsolescence
A marketing concept that incorporates into the original plan describing or defining the life of a product a finite time interval during which the product will be actively produced and offered for sale. At the end of the designated time interval, the product is to be deliberately made obsolete by the introduction of a new product, a different version of the existing product, or a new technology.

planned order
A shop or purchase order that is planned to satisfy net manufacturing requirements.

planner number
In manufacturing, an internal code number representing or identifying the planner responsible for the part marked with the related number.

plant
Generally, fixed assets such as land, buildings, machinery, furniture, and other equipment.

plant capacity
The maximum output capability of a production facility.

plant efficiency factor
A measure of merit that takes into account that, because of scheduling delays, machine breakdowns, maintenance time, and so forth, a portion of available hours cannot be used. For example, if, based on route sheets and other measurement methods, 100 products need 550 milling machine-hours per week and 138 machine-hours are unavailable during the week, the actual time required becomes 688 hours (550 + 138). In this example, therefore, the efficiency factor is 550 divided by 688 or 0.80. Plant efficiency factors generally range from 0.50 to 0.95.

plant fund
A fund established for the acquisition of land, buildings, improvements, and equipment.

plat
A map intended to show the division of land into lots or parcels.

plat book
A public record of maps that show the division of land into streets, blocks, and lots and that give the measurements of the individual parcels. Also known as *lot book*.

platted land
Land that has been surveyed and divided into lots delineated on a plot or map. The term is usually used in connection with land intended for development as building sites.

platykurtic distribution
A statistical distribution that is relatively flat, not peaked. See KURTOSIS and LEPTOKURTIC DISTRIBUTION.

pleading
See COMPLAINT.

pledged asset
An asset that has been placed in trust or given as security for an obligation, loan, or mortgage. Also known as *hypothecated asset.*

PL/1
See PROGRAMMING LANGUAGE 1.

plus tick
See UP TICK.

PMMI
Initials for *Packaging Machinery Manufacturers Institute.*

point
In the securities market, when referring to the price of shares of stock, a point means $1. In the case of bonds, it means $10. In the case of market averages, it means a change of one whole integer; for example, if the Dow Jones average rises from 964.25 to 965.25, it has risen a point.

point estimate
In statistics, a single, finite number in a distribution.

Point Four Program
Part of the Foreign Economic Assistance Act of 1950, the program seeks to raise living standards in the underdeveloped countries by making available to them U.S. technical and financial assistance, largely in the areas of agriculture, public health, and education. Much of this work is now carried out by agencies of the United Nations and by the U.S. Agency for International Development.

point of purchase (POP)
The location within a retail establishment where the decision to purchase an item is actually made by the consumer. Also known as *point of sale.*

point of sale (POS)
See POINT OF PURCHASE.

Poisson, Siméon D. (1781–1840)
A French mathematician who formulated the use of the frequency distribution that carries his name. Its first uses were to ascertain the probability of deaths in the Prussian army resulting from the kick of a horse and the probability of suicides among women and children. It

now finds wide application in modern industry in determining the probable demand for various types of units of service within specific time periods. See POISSON PROBABILITY DISTRIBUTION.

Poisson distribution
See POISSON PROBABILITY DISTRIBUTION.

Poisson probability distribution
In statistics, this type of frequency distribution often applies when there are a large number of independent events or trials for each of which there is only a small probability that a certain outcome will occur. Also known as *Poisson distribution* and *law of improbable events*.

polar coordinates
Used in plotting relationships in which one of the variables is a magnitude and the other is a direction. The system is composed of circular grids concentric about the origin, and of radial lines, one of which serves as a reference for the measurement of direction angles.

pole
A measure of length equal to one rod or 16.5 feet.

policy method
In accounting, a method of depreciation determined by financial or social policy; sometimes used in public works projects.

policy proof of interest (PPI) clause
A clause applicable to ocean marine insurance indicating the insurance company recognizes that the insured has an insurable interest up to the face amount of the contract, the policy being stamped accordingly. Also known as a *full interest admitted (FIA) clause*.

political corporation
See PUBLIC CORPORATION.

political risk
In the securities market, the uncertainty of future returns from a security because of political developments, such as revolution, currency devaluation, nationalization of facilities, and so on. Also, see SECURITY RISK, FINANCIAL RISK, INTEREST RATE RISK, MARKET RISK, PURCHASING POWER RISK, and SOCIAL RISK.

polling the jury
In a court trial, the act of calling the name of each juror and inquiring what his or her verdict is before it is made a matter of record.

polynomial expression
An algebraic expression containing two or more terms. See MONOMIAL EXPRESSION, BINOMIAL EXPRESSION, and TRINOMIAL EXPRESSION.

poor man's goods
See INFERIOR GOOD.

POP
See POINT OF PURCHASE.

population
In statistics, a group that is sampled; also referred to as a *universe*. It may be made up of people, prices, wages, interest rates, inventories, or of virtually any quantifiable items or units. In sampling methodology, it is extremely important that the population or universe be clearly defined and that the sample be drawn strictly from the population or universe as it has been defined.

port
A harbor with piers and docks. Also the left side of a ship or other carrier, as determined while facing forward toward the front of the carrier. The opening in the carrier's side for handling freight. Also known as *larboard*, as distinguished from *starboard*.

portfolio
The total holdings of securities by an individual or an institution. It may contain bonds, preferred stocks, common stocks, and other securities of a variety of enterprises.

port of entry
A place designated by the government for handling specified import shipments.

POS
Initials for *point of sale*. See POINT OF PURCHASE.

position evaluation
The process whereby the worth of a position or job to an organization is analyzed and compared with other positions and jobs in the enter-

prise and is formally placed within the company's salary grade structure.

position guide
See JOB DESCRIPTION.

position power
Within an organization, an individual who is able to induce or influence the behavior of others because of his or her position in the organization is said to have *position power*. See PERSONAL POWER.

positive economics
The part of economics that is concerned with propositions about what is rather than about what ought to be. The essence of a positive proposition is its concern with matters of fact, not with matters of values and ethics. See NORMATIVE ECONOMICS.

post
In accounting, to enter an item on a record. Also, see POSTING.

Postal Rate Commission (PRC)
An independent regulatory agency with a permanent five-member board appointed by the president, who designates one member as chairman; not part of the U.S. Postal Service. The major responsibility of the PRC is to submit recommended decisions to the Postal Service in the matter of postage rates and fees and mail classifications.

Postal Service (USPS)
See UNITED STATES POSTAL SERVICE.

postclaim underwriting
The analysis of insurance claims for the purpose of determining whether the policy should be canceled. It is routine practice in many companies to refer large claims to the underwriting department. The practice is often employed where the insured party has a history of a large number of small claims and future risks appear unfavorable.

postdate
To affix a date on a document later than the date on which the document is written or executed. A postdated check cannot be cashed or deposited before the date appearing on its face.

post hoc ergo propter hoc
Latin for "after this, therefore because of this." A common fallacy in economics, the proposition assumes that because one event precedes another, the first event is the cause of the second.

posting
The bookkeeping process of transferring dollar amounts and their accompanying or supporting data from a book of original entry to a ledger. Also, an item in a ledger or an amount posted. See ENTRY.

post 30
See INACTIVE POST.

postwar reserve
A reserve created by many corporations out of profits earned during World War II. The intent was to provide funds for conversion or reconstruction of fixed assets to peacetime activities at the end of the war.

pound
The basic unit of currency in Cyprus, Egypt, Gambia, Ghana, Gibraltar, Ireland, Israel, Jamaica, Lebanon, Libya, Malta, New Zealand, Nigeria, Sudan, Syria, Turkey, and the United Kingdom. The pound is also known as a *lira* in Syria and Turkey.

poverty line
A criterion proposed by the Social Security Administration as the minimum level of subsistence income for a family; adjusted periodically to accommodate changes in the cost of living.

power
In industrial psychology, the ability to induce or influence behavior. See PERSONAL POWER and POSITION POWER.

power file
A filing system using motorized vertical shelves that usually operate in an automatic selection mode (in case of power failure the system can be operated manually by means of a crank). The file is a series of rotating shelves, similar in concept to a Ferris wheel, encased in a free-standing metal cabinet. Individual files are placed on the shelves and assigned locator numbers that correspond with the shelves. When a specific file must be accessed, the operator keys the locator number onto a key pad on the control panel and the appropriate shelf is moved into an accessible position.

power need

A motivational factor, the desire to control other persons or objects, to obtain their obedience, to compel or influence their actions, to determine their fate. An example might be the elation felt by a salesperson who persuaded a buyer to purchase his product instead of that of a competitor.

power of attorney

A legal document authorizing a person to act as the agent for the person granting the power. A general power of attorney authorizes the agent to act generally without restriction on behalf of the principal. A special power of attorney limits the agent to a particular or specific act, such as conveying a parcel of property or negotiating a specified contract.

power-plant insurance

Also known as boiler and machinery insurance, protects against losses caused by explosions of furnaces, steam boilers, engines, and electrical equipment. Standard fire policies usually exclude explosions of this type. Coverage is generally for bodily injury (BI) and property damage (PD).

PP

Initials for *parcel post.*

PPI

Initials for *parcel post insured.* Also, see POLICY PROOF OF INTEREST CLAUSE.

PPI clause

See POLICY PROOF OF INTEREST CLAUSE.

PR

Initials for *public relations.*

PRC

See POSTAL RATE COMMISSION.

preacquisition profits

The retained earnings of a corporation as stated immediately prior to being acquired by, or in any way having come under the control of, another corporation.

precoded questions

See OSGOOD SCALES.

predicted cost
See STANDARD COST ACCOUNTING.

preemptive right
The privilege to subscribe for a pro rata share of any new capital stock a corporation is about to issue, given to a stockholder in the corporation's charter or under the common law.

preferential hiring
An agreement or practice under which an employer gives first choice of available jobs to members of a particular trade union. Also known as *preferential shop*.

preferential shop
See PREFERENTIAL HIRING.

preferred stock
A class of stock with a claim on the company's earnings before payment is made on the common stock and usually entitled to priority, or preferred treatment, if the company is liquidated. Normally entitled to dividends at a special rate, when declared by the board of directors, before payment of a dividend on common stocks. The dividend rate depends on the terms of the issue. See COMMON STOCK and PARTICIPATING PREFERRED STOCK.

preferred-stock dividend
A dividend paid to the registered holders of preferred stock, usually at a fixed rate per quarter and expressed as a percentage or in dollars per share.

preliminary balance sheet
See TENTATIVE BALANCE SHEET.

premium
In securities trading, the amount by which the price of a security exceeds its nominal, face, par, quoted, or market value. In the case of a new issue of bonds or stocks, the premium is the amount the market price rises over the original selling price. The term also refers to a charge sometimes made when a stock is borrowed to make a delivery on a short sale. Also, it may refer to the redemption price of a bond or a preferred stock if it is higher than face value.

In wages for labor, the extra dollars paid above normal or standard rates for work performed at other than usual times, such as late shifts, weekends, and holidays.

prepaid asset
See PREPAID EXPENSE.

prepaid expense
An expenditure made for future benefits or for facilities, utilities, and goods to be used at some time in the future. Examples include prepaid rent, taxes, royalties, insurance premiums, stationery, and office supplies. Also known as *deferred charge, deferred expense, current asset,* and *prepaid asset.*

prepaid income
See DEFERRED REVENUE.

prepaid interest
The excess of the face value of a loan over the amount of money actually received by the borrower, or the difference between the two amounts; often classified as a prepaid expense.

prepay
To pay for a service or the use of a facility before the benefit or enjoyment is actually received.

prepayment
A business expenditure made in advance for items that will yield portions of their benefits in the present and in the future. Examples include advance premiums on insurance policies, expenses incurred in marketing a new product, and purchases of stationery supplies.

preproduction cost
The makeready time and expense required to initiate production on specific orders.

present value
The value today of future cash flows. For example, $100 to be received a year from now is worth less than it would be if it were in hand today. Also known as *present worth.* See DISCOUNTED CASH FLOW.

present value method
See DISCOUNTED CASH FLOW.

present worth
See PRESENT VALUE.

prestige need
In business management, the desire to be highly regarded by one's associates; the need for recognition. The need may motivate an individual to strive for higher status, inasmuch as prestige or recognition is implicit in a class-stratified society (or organizational structure) and may be made visible in the form of special privileges, perquisites, or office location and furnishings. The need may be associated with the acquisitive need and may or may not be related to the individual's need for achievement.

pretax earnings
See PRETAX INCOME.

pretax income
Income reported for accounting purposes before income taxes have been deducted. Also known as *pretax earnings*.

preventive maintenance
The periodic servicing, adjustment, and general upkeep of equipment to minimize the probability of catastrophic failure, major repair work, costly replacement, or extended down time.

price
In formal economics, a ratio reflecting the exchange value of a good or a service. For example, if the price of a dressed chicken is $1 and the price of a pound of coffee is $2.50, the ratio of exchange is 2½ to 1. Two and one-half chickens have a value equivalent to one pound of coffee—in a barter system. The price system measures the value of exchange in monetary terms. This is less clumsy than the barter system on a worldwide market basis, since money is the prime and common denominator used to measure the value of goods and services exchanged within markets. See MARKET.

price-consumption curve
In indifference-curve analysis, a line that connects the tangency points of price lines and indifference curves by showing the amounts of two commodities a consumer will purchase when his or her income and the price of one commodity remain constant while the price of the other commodity varies. See INDIFFERENCE CURVE.

price-earnings (P/E or P-E) ratio
In the securities market, the P/E ratio is calculated by dividing the current market price of a share of stock by the earnings per share for a 12-month period. For example, a stock selling for $50 a share and

earning $2.50 per share is said to be selling at, or to have, a price-earnings ratio of 20.

price index
A statistical device for comparing the amount by which prices have changed during a given period of time. A specific year is chosen as the base year and prices in all other years are measured as a percentage of the price in this base year.

price leader
An item of merchandise priced abnormally low. The purpose is to attract customers, generally in retail sales operations.

price leadership
In marketing, leadership by a dominant firm whose price sets the pace for other manufacturers to follow. The product setting the prevailing price is called the *price leader*. See PRICE SYSTEM.

price margin
See GROSS MARGIN.

price system
Adherence by firms in an oligopolistic industry, often tacitly and without formal agreement, to the pricing policies of one of the members of the same industry. Frequently, but not always, the price leader will be the largest firm in the industry, and other firms will simply follow the leader, charging the same price as it charges.

price takeoff method
See QUANTITY SURVEY.

price variance
A variance resulting from a change in the cost of materials and labor.

price-wage spiral
See COST-PUSH INFLATION.

prima facie
Latin for "at first view." In law, a prima facie case is one that stands as presented until contrary evidence is produced.

primary account
Any account to which external transactions are first carried. At some point in the accounting period, some or all of the primary accounts may

be transferred to secondary accounts. See SECONDARY ACCOUNT and THROUGHPUT ACCOUNTING.

primary distribution
See NEW ISSUE.

primary investment
The original purchase of shares of stock from a company, the moneys derived therefrom giving the company the capital it needs to function. See SECONDARY INVESTMENT.

primary offering
See NEW ISSUE.

primary storage
A computer memory in which instructions and data are contained. Also known as *main storage*. See STORAGE.

prime cost
The cost of direct materials and direct labor entering into the manufacture of a product; the total of direct costs minus direct and indirect overhead.

prime meridian
The main imaginary meridian line in a township and range system of land surveying. See MERIDIAN LINE.

prime rate
The rate of interest charged by commercial banks on short-term loans to preferred customers.

Prince, The
See MACHIAVELLI, NICCOLÒ.

principal
In securities trading, the person for whom a broker executes an order, or a brokerage firm buying or selling for its own account. The term may also refer to a person's capital, or the face amount of a bond or of a loan.

printed circuit
In electronics, a circuit in which the components or connections are printed, painted, or sprayed on an insulating surface with conducting

materials. The insulating surface is referred to as a *printed circuit board* (*PCB*).

printout
The printed output of a computer or a printing press.

prior-period adjustment
In accounting, an expense or income item that relates to a period prior to the date of a financial statement but is not recognized until after that date. If the amount of the item is significant, corrected financial statements may have to be published. If the amount is nominal, it may be absorbed in the period of discovery without special disclosure.

Privacy Act of 1974
See FREEDOM OF INFORMATION ACT OF 1974.

private carrier
An enterprise that uses its own carriers or transportation system to move its own goods. The firm is usually not engaged in interstate transportation and, when so engaged, is not regulated by the federal government but may be subject to local and state requirements. The private carrier system is feasible when an enterprise requires heavy utilization of carriers or where specialized transportation services are required.

private corporation
The common corporation created by and for private individuals for nongovernmental purposes. See CORPORATION.

private enterprise
See PRIVATE SECTOR.

private offering
The sale of securities by the issuer to a selected group of subscribers, usually without the intermediation of an investment banker.

private sector
That part of the economy not under direct government control. Included are private enterprise firms and the economic activities of nonprofit organizations and private individuals. Also known as *personal sector*, *private enterprise*, and *free enterprise*.

private siding
A railroad track that serves an industrial plant and is owned or rented by the plant.

probability theory
In statistical analysis, a mathematical theory concerned with determining the likelihood of the occurrence of a chance event; used to predict the behavior of a group, not of a single item in the group. Probability theory finds application in many business disciplines, such as in calculating average quality levels of products manufactured in quantity. It is especially valuable in the field of insurance for calculating general or special premiums. The mathematical technique holds that the probability of events ranges from 0 to 1; 0 states that the event will certainly not occur, 1 holds that the event is certain to occur.

From the insurance standpoint, the theory of probability holds that, other things being equal, and an equal number of risks being insured, the losses in the future should be the same as the losses in the past.

probability tree
See DECISION TREE.

probable life
The age already attained by a piece of equipment plus its expected life. The estimated total or service life of equipment.

probable-life curve
In statistical analysis, a curve deduced from measurements of the frequency distributions of the use and the mortality of equipment.

procedure flowchart
In management, a symbolic and systematic representation of a procedure used to modify, work on, or handle a form or document used in organizational activities.

procedure-oriented language
A problem-oriented data processing language that facilitates expression of a procedure as an explicit algorithm. Examples include FORTRAN, ALGOL, COBOL, and PL/I.

process
In court proceedings, an instrument of the court, issued under its seal in the name of the state before or during the progress of the trial, directing an officer of the court to act, or cause some act to be done, for a purpose directly related to the trial.

process chart
In production analysis, a graphic representation of events that occur during a series of actions or operations on the part of a worker. A technique developed by Frank B. and Lillian M. Gilbreth.

process costing
A method of cost accounting in which costs are charged to processes or operations and are averaged over the total of units produced.

product differentiation
Real or imagined differences created in products that are essentially the same. The means used may be in the company's branding, packaging, advertising, quality variation, design variation, or claims made for performance. The practice is most prevalent in consumer goods industries, for example, automobiles, cigarettes, cosmetics, household detergents, and nonprescription medications such as aspirin. The purpose of product differentiation is to develop consumer preferences for one brand over all others.

production control
The function of planning the manufacture of components and the assembly of finished goods to meet sales goals. Production control may include (1) translating sales plans into production plans, (2) estimating factory load and materials requirements, (3) preparing manufacturing timetables and shipping schedules, (4) scheduling work onto the factory floor, (5) generating and controlling work order documents, (6) monitoring actual performance against plans, and (7) expediting manufacturing activity to meet the dynamics of changing sales demands. See PRODUCTION PLANNING.

production controller
A code assigned to each part number to determine the production control group responsible for that part.

production method of depreciation
See SERVICE-YIELD BASIS.

production planning
The phase of production control specifically involved with analyzing sales demands and developing production programs and timetables to satisfy the demands. See PRODUCTION CONTROL.

productive capacity
The potential of the economy and of companies and industries for producing useful goods and services; limited by the stock of capital goods, the available labor force, and the level of technology.

productivity
The yield obtained from a process or product as a result of work done with or on it. Also, a wage theory holding that wages should be based on employee productivity. A chief drawback here is the lack of any generally accepted standard of productivity. The piece-rate plan of compensation approaches the theory.

productivity of capital
Output produced per unit of capital employed.

productivity of labor
Output produced per unit of labor employed, usually measured per worker or per worker-hour.

product layout
The arrangement of machines and equipment in a production or processing facility according to the sequence of operations required to fabricate and assemble the item. Machines and workers are specialized in the performance of specific operations; parts approach continuous movement. Also known as *line layout*. Product or line layout has found greatest application in assembly rather than in fabrication.

product life cycle
The complete life of a product generally comprising seven stages: (1) research and development, (2) introductory, (3) market development, (4) exploitation, (5) maturation, (6) saturation, and (7) decline. See GOPERTZ CURVE.

products liability insurance
Provides protection to the insured for liability that may result from defective products or from completed operations; intended to cover obligations for accidents that may result from mistakes in the manufacture or preparation of products or in the rendering of service work.

product tree
See CHRISTMAS TREE.

professional liability insurance
Available in several forms, issued to professional individuals and firms to cover liabilities resulting from the practice of their professions. The liability must be legally judged to be an obligation.

profitability index
If the discounted cash flow (or present value) method is used, the present value of the earnings of a project can be compared directly with the present value of the earnings of another, even if the investments are of different magnitudes. To compare two proposals, the size of the earnings must be related to the amount of the money that is risked. This is done by dividing the present value of earnings by the amount of investment. The resultant ratio is called the *profitability index*. The higher the index number, the better the project from a profitability viewpoint.

profitability ratios
A set of ratios of financial data focusing on the profit realized by an enterprise and its relationship to the revenue generated or the resources employed. Such ratios include the profit margin on sales defined as net profit divided by sales, and the return on total assets defined as net profit divided by total assets; sometimes analysts and investors use the ratio for return on equity, defined as earnings after taxes (EAT) divided by equity.

profit and loss (P&L) statement
A business firm's formal statement of revenues, costs, expenses, losses, and profits for a given period, grouped under appropriate headings. Also known as *income statement* or *earnings report*. See EARNINGS REPORT.

profit center
A department, division, unit, or other clearly identifiable segment of a business that for purposes of financial control is treated budgetarily as an entity, enabling expenses and revenues to be accounted as a measure of the center's performance. See COST CENTER.

profit-push inflation
In economics, a situation in which prices and business profits begin to rise before any increase in wages or other production costs takes place. The process stimulates labor unions to seek wage increases, thereby prompting sellers to make further price increases.

profits and commission insurance
Issuable to manufacturers possessing prepared goods that may be destroyed or damaged by fire and that are not easily replaced. It is written only for finished goods, not for work in process, and is especially applicable to seasonal products that may not be replaced in time for seasonal sales intervals. For example, goods manufactured for the Christmas season but destroyed by fire immediately prior to the start of the season may need protection for loss of the property and loss of profits. See CONSEQUENTIAL-LOSSES INSURANCE.

profit sharing
A method by which some of the profits of a business firm are distributed among employees in the form of money or shares of stock, the distribution usually being made at the end of the fiscal year. The amounts distributed may be in accordance with a predetermined formula related to years of service of the individual employee or they may be entirely at the discretion of a designated committee or of management.

profit-sharing plan
A formal plan under which employees share in the company's profits, usually in relation to their salary and service. Under a cash profit-sharing plan, the award is distributed each year. Under a deferred profit-sharing plan, contributions are invested and are paid out when the employee leaves the company, retires, or dies.

pro forma
Latin for "as a matter of form."

pro forma balance sheet
A balance sheet that depicts the status of business operations—assets and liabilities—at a specific point in time; preliminary in content, unaudited, not confirmed by a certified public accountant as to content or form.

pro forma invoice
A financial statement in the form of an invoice listing goods or services considered hypothetical in that they have not yet been delivered and probably have not yet been ordered. Prices are usually entered on the invoice. Such documents are used for budgetary purposes and are generally provided by a supplier who proposes to export the items listed on the invoice to an importer who may require the document for import license and customs evaluations.

pro forma statement
See PRO FORMA BALANCE SHEET and PROJECTED FINANCIAL STATE-MENT.

program
In data processing, the complete sequence of machine instructions and routines necessary to solve a problem through the use of a computer. See ROUTINE and SUBROUTINE.

program check
In data processing, a system for determining correct program and machine functioning either by running a program (or a sample problem with similar programing and a known answer) or by using mathematical or logic checks such as comparing $A \times B$ with $B \times A$. This check system is normally concerned with programs run on computers that are not self-checking internally.

programmable read-only memory
In data processing, a field-programmable memory is one the user can program. See READ-ONLY MEMORY.

programmed learning
Learning from material arranged in a series of sequential steps that enable the learner to proceed with a minimum of error and a maximum of reinforcement by his or her own self at his or her own pace. The technique has proved to be extraordinarily effective.

programmer
In data processing, a person who prepares problem-solving procedures and flowcharts and who may also write and debug routines.

programming
In data processing, the designing, writing, and testing of a plan for the solution of a problem through the use of an electronic computer.

Programming Language/1 (PL/1)
A multipurpose programming language developed by IBM for the Models 360 and 370 data processing systems.

program step
In data processing, a phase of one instruction or command in a sequence of instructions.

program stop
An instruction built into a computer program that will automatically stop the machine under certain conditions, or on reaching the end of the processing, or on completing the solution of a problem.

program tape
A tape that contains the sequence of instructions required for solving a problem and that is read into a computer prior to running a program.

progress billing
An accounting procedure based on work performed under contract and allowing for the billing of work at progressive levels of completion.

progression, principle of
The rule that the worth of a residence of lower value tends to be enhanced by association with many higher-valued residences in the same area.

progressive consumer
In market analysis, a consumer who would be receptive to an offer of a better product or service at a slightly higher price. See RETROGRESSIVE CONSUMER.

progressive tax
A tax whose percentage rate increases as the tax base increases. The U.S. personal income tax is an example. The tax is graduated so that, other things being equal and assuming no loopholes, a person with a higher income pays a greater percentage of his or her income than a person with a lower income. Also known as *equitable tax*. See REGRESSIVE TAX.

progress payments
Payments made at stages of a construction or manufacturing program as it moves toward completion.

projected financial statement
A financial statement for a future date or period of activity, as opposed to a statement of past performance, based on estimates of transactions to be conducted. Also known as a *pro forma statement* and *giving-effect statement*.

projection
In behavioral psychology the process whereby a person ascribes to others faults and wants of his or her own that are unconsciously perceived as unacceptable in his or her own behavior or personality.

project rate of return
See DISCOUNTED CASH FLOW.

PROM
Acronym for PROGRAMMABLE READ-ONLY MEMORY.

promissory note
An unconditional written promise, signed by the maker, to pay the bearer of the note or a person or organization so designated on the note a specific sum of money. The due date of the note may be some specified future date or may be on presentation of the note.

promissory warranty
See WARRANTY.

pro number
A serial number assigned by a carrier to its freight bill. The term *pro* is short for the word progressive.

proof of loss
Generally used in the event of loss for which insurance payment is requested, a form that identifies the claimant and the relevant policy number and describes the incident and the extent of the loss. A statement may also be required as to how, in the opinion of the insured, the loss occurred. Fraud in making the proof-of-loss statement automatically cancels the policy and removes any obligations on the part of the insurer.

propensity to consume
In Keynesian economics, a statistical phrase denoting the relation, expressed as a percentage, between total income and total consumer expenditures. The relation is expressed in the equation $P = C/Y$, where P = propensity to consume, C = consumer expenditures, and Y = income. For total income Y, some authorities use national income, others use gross national product, and still others use disposable personal income. See PROPENSITY TO SAVE and KEYNES'S LAW OF CONSUMPTION.

propensity to save
In Keynesian economics, a statistical phrase denoting the relation, expressed as a percentage, between total income and that part of the income not devoted to consumer expenditures. The relation is expressed by the equation $S = (Y - C)/Y$, where S = propensity to save, Y = income, and C = consumer expenditures. When the percentage is calculated on the basis of a specific increase or decrease in the total income and in that part of the income not devoted to the consumption expenditures between two chosen periods, it is called the *marginal propensity to save*. For total income Y, some authorities use national income, others use gross national product, and still others use disposable personal income. See PROPENSITY TO CONSUME.

property account
An account maintained for the recording of fixed assets.

property dividend
A dividend paid in the form of property other than cash, scrip, or the company's own bonds and stocks. Also known as *dividend in kind*.

property reserved
A British term for *accumulated depreciation*.

property risk
The possibility of damage to or destruction of property through theft, fire, or other peril.

property tax
A tax levied on real or personal property, the rate usually being determined by the taxing authority.

proportional tax
A tax whose percentage rate remains constant as the tax base increases, so that the amount of tax paid is a fixed proportion of the tax base. Property tax is an example. Thus if the tax rate remains constant at 10 percent, a taxpayer who owns $20,000 worth of property pays $2,000 in taxes; a taxpayer who owns $200,000 in property pays $20,000 in taxes.

proprietary
Descriptive of exclusive ownership of a product or service by a private person or company as property under that person's or company's con-

trol. A proprietary medicine is a patent medicine, that is, one that may be sold only by specified persons. However, proprietary drugs, such as aspirin and cough remedies, can be sold without a prescription. Used as a noun, an owner or proprietor. Also, see PTY.

proprietary interest
Net worth; the excess of assets over liabilities.

proprietorship
Ownership. See PROPRIETARY.

proprietorship account
See PROPRIETY.

propriety
The account maintained of the net worth of a business of an individual proprietor. Also known as *proprietorship account.*

pro rata distribution clause
In insurance, a clause that may be used when the insured property is located at more than one place. It defines the property without necessarily describing its specific location.

pro tanto
Latin phrase meaning "for so much." In a legal proceeding, a person may be liable pro tanto, *for such an amount.*

protection and indemnity (P&I) policy
Ocean marine insurance providing full liability coverage, usually written on a deductible basis.

protective inventory
See BUFFER INVENTORY.

protective patent insurance
See PATENT INSURANCE.

protective tariff
An import tax intended to shield domestic producers from foreign competition. Although not usually high enough to prohibit the importation of foreign goods, protective tariffs may put foreign producers at a competitive disadvantage in domestic markets. See REVENUE TARIFF.

proximate cause
A cause arising out of a wrongdoer's negligence or out of conduct deemed, under the rules of law applicable to the case and under the extent of the wrongdoer's duty, sufficient to hold the wrongdoer liable for the particular harm resulting in fact therefrom. As distinguished from a remote cause, or any supervening or concurring cause, for which the wrongdoer is not deemed chargeable under those rules.

proxy
A written authorization given by a shareholder to someone else for the purpose of representing him or her and voting his or her shares at a shareholders' meeting.

proxy statement
Information the Securities and Exchange Commission requires a company to provide to its stockholders as a prerequisite to solicitation of proxies from them in the matter of a security subject to the requirements of the Securities Exchange Act.

PRSA
Initials for *Public Relations Society of America, Inc.*

prudent man rule
Applied as an investment standard in some states; the legal requirement that a fiduciary, such as a trustee, may invest the fund's money only in securities specifically listed by the state. See LEGAL LIST. In other states, the trustee may invest in a security if it is one that a prudent man of discretion and intelligence, who is seeking a reasonable income and preservation of capital, would buy.

PS
See POSTAL SERVICE, U.S.

PSA
See PUBLIC SERVICES ADMINISTRATION.

PSFB
Initials for *Pacific Southwest Freight Bureau.*

PSG
See PSYCHOGALVANOMETER.

PST
See PACIFIC STANDARD TIME.

psychogalvanometer
Equipment that measures basal skin resistance (BSR) and indicates changes in the resistance of the skin through a galvanometric instrument. It is sometimes used as a tool for market research wherein changes in a consumer's skin resistance are measured as the subject is exposed to assorted products or ideas. The difficulty with such a technique is that, while it does indicate a change that may be related to reaction on the part of the subject, the nature of the reaction is open to interpretation. In other uses, such as in law enforcement work, the popular name for psychogalvanometer is "lie detector."

PT
Initials for *Pacific time*. See PACIFIC STANDARD TIME.

Pty
Abbreviation for *proprietary*. In many countries, equivalent to *Company* in the United States; a privately owned as opposed to a publicly held corporation.

public accountant
An accountant who offers his or her professional services to the public. See CERTIFIED PUBLIC ACCOUNTANT.

public corporation
A corporation created by the state to fulfill certain purposes, for example, a town, a city, a school district, a water district. Also known as *political corporation* or *public agency*. See CORPORATION.

public domain
The realm embracing property rights belonging to the community at large, subject to appropriation by anyone. The legal status of being unprotected by copyright or patent.

Public Health Service (PHS)
An agency of the Department of Health, Education and Welfare, the PHS consists of six operating units that directly affect consumers. See ALCOHOL, DRUG ABUSE, AND MENTAL HEALTH ADMINISTRATION, CENTER FOR DISEASE CONTROL, FOOD AND DRUG ADMINISTRATION, HEALTH RESOURCES ADMINISTRATION, HEALTH SERVICES ADMINISTRATION, and NATIONAL INSTITUTES OF HEALTH.

public lands
See PUBLIC DOMAIN.

public liability insurance
See LIABILITY INSURANCE.

public offering
The sale of securities to the general public, usually through the services of an investment banker.

public property
All real and personal property owned by the government.

public sector
That part of the economy in which decisions of a collective or public nature predominate; the realm of the government.

public service corporation
See QUASI-PUBLIC ENTERPRISE.

Public Services Administration (PSA)
A unit of the Social and Rehabilitation Service of the Department of Health, Education and Welfare, the PSA is responsible for joint federal and state social services programs that aid children, families, aged and handicapped individuals, and others who may or may not be receiving public assistance.

public utility
An industry in which there is public regulation of a vital good or service that is produced more efficiently by a single firm than it might be if produced on the basis of open competition by many firms. Industries supplying natural gas, electric power, and water supplies are examples of public utilities. Also, see QUASI-PUBLIC ENTERPRISE.

public warehouse
A business enterprise that receives, crates, stores, ships, and performs other related services for others. See BULK STORAGE WAREHOUSE, COLD STORAGE WAREHOUSE, COMMODITY WAREHOUSE, GENERAL MERCHANDISE WAREHOUSE, HOUSEHOLD GOODS WAREHOUSE.

public works
Construction projects, such as highways, canals, and dams, undertaken by the government for the use and benefit of the general public.

PUD
Initials for *pickup and delivery,* descriptive of a service offered by the carrier.

pull date
The date on which material for a shop order or kit is pulled from the stockroom and issued to the production floor.

pulling
See PICKING.

pulse repetition rate
The number of electric pulses per unit of time occurring at a point in a computer.

punch card or punched card
In data processing, a heavy-duty or stiff-paper card of uniform size and shape, intended to have holes punched in it in a meaningful pattern. The punched holes are detected by a reading device of mechanical design, using either mechanical fingers or electrical contacts. Some readers use photoelectric sensing of the punched holes. See HOLLERITH CODE.

punched-card data processing
A method of putting data into a computer system by means of cards with holes punched into them in accordance with a code for which the system has been programmed. Paper tape, similarly punched and in roll form, may be used as an alternative method for activating data processing systems designed to accept this medium.

punched-tape data processing
See PUNCHED-CARD DATA PROCESSING.

punching-rate
In data processing, the number of cards, characters, blocks, fields, or words of information placed in the form of holes distributed on cards or on paper tape per unit of time.

purchase and installment salesback
The buying of a property on the completion of construction and its immediate resale to the same person under a long-term installment contract.

purchase and leaseback
The buying of a property that is subject to an existing mortgage and its immediate leasing to the seller.

purchase methods
In manufacturing, methods by which purchases are made, depending on the nature of the demand in the plant and conditions in the market in which the goods are to be bought. Principal purchase methods are (1) by requirements, (2) for a specific future period, (3) market purchasing, (4) speculative, (5) by contract, (6) group purchasing of small items, and (7) scheduled buys.

purchase-money mortgage
A mortgage to secure part or all of the purchase price of the property mortgaged, given by the buyer to the seller or to a third person furnishing a loan to the buyer.

purchase-money obligation
A mortgage or other type of debt secured by a lien that has priority over any lien subsequently created.

purchase order
A document instructing a supplier to deliver goods, materials, or services per specifications and at a specified price and time. On acceptance by the supplier, the purchase order becomes a legal contract.

purchase requisition
An internal document authorizing the purchasing department to issue a purchase order.

purchasing power risk
In the securities market, the uncertainty of the purchasing power of future returns on investment because of changes in the price level. Also, see SECURITY RISK, FINANCIAL RISK, INTEREST RATE RISK, MARKET RISK, POLITICAL RISK, and SOCIAL RISK.

pure oligopoly
See OLIGOPOLY.

pure risk
A risk in which there is no possibility for gain, only for loss. This is the type of risk generally and specifically covered by insurance contracts. Also, see SPECULATIVE RISK.

put
See PUTS AND CALLS.

puts and calls
Options that give the holder the right to sell (put) or buy (call) a fixed amount of a specific stock at a specified price within a specified time period. Puts are purchased by those who think a stock price may go down, and they obligate the seller of the right to take delivery of the stock at the specified price. The purchaser of the put may then buy stock on the open market at the lower price, delivering it at the higher price, thereby realizing a profit. A call is purchased by one who thinks the stock price will rise and that he or she will acquire it at a value higher than stipulated in the option. Put and call contracts are usually written for 30-, 60-, or 90-day periods.

pyramid selling
A system of selling in which purchasers buy the right to sell a product. This right usually includes a requirement to purchase a minimum quantity of the product. Titles are often part of the purchase; among them are *distributor, dealer, agent, sales supervisor, representative,* and *area manager.* The technique takes on the form of a pyramid by the fact that the first purchaser resells the product and a title to another purchaser who may do the same thing in turn. The effect is to resell the rights to buy and sell even though, as is often the case, the product is never technically consumed. Pyramid selling has been made illegal in some countries, and where it is not directly illegal it has been repeatedly challenged.

qualification
A statement in an auditor's report directing the reader's attention to any important limitation or to any doubt or disagreement the auditor feels about any item reported.

qualified profit sharing
A form of deferred profit sharing that conforms to Section 401(d) of the Internal Revenue Code and thereby qualifies for special tax breaks.

qualified report
An audit report that contains one or more qualifications or exceptions.

qualified stock option
A stock option plan that qualifies for capital gains tax treatment. Under such a plan a stock must be awarded at market value, exercised over no longer than a five-year period, and then held for three years before it is sold; capital gains tax rates then apply.

qualified stock purchase
A formal, IRS-governed plan under which employees can purchase company stock at less than the market price at the time of purchase, on a payroll deduction basis, over a fixed period of time.

qualifying reserve
See VALUATION ACCOUNT.

quality control
Any of the processes and policies practiced by an enterprise to maintain a desired level of quality of operations or of product. Not limited to

production, quality control may encompass any aspect of the enterprise.

quantification
The expression of any statement in terms of numbers or specific quantities.

quantity discount
An allowance, in credit, cash, or goods, given by a seller to a buyer because of the size of an individual purchase. The practice does not violate federal laws dealing with price discrimination provided the seller can demonstrate that the allowance or discount is granted as a result of a saving to the seller. It may also be justified on the basis that the seller, acting in good faith, must meet a competitor's reduced price. A primary objective of laws against price discrimination is to prevent larger corporations from engaging in price competition with smaller firms, which generally produce in lower volumes than the larger firms.

quantity survey
A technical process for estimating the cost of a new construction, it involves detailed estimates of the quantities of raw materials to be used, the current price of the materials, and the labor costs. Also known as the *price takeoff method.*

quantity theory of money
In economics, a theory that states the relationship between the quantity of money and the price level in an economy. The equation used to express the relationship is $MV = PT,$ where M is the stock of money, V is the velocity of circulation of money, P is the average price level, and T is a measure of the flow of real goods and services, that is, the flow of real income. This is known as the *Fisher equation,* after the economist Irving Fisher. According to the theory, an increase in the quantity of money in circulation causes an increase in prices, assuming the supply of goods remains constant; conversely, a decrease in the amount of money in circulation will lower prices. Its first explicit formulation as a theory is attributed to John Locke (1632–1704). In part, it became one of the basic tenets of the classical school of economics.

quantum meruit
Latin for "as much as he deserved." In a court pleading, an allegation that the defendant owes the plaintiff as much as the plaintiff is reasonably entitled to for work and labor already performed.

quartile
In statistics, one of the points in a frequency distribution by which the distribution is divided into fourths; for example, the 75th, 50th, and 25th percentiles. See PERCENTILE.

quartile deviation
In statistics, one-half of the difference obtained by subtracting the first quartile from the third quartile in a frequency distribution.

quasi contract
Not a contract but an obligation imposed by law. It rests on the principle that one should not be enriched unjustly at the expense of another. For example, when a person comes into possession of money or property belonging to another, and the person should not in good conscience retain it, the law places on that person the quasi-contractual duty to return it. Or after rendering services to a person injured in an accident, a physician may recover for his or her services on a quasi-contract theory.

quasi corporation
A public or municipal body or organization (as a county) not specifically incorporated or vested with all the usual powers of a corporation but exercising certain corporate functions and rights in connection with public duties.

quasi-public enterprise
An essentially public organization, although under private ownership and control, such as a railroad.

Quesnay, François (1694–1774)
A French doctor of medicine, physician to Louis XV and Madame de Pompadour, influential among members of the king's court as a theorist in economics; founder of the physiocrats. He emigrated to the state of Delaware in the Unites States where he was commissioned by President Jefferson to draw up a system of education for the United States. One of his views was the forerunner of the theory that value is added by labor to commodities and materials. See PHYSIOCRATS.

quetzal
The basic unit of currency in Guatemala.

queue time
See WAIT TIME.

queuing problem
The condition that occurs when the impact of demand on production facilities exceeds production capabilities. See WAITING-LINE THEORY.

queuing theory
See WAITING-LINE THEORY.

quick asset
A current asset normally convertible into cash within a relatively short time period, in the order of one month. Examples are cash call loans, marketable securities, and a commodity or good that can be sold immediately on the open market at quoted prices. Also known as *liquid asset*.

quick deck
A summarized parts list—usually in the form of a deck of punched cards—showing the total quantities of all components required to put a product together.

quick-deck explosion
The technique that uses a deck of punched cards to break an assembly down directly into all its components without stopping at each level to check inventory availability.

quick ratio
See ACID TEST.

quiet enjoyment
The right of an owner or tenant to the use of property without interference.

quitclaim deed
See DEED, QUITCLAIM.

quota
In trade relations, a physical limit, mandatory or voluntary, set on the import of a product. In marketing-sales operations, the definition of a budget for orders in terms of a physical limit that becomes mandatory; a numerical quantity for performance stated in units or dollars, sometimes in both, and generally designated for a geographical region, a sales district, and an individual salesperson or sales account. The fulfillment of cumulative quotas ensures the attainment of the budget. Progress toward achievement of quotas is one tool of management for

quantitatively measuring the progress of a specific effort, program, or individual in the sales activity.

quota sampling
In statistical research and analysis, a nonrandom sampling method. Often used in field studies of the opinions and practices of segments of populations. A community may be divided into equal numbers of households, and from each of the groups or divisions an equal number or quota of households may be selected for interview or study or sampling.

quo warranto
Medieval Latin for "by what warrant." A court proceeding by which a government body attempts to oust a person from public office.

r
See COEFFICIENT OF CORRELATION and PEARSON, KARL.

RAB
Initials for *Radio Advertising Bureau.*

rabble hypothesis
Developed by Elton Mayo of Harvard University, who contended that too many managers perceived society as a horde or mob of unorganized individuals whose only concern was self-preservation or self-interest. These managers viewed people as dominated by physiological and safety needs, wanting to make as much money as possible for as little work as possible. In consequence, management operated on the assumption that workers on the whole were a contemptible lot. Mayo called this assumption the *rabble hypothesis*. He deplored the au-

thoritarian, task-oriented management practices the hypothesis created. See MAYO, ELTON.

rack jobber
In the wholesale marketing of such nonfood products as drugs, toilet articles, and housewares to grocery retailers, the rack jobber stocks merchandise into display racks he has himself installed. Rack jobbers are full-service merchant wholesalers who carry an extensive line of goods, sell on credit or consignment, and may provide a wide range of ancillary services. Many of the items in a supermarket section in which housewares, drugs, and toiletries are displayed are supplied by rack jobbers. Also known as *rack merchandiser*.

rack merchandiser
See RACK JOBBER.

racks
Storing equipment used in warehouses and storerooms. Some of the most common types are pallet, bin, tier, cantilever, flow-through, drive-through, A-frame, stationary, rollaway, adjustable-arms, fixed-arms, single-deck, and double-deck.

Railroad Retirement Act
See RAILROAD RETIREMENT BOARD.

Railroad Retirement Board (RRB)
A federal agency that administers a retirement pension system for retired railroad employees, their spouses, and their survivors. It also administers an unemployment insurance system, together with a reemployment service. The board was established by the Railroad Retirement Act of 1935 and consists of three members appointed by the president of the United States, with the consent of the Senate.

rail-trailer shipment
See TRAILERS ON FLATCARS.

Railway Labor Act
Passed in 1926, governs the labor relations of railroads engaged in interstate commerce. The act established collective bargaining and labor's right to self-organization, and prescribed methods to settle disputes. Amended in 1936 to include labor relations between airlines and their employees.

rain insurance
Issued primarily in conjunction with outdoor events to which the public pays admission. The coverage usually extends for a brief period, possibly in the order of a few hours, and specifies the perils of rain, hail, snow, and sleet. Policies may cover (1) loss of revenue because the event had to be canceled on account of unfavorable weather conditions and (2) expenses of preparing for the event, for the same reasons. See CONSEQUENTIAL-LOSSES INSURANCE.

rally
A brisk rise following a decline in the general price level of the stock market, or in an individual stock. Also known as *upswing, upturn,* and *uptrend.*

RAM
Initials for *random-access memory.* See RANDOM ACCESS.

rand
The basic unit of currency in the Republic of South Africa, Botswana, Lesotho, South-West Africa (Namibia), and Swaziland.

In production procedures, a short expression for random selection, a scheduling rule that does not assign priorities. The order to be processed next is selected at random from all the orders waiting in line at the processing station.

R&D or R and D
See RESEARCH AND DEVELOPMENT.

R&L
Initials for *rail and lake,* used to designate routing of freight.

R&O
Initials for *rail and ocean,* used to designate routing of freight.

random access
In computers, the means of obtaining information from or placing information into storage where the time required for access is independent of the location of the information. Effectively, random access can be achieved without time penalty. See SERIAL ACCESS and PARALLEL ACCESS.

random dispatching rule
In manufacturing, the sequencing of jobs to be run on a basis that is unrelated to any measure of effectiveness for that operation. For example, an operator given the option may choose to run those jobs that have the loosest time standards. See DUE-DATE RULE.

random sampling
In statistical analysis, a selection of data taken entirely by chance and in such a way that every individual or unit of measurement has an equal and independent opportunity for being included in the sample. See STRATIFIED SAMPLING.

R&T
Initials for *rail and truck,* used to designate routing of freight.

R&W
Initials for *rail and water,* used to designate routing of freight.

range
A strip of land six miles wide, determined by a government survey, running north and south. Also, one of the north–south rows of a township in a U.S. public-land survey that are numbered east and west from the principal meridian of the survey.

In statistics, the spread between the smallest and the largest number in the group or class. It is distinct from *average,* which indicates the central tendency of a sequence of numbers.

rangeland
Land unsuitable for cultivation but capable of providing forage for livestock.

rate basis number
In transportation, the number by which a given scale of class rates is identified for application to a specific shipment.

rate-buster
A pieceworker who takes advantage of rates to earn high bonus payments and does not join with fellow workers in holding production back to the bogey level agreed on unofficially by the group. The unpopularity of rate-busters derives from the fear felt by the other workers that management might react to relatively high bonus payments by cutting the rate of payment for piecework. Also known as *cowboy* or *high-flier.* See RESTRICTER.

rate group
In transportation, the group in which a given place is identified for the determination of rates in a tariff.

rate of exchange
The price that must be paid in one unit of currency to purchase another unit of currency.

rate-of-return pricing
A method for determining a selling price for an item by adding a mark-up that will produce a target return on investment.

rating
The financial or credit position of a person or a business enterprise as determined by another enterprise or by a credit-checking agency. In the securities market, the relative worth of a security as determined by any of several investment advisory services.

In the television industry, rating is the result of a survey that indicates the percentage of those television sets in use which are tuned to a specific channel or show at a specified time.

In insurance, rating is the measure of insurability, or risk taken by the insurer, and is used in the determination of the premium rate for coverage for specified perils.

rating schedule
Used to determine insurance rates for buildings that are specifically rated rather than class rated. See SCHEDULE RATES and CLASS RATES.

ratio
In statistics, the ratio of quantity x to quantity y is defined as x divided by y.

ratio chart
A graphic representation of statistical data that shows the rate of change in a series of values. It differs from an arithmetic chart, which shows finite amounts of change.

ratio-delay technique
Originated approximately in 1927 by H. C. Tippett of the Shirley Institute of the British Cotton Industry Research Association. Known in the United Kingdom as *snap reading;* more widely used in the United States, where it is also called *work sampling.* A technique for obtaining information about work behavior in the form of a probability percent-

age of occurrence over a time period. After the occurrences are defined, a large number of momentary or *snap* observations are made of the actual work and are applied to a statistical conclusion. An alternative to TIME AND MOTION STUDY.

rationalization
In human behavior, the equivalent of making excuses. For example, the tendency to blame someone else for one's inability to attain an objective or reach an important goal: "It was Homer's fault that I didn't get that promotion." Or the habit of talking oneself out of what one really desires: "I really didn't want to do that anyway." See FRUSTRATION.

ratios
Financial ratios are derived from balance-sheet data. Operating ratios are derived from items of income and expense. Ratios serve as a measure of merit of several aspects of an enterprise when data for one accounting period are compared with similar data from another period. Ratios may also be used to compare one organization with another or with an industry average or standard. See ACTIVITY RATIO, LEVERAGE RATIOS, LIQUIDITY RATIOS, and PROFITABILITY RATIOS.

raw materials
Basic items that come from farms, mines, and forests, and include such commodities as grain, wool, ore, tobacco, petroleum, and wood. Also, semifinished goods purchased for use as an ingredient or component of a finished product. See INDUSTRIAL GOODS.

RDS
See RURAL DEVELOPMENT SERVICE.

REA
See RURAL ELECTRIFICATION ADMINISTRATION.

reacquired stock
Capital stock that has been reverted in title to the issuing corporation, usually through repurchase, by donation, or in settlement of a debt to the issuing company. Reacquired shares that are not canceled are known as *treasury stock* or *treasury shares*. See REDEMPTION and TREASURY STOCK.

read
In data processing, the sensing of information contained in some source.

read in
In data processing, to sense information and transfer it to an internal storage medium. See READ OUT.

reading rate
In data processing, the number of cards, characters, blocks, fields, or words sensed by a sensing device per unit of time.

read-only memory (ROM)
A computer memory that permits the reading of a predetermined pattern of zeros and ones. This predetermined information is stored in the ROM at the time of its manufacture. See PROGRAMMABLE READ-ONLY MEMORY.

read out
In data processing, the process of removing information from internal storage and displaying it in understandable form. Also, the information removed from storage and displayed.

real account
In accounting, a term used in double-entry bookkeeping to indicate an account that is carried over from one accounting period to another. Asset and liability accounts are examples. Also known as *property account.*

real cost
In accounting, cost expressed in terms of physical units, such as bushels, pounds, tons, miles, and worker-hours. In economics, the cost of goods and services adjusted for factors such as inflation.

real estate
Land and land improvements, including buildings and attachments; also, standing timber and orchard trees. Also known as *real property,* in contrast to *personal property.*

real estate investment trust (REIT)
A special arrangement under federal and state law whereby investors may pool funds for investments in real estate and mortgages.

real gross domestic product
In economics, gross domestic product (GDP) data adjusted for current inflation.

real gross national product
In economics, gross national product (GNP) data adjusted for current inflation.

real income
Income measured in terms of the real goods and services it can buy. It can be calculated by dividing money income by a suitable index of prices.

real investment
In finance, an expenditure that creates a new capital asset. Real investments result in new capital formation.

realistic method
Also known as *inductive method*. See INDUCTION.

real property
See REAL ESTATE.

real time
In data processing, a real-time computation is one that is performed during the actual occurrence of the physical event to which the calculation pertains. Real-time processing makes it possible to use the results of a computation to guide or control the related physical event.

realtor
A licensed real estate broker who is an active member of a local real estate board that is affiliated with the National Association of Real Estate Boards (NAREB).

real wage
The purchasing power of a money wage.

reappropriation
In government accounting, legislative action that permits the government to continue to incur obligations under an expired or soon-to-expire appropriation.

rebate
An adjustment in a charge that has been paid to the supplier of a service or good, resulting in a return of a portion of the payment. If the adjustment was the result of an overcharge, the returned portion would be referred to as a *refund*. If the adjustment was made prior to payment, it may be referred to as a *discount*. See REFUND.

recapture clause
In a lease, a provision to terminate the lease if certain of its conditions are not met by the lessee.

receivable
A collectible money obligation, whether due yet or not. Usually referred to as *account(s) receivable* or *note(s) receivable*.

receivables turnover
A ratio of business activity; net sales divided by average receivables during the sales period.

receiver
A person appointed by the court for a specified time period to take charge of property while its disposition is being determined or an imposed objective is being attained. The property administered by a receiver is said to be "in receivership."

receiving
In business and industry, the department or section responsible for receiving and identifying all incoming material and transferring the material to stores or other areas within the company.

receiving (or receiver's) report
A document prepared by the receiver of a shipment as a formal record of goods received; generally used as a source document for warehouse and inventory accounting and to support shippers' and carriers' invoices. The report usually includes the name and address of the shipper, date the goods were received, name of the carrier, bill of lading number, description and quantity of goods, and signature of the person actually receiving the property on behalf of the consignee.

recession
A downturn in economic activity, one phase of the business cycle. Decreased investment, falling incomes, falling consumption, and increased unemployment are characteristic of this phase.

reciprocal switching
An arrangement made by two or more railroad companies whereby each agrees to absorb the other's local switching charges when serving the same location.

reciprocal trade agreements program
A plan for the expansion of U.S. exports through legislation authorizing the president to negotiate tariff reductions with other nations in

return for parallel concessions. The program is defined in the Reciprocal Trade Agreements Act of 1934 with subsequent amendments and related legislation. See TRADE EXPANSION ACT.

reclassify
In accounting, to break down a transaction into secondary classifications.

reconciliation
In accounting, determining and recording the items necessary to bring the balances of two or more related accounts or statements into agreement.

reconsignment
Changing the bill of lading provisions with respect to the consignee or destination while the goods are still in transit.

reconveyance
Transfer of the title of land from one person to the immediately preceding owner; commonly used when the performance or debt is satisfied under the terms of a deed of trust, thus allowing the trustee to convey the title he or she has held on condition back to the owner. See TRUST DEED.

record
In data processing, a group of related fields of information treated as a unit; thus a listing of information, usually in printed or printable form. Also may be used to indicate the inputting of data into a storage device.

In accounting, a book used to document a company's transactions.

Also, a publication related to ocean marine insurance; see AMERICAN BUREAU OF SHIPPING.

record date
The date on which the holder of a security must be registered on the shareholders' record book of the company in order to receive a declared dividend or to vote on company affairs.

recoupment
A legal right to deduct from a plaintiff's claim any payment or loss the defendant has suffered by reason of the plaintiff's wrongful act.

recovery
The upward phase of a business cycle in which the economy's income, output, and employment are rising and a growing degree of business

and consumer optimism is manifested by an expanding rate of capital investment and consumption.

recovery value
In accounting, estimated revenue from a resale or scrapping of a fixed asset. See SALVAGE.

rectangular–Cartesian coordinates
The line graph or Cartesian coordinate system is the most extensively used chart form in statistics. Two axes, or coordinates, each bearing a uniformly divided scale, are located at right angles to one another through a point of origin. One, the abscissa, is measured along the horizontal scale and is called the x-axis; the other, the ordinate, is measured along the vertical scale and is called the y-axis. The abscissa is positive in sign to the right of the point of origin, negative to the left. The ordinate is positive above the origin, negative below.

Reddin, William J.
Professor of business administration and theorist in organizational development and the management of change; credited with the 3-D Theory of Managerial Effectiveness. Based on studies conducted by Ohio State University and the University of Michigan on the relationships and task orientation characteristics of managers, the theory casts the results of the studies into negative and positive dimensions that define the behavioral characteristics and styles with respect to effectiveness.

redemption
In financial transactions, the act of buying back. For example, a debtor buys back or redeems his or her mortgaged property on completely repaying the debt, or the issuer of a bond buys back the bond from the holder.

redemption fund
See SINKING FUND.

redemption price
The price at which a bond may be redeemed before maturity, at the option of the issuing company. Also applies to the price the company must pay to call in certain types of preferred stock. See CALLABLE ISSUE.

red herring
In finance, a colloquialism for a preliminary prospectus prepared in conjunction with a proposed security offering filed with the Securities and Exchange Commission.

rediscount
A negotiable instrument, previously acquired by a bank at a discount, sold to a Federal Reserve Bank. The act or process of rediscounting such an instrument.

rediscount rate
When the Federal Reserve System was originated, loans were the chief earning asset of commercial banks. Since then, buying and selling marketable securities, particularly government securities, have become significant means for obtaining added liquidity. At one time, member banks were expected to borrow at the Federal Reserve when in need of funds; these borrowings were *rediscounts,* because loans of a commercial nature, already discounted once by member banks, were the basis for rediscounting at the Federal Reserve Banks. The rate of interest charged by the Federal Reserve is the rediscount rate. Also known as *discount rate.*

red label
A label that must be clearly visible and that is required on shipments of articles of hazardous nature.

redlining
The practice whereby banks and other institutional lenders deny mortgage credit to an entire declining neighborhood regardless of the condition of the specific property or the creditworthiness of potential borrowers.

reducing-balance method
In accounting, a method of depreciating an asset. The amount to be depreciated annually is derived by applying a fixed percentage to the diminishing balance of the asset account, or by applying a diminishing rate to the original cost of the asset. For example, an asset whose estimated useful life is ten years could be depreciated each year by a constant rate equivalent to 90 percent of the previous year's depreciation charge. Other constant rates may be selected, within IRS guidelines.

reefer
See REFRIGERATION CAR.

reference designator
A code that indicates the location of a part or assembly on an engineering drawing.

reference group
In industrial psychology, any group with which an individual identifies, such that he or she tends to use the group as a standard for self-evaluation and as a source for attempts to satisfy personal needs, goals, and objectives. The reference group may be one to which the individual already belongs or one he or she aspires to join.

reference record
In data processing, an output of a compiler that lists the operations and their positions in the final specific routine and contains information describing the segmentation and storage allocation of the routine.

refinancing
In the securities market, new securities may be sold by a company and the money used to retire other debts. For example, the receipts from a new issue of common stock may be used to redeem outstanding bonds in order to save interest costs.

reformation
An action to correct a mistake in a deed.

refrigeration car
Any vehicle or railroad car built with an icing compartment and ventilators, or with mechanically operated cooling equipment. Used in transporting perishable goods. Also known as *reefer*.

refrigerator van
British term for REFRIGERATION CAR.

refund
The return of an overpayment made for goods or services. The refund may be in the form of money, merchandise, services, or a credit voucher applicable to the purchase of new goods or services.

regeneration
In production procedures, a periodic explosion of the master schedule, down through the bills of material. The master schedule is compared with the quantity on hand and on order to determine net requirements. See EXPLOSION and MASTER SCHEDULE.

regional stock exchange
Any stock exchange in the United States except the New York and American stock exchanges.

register
In computers, a hardware device that stores a certain amount of bits or characters. In finance and accounting, the official list of shareholders in a corporation; also, a record for the consecutive entry of any class of transactions.

registered bond
A bond registered on the books of the issuing company in the name of the owner. It can be transferred only when endorsed by the registered owner. See BEARER BOND and COUPON BOND.

registered mail insurance
This provides all-risk coverage for currency, securities, bullion, and similar valuables when shipped by registered mail. It covers the period from the messenger's departure from the insured party's premises to delivery of the item to the person to whom it is addressed. This supplements the post-office insurance limits by as much as several millions of dollars in shipment value.

registered representative
Current expression for the older term *customer's man;* in a member firm of the New York Stock Exchange, a full-time employee who has met the requirements of the Exchange as to background and knowledge of the securities business. Also known as *account executive* or *customer's broker.*

registered trader
A member of the New York Stock Exchange who trades in stocks on the floor for an account in which he or she has an interest. Also known as *floor trader.*

registrar
Usually a trust company or a bank—or a person employed by such an institution—charged with the responsibility of preventing a company from issuing more stock than it is authorized to issue.

registration
Before a public offering of new securities may be made through the mails or in interstate commerce, the securities must be registered with the Securities and Exchange Commission (SEC) by the issuer. Before a

security may be admitted to dealings on a national securities exchange, it must be registered under the Securities Exchange Act of 1934. The application for registration must be filed with the exchange and the SEC by the company issuing the securities. The application must disclose information relating to the company's operations, securities, management, and purpose in making the public offering. Securities of railroads under the jurisdiction of the Interstate Commerce Commission, and certain other types of securities, are exempted.

regression
Human behavior that is essentially below an individual's age level. It is sometimes used as an outlet for frustrated feelings, most dramatically demonstrated by the child who throws a temper tantrum, or by the adult who, angered by a machine that exhibits technical defects and does not perform as it should, strikes or curses the machine. See FRUSTRATION.

In real estate transactions, an appraising principle holding that high-value property located in a neighborhood of lower-value property seeks the level of the lower-value property.

regression analysis
A statistical technique for obtaining estimates and confidence intervals when the sample size is very small. In many instances, a useful tool for making predictions. In simple regression analysis, a variable x is used to make predictions about a variable y. For each value of x there exists a conditional probability distribution of y.

regressive tax
A tax whose percentage rate decreases as the tax base increases. In the strict sense there is no regressive tax in the United States. However, if we compare the rate structure of the tax with the taxpayer's net income rather than the actual tax base, the term regressive applies to any tax that takes a larger share of income from low-income than from high-income taxpayers. Most proportional taxes are thus seen to have regressive effects. For example, a sales tax is the same for rich as for poor people, but the poor spend a larger percentage of their incomes on consumer goods, so that the sales taxes they pay represent a greater proportion of their incomes. See PROGRESSIVE TAX.

regulated investment company
An investment company that has met the requirements of the Investment Company Act of 1940 and has chosen to be regulated under this act.

Regulation Q
The Federal Reserve Board regulation setting the maximum rates member banks may pay on time and savings deposits.

Regulation T
The Federal Reserve Board regulation setting the maximum amount of credit that may be granted by brokers and dealers for the purpose of purchasing securities. See MARGIN.

Regulation U
The Federal Reserve Board regulation setting the maximum amount of credit that may be granted by a bank to customers for the purpose of purchasing securities.

Rehabilitation Services Administration (RSA)
A unit of the Office of Human Development of the Department of Health, Education and Welfare, the RSA provides federal support for state and federal programs of vocational training and rehabilitation that serve physically and mentally handicapped citizens, with special priority to persons with severe disabilities.

reinsurance
The sharing of risk among several insurance companies in cases where an insurance policy involves the possibility of a large indemnification and where the possibility of catastrophic loss exists. It is sometimes known as *insurance of insurance.* One insurance company procures insurance coverage from another, or from several others; often done without the awareness of the insured. The company buying the reinsurance is called the *reinsured;* the company selling it is called the *reinsurer.*

REIT
See REAL ESTATE INVESTMENT TRUST.

rejectable quality level (RQL)
See LOT TOLERANCE PERCENT DEFECTIVE.

related manager
In behavioral science, a manager who accepts others as he or she finds them. Such managers enjoy long conversations as a way of getting to know others better. This also enables them to obtain much useful information from their subordinates. They see organizations primarily as social systems and judge subordinates on how well they understand

others. They judge superiors on the warmth they show to subordinates. They require considerable and continuous contact with others. In stress situations they tend to become dependent on others and depressed. They value people but tend to undervalue the importance of the organization and its technology. They are sentimental; they fear rejection and conflict.

relationships behavior
The extent to which a leader is likely to maintain personal relationships between himself or herself and members of the group by opening channels of communication, delegating responsibility, and giving subordinates an opportunity to use their potential; characterized by socio-emotional support, friendship, and mutual trust.

relationships orientation (RO)
In reference to management style, the extent to which a manager has personal job relationships; characterized by listening, trusting, and encouraging. See AUTOCRAT, MISSIONARY, and TASK ORIENTATION.

relative component bar chart
See BAR CHART.

release clause
A stipulation that, on payment of a specific sum of money to the holder of a trust deed or mortgage, the lien on the specifically described lot or property shall be removed from the blanket lien on the whole area involved.

release of deposit
A form signed by all parties to an escrow, authorizing the distribution of funds deposited in escrow.

release of mortgage
See DEED OF RELEASE.

reliction
An increase of land caused by the permanent withdrawal of the water of a river, a stream, a lake, or the sea. The use of the incremental land accrues to the owner of the land that has been thus increased.

remedial law
See ADJECTIVE LAW.

remedy
The judicial means or court procedures by which legal and equitable rights are enforced; the relief obtained by such means or procedures.

renewal fund
A reserve fund established for the replacement or renewal of an asset. Also known as *replacement fund*.

rent
In ordinary conversation, most payments for temporary use of an item of property. Economists find it desirable to reserve the term for land rent, considering other such payments a return on the capital invested in improvements.

rent and rental value insurance
Written to provide coverage in the event that a building may become unusable, having been rendered untenable by fire. See CONSEQUEN-TIAL-LOSSES INSURANCE.

repair order
See REWORK ORDER.

replacement cost and depreciation insurance
Normally pays for fire losses on the basis of replacement cost less depreciation. The policy generally provides that the insured must use the proceeds only for the repair or replacement of the property and within a 12-month period. Also, if it pertains to a building, the same site must be used. Not available in all states. See CONSEQUENTIAL-LOSSES INSURANCE.

replacement fund
See RENEWAL FUND.

replacement method
A method of depreciation whereby an estimate is made of the cost of replacing an asset that is in use and has a limited life. The amount of the current depreciation expense, usually on a straight-line basis, is increased by a percentage derived from a comparison of the anticipated replacement cost with recorded original cost.

replacement theory
In accounting, a means of determining the optimum balance between the costs of breakdowns or failure versus the cost of replacement under conditions of uncertainty.

replevin
A lawful course of action for the recovery of goods claimed to be wrongfully taken or detained. The goods in contention may be delivered to the claimant upon that party's promise to (1) seek remedy and resolution and (2) return the goods if so ordered through the courts.

report program generator (RPG)
A computer language that can be used on several computers; stresses complete output reports based on information that describes the input files, operations, and output format.

representation
A statement made by a person concerning a material fact, intended to induce an insurer to enter into an insurance contract. A material false representation will void the contract even though it may have been innocently made. For example, in applying for health insurance, a person represents that he or she has not had major surgery within the period covered by a specific question on the application form. Shortly thereafter it is learned that the person did in fact have surgery and is still undergoing medical treatment for the disease necessitating the surgery. The policy may then be voided.

repressed inflation
In economics, a state of inflation that exists when the economy is essentially inflationary, aggregate demand exceeding the aggregate supply causing prices to exhibit a tendency to rise; however, effective government policy is preventing the rise in prices. Economists contend that an underlying disequilibrium in aggregate supply and demand, if allowed to remain uncorrected, is certain to cause inflation, regardless of any regulatory efforts. Also known as *suppressed inflation*.

reproduction cost
See COST OF REPRODUCTION.

repudiation
See ABANDONMENT.

repurchased stock
Capital stock bought back by an issuer from its stockholders.

requirements contract
A contract wherein one party to the contract agrees to purchase all his or her requirements of a particular product from another party to the contract.

requisition
A formal, written request for specified articles or services; usually an internal procedure.

res adjudicata
Also known as *res judicata,* the doctrine that once a controversy has been decided or judged on its merits, it is forever settled so far as the particular parties involved are concerned. The intent is to avoid recurrent and whimsical law suits.

research and development (R&D or R and D)
Usually used in connection with the conception and design of new products and the application of technical or engineering resources to the investigation of various alternative approaches to the physical creation of the products. Commonly abbreviated *R&D* or *R and D.*

reserve city bank
See COUNTRY BANK.

reserved material
In manufacturing, material on hand or on order that is assigned to specific future production orders. Also known as *assigned material, allocated material, mortgaged material,* and *obligated material.*

reserve fund
Cash or securities separated from working capital for some specific purpose.

reserve requirement
Established by the Federal Reserve Board, a certain percentage of their deposits that member banks are required to maintain in the form of reserves. The Federal Reserve may set requirements between the limits of 10 and 20 percent on demand deposits held by large reserve banks, and 7 to 14 percent on demand deposits held by smaller banks. Limits on time deposits may range from 3 to 6 percent for any member bank. The changes in reserve requirements are a powerful tool of the Federal Reserve for influencing the money supply. Raising or lowering the reserve requirement has the effect of reducing or increasing the money available for loans and credit.

reserve stock
See BUFFER INVENTORY.

reset rate
In data processing, the number of corrections per unit of time made by the control system.

residence
See DOMICILE.

residuary legatee
One who is entitled to receive the balance of an estate after specified bequests, taxes, and other liabilities have been satisfied.

resignation
In human behavior, a state that occurs when prolonged frustration in goal attainment creates a desire to withdraw from reality and the source of the frustration. This may occur in people with boring, routine jobs, resulting in their resigning themselves to the belief that there is little hope for personal improvement within their environments. See FRUSTRATION.

resistor-transistor logic (RTL)
Developed to overcome certain problems with direct-coupled transistor logic. In RTL, the logic is performed by resistors while the transistors are used to amplify the signal and to produce an inverted output from any positive input.

respondeat superior
Latin for "let the superior give answer." A master's liability for the acts of his or her agent.

responsibility costing
An accounting method that identifies costs with persons assigned to their control rather than with products or functions.

responsibility drift
The shifting of responsibility within an organization, caused, for example, by imperfections in delegations of authority, altered assumptions of responsibility, unforeseen overlapping of authority, changes in personnel, growth of individuals, and informal changes in objectives and in the operating environment.

restraining forces
A term used to indicate those forces in an organizational situation that act to restrain or decrease the motivating drives of individuals. Exam-

ples representing diminishing productivity of a work group are apathy, hostility, and poor maintenance of equipment. See FORCE FIELD ANALYSIS and DRIVING FORCES.

restricted cash
Cash deposits that can be withdrawn only under special conditions or for special purposes. Usual practice is to maintain such cash in a separate bank account.

restricted retained earnings
The portion of retained earnings not legally available for disbursement as dividends.

restricted stock option
An option granted at 95 percent of market value, exercisable over ten years; a form of stock option most prevalent from 1954 through 1964. Profits from the sale of this stock were taxable at capital gains rates. Since 1963, most stock options have conformed with the requirements for qualified options. See QUALIFIED STOCK OPTION.

restricter
A worker who performs or produces at a level considered to be the norm for the group of which he or she is part. See RATE-BUSTER.

restrictive license
An agreement whereby a patentee permits a licensee to sell a patented product under restricted conditions. The restrictions imposed by the patentee may include the fixing of the geographic area the licensee may sell in, the level of the licensee's output, or the price the licensee may charge in selling the patented good.

retail accounting
An accounting method generally used by retail stores and advocated by the NATIONAL RETAIL MERCHANTS ASSOCIATION.

retained earnings
Accumulated net income less distributions to stockholders, and transfers to paid-in capital accounts. Also known as *earned surplus, retained income,* and *undistributed profits.*

retirement allowance
An annuity or pension payable to an employee who has retired from active service.

retirement method
In accounting, a method of depreciation formerly used by public utilities; now obsolete.

retrogressive consumer
In marketing analysis, a consumer who is eager to economize on an existing product or service. See PROGRESSIVE CONSUMER.

retrospective rating
A method of adjusting the amount of a premium to the actual loss experienced during the period covered by an insurance policy.

revenue bond
A bond issued by a government for the purpose of financing the construction or purchase of or additions to income-producing facilities. Repayment of such bonds and the periodic payment of interest on them are dependent on earnings. Familiar examples are bonds used to finance toll roads, bridges, sewers, and transit systems.

revenue deduction
In municipal accounting, an expense, tax, or uncollectible account receivable of a municipal utility or other self-supporting enterprise.

revenue expenditure
In accounting, equivalent to expense charged to operations.

revenue receipts
In accounting, revenue that has been collected in cash for a given period of operations.

revenue reserves
A British expression for the portion of the net worth or total equity of an enterprise that represents retained earnings available for withdrawal by proprietors.

revenue sharing
A plan by which the federal government turns over a portion of its tax revenues to state and local governments each year.

revenue tariff
An import tax usually applied to products that are not produced in the importing country, for example, tin, coffee, and bananas in the case of

the United States. Typically, rates on revenue tariffs are modest. See
PROTECTIVE TARIFF.

reverse split or reverse splitup
The recall of shares by the issuer, who then reissues fewer shares in
exchange. Also known as *splitback* and *splitdown*. See SPLIT.

revocable trust
A trust that can be terminated by its creator.

revolving fund
A fund whose resources are continuously expended, replenished, and
expended again. An example is an asset available for loans the repay-
ments of which are available for other loans. In government or institutional accounting, a revolving fund is one created by an appropriation
or issue of securities for the purpose of providing working capital that
is to be replenished through revenues or transfers from users of the
fund's facilities.

rework order
A manufacturing order to rework or salvage defective parts or products. Also known as *repair order* and "spoiled work order."

RIAA
Initials for *Recording Industry Association of America.*

rial
The basic unit of currency in Iran and Oman.

Ricardo, David (1772–1823)
Born in London, Ricardo entered his father's stock brokerage firm at
age 14 after a brief education in Holland. His strong professional skills
enabled him to enter the exchange, trading on his own account, from
which effort he was reported to have earned a significant fortune. He
studied mathematics and science privately. Stimulated by Adam
Smith's *Wealth of Nations,* he also studied political economy. In 1819
he became a member of Parliament and took an active part in discussions of bank reform, taxation, and national debt reduction. Ricardo
was a founder of the Political Economy Club in London. He authored
many pamphlets and articles on economics. His main work, *On the
Principles of Political Economy and Taxation,* which was published in
1817, contains discussions, considered original at the time, on the
theory of value and distribution, wages, rent, profit, prices, money,

and the comparative-costs principle in foreign-trade theory. Ricardo's work has been, and still is, used as source and reference material.

rider
See ENDORSEMENT.

riel
The basic unit of currency in Cambodia.

right of way
An easement, temporary or permanent, permitting the construction and operation of a railway, road, power line, or pipeline over another's land. See EASEMENT and LICENSE.

rights
A company wanting to raise more funds by issuing additional securities may give its stockholders the opportunity to buy the new securities ahead of others, in proportion to the number of shares each owns; the piece of paper evidencing this offer is called a *right*. The additional stock is usually offered to stockholders below the current market price; rights therefore ordinarily have a market value of their own and are often actively traded. With few exceptions, rights must be exercised within a relatively short span of time. Failure to exercise or sell rights may result in loss of the right to the stockholder. See WARRANT and PREEMPTIVE RIGHT.

right to work
In industrial relations, a term used to describe the rights guaranteed by law banning union security agreements that depend on contracts with management making employment conditional on membership in labor organizations. Legislation in more than one-third of the states of the United States is supported by Section 14b of the Labor-Management Relations Act of 1947, which makes it illegal to join in a contract that provides for a union shop. See TAFT-HARTLEY ACT and YELLOW DOG CONTRACT.

ring shift
See CYCLIC SHIFT.

riparian owner
One who owns land bounding a river or watercourse.

riparian right
The prerogative of a landowner to use the water on, under, or adjacent to his or her land. Also known as *aquatic* or *water right*.

risk
In insurance, the possibility of loss. Insurance tends to provide for full or partial compensation in the event an insured article is damaged or destroyed. See PURE RISK and SPECULATIVE RISK.

risk manager
An insurance specialist who diagnoses risks to which a project or enterprise may be subjected and prescribes appropriate action with respect to insurance coverage.

riyal
The basic unit of currency in Saudi Arabia and the Yemeni Arab Republic.

RL&R
Initials for *rail, lake, and rail,* used to designate routing of freight.

RMMTB
Initials for *Rocky Mountain Motor Tariff Bureau.*

RO
See RELATIONSHIPS ORIENTATION.

robbery insurance
Protects the insured from loss of property, money, and securities through robbery either on or off the premises. Robbery is defined as taking of property from a person in charge of it by force or threat of violence. Coverage may also include property on the insured's premises damaged in the course of the robbery.

Robinson, Joan Violet
Born in 1903 in Cambridge, England, the daughter of Major General Sir Frederick Maurice, Mrs. Robinson graduated from Girton College, Cambridge, and became one of the leading faculty members in economics at Cambridge. Her first book, *Economics of Imperfect Competition* (1933), gained wide attention. In *Essays on the Theory of Employment* (1937) she applied Keynesian concepts to specific conditions and situations. Subsequent works of hers were published in 1942, 1952, 1956, 1959, and 1962. Her articles have appeared in various pro-

fessional journals. Her theories, described as socialistic, contend that profit has no economic justification and that income should be redistributed to favor the weak and poor among the world's population.

Robinson-Patman Act
Passed by Congress in 1936 to amend the Clayton Antitrust Act; prohibits a seller from discriminating in price among his customers if the effect of such discrimination might be to substantially lessen competition, promote monopoly, or injure, prevent, or destroy competition with the buyer, seller, or customers of either one. The act makes it unlawful for a buyer to induce or receive such a discriminatory price in the circumstances described. Price differentials are permitted if they represent actual differences in the cost of manufacture or sale, if they are necessary to meet competition in good faith, or if the goods are seasonal, obsolescent, or distress merchandise.

Rochdale principles
A set of criteria for conducting and operating a consumer cooperative, named after the city of Rochdale, England, where it is believed Charles Howarth and a group of fellow workers in 1844 organized one of the earliest successful cooperative enterprises.

rod
A measure of length equal to 5.5 yards or 16.5 feet.

rollaways
A mobile lateral filing system consisting of self-contained shelving modules mounted on tracks in double-row arrangements. Front stacks glide back and forth to allow access to stationary stacks.

rolling budget
See CONTINUOUS BUDGET.

rolling forecast
A continuing series of periods of marketing activity in the form of a budget. See CONTINUOUS BUDGET.

rollover
The renewal of a short-term debt at the option of the borrower under an agreement with the lender.

rollover bonus
A bonus partially paid out in the year in which it is earned, the remainder being paid over the following several years.

ROM
See READ-ONLY MEMORY.

round lot
In the securities market, a unit of trading or a multiple thereof. On the New York Stock Exchange the standard unit of trading is 100 shares in stocks and a par value of $1,000 in the case of bonds. The unit of trading in some inactive stocks is 10 shares. See INACTIVE STOCK and ODD LOT.

round off
In the presentation of numerical data, to simplify with the express intent of displaying only significant figures. For example, assume the exact annual sales volume of an enterprise is $4,567,332.89. The precise figure is important in bookkeeping; however, for others the amount may be presented as $4,567,333, as $4,567 thousands, or more commonly in informal presentations as $4.6 million. Thus a figure may be rounded off to its most significant digits, depending on the degree of precision required and the occasion.

round sum
A figure whose final digits have been rounded off. See ROUND OFF.

route sheets
At each stage of a manufacturing process a part is analyzed to determine the operations required and to select and specify the functions required to complete the processing. The routing of the part is summarized on *route sheets*. These show (1) the operations required and their sequence, (2) the machines or equipment to be used, and (3) the setup and run time per piece. For a standard part intended to be produced repeatedly to fill needs, route sheets are maintained and accepted as partially descriptive of the manufacturing methods. See OPERATION SHEETS and METHODS MANUAL.

routine
A set of coded instructions arranged in proper sequence to direct the computer to perform a desired operation or sequence of operations; a subdivision of a program. See PROGRAM and SUBROUTINE.

RPG
See REPORT PROGRAM GENERATOR.

RQL
Initials for *rejectable quality level*. See LOT TOLERANCE PERCENT DE-FECTIVE.

RSA
See REHABILITATION SERVICES ADMINISTRATION.

r²
See COEFFICIENT OF DETERMINATION and COEFFICIENT OF CORRELATION.

RTL
See RESISTOR-TRANSISTOR LOGIC.

ruble
The basic unit of currency in the USSR.

rule off
To underscore the last entry in a journal or the last posting in a ledger account. Its purpose is to indicate that no further entries are to be made above the rule-off line and that a total of transactions has been reached.

rule of reason
A criterion for judging alleged infringements of the antitrust laws. The rule of reason was first adopted by the U.S. Supreme Court in 1911 in the cases of *Standard Oil Company* v. *United States* and *United States* v. *American Tobacco Company*. The rule of reason holds that size alone is not to be considered evidence of monopoly; the intent to restrain trade or to monopolize is set forth as the decisive factor.

rule of 72
Approximate formula for expressing the relationship between the number of years, y, required for a quantity to double if it grows at an annual rate of compound interest, r. The formula is $yr = 72$. Therefore, $y = 72/r$ and $r = 72/y$.

runaway inflation
See HYPERINFLATION.

runaway shop
A business organization that moves from one location to another primarily to escape unionization of its employees or the application of labor laws. It is possible for geographically centered industry to make a

similar physical move for the same reasons, or to take advantage of a lower-cost labor market or more favorable taxation.

runout list
A list of items to be scheduled into production in sequence by the dates on which the present available stock is expected to be exhausted.

rupee
The basic unit of currency in India, Mauritius, Nepal, Pakistan, and Sri Lanka.

rupiah
The basic unit of currency in Indonesia.

Rural Development Service (RDS)
An agency of the Department of Agriculture, RDS coordinates social and economic development programs in rural areas of the nation, including a wide range of assistance measures for communities of 10,000 population or less.

Rural Electrification Administration (REA)
An office of the Department of Agriculture, REA finances electric and telephone facilities in rural areas of the United States and its territories. About 1,000 rural electric and 900 rural telephone utility systems in 47 states have received loans from REA. It does not own or operate rural electric or telephone facilities. Its function is to provide self-liquidating loans and technical assistance in order to assure adequate and dependable electric and telephone service to rural locations under rates and conditions that permit full and productive use of these utility services.

ryal
The basic unit of currency in Khmer Republic.

SA
See SOCIÉTÉ ANONYME.

sabbatical year
Originally a year of rest for the land observed every seventh year in ancient Judea; in modern practice, a leave granted every seventh year, with or without pay, for the purpose of travel, research, or rest.

safety stock
See BUFFER INVENTORY.

St. Lawrence Seaway Development Corporation
A branch of the U.S. Department of Transportation; administers operation and maintenance of the U.S. portion of the St. Lawrence Seaway, including toll rates.

Saint-Simon, Claude Henri de Rouvroy, Comte de (1760–1825)
A Parisian who fought in the American Revolution and supported the French Revolutionists. He wrote several books, including *The New Christianity,* in which he expounded public ownership of private industry. No idlers, rich or poor, were to be tolerated. He had many followers, among them the philosopher Auguste Comte and Ferdinand de Lesseps, the engineer who built the Suez Canal.

salary roll
The payroll for salaried employees.

salary structure
The minimum and maximum dollar limits within which jobs are ranked according to compensation values. Usually, the structure consists of a series of coded grades, with each grade having a range of salary levels.

sales journal
In accounting, the book of original entry that is used for recording individual sales or classes of sales by product, department, or other aspect of the enterprise.

sales load
Commissions and other selling expenses used in determining the price of a share to an investor.

sales revenue
Total sales in dollars, usually for a specific period of time.

sale value
The price at which an asset can be sold, less any costs that are to be incurred in effecting the sale.

salvage
The actual or appraised selling price of an asset in the form of second-hand material, junk, or scrap. The term also applies to both the sale of merchandise through channels that are not ordinarily used for the class of product and to the value received less any cost of disposition. Also, the value of an asset remaining after a disaster such as fire or wreck, or from the retirement or scrapping of the asset.

salvage value
See SALVAGE.

SAM
In data processing, an acronym for *sequential-access memory*. See SEQUENTIAL MEMORY.

Also, acronym for *Society for the Advancement of Management*.

sampling
In statistics, the selection for study of a set of data from the total population or group. See RANDOM SAMPLING and STRATIFIED SAMPLING.

Samuelson, Paul Anthony
An American economist who has written extensively on all aspects of economic theory. Samuelson won the Nobel Prize in economic science in 1970. Born in Gary, Indiana, in 1915, he received a PhD from Harvard University in 1941 and has been a member of the faculty of the Massachusetts Institute of Technology since 1940. In the early 1960s,

Samuelson served as economic adviser to Presidents John F. Kennedy and Lyndon B. Johnson.

sanction

Literally, *enforcement*. A sanction is the penalty for the breach of a law. Redress for civil injuries is called *civil sanction*. Punishment for violation of a criminal law is called *penal sanction*.

S&P

See STANDARD & POOR'S CORPORATION.

S&P 500

See SHARE INDEX.

sandwich building

A real estate term for a structure that does not have its own side walls but uses the walls of the adjoining buildings.

SARL

See SOCIÉTÉ À RESPONSABILITÉ LIMITÉE.

SAR plan

See STOCK APPRECIATION RIGHTS.

SARs

See STOCK APPRECIATION RIGHTS.

satisfice

In economics, a concept to convey the idea that in reality commercial firms do not seek to maximize profit but rather to achieve certain levels of satiation. For example, they try to attain a particular target level or rate of profit, and they try to achieve a specific share of market or a certain level of sales.

savings

The excess of income over comsumption for a given period of time. Often referred to as *current savings*.

savings and loan association

A cooperative whose purpose is the promotion of thrift and home ownership. It is state-incorporated as a building and loan association but federally incorporated as a savings and loan association. A savings and loan association is also known as a *cooperative bank*.

savings bank
A bank that accepts only savings accounts and cannot create demand deposits (checking accounts). Savings and loan associations and mutual savings banks are examples of savings banks. In 1978 tests were under way in several states wherein savings banks were allowed to create checking accounts.

savings bank life insurance (SBLI)
Life insurance sold over the counter by mutual savings banks as authorized by law in some states.

savings bond
A debt security sold by the U.S. Treasury to individual investors. These are fully registered securities, usually sold in small amounts to make them affordable to the majority of the population.

savings plan
A formal compensation plan designed to provide a supplemental source of income in addition to a retirement plan for retirees, as well as a source of savings and capital accumulation for employees; also known as a *thrift plan*. Under the typical plan the individual contributes a percentage of pay, which is matched by the company and invested in one of several employee-selected investment options.

sawtooth diagram
In statistics, a graphic depiction of quantity versus time. The name derives from the fact that when the points of the graph are joined by straight lines, the result resembles an enlarged drawing of the teeth of a saw blade.

Say, Jean-Baptiste (1767–1832)
A French economist who formulated the statement known as *Say's law*, which states that since the production of any article creates an equivalent demand for some other article, total supply must equal total demand, and so there can be no such things as overproduction and unemployment. This principle was generally accepted until JOHN MAYNARD KEYNES rejected it in his influential *General Theory of Employment, Interest, and Money* in 1936.

SBA
See SMALL BUSINESS ADMINISTRATION.

SBC
Initials for *small-business computer*.

SBDIC
See State Business and Industrial Development Corporation.

SBICs
See small business investment companies.

SBLI
See savings bank life insurance.

SCA
See société en commandité par actions.

Scanlon plan
A cash-incentive program for employees based on sharing the savings from a reduction in labor costs from a described standard. The plan was developed in the 1930s and 1940s by Joseph Scanlon of the Massachusetts Institute of Technology and implemented with the cooperation of the United Steelworkers' Union. The plan also incorporated an employee-suggestion incentive.

scatter
In statistics, the variation of data about a central point in a frequency distribution. See central tendency and scatter diagram.

scatter diagram
A diagram of coordinate axes and points, designed to show relations between two or more variables. Its purpose is to simultaneously depict central tendencies, such as regressions, and tendencies toward scatter or dispersion.

scenario
A term used in corporate planning to describe a broad assessment of the organization's direction in the light of estimates or forecasts of the various economic, technological, political, and social environments that may affect its future.

schedule coverage
An insurance policy that defines a number of risks of the same general type to be covered under a single policy (rather than under separate policies for each risk). For example, the insured who has four properties may insure all four under a schedule policy. It is the equivalent, in short form, of four separate specific policies. See specific coverage.

scheduled costs
See STANDARD COST ACCOUNTING.

schedule pull date
In manufacturing, the date a kit is scheduled to be pulled. See PICKING.

schedule rates
These rates are applied to insurance risks where there is enough variation to make it unfair to apply general class rates. The rates for such
risks are usually determined after a physical inspection of the property
by a representative of the insurance company's rating bureau. Also
known as *specific rates*. See CLASS RATES.

schilling
Basic unit of currency in Austria.

Schumpeter, Joseph Alois (1883–1950)
Born in Austria, emigrated to the United States, where he taught at
Harvard University. An economist with an international reputation, he
is well known for his writings on the economic processes of equilibrium, business-cycle theory, and capitalism. See INNOVATION THEORY.

scientific method
A disciplined mode of inquiry characterized by the processes of induction, deduction, and verification. The essential steps of the scientific
method consist of (1) recognition and definition of a problem, (2) observation and collection of relevant data, (3) organization and classification of data, (4) formulation of hypotheses, (5) deductions from these
hypotheses, and (6) testing and verification of the hypotheses. All scientific laws may be modified or challenged by alternative theoretical
formulations.

SCORE
Acronym for *Service Corps of Retired Executives,* an organization of
volunteer business executives who have retired from active business
operations and, without financial remuneration, provide consultation
services to small business enterprises. Formed in 1964 and sponsored
by the SMALL BUSINESS ADMINISTRATION (SBA).

scrap factor
A production process will probably produce some bad parts or products. Some part of its total capacity will be used up in this way, so
allowances must be made in scheduling time. For example, if all esti-

mates indicate an expectation of 4 percent scrap in a milling operation with 597 available machine-hours per week, the requirement must be increased by the scrap factor of 1.04 (approximately) to a total of 621 machine hours (approximately). See PLANT EFFICIENCY FACTOR.

scrap value
See SALVAGE.

scrip
A fractional or temporary share of stock or other security. It may be issued in connection with a recapitalization or reorganization and is ultimately converted into regular certificates. Also, scrip is paper "money" issued by corporations to pay wages and is accepted in exchange for merchandise by the corporations' stores.

scrip dividend
A dividend paid in promissory notes referred to as *scrip*. The notes may be negotiable, bear interest, mature at different dates, and call for payment in cash, stock, bonds, or property.

SCS
See SOCIÉTÉ EN COMMANDITÉ SIMPLE.

SD–BL
Initials for *sight draft–bill of lading*. See SIGHT DRAFT.

SDRs
See SPECIAL DRAWING RIGHTS.

seasonal dating
An aspect of credit terms given to customers. During periods of slack sales, firms may sell to customers without requiring payment for some time to come. This extension of the credit period is referred to as seasonal dating; the practice may be employed to stimulate demand from customers who cannot pay until later in the season. Seasonal dating may also serve to reduce or avoid inventory-carrying costs on the part of the firm.

seasonal fluctuations
Patterns of orders or sales that last for periods of less than one year. For example, retail sales generally increase at Easter and Christmas time, and agricultural activity increases during the summer and declines during the winter. Also called *seasonal variations*. See CYCLICAL FLUCTUATIONS.

seasonal inventories

Inventories whose levels are adjusted to absorb seasonal fluctuations in demand. Many products have reasonably predictable seasonal demand patterns. Where this is true, management has the choice of either using seasonal inventories or, if applicable, changing production rates over the year to absorb fluctuating demand. A financial analysis of the options is usually the guiding factor in decision making.

seasoned security

A listed stock with narrow price fluctuations which yields regular quarterly dividends and is backed by net assets and an earning capacity considered adequate to protect the investor in such stock.

seat

Figure of speech for a membership on an exchange.

SEC

See SECURITIES AND EXCHANGE COMMISSION.

secondary account

An account that is based on internal transactions involving transfers from primary accounts and other secondary accounts. These include a finished-product account, a bad-debt account, and a retained-earnings account. See PRIMARY ACCOUNT and THROUGHPUT ACCOUNTING.

secondary boycott

Attempts by a union through strikes, picketing, or other methods to stop one employer from doing business with another employer. Secondary boycotts are outlawed by the Labor-Management Relations (Taft-Hartley) Act of 1947.

secondary distribution

See SECONDARY OFFERING.

secondary investment

Following a primary investment, a secondary investment is the change of ownership of shares of a company's stock, such as occurs through buying and selling common shares on a stock exchange. See PRIMARY INVESTMENT.

secondary offering

The redistribution of a block of stock some time after that stock has been sold by the issuing company. The sale is handled by a securities firm or group of firms, and the shares are usually offered at a fixed price that is related to the current market price of the stock. Usually the block is a large one, such as might be involved in the settlement of an estate. The security may be listed or unlisted. See NEW ISSUE.

second mortgage
A mortgage that differs from a first mortgage only in that it constitutes a second, or junior, lien or encumbrance on the property. In the case of default, the claims of the first mortgage are given priority over those of the second.

secret partner
A limited partner who takes an active role in the management of a partnership but is not generally known to be so engaged.

secret reserve
Same as HIDDEN RESERVE.

section
A real estate term referring to a tract of land containing 640 acres or one square mile, forming one of the 36 subdivisions of a township in a government public-land survey.

secular price
A price resulting from the interaction of economic forces over a period of years.

secular trend
A definite tendency to change in a particular direction because of long-term economic influences. Secular trends are used mainly to predict the growth rates of various industries.

secured account
Any account against which collateral or other security is held.

secured creditor
A person whose claim against another is protected by collateral, or by a mortgage or other lien.

secured liability
An obligation against which specific assets have been pledged or guarantees given.

Securities Act of 1933
A securities trading law requiring full and fair disclosure of information about companies selling securities to the general public. The intent was to make it possible for investors to evaluate new issues on an informed, factual, and realistic basis. While the investor has the burden of making the choice of securities, the law assures the accuracy of information on which the decision or selection is based. The act required the registration of securities information with the Federal Trade Commission; this information is also made available to prospective investors in a document referred to as a *prospectus*. The act is also known as the *Truth-in-Securities Act*. See SECURITIES EXCHANGE ACT OF 1934.

Securities and Exchange Commission (SEC)
An independent agency comprised of five commissioners and headed by a chairman, all of whom are appointed by the president for staggered five-year terms. SEC's purpose is to regulate the issuance and trading of securities (stocks and bonds). SEC protects the public in the investment and trading of securities by (1) requiring disclosure of information by companies having publicly held securities, (2) overseeing the securities markets, and (3) taking enforcement action through the courts or administrative proceedings, or both. SEC administers the Securities Act of 1933, the Securities Exchange Act of 1934, the Trust Indenture Act of 1939, the Investment Company Act of 1940, the Investment Advisers Act of 1940, and the Public Utility Holding Company Act of 1935.

Securities Exchange Act of 1934
A securities trading law that extended federal regulation of the securities trading industry and established the Securities and Exchange Commission (SEC). The act empowered SEC to regulate trading procedures and practices of most stock exchanges in the United States as well as the activities of brokers and dealers and the procedures used in bringing company business to shareholders for their approval. The Securities Act of 1933, predecessor to the act of 1934, had been administered by the Federal Trade Commission.

Security Council
A permanent council of the United Nations, concerned with the keeping of international peace. It has five permanent members and ten members elected by the General Assembly for two-year terms. The permanent members are the United States, France, the United Kingdom, the USSR, and the People's Republic of China.

security risk
In the securities market there are several classic types of risk that the investor must recognize. See FINANCIAL RISK, INTEREST RATE RISK, MARKET RISK, POLITICAL RISK, PURCHASING POWER RISK, and SOCIAL RISK.

selective gravity, law of
See LAW OF SELECTIVE GRAVITY.

self-fulfilling prophecy
A forecast that is made more realizable because special effort is given toward its fulfillment. This may happen in marketing where a decision that a particular product or market is most (or least) promising is followed by a concentration (or lack) of effort to achieve the forecast result.

self-insurance
Often confused with noninsurance, which means not taking out an insurance policy; however, self-insurance as practiced by large companies means the actual setting aside of a reserve fund that may be used in the event of loss.

sell-and-leaseback agreement
An arrangement whereby a business that owns and occupies improved real estate sells it to an investor and takes a long-term lease on the property, which it continues to occupy. The agreement may include an option to repurchase the property at the termination of the lease.

seller's market
A favorable condition for sellers within an industry when the demand exceeds the supply. Generally, under such conditions, prices tend to move upward. See BUYER'S MARKET.

seller's option
A special transaction on an exchange that gives a seller of a security the right to deliver the security at any time within a specified period, ranging from not less than six business days to not more than 60 days.

selling expense
Not to be confused with *cost of sales,* selling expense (or cost) is a class of expense incurred in the activities of selling or marketing. Examples of selling expense include advertising, sales commissions,

marketing staff salaries and related costs, while cost of sales includes direct and indirect manufacturing costs. See COST OF SALES.

semilogarithmic coordinates
Coordinates in a chart based on one axis bearing a logarithmic scale, usually the ordinate or y-axis, and on one bearing a uniform scale.

semimanufactured goods
Raw materials that have been partially processed but will be sold or delivered to another manufacturer for further processing. Among such materials are pig iron, leather, industrial chemicals, and sheet aluminum. See RAW MATERIALS and INDUSTRIAL GOODS.

semitrailer
A freight-carrying vehicle that has no power of its own. It is attached to a tractor to obtain motive capabilities.

semivariable cost
An operating expense that varies, not necessarily at the same rate, with production rates.

senior mortgage
See FIRST MORTGAGE.

senior security
A term that is applied to a class of securities (bond, note, or share) to indicate its preference over another class of securities in the event of liquidation. For example, a first mortgage is a senior security as compared with a second mortgage. Preferred stock is senior to common stock. A senior security is superior to a junior security.

sensitivity training
A group training method intended to develop the ability to see one's self as others do.

sentinel
A data processing term. See FLAG.

separable cost
A cost that may be identified with a specific product or service.

separated manager
A manager who is very concerned with correcting deviations. He tends to write more than talk and, partly because of this, has relatively little personal communication in any direction. His perspective tends to be dictated by past experiences. He takes great interest in rules and procedures and judges others on how well they adhere to them. He values intellect in his superiors but not in others. He does not enjoy nonroutine work. The greatest fear he has about himself is that he might let emotion, softness, or dependence on others influence his judgment. His fear of others is they might act irrationally and violate the system.

sequential
In statistics, anything arranged in numeric sequence, usually in an ascending order.

sequential memory or sequential-access memory
Same as SERIAL MEMORY.

serial access
In data processing, a technique for obtaining information from or placing information into storage, where the time required for such access depends on how long it takes for other storage locations to be processed in turn. See PARALLEL ACCESS, RANDOM ACCESS, and SERIAL MEMORY.

serial-access memory
See SERIAL MEMORY.

serial bond
An issue that matures in relatively small amounts at periodic stated intervals.

serial computer
A computer in which digits for data lines are handled sequentially by separate units of the computer. See PARALLEL COMPUTER.

serial memory
In data processing, an information storage and retrieval technique in which time is one of the factors used to locate any given bit, character, word, or group of words appearing one after the other in time sequence, and in which a variable waiting time of from zero to many word times is included in the access time. A storage is said to be serial by word when the individual bits comprising a word appear serially in

time. A storage is said to be serial by character when the characters representing coded decimal or other nonbinary numbers appear serially in time. Also known as *sequential-access memory, sequential memory, serial-access memory,* and *serial storage*.

serial storage
See SERIAL MEMORY.

serial transfer
A method of data transfer in which the characters of an element are transferred in time sequence over a signal path. See PARALLEL TRANS-FER.

service life
The period of usefulness of an asset to the owner of the asset. Service life may be used as the basis for calculating depreciation.

Servicemen's Indemnity and Insurance Act
Enacted in 1951 to provide free life insurance in the amount of $10,000 for all servicemen. The program was repealed in 1956. Effective January 1, 1957, servicemen were brought under the coverage of OASDI. See also SOCIAL SECURITY ACT.

service unit
In manufacturing, an item of work or a single performance of an operation.

service-yield basis
A method of depreciating an asset whereby cost is spread over the useful life of the asset in proportion to service units consumed or outputted by the asset. Also known as *production method of depreciation* or *unit-of-product method*.

servomechanism theory
A means for automatically filtering out spurious information on certain types of decision making in management. Also, a method of studying operations that involves the feedback of information and the design of management controls in the form of systematic checks and balances. The name *servomechanism* indicates a closed loop wherein an action at one point in the loop causes a similar reaction at other points.

set
In data processing, to place a storage device in a prescribed state; also, to place a binary cell in one specific state.

In statistics, a collection of elements having some feature in common or bearing a certain relationship to one another; for example, all even numbers, geometrical figures, terms in a series, a group of irrational numbers. All positive even integers less than 100 may be a set or a subset.

set of accounts
The journals, ledgers, forms, accounts, records, and files that are maintained under an accounting system.

settlement options
The provisions of a special compensation plan that govern the form and timing of the payout of benefits, used particularly with pension, profit-sharing, and thrift plans.

set up (SU)
Designation for an article that is ready for use, completely assembled. The opposite of KNOCKED DOWN.

setup time
The time required for changing a machine or a method of production from one product or process to another.

seventy-two
See RULE OF 72.

several contract
A contract in which each party makes a separate promise and is separately liable therefor. There may be several promises in the same contract. If the promisors make a single promise, the obligation is joint. This accounts for the use of the phrase in contracts: "We jointly and severally promise."

SFA
Initials for *Southern Freight Association*.

SFP
See STANDARD FIRE INSURANCE POLICY.

shadow stock option
See PHANTOM STOCK OPTION.

share bonus
British term for *splitup*. See SPLIT.

shareholder
Same as STOCKHOLDER.

share index
An index serving as an indicator of the overall fluctuations of a stock market. One of the best known of the various indexes of the U.S. markets is the Dow-Jones averages, a composite of four different groupings of stocks: the industrial average—30 stocks that account for 20 percent of the value of all common stocks listed on the New York Stock Exchange (NYSE), oldest of the market indicators but no longer considered representative of the state of American industry; the utilities average—15 stocks of selected gas and electric companies; the transportation average—stocks of 20 firms, including airlines, railroads, and trucking companies; and 65 stocks—a combination of the industrial, utilities, and transportation averages. Standard & Poor (S&P) publishes a composite index of 500 stocks. The S&P-500 index is based on the aggregate value of shares of major firms with each stock's price weighted by the numbers of shares outstanding. The New York Stock Exchange index is a weighted index of all common shares listed on the NYSE, based on the close of the market on December 31, 1965, with an index of 50.00. Point changes on the NYSE index are converted to dollars and cents. The American Stock Exchange (ASE) publishes an index calculated to reflect the actual prices of all stocks and warrants listed on the ASE. The National Association of Securities Dealers Automated Quotations (NASDAQ) publishes an index of 2,350 common stocks that are traded over the counter by brokerages, rather than on a stock exchange.

share-premium account
British term for *capital surplus* or *paid-in surplus*. See CAPITAL SURPLUS.

sheriff's deed
See DEED, SHERIFF'S.

Sherman Act
A federal law passed by Congress in 1890 prohibiting contracts and combinations of companies that restrict or tend to monopolize trade. The act imposes civil and criminal penalties for violations and provides for the granting of injunctions. The federal government as well as private parties can sue under the statute. It is largely supplanted by the Clayton Act of 1913 and the Federal Trade Commission Act of 1914, which are more specific.

Shewhart, Walter (1891–1967)
Credited with the development and introduction to industry of statistical quality control in 1931. Statistical quality control concepts grew rapidly, and the application of probability data to the control of product quality became fairly general practice, especially with the onset of World War II.

shift register
In data processing a register in which the characters may be shifted one or more positions to the right or left. In a right shift, the rightmost character(s) may be lost. In a left shift, the leftmost character(s) may be lost.

shilling
Basic unit of currency in Kenya, Somalia, Tanzania, and Uganda.

ship chandler
An individual or a company that sells ships' equipment and supplies.

shippers export declaration
A form required by the U.S. Treasury on export shipments. The form lists details concerning the goods to be shipped.

shipper's weight, load, and count
Car load or truck load shipments loaded and sealed by shippers where the contents have not been verified by the carriers as to weight or quantity.

shopping goods
Consumer goods whose price, fashion, quality, and service are relatively important to the buyer. Generally bought infrequently, they are of high unit value, and the buyer may spend considerable time in shopping for price and quality, often at outlets located some distance from the consumer's residence. Items in this class include furniture, automobiles, jewelry, china, and furs. See CONVENIENCE GOODS and SPECIALTY GOODS.

shortage
In marketing and manufacturing, that part of a shipment that is undelivered.

shortage status
See JOB SHORTAGE.

short covering
In securities trading, the purchase of stock in order to return stock that was previously borrowed to make a delivery on a short sale. See SHORT SALE.

shortfall
The gain from a sale of an investment owned for a brief period, such as six months.

short rate
The disproportionate amount of an insurance premium returned when an insured cancels the policy. The insurance company retains a portion of the unused premium as a cancellation penalty.

short sale
A person who believes that a stock will decline and sells it even though he does not own any has made a short sale. By example, a trader instructs his broker to sell short 100 shares of XYZ. The broker borrows the stock in order to deliver the 100 shares to the buyer and deposits the money value of the borrowed shares with the lender. In time, the short sale must be covered by purchasing the same amount of borrowed stock for return to the lender. If the trader can buy the XYZ shares at a lower price than that obtained in the short sale, he may realize a profit, after deducting taxes and commissions. Obviously, a loss may also be suffered. Exchange and federal regulations govern the conditions under which a short sale may be made on a national securities exchange.

short-term debt
Any current liability, including the maturing portion of a long-term liability. Short-term debts are usually payable within the next 12-month period.

short-term equilibrium
A time period that is long enough to permit market supply to vary within the limits of existing productive capacity. See EQUILIBRIUM.

short-term liability
See SHORT-TERM DEBT.

short ton
2,000 pounds. Commonly used in the United States; the LONG TON is the preferred unit in the United Kingdom and other English-speaking countries.

sidetrack
A siding or length of track branching from a through track of a railroad, usually paralleling the through track.

sidetrack agreement
A contract between a railroad and a shipper or receiver to cover mutual responsibilities for the use of a sidetrack.

sight draft
A written order drawn by one party (drawer) ordering a second party (drawee) to pay a specified amount of money upon demand (usually supported by particular documentation of a transaction) to a payee. See TIME DRAFT.

sight test
In auditing, an examination of accounts without formal analysis.

sigma (σ)
A common designation for the STANDARD DEVIATION.

sigma chi (σ_x)
Denotes the population standard deviation in a probability distribution.

signaling rate
In data processing, the rate at which signals are transmitted.

silent partner
A member of a partnership who takes no active part in the management of the enterprise. This type of partnership enables persons to invest in the business without taking an active part in operations but allows others to handle the day-to-day management situations. A silent partner is a limited partner, one whose financial liability in the business is limited to the extent of his actual investment; however, if the silent partner takes an active part in management the personal liability is the same as that of a full partner.

SIMO chart
Acronym for *simultaneous motion cycle chart;* in manufacturing, a detailed, systematic symbolic representation of a method of work. Usually, motion pictures are used to study the body movements of a worker, most often at one workplace. The process elements isolated in this phase of the analysis are coded by therblig symbols. See THERBLIG CHART.

simple interest
The charges made by a lender for the loan of money or for a deferment of the collection of an account. It is calculated by applying an interest rate against the principal of the loan only. Compare COMPOUND INTEREST.

simple journal
In accounting, a book of original entry that contains only two money columns, one for debits, the other for credits.

simple trust
A trust that must distribute its income currently but does not distribute capital before its termination. See COMPLEX TRUST.

simultaneous access
See PARALLEL ACCESS.

single-entry bookkeeping
A system of bookkeeping in which only records of cash and of personal accounts are maintained. Usually, there is not a detailed record of gains and losses. In business operations where transactions are infrequent and receivables, payables, and assets other than cash are few in number, carefully maintained single-entry bookkeeping may be adequate. See DOUBLE-ENTRY BOOKKEEPING.

single-level bill of materials
In manufacturing, a list of components or raw materials for a single assembly level.

single-line store
A type of retail sales establishment that carries a wide variety of one line of merchandise. The goods handled are related items, such as might be found in a sporting goods shop, a furniture store, or a large men's clothing store where one could expect to find a selection of suits, ties, shirts, socks, shoes, and accessory items.

single-premium-payment life insurance
See STRAIGHT LIFE INSURANCE.

sinking fund
Cash or other assets, and the interest or other income earned thereon, set apart for the retirement of a debt, such as the redemption of stocks or bonds. To assure its integrity or safety, the sinking fund may be

invested in such conservative areas as certificates of deposit or in U.S. government bonds, treasury notes, and bills.

sinking fund bond
Any issue of a bond that requires the issuer to set aside periodically a sum that, with interest, will meet the redemption price of the bond or will be equal to a specified fraction of the total.

sinking fund method
A method of depreciating an asset that consists of setting aside periodically equal amounts of money that, with compound interest, will produce a sum equal to the original cost or exact replacement cost of the asset at the end of its useful life.

sinking fund reserve
An appropriation or designation of earned surplus for the retirement of an outstanding obligation.

SIR
Initials for *Society of Industrial Realtors*.

Sismondi, Jean Charles Léonard Simonde de (1773–1842)
A Swiss historian and economist, his views on economics were published in *New Principles of Political Economy* (1819). A critic of laissez faire and Say's law, he maintained that unchecked free enterprise results in unemployment, perpetuating the periodic economic crises of the business cycle, and that overproduction forces manufacturers to turn to foreign markets for their sales, causing imperialism and wars. Sismondi advocated government intervention to guantee workers decent wages and social security, and he encouraged employment in public works to keep workers away from the overproducing industries where they might not be able to earn subsistence-level wages.

site audit
An audit conducted on the premises of the organization being examined, especially in financial examinations performed by government agencies such as the IRS.

situational manipulation
The management of a situation for the sole purpose of improving personal effectiveness rather than managerial effectiveness. The basic motive on the part of the manager who manipulates a situation may be the desire for power, status, or promotion when these may not actually

lead to improved managerial effectiveness. Thus the practice is generally referred to as *situational manipulation* rather than *situational management*.

situational sensitivity
In organizational behavior, the skill in appraising situational elements in terms of task and relationships demands. See RELATIONSHIPS ORIENTATION and TASK ORIENTATION.

situs
A legal term meaning *place* or *situation*. The situs of personal property is the domicile of the owner. The situs of land is the state or county in which the land is located.

SI units
See INTERNATIONAL SYSTEM.

skewness
An asymmetrical statistical distribution (values are not equidistant from the central point). In a right-skewed, or positively skewed, distribution the tail of the curve extends toward the higher values. The mean of a positively skewed distribution is greater than the median, which is greater than the mode. In a left-skewed distribution, also known as negatively skewed, the tail extends to the lower values. In a negative skew the mode has a higher value than the median, which has a higher value than the mean. Distributions with a negative skew are much less frequently encountered than those with a positive skew.

skimming
A pricing policy that may be practiced by a company with a unique product or service (the uniqueness may be temporary, depending on the competition's ability to bring a similar product to market) in an effort to maximize profit margins. The product is initially offered at a high price and reduced periodically in order to achieve market saturation and thereby theoretically render the competitor impotent in the market.

SKU
See STOCKKEEPING UNIT.

slander
In law, a false and defamatory oral statement that tends to injure the reputation of a person. See DEFAMATION and LIBEL.

slander liability insurance
Available to radio and television broadcasting stations, credit bureaus, and other organizations that may face accusations of oral defamation of character. Usually written with a high dollar-value deductible clause. The insured company is required to conduct its own legal defense.

sliding parity
See CRAWLING PEG.

sling
A large net into which freight is placed for hoisting into or out of a ship.

small business
A general term related to the quantification or size of an enterprise. Definitions of small business are varied. For example, the Bureau of the Census references the number of employees within the enterprise; the Internal Revenue Service references sales volume; Dun & Bradstreet references net worth. The Small Business Administration exercises considerable latitude in defining the difference between "small" and "big"—according to type of business (manufacturing, wholesaling, retailing, service) and the dominance of the enterprise within its specific field of endeavor. According to the Internal Revenue Service, based on 1974 data, small businesses represented 96.7 percent of all business enterprises and generated 53.5 percent of all sales receipts.

Small Business Administration
SBA is an independent agency established by Congress under the Small Business Act and the Small Business Investment Act. These direct SBA to help small business firms solve their financial problems, overcome the effects of natural disasters, sell to or buy from the government, strengthen their management and production capabilities, and generally increase their growth and prosperity. SBA is headed by an administrator appointed by the president. See SMALL BUSINESS INVESTMENT ACT and SMALL BUSINESS INVESTMENT COMPANY.

Small Business Development Center Act of 1977
An act of Congress intended to create a pilot program providing for small business development centers in 15 states. Each state would present a plan to the Small Business Administration (SBA) stating which universities or private groups would participate. The centers would provide nonfinancial assistance for small business. Businessmen and university professors would staff the centers. On April 10, 1978,

the House of Representatives passed an omnibus small business bill that included expansion of the SBA's development center pilot program into a national program, with grants to be made on a 50/50 matching basis. Under this bill, federal funds are to be allocated on the basis of the portion of the population served, as a percentage of the total U.S. population.

Small Business Investment Act
Enacted in 1958 by the federal government to help solve the small business firm's problems in obtaining long-term financing, the act authorized the Small Business Administration to license and regulate small business investment companies. See SMALL BUSINESS INVESTMENT COMPANY.

Small Business Investment Company
A privately and publicly owned but government-regulated company whose sole purpose is to provide long-term financial assistance and management services to small business firms. SBICs are licensed and regulated by the Small Business Administration, from which they may also obtain favorable financing. See SMALL BUSINESS ADMINISTRATION.

smallest processing time rule
In manufacturing, a dispatching rule that directs the sequencing of jobs in ascending order according to the time required to process. Following this rule, the maximum number of jobs per time period will be processed. The result is that the average lateness of jobs is minimized, but some jobs will of necessity be very late. Also known as *least processing time* (LPT) and *shortest operating time* (SOT).

SMCRC
Initials for *Southern Motor Carriers Rate Conference.*

SME
Initials for *Society of Manufacturing Engineers.*

Smith, Adam (1723–1790)
A production economist, educated at Glasgow and Oxford universities, who gained attention at the time the factory system began to emerge. In 1776 Smith wrote *The Wealth of Nations,* in which he observed three basic economic advantages from the division of labor: (1) the development of a skill or a dexterity when a single task was performed repetitively by the individual, (2) the saving of time normally lost in changing from one activity to the next, and (3) the inven-

tion of tools and machines that followed when people specialized their efforts on tasks of restricted scope. His book was an important milestone in the development of production economics.

smoothing
In statistical analysis, any method that removes irregularities in data, including unusual perturbations in a curve that may have been caused by nonrecurring operating conditions.

SMPTE
See Society of Motion Picture and Television Engineers.

snap reading
See ratio-delay technique.

SNC
See société en nom collectif.

SNOBOL
Acronym for *String-Oriented Symbolic Language,* a computer programming language developed at Bell Telephone Laboratories. snobol is especially applicable for programs dealing with text editing, linguistics, compiling, and symbolic manipulation of algebraic expressions.

Social and Rehabilitation Service
An agency of the Department of Health, Education, and Welfare, SRS helps the states to provide monetary, medical, and social services to people in need. SRS works with the state and local governments and with private and voluntary agencies through ten regional offices. See Assistance Payments Administration, Medical Services Administration, and Public Services Administration.

social balance
The relative distribution of resources between the public and private sectors.

social benefits
A gain that accrues to individuals and to society as a whole, but for which the individual does not have to pay directly. Highway construction and police and fire protection are examples.

social costs
A disadvantage to society that may result from private production but that is not necessarily reflected in the money costs to the individual

producer of acquiring the resources needed for production. Pollution is a social cost of production that the market system does not measure.

socialism
An economic system whose basic feature is the ownership of all or most production activity by the government rather than by individuals. In revolutionary socialism, the government owns all factors of production (other than human services), thus eliminating property as a source of individual income; it controls the economy through centralized planning. In democratic socialism, the private sector retains control of agriculture, services, and nonvital industries; the government attempts to redistribute wealth through taxation and social welfare programs. See CAPITALISM and COMMUNISM.

social overhead capital
The capital of a society, consisting of facilities for energy production, communications, transportation, and education. Also known as the *infrastructure of a society.*

social risk
In the securities market, the uncertainty of future returns from a security because of shifts in public attitudes. This may involve changing consumption patterns, pollution, and population control, for examples. See FINANCIAL RISK, INTEREST RATE RISK, MARKET RISK, POLITICAL RISK, PURCHASING POWER RISK, and SECURITY RISK.

Social Security Act of 1935
The first major government venture into the field of social insurance. Old Age, Survivors, and Disability Insurance (OASDI) is one of its programs; however, the act is a comprehensive piece of legislation that includes old-age assistance and unemployment compensation, plus several smaller programs such as aid to the blind, aid to dependent children, public health, and maternal and child care.

Social Security Administration
An agency of the Department of Health, Education, and Welfare, SSA is responsible for monthly benefits to insured persons and their dependents in the event of the retirement, disability, or death of the insured, and administers a health insurance program (Medicare) for persons age 65 and over and for some under 65 who are disabled. SSA also administers a federal program of supplemental security income (SSI) to provide cash-assistance payments to the aged, blind, and disabled, and a program of aid to families with dependent children (AFDC).

social security integration
The technique whereby a pension or profit-sharing retirement plan is discounted for social security benefits. This is done by applying a formula, by excluding certain earnings from the benefits, calculation, or by subtracting social security benefits under the so-called offset approach.

sociedad anonima
See SOCIÉTÉ ANONYME.

sociedade em comandita por ações
A partnership limited by shares under Portuguese law.

sociedade em comandita simples
General partnership under Portuguese law.

sociedad en comandita
A limited partnership operating under Spanish law.

sociedade por cotas
A limited-liability company under Portuguese law. The word *Limitada* must be included in the name of a company operating under this law.

società a responsibilità limitata
A private limited-liability company under Italian law.

società de fatto
A partnership in fact, operating under Italian law. Although the arrangement is equivalent to a partnership, it is not necessarily formalized by a written contract.

società in accomandita per azioni
A partnership limited by shares under the Italian Commercial Code.

società in nome collettivo
A general partnership under the Italian Commercial Code.

società non azionare
A nonstock company organized under the Italian Commercial Code.

società per azioni
A joint-stock company under Italian law.

società semplice
A private parnership operating under the Italian Commercial Code.

société anonyme
A joint-stock company under French, Belgian, Luxembourgian, and Swiss laws in which shareholders are liable only to the extent of the amount of capital invested. In France the company must have at least seven shareholders, and a share capital of at least 500,000 francs if it is subscribed to by the public or a minimum of 100,000 francs if there is no public subscription. In Switzerland, it is also known as *Aktiengesellschaft*. *Société anonyme* may be abbreviated *SA*. In Spanish, SA is the abbreviation for *sociedad anonima*.

société à responsabilité limitée
A private limited partnership under French and Luxembourgian law for a company with 2 to 50 partners whose liability is limited to the extent of their contributions. Shares are not freely negotiable and may be transferred to third parties only with the agreement of partners representing at least 75 percent of the capital.

société en commandité
See KOMMANDITGESELLSCHAFT.

société en commandité par actions
A partnership under Belgian, French, and Luxembourgian law; equivalent to the American limited partnership. Certain partners are liable for the debts of the partnership while the liabilities of the other partners are limited to the extent of their financial participation. In 1966 France discontinued the setting up of companies under this law, preferring the SOCIÉTÉ EN COMMANDITÉ SIMPLE.

société en commandité simple
A limited partnership under Belgian, French, and Luxembourgian laws.

société en nom collectif
A partnership under Belgian, French, Luxembourgian, and Swiss laws in which all partners are jointly and separately liable for the actions of the partners.

société simple
A simple partnership under Swiss company law. Also known as *einfache Gesellschaft*.

Society of Motion Picture and Television Engineers

Founded in 1916 by C. Francis Jenkins, this professional association grew from 24 original members to approximately 8,000 members in the 60 subsequent years.

soft currency

A currency whose exchange rate is tending to fall because of persistent balance-of-payments deficits or because of the building up of speculative selling of the currency in anticipation of a change in the exchange rate.

soft loan

A loan bearing no interest rate, or a rate that is abnormally below the true cost of the capital lent. The International Bank for Reconstruction and Development, working through its affiliate, the International Development Association, gives soft loans to developing countries for long-term capital projects.

In international trade, a soft loan is a loan that is to be repaid in the borrower's currency instead of in the lender's currency, gold, or a reserve currency. The loan is actually a disguised gift because the country that is repaid in "soft" currency cannot spend it without disrupting the borrowing country's economy. This circuitous method for making a loan is used to save the borrower's face and to counter voter objections in the donor country.

software

The programs and routines used to enable a computer and its peripherals to perform their functions.

sol

Basic unit of currency in Peru.

sole proprietorship

A business venture that is wholly owned by one individual.

SOP

Short for *standard operating procedure*. A written, detailed description of a routine operation, sometimes an unwritten procedure that has become standardized through practice.

Sorel, Georges (1847–1922)

A French social philosopher. Sorel studied engineering at the Ecole Polytechnique in Paris. In 1882 he became active in syndicalism. His best-known book is *Reflexions sur la Violence,* 1908. Sorel admired both fascism and bolshevism, and any movement that planned to remove the bourgeoisie. See SYNDICALISM.

sort
In data processing, to arrange items of information according to some definite rules, usually referring to a key or field contained in the items or records. For example, a digital sort involves sorting the keys first on the least significant digit, then on each higher-order digit, until the items are sorted on the most significant digit.

SOT
Acronym for *shortest operation time.* Also known as *minimum processing time per operation.* See SMALLEST PROCESSING TIME RULE.

sound value
In accounting, the replacement cost less depreciation and deferred maintenance for fixed assets. A term generally used in appraising the present value of an asset.

source language
The original form in which a computer program is prepared prior to processing by the machine.

source program
A computer program written in a language designed for ease of expression of a class of problems or procedures (for instance, symbolic or algebraic). A generator, assembler translator, or compiler routine is used to perform the mechanics of translating the source program into an object program in machine language.

SpA
See SOCIETÀ PER AZIONI.

span of control
A theory and practice of management holding that a supervisor, manager, or executive cannot operate efficiently if he has more than a limited number of subordinates reporting directly to him. Generally, the higher the level of work, the smaller the number of directly reporting subordinates. For example, the span of control for a general manager might be limited to six to nine subordinates while that of a shop floor supervisor might include several hundred.

special assessment
Charges levied by a municipal government on those who will benefit most from an improvement or service (such as installing pavements or sewers). Often bonds are issued to finance the work, and interest and payments on the principal are included in the taxes of those who benefit from the improvement or service.

special audit
An audit or inspection of financial records and accounts that has a limited and specified scope. Also known as *limited audit*.

special bid
The purchase of a large block of stock on the floor of the New York Stock Exchange. In a special bid, the bidder for the block of stock will pay a special commission to the broker who represents him or her in making the purchase. The seller does not pay a commission. The special bid is made on the floor of the exchange at a fixed price that must not be below the last sale of the security or the current bid on the regular market, whichever is higher. Member firms may sell this stock for customers direct to the buyer's broker during trading hours.

special contingency reserve
A reserve established to support an anticipated future need, expense, or loss. See GENERAL CONTINGENCY RESERVE.

Special Drawing Rights (SDRs)
Supplementary reserves established in 1969 in the form of account entries on the books of the International Monetary Fund. The reserves are allocated among participating countries in accordance with their quotas, and can be drawn upon by governments to help finance balance-of-payments deficits. They are intended to promote an orderly growth of reserves that will help the long-term expanding needs of world trade. When issued as a substitute for gold, SDRs are also known as *paper gold*.

special fund
In municipal accounting practice, a fund that must be used in accordance with specified legal or administrative restrictions; also any fund other than a general fund.

specialist
A member of a stock exchange who specializes in very few stocks or even a single stock. The two main functions of a specialist are (1) to

maintain an orderly market, insofar as reasonably practicable, in the stocks in which he is registered as a specialist, and (2) to act as a broker's broker. To maintain an orderly market, the specialist buys or sells for his own account, within reasonable limits, when there is a disparity between supply and demand. There are about 350 specialists on the New York Stock Exchange. See DEALER.

specialist block purchase
The purchase by a specialist for his own account of a large block of stock outside the regular exchange market. Such purchases may be made only when the sale of the block could not be made in the regular market within a reasonable time and at reasonable prices, and when the purchase would aid the specialist in maintaining a fair and orderly market.

specialist block sale
Opposite of SPECIALIST BLOCK PURCHASE.

specialization
Division of production activities among individuals and regions so that no one person or area is self-sufficient. Total production is increased by specialization, thus permitting all participants to share in a greater volume of output through exchange or trade.

specialization of labor
The division of tasks into their component operations so that each worker becomes a specialist in one operation (or a small number of similar operations). The worker thus achieves maximum efficiency, and the time usually spent in shifting from one type of task to another is eliminated. Also known as *division of labor*.

special offering
A large block of stock requiring special handling. Occasionally a large block of stock becomes available for sale and, because of its quantity and market, may call for special treatment. A notice is printed on the ticker tape announcing that the stock will be offered for sale on the exchange floor at a predetermined price. Member firms of the exchange may buy this stock for customers directly from the seller's broker during trading hours. The price is usually based on the last transaction in the regular auction market. If there are more buyers than shares of available stock, allotments are made. Only the seller pays a commission on a special offering.

special order
See JOB ORDER.

special partner
See LIMITED PARTNER.

special-purpose computer
A computer designed to solve a specific class or narrow range of problems.

special revenue fund
In municipal accounting practice, a fund used to finance specific activities. A fund of this type may be authorized by statutory or charter provisions to pay for identified activities with some special form of continuing revenues such as specific taxes.

special-talent insurance
A highly specialized form of career insurance, generally providing indemnity for the loss of a member or function of the body related directly to the financial success of the insured. Examples are insurance for the hands of a well-known pianist, the legs of a famous dancer, the voice of a popular vocalist, the fingers of a dentist, or a facial or bodily characteristic of a well-known or readily recognized performer or public personality whose disfigurement might diminish or end the person's career.

specialty goods
A class of consumer goods offering distinctive qualities for which the consumer may have a strong preference. Such products are very similar to shopping goods except that price is not the principal consideration in the purchase. One example is a brand of candy, available only at a particular store, for which the consumer is willing to make a special trip. Specialty goods also include appliances and other high-priced items such as automobiles. See CONVENIENCE GOODS and SHOPPING GOODS.

specialty store
A retail establishment that stocks and sells a limited variety of merchandise but offers a wide selection within a category of goods. Examples include stores specializing in dinette furniture, beds, or musical records and tapes.

special warranty deed
In real estate, a deed that, instead of guaranteeing the title from the sovereignty to the last grantee, merely guarantees the title against claims arising by, through, or under the grantor.

specie
Coin money, as distinct from paper money.

specific address
A data processing term. See ABSOLUTE ADDRESS.

specific cost
A cost that is readily identifiable with a particular product or service.

specific coverage
A specific insurance policy, written for a definite amount on one item of property at one location.

specific duty
A tariff levied as a fixed money charge per physical unit, such as pennies per kilogram.

specific rates
See SCHEDULE RATES.

speculation
The employment of funds by a trader. Safety of principal is a secondary factor, opportunity for significant, rapid appreciation being the primary motive. The speculator may buy and sell a security during the same day or speculate in an enterprise that he does not expect to be profitable for years but that he considers worth the risk. Speculation is not limited to the securities market. It may also involve the buying and selling of real estate, buildings, and goods and commodities for relatively short-term investment purposes.

speculative risk
A risk in which there is both a chance of loss and an element of gain. A business venture and a gambling transaction are examples of speculative risk. See PURE RISK.

Spencer, Herbert (1820–1903)
British philosopher. Educated by his father and his uncle, Spencer started to work for a railway at the age of 17. He became an engineer

and one of the editors of the *Economist* in 1848. His work *Social Studies* appeared in 1850. His *Programme of a System of Synthetic Philosophy* was completed in 1896, and in 1898 his work *What Is Social Revolution* was published. Spencer applied the ideas of organic evolution, which he had formulated before Darwin, to the social organism. He held that government was a necessary evil that has only the duty to protect and enforce economic contracts. Spencer is credited with having originated the phrase "survival of the fittest."

SPFFC
Initials for *Southern Ports Foreign Freight Committee.*

spillover effects
Benefits or costs associated with the production or consumption of a good that spill over to parties other than the buyer or seller. See EX-TERNALITIES.

spinoff
The transfer by a corporation of a portion of its assets to a newly formed company in exchange for the latter's capital stock.

split
In the securities market, the division of the outstanding shares of a corporation into a larger number of shares. For example, a 2-for-1 split by a company with a million shares outstanding results in 2 million shares outstanding. Each holder of 100 shares before the split has 200 shares after the split; however, his equity in the company remains the same. Usually, splits must be voted by directors and approved by shareholders. One of the primary reasons for a split is that the resultant drop in price per share stimulates trading in the market and encourages new buyers, thereby increasing the demand and hopefully increasing the market value of the individual share.

splitback
See REVERSE SPLIT.

splitdown
See REVERSE SPLIT.

splitoff point
In accounting, when two or more products are involved in the same or similar operations, the point at which joint costs end and costs that can be identified with individual products begin.

splitup
See SPLIT.

SPMC
Initials for *Society of Professional Management Consultants*. Founded in 1959 as an individual accrediting body.

spoiled-work order
See REWORK ORDER.

spot cash
Cash that is readily available, usually in hand, for an immediate purchase.

spot price
The price of a commodity available for immediate sale and delivery. The commodity is referred to as a *spot commodity*.

spread sheet
A worksheet for the analysis of a group of related accounts or classes of accounts.

sprinkler leakage insurance
Installation of a sprinkler system may result in reduced fire insurance rates; however, the action of the sprinkler may represent a separate hazard. Sprinkler-leakage insurance provides indemnity for accidents resulting from sprinkler discharge where there is no fire. In the case of fire, damage caused by the sprinkler operation may be covered as a proximate result of the fire. See PROXIMATE CAUSE. Also see SPRINKLER-LEAKAGE LIABILITY.

sprinkler-leakage liability
A third-party coverage, this casualty insurance protects the installer of a sprinkler system against claims for damage resulting from the operation of his sprinkler system for which he might be considered legally liable to another. Coverage is applicable only if the insured is legally responsible to the third party. See THIRD-PARTY RIGHTS.

SPRL
Société de personnes à responsabilité limitée. A Belgian private limited company in which shares are not negotiable and only individuals may hold shares.

spur track
A track extending a fairly short distance from a regular railroad track. Used as a convenience for pickup and delivery of goods, spur tracks are sometimes laid directly to a dock of a warehouse or producer.

SRA
Initials for *Society of Real Estate Appraisers*.

SR&CC
Strikes, riots, and civil commotions; ocean marine insurance. See FC&S.

SRL
See SOCIETÀ A RESPONSABILITÀ LIMITATA.

SRS
See SOCIAL AND REHABILITATION SERVICE.

SS
Abbreviation for *shipside* or *steamship*.

SSA
See SOCIAL SECURITY ADMINISTRATION.

SSI
Initials for *supplemental security income*. See SOCIAL SECURITY ADMINISTRATION.

staff auditor
A member of the accounting or financial division of a corporation assigned the duties of examining and inspecting the accounts of an economic unit of the corporation.

stagflation
An economic term invented in the late 1960s to describe the state of the U.S. economy; a combination form of stagnation and inflation. It is intended to depict the simultaneous occurrence of the rising-prices aspect of inflation and the insufficient economic expansion that characterizes stagnation, the combination causing an increase in unemployment.

Standard & Poor's Corporation

An organization that publishes financial data on enterprises that have issued securities. A subscription service, it also rates securities and offers advisory services. Often referred to by its initials *S&P.*

standard cost

See STANDARD COST ACCOUNTING.

standard cost accounting

Estimates or forecasts of costs to be incurred in the production of goods or the delivery of services. Such costs become known as *standard costs*. The estimates or forecasts are based on assumptions of specific conditions. After the acquisition of experience, actual costs are accumulated and compared with standard costs as a measure of efficiency.

standard costing

In accounting, the process of pricing goods or services at standard cost.

standard-cost system

A method of accounting whereby standard costs are the basis for credits to work-in-process accounts. Standard costs may be applied to charges for materials, labor, and other costs related to work in process. Physical and book inventories may be recorded at standard-cost values. Differences between standard costs and actual costs are carried to variance accounts.

standard deviation

The most widely used measure of variation in statistical analysis, denoted by the Greek letter sigma, σ. This measure of variation has been accepted almost universally as the most effective and suitable measure of the variability of a set of numerical data. The standard deviation is a measure that considers how far from the *mean* each of the items in a frequency distribution is location. In this way it measures the extent of variation in the distribution. The more spread out the distribution, the larger the standard deviation; the more concentrated the distribution, the smaller the standard deviation.

standard error

The standard deviation of a sampling distribution. See STANDARD DEVIATION.

standard fire insurance policy
A standard form for fire insurance policies, adopted by most of the United States, the District of Columbia, and Puerto Rico. Introduced in 1943, it is known variously as *New York form, SFP, standard fire policy,* and *165-line policy* to distinguish it from previous New York standard fire policies.

standard fire policy
See STANDARD FIRE INSURANCE POLICY.

standard gauge
The distance between the rails of the majority of North American railroads, standardized at four feet, eight and one-half inches.

standard labor rate
An employee's base pay, plus any incentives and premiums in money, estimated to be attainable under efficient working conditions.

standard labor time
The time, in terms of man-hours of a specified quality, estimated to be required to produce a specific quantity of goods or services.

standard machine time
The time allocated or forecast to be required for the use of a machine in a specific operation in a production process. It may be referenced to a specific quantity of output of units produced against a time base. Setup and teardown time may be included in the total machine time allocation.

standard method
A series or set of operations proved to the satisfaction of management to be desirable in carrying out a work order, process, or other production function.

standard metropolitan area
An area defined by the Bureau of the Census as a county or a group of contiguous counties containing a city with a population of 50,000 or more.

standard order quantity
See ECONOMIC ORDER QUANTITY.

standard of living theory
A wage theory which holds that employees should be paid more than a subsistence wage. Wage levels, it maintains, should be such that employees can afford higher education and some of the luxuries of life, such as recreation.

standard preparation time
A standard value or measure of setup or makeready time for a production operation. It is determined from a statistical study of historical or pilot-run efforts.

standard profit
The net amount that should be earned per unit of production when a job or a service is performed under an accounting method of standard costs. See STANDARD COST ACCOUNTING.

standard-run quantity
See ECONOMIC ORDER QUANTITY.

standby costs
See FIXED COSTS.

standing cost
See FIXED COST.

standing order
A continuing work order that directs the production of an item to meet specified sales objectives.

staple
The chief commodity traded in a market. Also, raw materials, or a linen, wool, cotton, or synthetic fiber.

starboard
The right side of a ship when facing forward toward the bow.

state business and industrial development corporation
Created by legislation of the individual states, SBIDCs exist to increase statewide prosperity and employment by assisting small and medium-size businesses with equity investments and long-term loans. SBIDCs are not owned, managed, or leveraged by the state. Usually, oil companies, utilities, and major retail chains are stockholders in SBIDCs and provide equity funds in states where SBIDCs make investments.

Banks, savings and loan companies, and insurance firms are SBIDC members; they fund long-term loans. See SMALL BUSINESS INVESTMENT COMPANIES.

stated capital
The dollars received by a corporation from the purchasers of its capital stock. Also known as *declared capital*.

stated value
The value given by a corporation to its capital stock for any of various taxation purposes. Also known as *declared value*.

state farms
In the Soviet Union, lands that are owned and operated as state enterprises under elected or government-appointed managing directors. Workers and technicians are hired to run the farms, and are usually paid set wages as well as bonuses if their output exceeds a basic norm.

statement
In accounting, a summary of transactions between a customer and his supplier for a fiscal period, usually a calendar month. Also, a formal presentation of classes of accounts and the related amounts, prepared as a summary of the financial condition and operating results of a company for a fiscal period, usually 12 months.

statement of identity
A questionnaire by which real estate title companies are helped in identifying a person; such a statement is essential, for example, when records show more than one person with the same name. See TITLE COMPANY.

statement of sources and application of funds
An item on a financial statement indicating the origin of capital and the uses to which such capital is put. The British equivalent term is *capital reconciliation statement*.

statistical inference
In statistics, a general statement about a group or population on the basis of imperfect information about that group. For example, by taking a random sample of voters, we may obtain information on voting intentions. However, this information is imperfect because it does not describe with certainty what all the voters will actually do. Nevertheless, it is possible to generalize on the basis of the sample. The theory

of statistical inference is primarily concerned with the degree of confidence that can be placed on the generalizations, and with the margins of error that may be involved.

statistics
A body of techniques or rules for the collection, presentation, and analysis of quantitative information. Statistical information plays an important role in business decision making. See STATISTICAL INFERENCE.

status symbols
Visible marks of the status of the various positions in a group or an organization. Status symbols serve as clues that enable the members of a group or organization to perceive the status of other members and thus guide their behavior accordingly. Status symbols often come to be prized as symbols of success rather than as items of comfort or beautification.

statute
A law passed by the legislative body of a state.

steamship freight contract
An agreement between a shipper and a steamship line for space and rates.

stepped cost
A cost that increases in steps with increased volumes of activity.

stochastic inventory models
In manufacturing, inventory models where the demand is not known but can be described as a random variable with some known probability distribution. See DETERMINISTIC INVENTORY MODELS.

stock
The legal capital of a corporation obtained through the issuance and sale of marketable certificates or shares.

stock appreciation rights
An executive compensation plan intended to reduce the risk of market declines that may be experienced with conventional stock options. Such a plan also eliminates the need for cash investment. A stock appreciation right (SAR) is a provision attached to a nonqualified stock option that allows the holder, in lieu of exercising the option, to receive

in cash, stock, or a combination of them an amount equal to the appreciation value of the option. Payment is received directly from the company, and the related stock right is then canceled. One of the advantages of SARs is that they relieve executives of the need to borrow large sums of money to purchase options. At the same time, the executive receives cash immediately; the six-month holding period that the Securities and Exchange Commission (SEC) requires if an individual exercises an option to buy stock—a period during which the stock could decline—is eliminated. Also, the cash payments can provide funds to pay taxes on gains.

Stock-Clearing Corporation
A subsidiary of the New York Stock Exchange that acts as a central agency for clearing firms in providing a clearing operation through which transactions made on the floor are confirmed and balanced; it also provides a settlement operation to handle the physical delivery of securities and money. See CENTRAL CERTIFICATE SERVICE.

stock company
A company organized for the purpose of writing insurance coverage and registered as a corporation owned by stockholders who need not necessarily be policyholders. The initial capital subscribed by the stockholders constitutes the company's working capital. Income must be earned from premiums paid by policyholders. In most respects, the financial operations are like those of a general corporation. Also see MUTUAL INSURANCE COMPANY.

stock discount
The excess of par value over paid-in capital. At one time this was treated as a deferred charge. It is now generally considered a debit-valuation account to be combined, before exposure on the balance sheet, with the capital-stock account to which it is related, or to be subtracted on the face of the balance sheet from that same capital-stock account.

stock dividend
A dividend paid in securities rather than cash. The dividend may be additional shares of the issuing company or shares of another company, usually a subsidiary of the issuing company.

stock exchange
A market in which securities are bought and sold. The principal stock exchange in the United States is known as the New York Stock Ex-

change and is located on Wall Street in New York City. There are many other exchanges in large cities. The principal stock exchange in Britain is known as the Stock Exchange, located on Throgmorton Street in London. Continental European exchanges are often referred to by the French name *bourse*.

stockholder
The person of legal record who owns one or more shares of the capital stock of a corporation. Stockholders are in effect owners of the corporation and as such have the power to establish basic corporate policies. This power is rarely exercised, however, because it is difficult for a collective of stockholders to practice direct control of the corporation. Stockholders vote annually for members of the board of directors and on other key issues.

stockholder of record
A stockholder whose name is registered on the books of the issuing corporation.

stockkeeping unit (SKU)
Units of finished-goods inventory. For example, a company with 75 items of finished-goods inventory is said to have 75 SKUs.

stock option
See OPTION.

stock-option cancellation
A program under which a company cancels outstanding stock options whose exercise price is substantially higher than the current market price. The company then issues new, lower-priced options to replace the canceled options.

stockout
The lack of materials and supplies that are normally expected to be on hand in stores or inventory.

stock-purchase warrant
See WARRANT.

stock register
A corporate record containing the details of the issuance of stock certificates and of the disposition of those returned for transfer or for cancellation.

stock split
See SPLIT.

stock-transfer book
A record or journal in which transfers of capital stock are entered; maintained by the company that issues the stock or by its transfer agent.

stop-limit order
In securities trading, a stop-limit order to *buy* becomes a limit order executable at the limit price, or at a better price if obtainable, when a transaction in a security occurs at or above the stop price after the order has been presented to the trading floor. A stop-limit order to *sell* becomes a limit order executable at the limit price, or at a better price if obtainable, when a transaction in the security occurs at or below the stop price after the order has been presented to the trading floor. See MARKET ORDER.

stopoff
An arrangement that allows a carload or truckload to be started at one point and stopped at another while en route to its final destination for completion of loading or partial unloading.

stop order
In securities trading, an order to buy or sell a specified quantity of securities at a specified price or better. A stop order to *buy* becomes a market order when a transaction in the security occurs at or above the specific price after the order is presented to the trading floor. A stop order to *sell* becomes a market order when a transaction in the security occurs at or below the specified price after the order is presented to the trading floor. A stop order may be used in an effort to protect a paper profit or limit a possible loss to a specific amount. Since it becomes a market order only when the specified price is reached, there is no certainty that it will be executed at that price. See MARKET ORDER.

stoppage in transitu
In law, the right of a seller of goods that have not been paid for, upon learning that the buyer of the goods is insolvent, to stop the goods in transit and hold them as security for the purchase price.

storage
Used interchangeably with *memory,* storage pertains to a device in which data can be stored and recalled at a later time.

storage capacity
The number of elementary pieces of data that can be contained in a storage device. Also referred to as *memory capacity*.

storage disk
See MAGNETIC DISK.

storage dump
In data processing, a listing of the contents of a storage device, or selected parts of it. Also known as *core dump* or *memory dump*.

storage in transit
A tariff privilege that permits freight to be stopped and stored en route, with the rate from point of origin to point of destination applicable.

stored-program computer
A computer capable of performing sequences of internally stored instructions and usually capable of modifying those instructions as directed.

storekeeper's burglary and robbery policy
An insurance policy designed specifically for small business firms. It covers low-limit losses similar to those described in a comprehensive crime policy. See COMPREHENSIVE CRIME INSURANCE.

storekeeper's liability insurance
A package policy designed for the small retail store operation; roughly comparable to COMPREHENSIVE GENERAL LIABILITY INSURANCE.

stores
Supplies and raw materials used in the manufacture and distribution of goods; also, such items used in the maintenance of a plant and its equipment.

stores ledger cards
In manufacturing, cards on which are maintained records and data related to material on hand and on order.

stowage
A marine term that refers to the loading of freight into a ship's holds.

straddle
The purchase of a *put* and a *call* for a single security at the same market price; also known as a *double option*. The purchase of two puts and one call is referred to as a *strip,* and of one put and two calls as a *strap.* Speculators in securities make use of straddles as one means of protecting holdings whether the prices of the securities go up or down. See PUTS AND CALLS.

straight deductible
In insurance, the most common form of deductible clause; it provides that there is no coverage for small losses, typically in the amounts of $25, $50, or $100. In some policies the deductible clause is mandatory. In others, it is optional and may be inserted into the policy with a corresponding reduction in premium payments. See DEDUCTIBLE CLAUSES.

straight lease
A lease for a fixed, agreed-upon price for a specific period, with regular payments of equal amounts. Also known as *flat lease*.

straight life insurance
Premiums are paid by the insured throughout his or her lifetime. When death occurs, the face value of the policy is paid to the beneficiary. This type of policy has cash surrender or loan value. Also known as *ordinary life* and *whole life* insurance. A variation is the limited-payment contract wherein premiums are paid for a finite number of years, usually 20 or 30. After that period, protection continues for the life of the insured without further payments of premiums. Also, the single-premium payment life policy may be offered, which requires only one payment for lifetime coverage.

straight-line method
A depreciation method that assumes that assets depreciate at a uniform rate, in equal amounts for each year of the asset's useful life. Thus, if a machine is estimated to have a ten-year life, one-tenth of its cost is taken as depreciation in the first year, one-tenth in the second year, and so on until the tenth year, when the residual value is estimated to be at zero dollars. See DEPRECIATION METHOD.

straight-line scheduling
See GAPPED SCHEDULE.

strap
See STRADDLE.

stratified sampling
A selection of data for study in which the total number of individuals or measurement units in the population is first divided into a number of nonoverlapping groups according to some criterion and a random sampling taken within each group. The number of cases in each group is proportional to that group's representation in the total population. See RANDOM SAMPLING.

Street
Colloquial expression for the New York financial community in the Wall Street area.

street name
Securities held in the name of a broker instead of the customer are said to be carried in a *street name*. This occurs when the securities have been bought on margin or when the customer wishes the security to be held by the broker.

strikes, riots, and civil commotions (SR&CC)
An ocean-marine-insurance consideration. See FC&S.

strip
See STRADDLE.

structural unemployment
The displacement of workers as a result of technological change in production processes, a new invention, or a shift in demand toward new products and services.

Student's t-distribution
See "t"-DISTRIBUTION and GOSSET, W. S.

stumpage
A commercial real estate term that has several meanings, including the log-feet derivable from the standing timber in a forest, the price paid for the right to remove timber from land, or the portion of the cost of timberland that is assigned to the lumber that has been or is to be removed.

style adaptability
A term for the range of behavior within which a leader can vary his or her style. The leader will be effective if the variation is appropriate to the situation, ineffective if the style is inappropriate. See STYLE DRIFT, STYLE FLEXIBILITY, STYLE RESILIENCE, and STYLE RIGIDITY.

style drift
In organizational behavior, the inappropriate variation of a manager's basic style of behavior, so that managerial effectiveness is decreased. See STYLE FLEXIBILITY, STYLE RESILIENCE, and STYLE RIGIDITY.

style flexibility
In organizational behavior, the skill of a manager in varying his or her basic style of behavior appropriately to meet a changing situation, so that managerial effectiveness is increased. See STYLE DRIFT, STYLE RESILIENCE, and STYLE RIGIDITY.

style resilience
In organizational behavior, the tendency of a manager to maintain a single, appropriate basic style, so that his effectiveness as a manager is increased. See STYLE DRIFT, STYLE FLEXIBILITY, and STYLE RIGIDITY.

style rigidity
In organizational behavior, the tendency of a manager to maintain a single, inappropriate basic style, so that his effectiveness as a manager is decreased. See STYLE DRIFT, STYLE FLEXIBILITY, and STYLE RESILIENCE.

SU
See SET UP.

subassembly
In manufacturing, a low-level assembly or minor assembly of individual components or materials later combined with other subassemblies to form a high-level assembly or an end product.

subjective value
In accounting, a value assigned to an asset by management without supporting verification from an independent source, possibly without relation to market value, and usually based on opinion or experience rather than on hard data.

subliminal advertising
Presentation of messages or images on such media as television screens and flashing signs at a rapid rate (measured in microseconds) so that they make an impact on the subconscious mind of the viewer without being seen consciously. Subliminal advertising is illegal in some countries because it is considered to be a brainwashing technique that takes unfair advantage of the viewer. See TACHISTOSCOPE.

suboptimization

A term used in operations research (OR) to describe a problem solution that is best from a narrow point of view but may not necessarily be in the best interests of the overall company. For example, a department manager who expounds and exercises a policy of "no overtime under any conditions" may be suboptimizing.

subordinated debt

A debt that ranks below the actual amounts owed to general creditors. In times of financial embarrassment, an arrangement is sometimes made between a creditor and a debtor to subordinate a specific debt, where the creditor has faith in the business future of the debtor.

subpoena

A process issued by a court requiring the attendance of a witness at a trial or hearing.

subrogation

The right of an insurance company, after paying the insured's loss in accordance with the amounts described in the policy, to take over all the insured's legal rights against negligent third parties. If not for subrogation, the insured might attempt to collect twice for the same occurrence, once from the insurance company and again from the negligent third party.

Also, the transfer of a legal claim or right from one person to another. For example, when a creditor is unable to collect on a promissory note, the note may be transferred to a third party, who pays the original creditor and sues the debtor who defaulted on the loan.

subroutine

A set of instructions, part of a larger routine, that directs the computer to carry out a well-defined mathematical or logical operation.

subscribed capital stock

That part of the capital stock of a corporation against which unpaid subscriptions are outstanding. As subscriptions become fully paid, capital stock is issued.

subscription right

See WARRANT.

subset

See SET.

subsidiary accounts
A group of similar accounts that relate to the same activity or object and that are maintained in a separate record and controlled by an account in the general ledger.

subsidiary ledger
A supporting ledger containing a group of accounts. Examples are an expense ledger, customers' ledger, creditors' ledger, and a departmental ledger.

subsidy
A grant of financial aid, usually by a government agency, to a person or institution. One form of subsidy, called a *grant-in-aid,* is restricted to special purposes. Also see SUBVENTION.

substantial performance
In law, the complete performance of all the essential elements of a contract. Only those items that are trivial, inadvertent, and inconsequential may be omitted or performed in a manner that deviates from the terms of the contract. Compensation for defects may be substituted for actual performance.

substitution effect
As the price for a commodity, good, or service is increased beyond a critical level, consumers will seek lower-priced alternatives or substitutes. When such a phenomenon occurs and is successful, the tendency is for the original commodity, good, or service to become reduced in price in response to overproduction, high inventories, or the law of supply and demand. See EQUILIBRIUM.

subvention
A grant by a government, a foundation, or an institution to an individual or an organization for charitable, literary, scientific, or other similar purpose.

sucre
Basic unit of currency in Ecuador.

suits against the insurer
The majority of insurance contracts provide a clause that no legal action may be brought against the insurer unless all the provisions of the policy have been complied with. Also, it is usual to provide a statute of limitations within which all claims must be initiated in order to be valid. The time period is usually 12 months.

summary prospectus
A prospectus in short form permitted by the Securities Exchange Commission under regulations relating to promotional activities of dealers in SEC-registered securities.

summation notation
In statistics it is desirable to have a simplified notation for the sums of large numbers of terms that appear frequently. A variable is denoted by the letter X (capital, italics). Successive observations are noted as X_1, X_2, X_3, and so on, with X_n denoting the last observation in the series. The Greek capital letter sigma Σ is used to indicate the sum of n observations.

summons
A writ issued by a court to the sheriff directing him to notify the defendent that the plaintiff claims to have a cause for action and that the defendent is required to answer. If the defendant does not answer, a judgment may be taken by default.

sum-of-the-digits method
See SUM-OF-THE-YEARS DIGITS METHOD.

sum-of-the-years digits method
A method of depreciation of a fixed asset that allows depreciation to be taken at an accelerated rate in the early years of the asset's useful life. To calculate the depreciation rate that is to be taken each year, a fraction is developed in which all the years of useful life (n) of the asset are added together ($1 + 2 + 3 + \cdots + n$) and used as the denominator. For the first year, the numerator is n, for the second year it is $n - 1$, for the third year, $n - 2$, and so forth. For example, for an office machine with a useful life of five years ($n = 5$), the denominator of the fraction is 15. Depreciation the first year is 5/15th of the acquisition cost of the asset; it is 4/15th the second year, 3/15 the third year, and so on. In the final year the total remaining value of the asset may be fully depreciated, ignoring for purposes of this example any recoverable market value for the asset. Also known as *sum-of-the-digits method*. See DEPRECIATION METHODS.

Sunday contract
In states having blue laws, a contract executed on Sunday is not valid. The dating of such a contract as of any day other than Sunday does not make it valid if it was actually signed on Sunday. See BLUE LAWS.

sunk costs
In accounting, costs that have been incurred and are not reversible in the event of a decision to discontinue an incompleted project.

sunspot theory
A theory of business cycles proposed in England during the late 19th century. It held that sunspot cycles (disturbances on the surface of the sun) exhibited an extremely high correlation with agricultural cycles for a number of years; therefore, sunspots must affect the weather, which influences argicultural crops, which affect business conditions. This theory received worldwide popularity when it was first introduced, but then fell into disrepute because the high correlation between sunspots and agricultural cycles did not endure; it was the result of accidental rather than causal factors. Also known as the *astronomical theory of the business cycle*. See JEVONS, WILLIAMS STANLEY.

superintendent
A title sometimes used to denote the manager of a factory or a division; equivalent to *general foreman* or *works manager* in some countries.

supermarket
The supermarket initially was intended to appeal to people with limited incomes by offering low prices and minimum services. The first supermarkets were located in warehouses, had poor lighting, and offered extremely simple displays of goods, primarily foodstuffs. Modern supermarkets are generally large, well lit, and air-conditioned, with well-organized displays of assorted goods, including a wide variety of household merchandise. Except for the feature of self-service, they have come to resemble large versions of the old-time GENERAL STORE.

supervisor
In general, any person who directs the activities of others. Often this title is applied to a group leader who heads a section within a department.

supervisory routine
See EXECUTIVE ROUTINE.

supplemental appropriation
In government accounting, a Congressional grant of funds that has the effect of increasing an appropriation that has been previously approved.

supplemental security income
See SOCIAL SECURITY ADMINISTRATION.

supplementary cost
In accounting, the cost of a product that is not included in prime-cost data.

supplies
Materials that are essential to the operation of a business but are not physically incorporated into the products or parts manufactured by the firm. Supplies include wrapping paper, machine oil, cleaning materials, and fuel for the operation of the machinery. See INDUSTRIAL GOODS.

supply
The amount or quantity available of a good, service, or resource.

supply curve
The graphic representation of the quantity of a commodity available at different price levels. See SUPPLY SCHEDULE.

supply schedule
The quantities of a commodity that producers will supply at each price level.

support deed
An instrument used in the transfer of property in which the consideration is the support for life of the grantor by the grantee.

supporting style
In organizational behavior, the basic managerial style a manager uses next most frequently after the dominant style. See DOMINANT STYLE and OVERREJECTED STYLE.

suppressed inflation
See REPRESSED INFLATION.

surety bonds
See FIDELITY AND SURETY BONDING INSURANCE.

surplus value
According to the theories of Karl Marx, surplus value is the difference between the value that a worker creates as determined by the labor time embodied in the goods he produces, and the value that he receives

as determined by the subsistence level of wages. This surplus, Marx contended, is appropriated by the capitalist, and is the incentive for the development of the capitalistic system.

surrender value
The portion of premiums paid or another amount recoverable on an insurance policy if the policy is canceled immediately after having been issued.

surtax
A tax imposed on a tax base in addition to a so-called normal tax. Note that a surtax is imposed on an existing tax base. It is not a tax on a tax as is popularly believed.

surviving company
A company operating as an entity that has acquired the assets of other companies and continues the operations of those it has acquired but under its own name.

survivor-life curve
A curve that displays the residual or remaining life spans of people or things that are living or are in use at a specific point in time. See MORTALITY CURVE.

suspense account
An account in which receipts or disbursements are carried on a temporary basis, pending classification or identification.

sweat equity
The lending or substitution of services and labor for money.

sweetheart agreement
A substandard labor contract negotiated by a dishonest union leader in return for private payments from an employer; a violation of U.S. federal labor relations laws. A union engaging in these practices, if detected, cannot be certified as a bargaining agent.

SWFB
Initials for *Southwestern Freight Bureau.*

switching
The transfer of cars from one location or track to another within a local railroad area.

switch order
In securities trading, an order for the purchase or sale of one stock and the sale or purchase of another stock at a stipulated price difference.

SWL&C
See SHIPPER'S WEIGHT, LOAD, AND COUNT.

symbolic notation
In data processing, a method of representing a storage location by one or more figures.

synchronous computer
A computer in which all operations and events are controlled by equally spaced pulses from a clock. See CLOCK.

syndicalism
An economic system, combining features of anarchism and socialism, which demands the abolition of both capitalism and the state as instruments of oppression, and in its place the reorganization of society into industrywide associations or syndicates of workers. The syndicates—fundamentally trade unions—would replace the state. Each syndicate would then govern its own members in their activities as producers but leave them free from interference in all other matters. The chief exponent of syndicalism was the French social philosopher GEORGES SOREL (1847–1922), some of whose views later influenced the growth of fascism.

syndicate
In the securities market, a group of investors or investment bankers who together underwrite and distribute a new issue of securities or a large block of an outstanding issue. See INVESTMENT BANK.

Système International d'Unités
See INTERNATIONAL SYSTEM.

systems analysis
Generally, an analytic study of a complex problem that requires deciding among several alternative solutions. In any of the several disciplines of business management, systems analysis is the examination of an activity, procedure, method, or technique. The objective is generally to determine what must be accomplished and what methods must be employed to accomplish the goals that have been established.

When systems analysis is applied to the business itself, a company is viewed as a system in terms of input and output so that decision making will become more objective and quantitative. Each department is treated as a subsystem of the main system (rather than as an independently functioning entity), and the interaction (input and output) of the various activities is taken into account. Because of the complex data, a computer is usually essential to process and transmit the required information rapidly.

TA
See TRANSACTIONAL ANALYSIS.

TAA
Initials for *Transportation Association of America.*

tableland
A high plain of land.

tabular data
Data, too complex to be made part of a sentence or of a text, arranged by columns and rows in formal statistical tables. See TEXTUAL DATA.

T account
A convention in accounting practice that presents data in a two-column format, with a vertical line separating the two columns and a horizontal line centered over the top of the vertical. The title of the account is written along the horizontal line. Entered on the left side of the line are the assets or debits, and on the right side the liabilities or credits. Adding to an asset is referred to by accountants as *debiting* the asset,

while adding to the liabilities or ownership is referred to as *crediting* the account involved.

tachistoscope
In marketing, a device used to calculate the optimum time for displaying a message or an image, the purpose being to determine what length of time is most effective in getting an advertiser's message across. Subjects look into an aperture in the device, and the messages or images are flashed for varying lengths of time, usually measured in microseconds. See SUBLIMINAL ADVERTISING.

tacit
In legal proceedings, those rules that are generally understood to be the law by reason of custom and mores.

Taft-Hartley Act
Popular name for the Labor-Management Relations Act of 1947; it amends the National Labor Relations Act of 1935 (popularly known as the Wagner Act). While retaining the rights given to labor by the 1935 act, it also (1) outlaws unfair labor practices, such as coercing workers into joining unions, failure to bargain in good faith, jurisdictional strikes, secondary boycotts, and featherbedding; (2) outlaws the closed shop but permits the union shop; (3) requires unions to file financial reports with the National Labor Relations Board and union officials to sign non-Communist affidavits; (4) prohibits strikes to be called before the end of a 60-day notice period prior to the expiration of a collective bargaining agreement; and (5) enables the president to obtain an 80-day injunction against strikes for certain reasons.

takedown
In data processing, the actions performed at the end of an equipment operating cycle to prepare the equipment for the next setup; for example, removing the tapes from the tape handlers at the end of a computer run is a takedown operation.

takeout loan
A long-term loan that replaces an interim construction loan.

takeover
The acquisition of a business by another through purchase, exchange of capital stock, or any other device.

tala
The basic unit of currency in Western Samoa.

talisman
A juror summoned to fill up a panel for the trial of a particular case. Also known as *venireman*.

tandem option
A combination qualified and nonqualified stock option used between 1969 and 1973 but rendered ineffective by Internal Revenue Service rulings.

tangible asset
Any asset that exists physically, as opposed to an intangible asset.

tangible choses
See ASSIGNMENT.

tangible value
The worth of tangible assets such as plant and equipment and current assets.

tank car
A car for transporting bulk liquid freight; the car is sometimes divided internally into compartments.

tape drive
The mechanism that moves magnetic or paper tape past sensing and recording heads. Also known as *tape transport*.

tape transport
See TAPE DRIVE.

TAPPI
Initials for *Technical Association of the Pulp and Paper Industry*.

tare weight
The weight of packing material; in carload shipments, the weight of the empty freight car.

target program
See OBJECT PROGRAM.

tariff
A schedule of duties authorized by a government and imposed on commodities imported or exported. The intent may be to generate revenue for the government or to protect domestic suppliers. See REV-

ENUE TARIFF and PROTECTIVE TARIFF.

Also, in transportation, a publication that sets forth the charges, rates, and rules of transportation companies.

tariff harmonization
A tariff reduction that narrows the disparity among tariff rates on the same item.

tariff rates
See CLASS RATES.

task behavior
The tendency of a leader to organize and define the roles of the members of his or her group and to explain what activities each is to do and when, where, and how the tasks are to be accomplished; characterized by the endeavor to establish well-defined patterns of organization, channels of communication, and ways of getting jobs accomplished.

task force
An ad hoc committee, usually active for a limited term, assigned the task of identifying and recommending specific solutions to problem areas.

task orientation (TO)
In reference to management style, the extent to which a manager directs his own and his subordinates' efforts toward completion of a task; characterized by relatively low people orientation. See RELATIONSHIPS ORIENTATION, AUTOCRAT, and EXECUTIVE.

task style
A style of leadership guided by the belief that efficiency in operations results from arranging conditions of work in such a way that human elements interfere to a minimum degree. See MANAGERIAL GRID.

TAT
See THEMATIC APPERCEPTION TEST.

tax-anticipation note
In municipal accounting, a note issued in prospect of the collection of property taxes and scheduled to be repaid from the collected taxes.

tax avoidance
The management of financial matters so as to lower taxes as much as is legally possible. See TAX EVASION.

tax base
In economics, the object on which a tax is levied, such as sales, property, income, and so on. For example, the base may refer to objects owned by an individual or to the aggregate real estate of a community.

tax certification
The confirmation by city and county treasurers that no taxes remain unpaid prior to the acceptance of a warranty deed for recording; required in some states in real estate transactions.

taxes receivable
In municipal accounting, the uncollected portion of current and delinquent taxes.

tax evasion
Taxes owed but deliberately not paid; an illegal position. See TAX AVOIDANCE.

tax-exempt bond
A debt security of a state, city, or other public authority, the interest receipts of which are exempt from federal income taxation. See MUNICIPAL BOND.

tax ferret
A volunteer citizen or a special agent employed by a government agency to discover taxable property escaping assessment by the regular assessing agencies. Such agents are compensated in proportion to the assessment of property they discover or the amount of taxes collected thereon.

tax lien
A duly recorded claim of a government agency on property, pending the payment of taxes levied against it or its owner.

Tax Reduction Act Stock-Ownership Plan (TRASOP)
Created in 1975, the plan allows employers to claim as credit against taxes an amount equal to one percent of their capital spending if the money saved is used to buy company stock for employees who pay nothing for it.

Taylor, Frederick W. (1856–1915)
Considered the father of scientific production management. Carl Barth, Henry L. Gantt, Harrington Emerson, and Frank and Lillian Gilbreth, among other well-known authorities, worked within Taylor's

philosophy, first formulated in *The Principles of Scientific Management* (1911). Essentially, Taylor stated that scientific methods could and should be applied to all management problems, and that methods by which work was accomplished should be determined through scientific study and investigation. His ideas developed into the fields of methods engineering and work measurement. It is claimed by some that Taylor's work laid the foundations for human engineering and industrial relations sciences.

TCFB
Initials for *Transcontinental Freight Bureau*.

TDCC
Initials for *Transportation Data Coordinating Committee*.

t-distribution
In statistics, a symmetrical distribution of a population, like the normal distribution but more spread out. Used where the standard deviation of the population is unknown and an estimate of it, obtained from a small sample, has to be used. The problem was first studied by W. S. Gosset, a statistician for Guinness's Brewery. See GOSSET, WILLIAM S.

Teamsters Union
The largest trade union in the United States and Canada, established in 1903. Its full name is International Brotherhood of Teamsters, Chauffeurs, Warehousemen and Helpers of America. The union represents approximately two million members.

team style
A style of leadership whose basic premises are that work is accomplished through committed people and that interdependence through a common stake in the organization's purpose leads to relationships of trust and respect. See MANAGERIAL GRID.

team track
A track established by a railroad for general use of the public in loading and unloading freight cars.

tear sheet
A sheet or an actual page removed from a periodical. The sheet contains an actual reproduction of an advertisement and is often used as a document in support of an invoice to the advertiser, proof that the advertisement did in fact appear as ordered.

technical analysis
In the securities market, the technique of analyzing factors of supply and demand to determine the direction of security prices.

technological change
In economics, increase in the inventory of knowledge used in the production of goods and services.

technology
An entire inventory of knowledge and skills, usually applied to specific technical disciplines.

telescoping
See OVERLAPPED SCHEDULE.

telex
A telegraph service giving instant printed communications between subscribers who operate typewriterlike instruments for such communications.

template
A graphic aid in visualizing and planning the physical layout of a facility. Two-dimensional and block templates depict, to scale, the outlines of the maximum projected areas of machines and equipment. Three-dimensional templates are scale models that add an element of realism and aid in the comprehension of height as well as length and width situations. In constructing templates, a heavy cross-sectioned or quad-ruled sheet is often used for the base; this provides the scale to minimize the need for repetitive measuring.

tenancy at sufferance
A continued tenancy after a lease expires, the owner permitting a tenant to continue in possession on a temporary basis.

tenancy by the entirety
An estate existing between husband and wife, with equal rights of possession and enjoyment during their joint lives and with the right of survivorship.

tenancy in common
The ownership of equal or unequal undivided interests in property by two or more persons, without the right of survivorship.

tenancy in partnership
The ownership by two or more persons who unite their property in a lawful business venture.

tenant
One who holds land by any kind of right or title, whether permanently or temporarily.

tenant in fee
One who owns land to hold to himself and his heirs forever. This is the highest estate known to law.

ten-day escrow law
See BULK SALES LAW.

tender
In securities trading, an offer to purchase outstanding stock from the stockholders. Usually made by a corporation or an individual to gain control of a company or to simplify the corporate structure of the company making the tender. The price offered is usually above the market price. However, if there is no limit to the number of shares the maker of the tender will purchase, the market price rapidly moves to the higher price represented by the tender.

tender bid
In marketing, a tender is a specification for the purchase of goods and services published by a government agency, inviting suppliers to bid competitively their specific offerings. Usually, the suppliers' responses are considered confidential until the date and hour of the openings of the suppliers' bids, at which time they become public knowledge. Terms and conditions under which a tender bid may be accepted or rejected are given in the original tender specification.

tender specification
See TENDER BID.

Tennessee Valley Authority (TVA)
A government-owned corporation that conducts a unified program of resource development for the advancement of economic growth in the Tennessee Valley region. The authority's program of activities includes flood control, navigation development, electric power production, fertilizer development, recreation improvement, and forestry and

wildlife development. Although its power program is financially self-supporting, other programs are financed primarily by appropriations from Congress.

tentative balance sheet
A balance sheet in work form, intended for discussion, review, or any other managerial purpose prior to its publication in final form.

tenure
The time limit of a person's right to public office. *Term* signifies a limited period; *tenure,* an indefinite period.

In U.S. educational institutions, the tenure system is intended to provide job assurance for staff teachers and instructors.

term bonds
Bonds that mature at the same date.

terminal account
A general or expense ledger account appearing as an item on a balance sheet or income statement. Also, any account that is not changed; in which transactions are not transferred, reclassified, or reallocated; and that is considered closed as entered in its classification.

terminal charge
A charge made for a service performed in a carrier's terminal area.

term insurance
Provides protection for a specific period of time, without savings, investment, or cash-value features. Usually written for 5-, 10-, or 15-year periods, although some companies issue policies for longer terms than 15 years.

testator
A person who has died and left a will.

testatrix
A female TESTATOR.

test check
The verification of selected items in an account as an indication of the probability of, or the development of an opinion concerning, the accuracy of the entire account or record.

textual data
Data simple enough to be presented as an integral part of a text or a sentence. For example, the following data are readily understood even though presented as a sentence: Annual personal income in the United States in 1948 was $209.5 billion, and by 1953 it had risen to $284.5 billion. See TABULAR DATA.

TF
See TILL FORBID.

T-group training
A method of sensitivity training developed in 1947 by Leland P. Bradford, Kenneth D. Benne, and Ronald Lippitt in Bethel, Maine, to help individuals learn how others perceive their behavior. It is based on the assumption that a number of individuals meeting in an unstructured situation with an open climate will develop working relations with each other and learn a great deal about themselves by observing how they are perceived by other group members. The training is intended to help the individual develop the ability to analyze and become more sensitive to the processes of human interaction and to acquire concepts for ordering and controlling these phenomena.

thematic apperception test (TAT)
A personality test, sometimes used by industrial psychologists or personnel managers trained in the method, in which the person being tested is shown a set of pictures that can be interpreted in a variety of ways. The person invents a story based on what the picture conveys to him or her. The story is then used as the basis for analysis of the person's personality.

theory of interest
See LIQUIDITY PREFERENCE.

Theory X
A theory of human nature and human behavior postulated by Douglas McGregor to explain managers' behavior toward their subordinates. Theory X assumes that the average human being has an inherent dislike of work and will avoid it if possible; that most people must be coerced, controlled, directed, threatened with punishment to get them to put forth adequate effort; and that the average human being prefers to be directed, wishes to avoid responsibility, has relatively little ambition, and wants security above all. Also known as the *traditional view of*

direction and control. See McGregor, Douglas, Theory Y, and Theory Z.

Theory Y

A theory of human nature and human behavior postulated by Douglas McGregor to explain managers' behavior toward their subordinates. Theory Y assumes that the expenditure of physical and mental effort in work is as natural as in play or rest; that human beings will exercise self-direction and self-control in the service of objectives to which they are committed; that commitment to objectives is a function of the rewards associated with their achievement; that the average human being accepts and seeks responsibility under proper conditions; and that the intellectual potentialities of the average human being are only partially utilized. Also known as the *integration of individual and organizational goals.* See McGregor, Douglas, Theory X, and Theory Z.

Theory Z

In organizational behavior, a theory of human conduct, drives, and needs whose premises are that human beings have a will, they are open to good and evil, situations drive them, reason motivates them, interdependence is their basic mode of interaction, interaction is their social unit of importance, and objective best describes their view of themselves. Theory Z is an outgrowth of Theory X and Theory Y, postulated by Douglas McGregor in his book *The Human Side of Enterprise.* See McGregor, Douglas, Theory X, and Theory Y.

therblig chart

A detailed, symbolic and systematic analysis of work performed by a worker's body members, usually when the work is performed at one workplace. Through the use of symbols, a therblig chart provides a great amount of qualitative information. It is usually used where there is a large volume of work, especially when two hands are involved in the work. A therblig deals in the fundamental motions involved in a time and motion study. Therblig is the name of its inventor, Gilbreth, spelled backward. See Gilbreth, Frank Bunker.

thin market

A securities market in which there are comparatively few bids to buy or offers to sell, or both. The phrase may apply to a single security or to the entire stock market. Price fluctuations between transactions are usually larger in a thin market than when the market is liquid (opposite of thin in trading terminology). A thin market in a particular security may reflect lack of interest in that issue or a limited supply or a limited demand for stock in the market.

third mortgage
A mortgage inferior to the first and second mortgages.

third-party liability insurance
See LIABILITY INSURANCE.

third-party rights
An insurance contract is generally between two parties, the insured party and the insurance company. Under certain conditions, such as where an insurance company offers a life insurance contract that specifies a beneficiary who would eventually receive the payment, the rights of the third party, the beneficiary, are recognized.

third-party risk
See LIABILITY RISK.

third world
The entirety of the poor nations that are burdened by problems of underdevelopment, poverty, illiteracy, and technological backwardness.

three-by-threes
In some states, an arrangement designed to avoid the applications of subdivision laws by dividing the acreage into three parcels and transferring them to others who redivide each parcel into three parcels, and so on.

Three-D management style theory
See REDDIN, WILLIAM J.

three-fourths loss clause
In regard to fire insurance, a clause providing that under no circumstances will the insurance company pay more than three-fourths of the amount of the loss, no matter how much insurance coverage may be in force. See THREE-FOURTHS VALUE CLAUSE.

three-fourths value clause
In regard to fire insurance, a clause providing that under no circumstances will the insurance company make a loss payment for more than

three-fourths the value of the building. However, it is possible for partial losses to be paid in full. See THREE-FOURTHS LOSS CLAUSE.

thrift plan
See SAVINGS PLAN.

through lot
A parcel of land having frontage on two streets.

throughput accounting
An accounting system that enables original expenditures recorded in primary accounts to be identified in secondary accounts and financial statements. See PRIMARY ACCOUNT and SECONDARY ACCOUNT.

through rate
A transportation rate that applies from origin to destination.

tical
The basic unit of currency in Thailand.

ticker
The instrument that prints prices and volume of securities transactions in cities and towns throughout the United States and Canada. Modern techniques enable the data related to these transactions to be displayed within minutes after the transactions have taken place.

tickler
Jargon for *reminder*. A tickler file is maintained by some managers as a matter of style. Items may be entered into the file according to a specific date, time, or subject and accessed for use on the appropriate occasion.

tide and overflow land
All land over which the tide ebbs and flows as measured from the line of ordinary high tide to the line of mean low tide.

tie-in sale
A practice whereby a seller requires the buyer to purchase one or more additional or *tied* products as a condition for purchasing the desired or *tying* product. Also known as *tying contract*.

tight money
A monetary policy that has a restrictive impact on economic activity; usually associated with high interest rates.

till forbid (TF)
In advertising, an instruction to a publication in which space has been ordered for the marketer's advertisement. The initials TF, when appearing on the purchase order for the space, indicate that the specified advertisement shall appear in every issue of the publication until the advertiser or its agent issues a change order.

time-adjusted return
See DISCOUNTED CASH FLOW.

time and motion study or time-motion study
In manufacturing, systematic observation, analysis, measurement, and correlation of the time required to perform a set of human motions in the fulfillment of a specific task. Also see MOTION STUDY.

time certificate of deposit
See CERTIFICATE OF DEPOSIT.

time cost
See PERIOD COST.

time deposit
A deposit in a financial institution requiring at least 30 days notice before a withdrawal may be effected. Most savings accounts are time deposits; however, few financial institutions exercise the 30-days-notice requirement.

time deposit—open account
A type of savings account into which a depositor may place funds at any time. A request in writing must be made to withdraw money from this type of account.

time draft
A draft payable within a specified time—usually 30 days—after acceptance by the drawee.

time order
An order to buy or sell a security that becomes a market or limited price order at a specified time.

time-phased planning
See TIME-SERIES PLANNING.

time series
Statistical data collected, observed, or recorded at successive intervals of time. A frequency distribution on the horizontal axis if the distribution is plotted on a graph.

time-series planning
In materials planning, a technique whereby the demand is expressed by specific time periods extended into the future and order release dates are based on the anticipated levels of inventory that will be on hand in these future time periods. Also known as *time-phased planning*.

time sharing
The simultaneous use of a single computer by more than one person or customer. The computer operation is usually handled so rapidly that each user has the impression of being the sole user.

times-interest ratio
The relationship between net income from interest on a long-term obligation and a period of time, usually a single year or the average of several years. It is sometimes used as an indicator of the relative safety of an investment.

time ticket
A report of time spent in performing a labor task; usually in the form of a handwritten report or a punched card. Also known as *job ticket*.

time zone
See ZONE TIME.

TIO
Initials for *Television Information Office*.

Tippett, L. H. C.
Acknowledged to be the developer of a work-sampling procedure to determine standards for such elements of production as delays and work time. Although Tippett introduced his theories in 1934, they lay dormant until the 1950s when some progressive companies put them to work. Tippett's work-sampling procedure is used extensively in the 1970s.

TIR carnet
Transport International Routier Carnet; an international customs document for road transportation of goods intended as samples, as demonstrators, or for exhibits, the equipment or goods to be used on a temporary basis and afterward returned to the country of origin. Under the TIR carnet system, the goods are sealed in a container by customs officials before export and can then be carried to any participating customs office destination abroad with a minimum of customs examination and documentation in the countries passed through en route. The intermediate countries waive the payment of deposits of duties. See ATA CARNET.

title
Evidence that the owner of land is in lawful possession thereof; an instrument evidencing such ownership. Title may be used in connection with real property or goods other than terra firma.

title company
A company that insures titles and issues title insurance policies to property owners.

title deeds
The successive deeds on which real estate title rests.

title defect
A fault or cloud in the real estate title.

title insurance
Protection to a property owner against loss because of a defect, fault, or cloud in a title.

Title I loan
A loan insured by the Federal Housing Administration for up to $3,500 for home repair and improvement.

title policy
See TITLE INSURANCE.

title report
In real estate transactions, a description of the condition of a title, made by a licensed title insurance company as a preliminary to issuing a title policy.

title search
An examination of public records to determine the ownership and en-cumbrances affecting real property. Also known as *examination of title*.

Title II loan
Any loan insured by the Federal Housing Administration not included in Title I.

TL
In freight-handling terminology, the abbreviation for truckload. See CARLOAD.

TO
See TASK ORIENTATION.

TOFC
See TRAILERS ON FLATCARS.

TOFCEE
Actual spelling is TOFC, but popularly pronounced *tofcee,* as in *toffsee*. See TRAILERS ON FLATCARS.

token money
A government-issued object, either paper or metal, whose value as money is greater than the market value of the materials of which it is composed. Examples are pennies, nickels, dimes, and dollars.

tolerance
The amount and direction (plus or minus) of the deviation from a basic dimension. Also, the allowable difference in dimensions between two mating parts.

Torrens, Sir Robert (1780–1864)
A soldier, member of Parliament, and political economist, Torrens was one of the first economists to attribute production of wealth to the joint action of land, labor, and capital, and to state the law of diminishing returns. His son, Sir Robert Richard Torrens (1814–1884), emigrated to Australia in 1840 and originated the Torrens Land-Title System.

Torrens certificate of title
In some states, the evidence of ownership issued to a landowner by a circuit court and entered in the register of titles by the county recorder.

Torrens property
Real property to which a Torrens certificate of title has been issued by the circuit court.

Torrens title system
A method of land registration still in use in some states but generally replaced by the faster, less expensive title insurance system.

tort
A wrongful act committed by one person against another or that other's property; the breach of a legal duty imposed by law other than by contract. The word tort means "twisted" or "wrong."

total equity
In the United Kingdom, equivalent to the U.S. term *equity*.

Towne, Henry Robinson (1844–1924)
One of the founders of Yale & Towne Manufacturing Company; considered one of the pioneers in the use of scientific management techniques.

TR
See TRAVELING REQUISITION.

trace
An auditor's term for the process of ascertaining whether or not an item has been disposed of in accordance with the facts as reported.

traceable cost
A cost element whose origin can be identified even though it may have been transferred from one account to another.

trackage right
The privilege granted one railroad to operate over the tracks of another railroad.

tracking signal
In exponential smoothing theory, the ratio of the cumulative algebraic sum of the deviations between the forecasts and the actual values to the mean absolute deviation. It is used to signal when the validity of the forecasting model might be doubtful. See MEAN ABSOLUTE DEVIATION.

tractor or **tractor truck**
A self-powered unit of equipment without freight storage or carrying capability of its own. Used to pull trailers and semitrailers.

trade acceptance
A bill of exchange drawn on the buyer by the seller of merchandise and unconditionally accepted by the buyer. Made out in accordance with the terms of the contract between the seller and the buyer. See BILL OF EXCHANGE.

trade account payable
An amount owed to a supplier by a company that has received goods or services provided by the supplier.

trade account receivable
An amount owed to a supplier by a company to which the supplier has delivered goods or provided services.

Trade Agreements Act
A 1958 act of Congress that provides authority for oil import quotas. See RECIPROCAL TRADE AGREEMENTS PROGRAM and TRADE EXPANSION ACT.

trade association
A nonprofit organization sponsored by business firms in the same kind of business and designed to protect and advance their common interests.

trade balance
The difference between the value of goods exported by a nation and those it has imported.

trade discount
A discount allowed by their suppliers to a class of customers, such as electrical appliance or business machine dealers. It is based on a published list or suggested end-user price, is usually offered on the basis of volume purchases by the dealers, and is not related to date of payment.

Trade Expansion Act
Enacted in 1962 as part of the Reciprocal Trade Agreements Program, this act broadens the powers of the president to (1) negotiate tariff reductions on broad categories of goods; (2) lower or eliminate tariffs on goods for which the European Common Market and the United

States together account for at least 80 percent of total world exports; (3) lower tariffs by as much as 50 percent on the basis of reciprocal trade agreements, provided that such agreements include most-favored-nation clauses; and (4) grant vocational, technical, and financial assistance to American employees and business firms whose industries are adversely affected by tariff reductions.

trade investment
In the United Kingdom, an investment by one business firm in another for the purpose of protecting or expanding the investor's activities. Usually represented by a minority ownership of capital stock.

trade liability
A current account, note, charge, or debt that is payable for goods purchased and services received; any current liability with the exceptions of wages and unpaid taxes.

trademark
A word, name, symbol, device, or any combination of these, adopted and used by a manufacturer or merchandiser to identify its goods and distinguish them from those manufactured or sold by others. The primary function is to distinguish one entrepreneur's goods from another's. A trademark may be owned by an individual, a firm, a partnership, a corporation, or an association or other collective group. Application for registration of a trademark is made to the Commissioner of Patents, Washington, D.C. If granted, the trademark registration is valid for 20 years, renewable so long as the mark is still in use in commerce. In the event of transfer of business ownership, a trademark may be assigned, sold, or traded as an asset along with the goodwill of the business using it.

trade name
The name by which a product or a service is known. It may or may not be registered as a trademark.

trade note receivable
A customer's promissory note, pledging payment for goods supplied or services rendered.

trade payable
An amount of money owed to a creditor for goods or services received. Also known as *account payable*.

trade price
The price charged to regular customers who purchase continuously or in large volume for resale to their own customers. It is usually the list price or suggested end-user price less an applicable discount.

trader
One who buys and sells goods, commodities, or securities for his or her own account for short-term profit. See SPECULATION.

trade receivable
An amount of money invoiced to a customer for goods delivered or services rendered. Also known as *account receivable*.

trade union
A labor union whose membership is limited to people who are engaged in the same trade rather than the same craft, industry, or company. See CRAFT UNION and INDUSTRIAL UNION.

trading company
A company organized to carry on commerce with foreign nations or with other trading companies in overseas territories.

trading limit
One of the prices above or below which trading on commodity exchanges is not allowed during any one day. Also, the maximum number of contracts an individual is allowed to hold at one time in commodities covered by regulation.

trading market
A securities market that does not exhibit a definite price trend and with few traders who are other than professionally engaged in the trading of securities.

trading on the equity
Taking the profit derived from borrowing capital at a low rate and employing it in a business or venture that yields a higher rate.

trading post
One of 18 horseshoe-shaped trading locations on the floor of the New York Stock Exchange at which stocks assigned to each location are bought and sold. About 75 stocks are traded at each post. See INACTIVE POST.

trading profit
Usually the first item listed in a British income statement, equivalent to gross profit in the U.S. method of reporting. Also, in the securities market, the profit derived from speculation.

traffic manager
A job function and title believed to have originated in the latter part of the nineteenth century within large industrial corporations. The title was conceivably taken from the railroad industry, which already had such a title and from which the first industrial traffic managers were hired. The function has grown to include the management, organization, and control of all aspects of transportation, including the purchase of transportation services by shippers or consignees to effect the efficient movement of people and property from one point to another.

trailer
The storage unit of a tractor-trailer combination into which freight is loaded. See SEMITRAILER.

trailers on flatcars (TOFC and TOFCEE)
A method of containerization that enables exceptionally large packages to be loaded directly onto a railroad flatcar or into the interior of an airfreighter fuselage. A common sight is that of an overland trailer secured to the deck of a railroad flatcar, in which case the trailer itself becomes a container.

trait theory
A management leadership theory whose premise is that more effective leaders have special qualities not possessed by less effective leaders. In popular language, the theory contends that leaders are born, not necessarily made. With the growth of the behaviorial sciences, the trait theory has been significantly discounted.

tramp service
The service offered by vessels operating as contract rather than common carriers, following no fixed route and not adhering to a regular schedule. See LINEAR SERVICE and TRAMP STEAMER.

tramp steamer
A steamship that does not operate on regular runs or schedules and that usually carries a combination of passengers and freight. See TRAMP SERVICE.

transactional analysis (TA)
A concept of interpersonal actions, reactions, communications, and noncommunications. It hypothesizes three role states in which the human mind operates: Parent, Adult, and Child. The Parent may be nurturing, patient, or scolding and authoritarian in behavior. The Adult is usually logical and highly self-controlled. The Child is emotional, demanding, at times creative, but generally self-centered. As behavioral patterns move from state to state, or level to level, *games* may be played deliberately or intuitively; attempts are made at manipulation. The concept was formulated by Dr. Eric Berne in his book *Games People Play* (1964).

transactions motive
Desire on the part of households and businesses to hold some of their assets in liquid form so that they can engage in day-to-day spending activities. The motive is influenced primarily by the level of income rather than by changes in the interest rate, and in the modern theory of interest it is considered to be one of the chief sources of demand for loanable funds.

transcribe
In accounting, to post as from an invoice to a journal, from a journal to a ledger, or from a ledger to a trial balance or financial statement. Also, to transfer a dollar amount or quantity of goods or services from one record or account to another.

In office procedures, to transfer information to a typewritten page from another recorded form, such as stenographic notes or recorded tapes.

transfer
Either of two different operations in the securities market. One, the delivery of a stock certificate from the seller's broker to the buyer's broker and the legal change of ownership; normally accomplished within a few days of the initial transaction. Two, the recording of a change of ownership on the books of the corporation by the transfer agent. When the purchaser's name is recorded on the books of the company, dividends, notices of meetings, proxies, financial reports, and all pertinent literature sent by the issuer to its holders of securities are mailed directly to the new owner of record.

transfer agent
The officer, bank, or trust company that keeps a record of the name of each registered shareowner, his or her address, and the number of

shares owned, and who sees that the certificates presented for transfer are properly canceled and that new certificates are issued in the name of the new owner.

transfer ledger
A binder for filled ledger sheets or closed accounts.

transfer payment
A disbursement by the government for which it receives no goods or services. Items such as Social Security payments to the aged, unemployment compensation, and certain business subsidies are included because they channel tax revenues back to businesses and households without directly absorbing resources.

transfer tax
A tax imposed by New York State when a security is sold by or transferred from one person to another. The tax is paid by the seller.

transistor-transistor logic (TTL or T²L)
Evolved from a need for more speed than could be achieved with diode-transistor logic.

transit number
An identification number printed on the faces of checks issued by banks in the United States. It consists of a group of three sets of numbers, usually in the upper right-hand corner, arranged as in this example: $\frac{11\text{-}24/277}{1210}$. The 11 is a code for the Federal Reserve city; 24 represents the bank's name; 277, the branch name; 12, the Federal Reserve district; 1, the Federal Reserve Bank or branch; and 0, the class of account. The code was developed by the American Banking Association.

transportation average
See SHARE INDEX.

transportation insurance rating bureau
Performs the same functions for mutual insurance companies as the Inland Marine Insurance Bureau does for stock companies. See INLAND MARINE INSURANCE BUREAU.

transportation inventory
Inventories that exist because material must be moved. For example, if it takes two weeks to replenish a branch warehouse on the other side of a geographical region, inventory equivalent to approximately two weeks of requirements will normally be in transit; this is therefore considered to be *extra* (or *transportation*) *inventory*. Sometimes refered to as *movement inventory*.

transship or tranship
To transfer freight from one carrier to another.

TRASOP
See TAX REDUCTION ACT STOCK-OWNERSHIP PLAN.

traveler
In industrial production, a copy of the manufacturing order that moves the work through the shop.

traveler's check
A draft issued by a bank or express company that is payable on presentation by any correspondent of the issuer.

traveling auditor
A staff auditor whose function is to examine branches and divisions of a corporation at outlying locations as an aid to corporate control.

traveling requisition (TR)
A purchase requisition made up once and reused each time the raw material or product is to be reordered so that new requisitions do not have to be written repeatedly.

treasury bill
A short-term obligation that matures in 13 or 26 weeks, sold by the U.S. government primarily through competitive bidding to meet current needs for working funds that are not fulfilled by receipts from income taxes paid. The return to investors on these government securities, the so-called *bill rate,* is determined by the difference between the price paid for the bill and the price received when the bill matures. This rate reflects the supply of bills and the demand for these securities by major buyers, including commercial banks, Federal Reserve Banks, lending institutions, insurance companies, and other investors. Because of the high quality of the bills, the yield on them is relatively low.

treasury department
See DEPARTMENT OF THE TREASURY.

treasury stock
Stock issued by a company but later reacquired. It may be held in the company's treasury indefinitely, reissued to the public, or retired. Treasury stock receives no dividend and grants no voting right when held by the company. See REACQUIRED STOCK and REDEMPTION.

Treaty of Accession
An amendment to the Treaty of Rome, which in 1957 founded the European Economic Community (EEC), or the Common Market. The Treaty of Accession became effective on January 1, 1973, and joined Denmark, the Irish Republic, and the United Kingdom to the EEC. The treaty also provided for the new member states to join the European Atomic Energy Community and the European Coal and Steel Community, originally established by the Treaty of Paris in 1951. See TREATY OF ROME and EUROPEAN ECONOMIC COMMUNITY.

Treaty of Paris
Established the European Coal and Steel Community among the founder members of the Common Market in 1951. The treaty was the prototype for the European Economic Community, established by the Treaty of Rome in 1957.

Treaty of Rome
Signed by its founder members France, West Germany, Italy, the Netherlands, Belgium, and Luxembourg on March 25, 1957, the treaty created the European Economic Community, which came into effect on January 1, 1958. See TREATY OF ACCESSION and EUROPEAN ECONOMIC COMMUNITY.

Treaty of the Meter, 1875
See METRIC CONVERSION ACT OF 1975.

trend bucker
A colloquialism for a company whose sales and earnings do not decline when the general economy recedes.

triadic product test
A term used by market researchers for a product test in which a consumer is presented with three unmarked products, two of which are

identical, and is asked to pick out the one that is different. With a large enough sample, it is possible statistically to eliminate the guesses made by some consumers and to determine whether or not the different product is in fact perceived as different by the consumer. See MONADIC PRODUCT TEST and DIADIC PRODUCT TEST.

trial balance
A term applied to the preparation of a list of account balances abstracted from a customer's ledger or other subsidiary ledger for the purpose of testing their totals and comparing them with those in the related control account. The trial balance is the basic summary of the total debits and total credits in a ledger preliminary to preparing a financial statement.

triaxial coordinates
The percentage composition of a mixture of three components may be represented by a point on triaxial coordinates. The chart is in the form of an equilateral triangle, the altitude of which represents 100 percent of each of the three components. The usefulness of such a diagram depends on the geometric principle that the sum of the perpendiculars to the sides from any point within an equilateral triangle is a constant and is equal to the altitude.

trigger price mechanism
A minimum price level established by the U.S. government for specified imported goods. In the event that the price of any of the goods drops below the "trigger" level, the Treasury Department begins an investigation to determine whether dumping has occurred. For example, in early 1978, at a joint meeting of a Japanese delegation and the U.S. Council on Wage and Price Stability, in which data were studied for costs of materials, labor, overhead, and depreciation, it was determined that the "trigger" price for 17 steel products that make up 75 percent of the market would be set at $330 per ton, or 5.7 percent less than the price for comparable U.S.-made products on the East Coast.

trinomial expression
An algebraic expression composed of three terms. See MONOMIAL EXPRESSION, BINOMIAL EXPRESSION, and POLYNOMIAL EXPRESSION.

trip transit policy
Provides insurance coverage for single shipments of owner's goods, equipment, household furniture, machinery, and general merchandise.

Covers the interest of the shipper only; does not provide protection for the carrier. Although usually written on a specified-perils basis, the insurer may write the policy on an all-risk basis for preferred accounts.

trover
Legal action to recover the value of property that has been seized illegally. See DETINUE.

truckload (TL)
See CARLOAD.

truck wholesaler
Combines selling, delivery, and collection in one operation. Maintains a warehouse and operates one or more trucks that are driven to customer locations where the merchandise is dispensed. Usually deals in perishable and semiperishable goods; therefore makes frequent calls at customer locations, a service that appeals strongly to suppliers and dealers. Also known as a *wagon distributor* or *wagon jobber*.

trunk line
A system or main line for handling long-distance transportation, traffic, and communications. A main supply channel such as a natural-gas main or other fuel-feed line. A direct communications link such as a telephone circuit between two switchboards or main terminals.

trust
The right of property, real or personal, held by one for the benefit of another.

trust-and-agency fund
In municipal accounting, a fund consisting of money and property received and held by a municipality or an institution as trustee or custodian, or in the capacity of an agent for certain individuals or government units.

trust deed
A conveyance of a title to a trustee to be held until a loan or a performance secured by a note is paid or completed, at which time the title is reconveyed. See RECONVEYANCE.

trustee
One who holds property in trust for another to secure the performance of an obligation.

trust estate
An estate subject to a trust or being held in trust.

trust fund
A fund held by one person, the trustee, for the benefit of another, the affairs of the trust being conducted in accordance with the provisions of a formal trust agreement. Various states have passed legislation governing the conduct of the trustee.

Trust Indenture Act of 1940
Passed by Congress to provide protection for bondholders by regulating the actions of the trustee as outlined in the bond indenture.

trust mortgage
A mortgage to a person or a corporation as trustee, who holds the security for the benefit of others in accordance with the terms and conditions set forth in the instrument. Such a mortgage may be given to secure an issue of bonds sold by the mortgagor to various persons and transferable at their will. The mortgage is given to a trustee who acts for and on behalf of all bondholders.

trustor
The borrower in a trust deed. One who deeds his or her property to a trustee in a trust deed transaction.

Truth-in-Securities Act
See SECURITIES ACT OF 1933.

T²L
See TRANSISTOR-TRANSISTOR LOGIC.

TTL
See TRANSISTOR-TRANSISTOR LOGIC.

tugrik
The basic unit of currency in Outer Mongolia.

turnaround
The situation wherein a company's trend of declining sales and/or earnings is reversed.

turnover
In accounting, the number of times in a stated period that various assets are consumed and replaced. When used in ratio analysis, one of the indicators of the specific performance of management and the firm. Also, the financial statements of companies in the United Kingdom use the term as the equivalent of the U.S. term *gross sales,* the first item on an earnings report.

TVA
See TENNESSEE VALLEY AUTHORITY. Also, the initials for the French term *taxe à la valeur ajoutée.* See VALUE-ADDED TAX.

TVB
Initials for *Television Bureau of Advertising.*

two-bin system
A simple system of inventory control in which relatively small items are stored in two bins of equal size. When the first bin is emptied, a replenishment quantity is ordered. When the material is received, the first bin is refilled and the excess is put into the second bin. See VISUAL REVIEW SYSTEM.

two-dollar broker
A member on the floor of the New York Stock Exchange who executes orders either for other brokers having more business at that time than they can handle themselves or for firms that do not have their Exchange member-partner on the floor. The term derives from the time when these independent brokers received $2 per hundred shares for executing such orders. The fee today varies with the price of the stock.

two-tier board
An executive board composed of the two highest levels of management in a corporate structure. One is a part-time board of supervisors chosen by stockholders. This supervisory board appoints a full-time management board that may include representatives chosen by employee nominations. Although the supervisory board approves annual budgets, determines operating policies, and responds to reports and advice from the management board, it takes no part in day-to-day operations. The management board appoints the general manager and the department heads and is responsible for day-to-day operations.

tying contract
See TIE-IN SALE.

Type I error
In hypothesis testing, the error committed in rejecting a hypothesis that should really have been accepted. See TYPE II ERROR.

Type II error
In hypothesis testing, the error committed in accepting a hypothesis that should actually have been rejected. See TYPE I ERROR.

UCC
Initials for *Uniform Classification Committee*. Also see UNIFORM COMMERCIAL CODE.

UFC
Initials for *uniform freight classification*.

UL
See UNDERWRITERS LABORATORY.

ultra vires
Latin for "beyond power." The acts of a corporation are ultra vires when they are beyond the power or capacity of the corporation as granted by the state in its charter to the corporation.

UMTA
See URBAN MASS TRANSPORTATION ADMINISTRATION.

UMWA
See UNITED MINE WORKERS OF AMERICA.

UN
See UNITED NATIONS.

unadmitted asset
An asset determined to have little or no liquidation value. In reporting the financial position of an insurance company, such assets are segregated and deducted as a group. Also referred to as *inadmitted asset* and *nonadmitted asset*.

unallotted appropriation
In government accounting, the remainder of an appropriation available for purposes defined by the original appropriation determination.

unamortized debt discount
The portion of debt discount that remains and is to be spread over future fiscal periods. Usually appears as a prepaid expense, if related to a bank loan, or as a deferred charge, if related to a long-term bond issue.

unapplied cash
In municipal accounting, cash not reserved for a specific purpose and available for use within the fund of which it is part.

unappropriated budget surplus
In municipal accounting, the excess of the estimated revenues of a fund over the original appropriation for a given period of time.

unappropriated earned surplus
The part of earned surplus that has not been transferred to a subordinate account or earmarked for a specific purpose. Such surplus therefore remains available for distribution in the form of dividends.

unappropriated income
An account set up for budgetary control to which is credited the excess of income, according to a related and approved expense or earnings budget.

unavoidable cost
A cost that cannot be eliminated but must be continued even under a program of business retraction. Also, a fixed cost.

unbilled cost
A recoverable cost that may be identified with specific and uncompleted contracts for goods and services. Such uncompleted contracts are classified as assets or receivables.

UNCDF
See UNITED NATIONS CAPITAL DEVELOPMENT FUND.

uncertainty
In business economics, a state of knowledge in which the probabilities of outcomes resulting from specific actions are not known and cannot be predicted because they are subjective rather than objective phenomena. Uncertainties are therefore not insurable and cannot be integrated into the firm's cost structure.

unclaimed dividends
The dollar amount of the dividend checks not yet cashed by stockholders or not yet in their hands.

unclaimed wages
Wages earned but not claimed by employees, although cash is available to make the payments. Also, wage checks not yet presented for payment.

UNCTAD
See UNITED NATIONS CONFERENCE ON TRADE AND DEVELOPMENT.

underconsumption theory
A theory of business cycles whose premise is that recessions result from the lag of consumer expenditures behind output because too large a proportion of society's income is not spent on consumption. According to the theory, society distributes income too inequitably to enable people to purchase all the goods produced.

underdeveloped nation
In comparison with the more advanced countries, a nation that tends to exhibit (1) a poverty level of income and hence little or no savings, (2) a high rate of population growth, (3) a substantial majority of its labor force employed in agriculture, (4) a low proportion of adult literacy, (5) extensive unemployment that may be disguised, and (6) heavy reliance on a few items for export. Also referred to as *less developed nation*.

underemployment
Circumstances where skilled workers are employed at jobs for which they are overqualified, either by education or experience. Also, the situation where workers put in less than a standard number of hours per week at their jobs, sometimes done to provide employment for other workers who might otherwise become unemployed. Also known as *disguised unemployment*.

underlying company
A company that is part of a larger consolidated organization and is kept in existence only because of nontransferable rights or franchises that it possesses.

underlying mortgage
A mortgage that has priority over a larger one.

underlying security
A security issued by a subsidiary company and guaranteed by the parent company.

underwriter
In the securities market, an agent acting between a corporation issuing new securities and the public. The usual practice is for one or more underwriters to make an outright purchase of a corporation's new issue of stocks or bonds and to form a syndicate to sell the securities to individuals and institutions. Underwriters also distribute very large blocks of securities, perhaps held by an estate. Thereafter, the market in the securities may be over the counter, on a regional stock exchange, on the American Stock Exchange, or on the New York Stock Exchange. Also known as an *investment banker*.

Underwriters Laboratory (UL)
The UL label that appears on many products is the symbol of approval by the Underwriters Laboratory, maintained by the National Board of Fire Underwriters for the purpose of testing products or parts for safety with regard to fire hazard. Products that are not approved are referred to the manufacturer with suggestions for improvements that might lead to approval. See NATIONAL BOARD OF FIRE UNDERWRITERS.

undistributed profit
The profit of an activity before division among the interested parties. Also known as *earned surplus*. See RETAINED EARNINGS.

undivided account
See DIVIDED ACCOUNT.

undivided interest
The interest of co-owners in a property in which their individual interests are undistinguishable from one another.

undivided profit
The undistributed amount of a corporation's net income not yet formally transferred to retained earnings; a term generally used on the financial statements of banks where undivided profits are often combined with earned surplus under the heading *surplus and undivided profits*.

UNDP
See UNITED NATIONS DEVELOPMENT PROGRAM.

unearned increment
In accounting, any increase in the value of property due to circumstances beyond the control of the property owner and not attributable to direct expenditures or efforts. An example would be the increased market value of a piece of real property caused by improvements made to neighboring properties.

unearned revenue
Revenue or income not yet earned although already received.

unemployment compensation
See UNEMPLOYMENT INSURANCE.

unemployment insurance
Administered by each individual state and financed by payroll taxes imposed on employers, it provides income for a specific period of unemployment for persons laid off from their jobs and willing and able to accept employment if offered. In a few states employees are required to make contributions to the state unemployment compensation fund. Also known as *unemployment compensation*.

unemployment rate
The percentage of the civilian labor force that is out of work, as measured by the Bureau of Labor Statistics.

unencumbered allotment
In government accounting, the portion of an allotment or allocation that has been neither expended nor encumbered.

unencumbered appropriation
In government accounting, the portion of an appropriation that has been neither expended nor encumbered. Also known as *unencumbered balance*.

unencumbered balance
See UNENCUMBERED APPROPRIATION.

unencumbered land
Land free and clear of money claims against the title.

UNESCO
See UNITED NATIONS EDUCATIONAL, SCIENTIFIC, AND CULTURAL ORGANIZATION.

unexpended appropriation
In government accounting, the portion of an appropriation that has not yet been expended, although it may be committed in whole or in part. Also known as *unexpended balance*.

unexpended balance
See UNEXPENDED APPROPRIATION.

unexpired cost
An expenditure, including prepaid expenses, whose benefits will be realized in the future.

unfair competition
Outlawed by the Clayton and Sherman Antitrust Acts, the practices of using false or misleading advertising, misappropriating a competitor's trademark, applying discriminatory pricing, selling below cost (called dumping), making preemptive purchases of raw materials, establishing exclusive contracts with distributors or dealers whereby they are required to sell or prohibited from selling a competitor's goods or services, securing rebates from suppliers, or using any technique that unfairly takes advantages of a competing firm.

UNIDO
See UNITED NATIONS INDUSTRIAL DEVELOPMENT ORGANIZATION.

uniform accounting system

A system of accounts common to similar organizations. Trade associations, for example, propose accounting systems that are uniform in application to all members of their particular associations. Federal and state regulatory agencies, such as public utility commissions, may develop and strongly recommend uniform accounting systems for organizations and institutions that come under their purview.

Uniform Commercial Code (UCC)

Because of the differences between the laws of the states of the United States, especially as applied to business, confusion may exist as persons accustomed to the laws of one state do business in other states. To relieve such difficulties, many states have adopted certain uniform laws that are essentially the same from state to state. A Uniform Commercial Code embodying many of the uniform laws has been enacted and adopted by many states to simplify, clarify, and modernize the law governing commercial transactions; to permit the continued expansion of commercial practices through custom, usage, and agreement of the parties; and to make the law uniform among the various state jurisdictions.

unilateral contract

A one-sided agreement wherein one party, the offeror, calls for the performance of an act by the performer, the offeree, in exchange for a promise by the offeror. When the offeree performs the act, a unilateral contract results. A promise is given in exchange for the performance of an act. The offeree is in no way obliged to perform the act, and on having performed it is under no further obligation. The contract comes into being with the performance of the act, and once it is in existence only the offeror who made the promise is under an obligation.

unintended investment

Unforeseen buildup of inventories in the economic system. Actual saving and actual investment are brought into equality in the economy by this means.

union shop

A place of employment that requires newly employed workers to become members of the union after a specified period of time on the job.

unique selling proposition (USP)
The sales features of a product or service that are unique to the offer. Often used as the theme of a marketer's advertising, sales promotion, or merchandising program.

unissued capital stock
The part of the capital stock that has been authorized for issue but has not in fact been issued.

unitary elasticity
See ELASTICITY OF DEMAND.

unit cost
In accounting, the cost of a selected unit of a good or a service. For example, dollar cost per kilogram, labor hour, machine hour, and so on.

United Mine Workers of America (UMWA)
An industrial union that represents workers in the coal mines and coal-processing industries of the United States. It also has local unions in Canada. Organized in 1890, the UMWA belonged to the American Federation of Labor (AFL) until 1936. It helped form the Congress of Industrial Organizations in 1938, but withdrew in 1942. It has remained independent, except for a brief affiliation with the AFL in 1946 and 1947.

United Nations (UN)
Created officially by its 51 founder member nations on October 24, 1945, its principle objectives being to (1) maintain international peace and security; (2) develop friendly relations among nations; (3) cooperate in solving international economic, social, cultural, and humanitarian problems and in promoting respect for human rights and fundamental freedoms; and (4) be a center for harmonizing actions of nations in attaining these common ends.

United Nations Capital Development Fund (UNCDF)
Associated with the United Nations Development Fund, the UNCDF was established in 1966 to provide grants and low-interest capital loans to developing countries.

United Nations Conference on Trade and Development (UNCTAD)
A conference convened in 1964 in response to growing anxiety among the developing countries over the difficulties they were facing in their

attempts to bridge the standard-of-living gap between them and the developed nations.

United Nations Development Program (UNDP)
An agency of the United Nations set up in 1965 to assist in the growth and prosperity of developing countries through educational and economic projects.

United Nations Educational, Scientific, and Cultural Organization (UNESCO)
Established in 1946, it consists of a General Conference of United Nations member states, an executive board, a director general, and a secretariat based in Paris, France. UNESCO's objective is to work for peace and security by promoting collaboration among the nations through education, science, and culture in order to further universal respect for justice, for the rule of law, and for the human rights and fundamental freedoms affirmed by the charter of the United Nations.

United Nations Industrial Development Organization (UNIDO)
An agency of the United Nations formed in 1967 to mobilize resources for the promotion of industrial development and manufacturing in the developing countries.

United Nations Relief and Rehabilitation Administration (UNRRA)
An emergency organization established toward the end of World War II to supply basic food and clothing, machinery, and raw materials to the countries of Western Europe that had suffered extensive war damage. Financed by the United States and the British Commonwealth and extended to the Pacific arena at the end of the war, it was terminated in 1946 and the major task of rehabilitation was then taken over by the European Recovery Program.

United Parcel Service (UPS)
Originally conceived as a delivery service for retail stores, now operates as a nationwide common carrier. *Blue Label* service includes the use of containers in jet freighters.

United States Employment Service (USES)
Provides industry with a national consulting and publications service on employment, training, selection, and other matters related to personnel development and recruiting.

United States Government Life Insurance (USGLI)
Created in 1917 to provide life insurance coverage for servicemen during World War I. It was first administered by the U.S. Treasury Department, later by the Veterans Administration. See NATIONAL SERVICE LIFE INSURANCE.

United States of America Standard Code for Information Interchange (USASCII)
An eight-level code intended to provide information code compatibility between digital devices. Also referred to as *American Standard Code for Information Interchange* (ASCII).

United States Postal Service (USPS)
Created as an independent establishment of the executive branch by the Postal Reorganization Act of 1970, the USPS commenced operations on July 1, 1971. The Postal Service handles approximately 88 billion pieces of mail yearly and employs 655,000 people. It is headed by the Postmaster General and the Deputy Postmaster General, both of whom are appointed by, and sit on, the Board of Governors. The nine governors are appointed by the president with the advice and consent of the Senate for overlapping nine-year terms. The USPS is committed to the development of efficient mail-handling systems and operates its own planning and engineering programs. It is responsible for protecting the mails from loss or theft and for apprehending those who violate postal laws. There are about 30,000 post offices throughout the United States.

United States rule
A method of identifying the amounts of interest and principal included in a partial payment of an interest-bearing debt. Also known as *merchant's rule*.

unit-in-place method
A process for estimating the cost of erecting a building by estimating the cost of each component part, such as the foundation, floors, walls, windows, ceilings, and roof, including labor, materials, and overhead.

unitization
The process of fastening a group of packages or pieces together for shipment as a unit in domestic or overseas traffic. Often these items are on expendable pallets. See UNIT LOAD.

unit load
The result of bracing freight in railway cars under the floating load principle, by strapping two or more packages together to make them one large unit that is permitted to shift somewhat under impact. See UNITIZATION.

unit-of-product method
In accounting, a depreciation method. See SERVICE-YIELD BASIS.

unity of command
A management principle holding that an employee should receive orders from only one superior. See PARITY OF AUTHORITY and PARITY OF RESPONSIBILITY.

Universal Postal Union (UPU)
An agency of the United Nations (UN) responsible for promoting international cooperation in the development of international postal services. The UPU predates the UN, having been set up as the General Postal Union in 1924.

universe
In statistical analysis, the population, or large set of data, from which samples are drawn. Usually assumed to be infinitely large, or at least very large relative to the sample. See POPULATION.

unlawful detainer
The failure of a tenant to vacate premises after being notified of being in default.

unliquidated encumbrance
In government accounting, an encumbrance not paid or not approved for payment.

unpaid dividend
A declared dividend that has not yet been paid; an unclaimed dividend. Also, a passed dividend on cumulative preferred stock.

unproductive labor
In some accounting procedures, the same as indirect labor.

unproductive wages
Wages paid for UNPRODUCTIVE LABOR.

unqualified stock option
See NONQUALIFIED STOCK OPTION.

unrealized appreciation
In revaluating an asset, the excess over book value of the asset at the time of revaluation and recording, less allocated depreciation.

unrealized revenue
Revenue attributed to a completed business transaction and received in the form of an asset other than cash or other form of current asset. Such revenue does not appear on the income statement until the asset has been converted to or realized as cash.

unrecovered cost
The portion of an original investment that has not been amortized through depreciation or depletion. Also, uninsured losses caused by fire, theft, obsolescence, or market fluctuations.

unregistered stock
See LETTER STOCK.

unrelated business income
The portion of the income of an eleemosynary corporation that may be subject to corporate income taxation because the activity that produced the income is unrelated to the tax-exempt purposes of the corporation.

UNRRA
See UNITED NATIONS RELIEF AND REHABILITATION ADMINISTRATION.

unsecured account
A personal account supported only by the general credit of the debtor, without collateral or other tangible guaranty.

unsecured liability
A liability for which the creditor holds no security.

update
In data processing, to make a master file current by inserting changes required by current information or transactions.

upland

In real estate transactions, land above the line of ordinary high water, which adjoins submersible or submerged land; land situated in an area higher than its surroundings.

UPS

See UNITED PARCEL SERVICE.

upset price

In the case of equity proceedings in a bankruptcy, the amount established by the court as the lowest acceptable price for a firm's assets when offered at public auction.

More generally, the lowest price at which a seller is willing to sell. Also, the initial price asked at an auction before bidding is started.

up tick

In securities trading, a transaction made at a price higher than the preceding transaction. Also called a *plus tick*. A stock may be sold short only on an up tick or on a *zero-plus tick*. A zero-plus tick is a transaction at the same price as the preceding trade but higher than the preceding different price. See DOWN TICK.

UPU

See UNIVERSAL POSTAL UNION.

Urban Mass Transportation Administration (UMTA)

A unit of the Department of Transportation, UMTA assists communities throughout the country in meeting their residents' needs for safe and efficient mass transit systems.

URW Initials for *United Rubber Workers,* a labor union.

USASCII

See UNITED STATES OF AMERICA STANDARD CODE FOR INFORMATION INTERCHANGE.

U.S. customary system

A system of units of measurement derived from the British imperial system, although varying from it at some points, such as in liquid measures. The U.S. customary system and the British imperial system use the foot and the pound as basic units. See INTERNATIONAL SYSTEM.

USDA
See Department of Agriculture.

useful life
In accounting, the normal operating life of a fixed asset or its utility to the owner.

USES
See United States Employment Service.

USGLI
See United States Government Life Insurance.

USNS
Initials for *United States naval ship*.

USP
See unique selling proposition.

USPS
See United States Postal Service.

usurious
Descriptive of a contract made for a loan of money at a rate of interest higher than that permitted by statute.

USWA
Initials for *United Steelworkers of America,* a labor union.

utilitarianism
See Bentham, Jeremy.

utilities average
See share index.

utopian socialism
Advanced by a group of English and French writers in the early nineteenth century, a philosophy that advocated the creation of model communities, largely self-contained, where the instruments of production would be collectively owned and the government would be established primarily on a voluntary or wholly democratic basis. The leading propagator of the philosophy in England was Robert Owen (1771–1858), and in France, Charles Fourier (1772–1837).

VA
See Veterans Administration.

vacancy factor
The percentage of unoccupied space in a rental building during a specific accounting period.

valence
See EXPECTANCY THEORY.

validity
In statistical analysis, the extent to which a test or other measuring method or device measures what it is supposed to measure.

valorize
To attempt to determine the price of a commodity by setting an arbitrary market value, usually by government intervention as in buying up surpluses or making loans to producers to enable them to store their products for release to the market at more appropriate times. *Valorization* is also price fixing by cartels or by agreements.

valuation account
A reserve account that relates to and partly or wholly offsets one or more other accounts, including accumulated depreciation, allowance for bad debts, and unamortized debt discount.

value
In the use or exchange theory in economics, there have been three broad approaches to the analysis of value: (1) the general use theory based on the assumption that the value of a commodity is related to the use to which it is put; (2) the labor theory that asserts that value reflects

the cost of production measured in terms of labor time absorbed; and (3) the marginal utility theory that contends that the final small increment in demand and supply determines the value of commodities in exchange.

value-added tax (VAT)
A tax on consumption levied at each point where goods or services are exchanged in the course of their production and distribution until they reach the ultimate consumer. At each stage the tax is levied on the difference between the cost of the goods or services bought at the start of the specific stage and the price of the outputs sold at the end of the stage. For example, a retail firm may be taxed on the difference between the wholesale price it paid for goods and the retail price at which it sells them to consumers. VAT is a principal indirect tax in many countries, including the European Economic Community, and was introduced in the United Kingdom in 1973. The French term for value-added tax is *taxe à la valeur ajoutée (TVA)*.

value analysis
Usually performed by the purchasing department, the study of materials, parts, or components, purchased or manufactured. The purpose is to determine the value received for the dollars spent and to start specific action intended to improve that value.

valued policy
Insurance usually issued for property whose precise value may be difficult to establish, such as a work of art, a coin collection, or a rare book. Such a policy establishes a face amount for the value of the insured property, and in the event of loss within the terms of the policy, the face amount is paid. Another example is a life insurance contract under which the dollar amount is fixed and becomes payable on the death of the insured.

vara
A measure of length equal to 33 $\frac{1}{3}$ inches. It is used to some extent in Texas.

variable annuity
A pension benefit plan that fluctuates in value with the changes in the worth of the assets, typically common stocks, in which the pension fund is invested. The variable annuity was designed to provide an adjustment mechanism for inflation on the theory that stock prices would rise over time.

Also, a contract between an insurance or investment company and an investor under which periodic distributions differ as changes take place in the value of underlying equity securities.

variable budget
See FLEXIBLE BUDGET.

variable cost
An operating expense that varies in relation to sales or production volume, facility use, or other indicator of activity. Also known as *variable expense*.

variable cost ratio
The ratio between sales revenues and variable costs. One of many ratios by which the performance of management or a business may be measured.

variable expense
See VARIABLE COST.

variable price option
A form of nonqualified stock option under which the exercise price decreases as the stock price increases in relation to the stock price at the time of the award. Also known as *yo-yo option*.

variable-ratio plan
A formula investment plan under which an investor changes the ratio of certain types of securities in his or her portfolio, depending on whether the stock market is relatively high or relatively low.

variance
In accounting, the difference between corresponding items in comparative balance sheets or in income or other operating statements. Also, the difference over a period of a year or less between standard costs and actual costs; the difference between the expected or planned and the actual.

In statistics, mixed positive and negative quantities can be converted to all-positive quantities by the process of squaring. The average of the squared deviations from the mean, used as a measure of dispersion, is called *variance*.

In law procedures, a discrepancy between what is charged or alleged and what is proved or is offered as proof.

In real estate zoning, an exemption from the application of a zoning ordinance or regulation, permitting a use that varies from what is otherwise permitted. The exception or *variance* is granted by the appropriate authority in special circumstances to protect against an undue hardship wrought by strict enforcement of the zoning regulations.

variety store

A store carrying a wide range of relatively inexpensive goods for the household. Small appliances, dry goods, stationery, and notions are typical of the items offered. Also known as *five-and-ten, five-and-dime store,* and *five-and-ten-cent store.*

VAT

See VALUE-ADDED TAX.

VDU

See VISUAL DISPLAY UNIT.

Veblen, Thorstein Bunde (1857–1929)

Born in Wisconsin of Norwegian parents, a teacher of economics and sociology who was outspokenly critical of virtually all other economists and sociologists. His many books attracted international attention. His most famous, *The Theory of the Leisure Class* (1899), attacked the unequal distribution of wealth. See CONSPICUOUS CONSUMPTION.

vendee's lien

The encumbrance of a buyer for the return of his or her deposit in the event a seller defaults on a contract.

vendor

An outside company selling or supplying material or services.

vendor's lien

An unpaid seller's legal right to maintain possession of property until the purchase price has been recovered.

venire

A writ used to summon a jury to come into court. It is often used to mean *jury.*

venireman

See TALISMAN.

venue
In legal proceedings, the geographical area over which a court presides. The county in which a legal action is to be tried. A change of venue means a move to another county.

verifier
A keypunch machine with a keyboard, used to verify that the information has been properly punched into a card or tape. The machine signals when the punched hole and the depressed key on the keyboard do not agree.

vertical boring machine
A large machine tool in which the work rotates about a vertical axis, and the cutting tool moves radially or vertically into the work.

vertical merger
A merger involving firms that already exist in a buyer-seller relationship. For example, the merging of a manufacturing firm and its supplier of raw materials is a vertical merger.

vessel ton
A unit of internal capacity for ships equal to 100 cubic feet. Also known as *register ton*.

vested interest
An immediate right of present enjoyment, or a present fixed right of future enjoyment.

vested right
A right entitled to government protection and belonging so absolutely and unconditionally to a person that it cannot be defeated by the act of any private person or organization.

vested rights
A provision in a firm's pension plan whereby an employee who leaves the company, for whatever reason, may retain his or her pension rights in the form of a frozen or paid-up pension.

vestibule training
Used primarily for rapid introduction of new employees to a production environment, the training of these employees on equipment in a separate part of the plant. An attempt may be made to simulate the actual working condition to help the employees develop skills, to get

them used to the plant routine, and to allay their initial nervousness before they are assigned to actual production jobs.

vesting
The conveying of an irrevocable right to a benefit, usually after a specified number of years of continuous employment have been accrued within the same company; most prevalent in pension and profit-sharing plans.

Veterans Administration (VA)
An independent agency headed by an Administrator of Veterans Affairs appointed by the president, it provides medical care to eligible veterans of the armed services and their dependents, including hospitalization, home care, home nursing care, out-patient medical and dental care, and prosthetic devices. The VA also provides funds for educational assistance to qualified veterans, orphans and widows of veterans, children and wives of certain seriously disabled veterans, and certain categories of active-duty personnel.

viability
In economics, the ability of a nation or an economy to operate, develop, and survive. Sometimes used in reference to a business, an industry, a market, or a product.

virement
An administrative allocation of funds, or any transfer of funds from one account to another.

virtual monopoly
See NATURAL MONOPOLY.

vis major
Latin for "greater force," "superior force." Used in civil law to mean an act of God, an overwhelming force of nature that has consequences that are not preventable by any due and reasonable precautions and that under certain circumstances is held to exempt from contract obligations. See ACT OF GOD.

VISTA
See VOLUNTEERS IN SERVICE TO AMERICA.

visual display unit (VDU)
A component of a computer or central processing unit that uses a cathode-ray tube to display data in alpha-numeric or graph form as they are inputted to or outputted from the computer or central processing unit.

visual review system
One of the simplest methods of inventory control wherein the reordering of inventory is based on actually looking at the amount of inventory on hand. Usually applied to such low-value items as nuts, bolts, and washers stored in small bins. Also see TWO-BIN SYSTEM.

vocabulary
A list of operating codes or instructions available to the programmer for writing the program for a given problem for a specific computer.

void
Without legal effect. A contract that is void, for example, confers no rights or duties, creates no obligations.

voidable contract
A contract that remains valid until one party, who has the power of avoidance, exercises that power. An infant has the power of avoidance of his or her contract. A defrauded party has the power to avoid his or her contract.

volume discount
An allowance, in credit, cash, or goods, given by a seller to a buyer because of the aggregate size of the purchases in a series of transactions over a specific period of time. Distinguished from a quantity discount, which is usually related to a single transaction rather than a series. See QUANTITY DISCOUNT.

volume minimum weight
In motor carrier tariffs, the minimum weight to which any specific rate, other than truckload, applies.

volume rate
In motor carrier tariffs, any rate to which a volume minimum weight applies. See VOLUME MINIMUM WEIGHT.

voluntary alienation
The transfer of a title to another by a deed.

voluntary lien
An encumbrance placed on a property through the willing act of the owner, as in making a mortgage loan.

voluntary reserve
An allocation or earmarking of earned surplus or retained earnings for insurance, retirements, and other items not covered by contracts or commitments to outsiders.

Volunteers in Service to America (VISTA)
The creation of VISTA was authorized by Congress in 1964. Its purpose is to provide constructive opportunities for Americans to work on a full-time basis with locally sponsored projects designed to strengthen and supplement efforts to eliminate poverty and poverty-related human, social, and environmental problems in the United States and its territories, and to secure and exploit opportunities for self-advancement by persons afflicted with such problems. VISTA volunteer men and women are chosen from all ages and walks of life, and receive training for project assignments. Volunteers serve for up to two years, living and working among the needy. VISTA is an office of ACTION, an independent agency headquartered in Washington, D.C.

von Thünen, Joachim (1783–1850)
German landowner and economist who gained fame in the nineteenth century as a theorist in commodity distribution and plant location. In von Thünen's theory, transport expense is the primary factor in production locations of different agricultural commodities. Those commodities that cannot readily absorb the expense of transportation will be located near the market and vice versa.

voting trust
The transfer by two or more persons of their shares of stock of a corporation to a trustee who is to vote the shares and act for such shareholders.

voucher
A document serving as evidence of the disbursement of cash. A document authorizing the disbursement of cash. Written evidence of a business or accounting transaction.

voucher audit
An authorized individual's examination of a proposed disbursement. In government accounting, the postaudit of individual disbursements made by the comptroller general.

voucher check
A document showing details of a payment made, including date, amount, discount, deductions, invoice number, and other references to goods or services for which payment has been or is to be made. A voucher check may combine the features of a check, a formal receipt, and a detachable remittance record.

voucher index
An alphabetical list, in card-index or carbon-copy form, of persons or firms that are payees of the company. As a record of business done with each payee, it may also serve as a creditors' ledger. See VOUCHER SYSTEM.

voucher register
A journal or record, usually in columnar form, for the entry of vouchers. It enables the summarization, distribution, and posting to ledgers of the liabilities indicated by the vouchers, individually or in the aggregate.

voucher system
A system of accounting in which a voucher for an account payable is prepared with supporting documents attached for each transaction (or series of transactions) affecting a single account and, when approved, is usually entered in a voucher register.

WA
See WITH AVERAGE.

WADS
See WIDE AREA DATA SERVICE.

wage
Payment to an owner of resources who supplies the factor of production known as *labor*. Such payment includes salaries, commissions, bonuses, and so forth. Also, the price paid for the use of labor, usually expressed as a time rate such as so much per hour, day, week, or month, or less frequently expressed as so much per unit of work performed.

wage-fund theory
Developed by John Stuart Mill, the principle that wages depend on the relationship that exists at any particular time between the number of workers and the quantity of capital employed for the payment of wages. Mill held that the only way to increase wages is to reduce the number of workers or to increase the amount of capital used for the payment of wages. See MILL, JOHN STUART.

wage leadership
The influence exerted over the wage level of an entire industry or labor market by a wage settlement arrived at in one large industrial firm or in a group of firms.

wage-price controls
Government controls over the level of wages and prices in the economy.

wage-price guideposts
Conditions or standards set by the government in an effort to control the behavior of wages and prices.

wage theory
Any of the varying approaches to or theories for determining the wages paid to employees. See ABILITY TO PAY, STANDARD OF LIVING, MARKET THEORY, and PRODUCTIVITY.

Wagner Act
Popular name for the National Labor Relations Act, 1935. Named for its chief sponsor, Senator Robert F. Wagner of New York. See NATIONAL LABOR RELATIONS ACT.

wagon distributor
See TRUCK WHOLESALER.

wagon jobber
See TRUCK WHOLESALER.

waiting-line theory
Developed in 1905 by A. K. Erlang, a Danish telephone engineer seeking to determine the effect of fluctuating service demand on the utilization of automatic dialing equipment. Since the end of World War II, work on waiting-line models has been extended to solutions of production problems. Such models are among the most used of quantitative methods for scheduling the arrivals and introductions of materials into the manufacturing, repair, or service processes. Also known as *queuing theory*.

waiting period
Under the regulations of the Securities and Exchange Commission covering the issuance of a new security, the required waiting period of 20 days between the filing of a registration statement and its effective date. In some cases, a shorter waiting period may be granted. Where deficiences are found, a period of more than 20 days may be required.

Also, a form of deductible clause found most often in accident and sickness insurance policies, especially in those providing income benefits to the insured. A waiting period is specified as the number of days, usually following the occurrence, that must elapse before payments are to be made by the insurer. The longer the waiting period, the lower the premium rates. Some policies offer retroactive periods, which means that if the disability continues beyond the waiting period, payment is also made for the waiting period. See DEDUCTIBLE CLAUSES.

wait time
The time a job spends waiting to be moved or waiting to be worked on in the factory area. Also known as *queue time*.

waive
In legal proceedings, to intentionally give up or relinquish a known right or to perform an act that is not consistent with the claiming of a known right.

waiver
The voluntary relinquishment of a right or privilege without causing the insurance policy to be canceled. A premium waiver may become part of the contract terms, as when an incident temporarily prevents a business firm from conducting its affairs. The insurance company may have voluntarily relinquished or waived its right to premiums for the specified period of time.

wall-to-wall inventory
A technique for inventory control or movement whereby raw materials, parts, and assemblies enter a factory at one end, are processed through the facility, and eventually become an end product without ever having entered a formal stockroom area.

Walras, Léon (1834–1910)
A French-Swiss teacher of economics who advocated nationalization of land. Principally known as the first to develop a complete mathematical system for a whole economy, showing how it would tend toward equilibrium under his assumptions. See NEOCLASSICAL ECONOMICS and PARETO, VILFREDO.

want
In economic theory, a need or desire for an economic good or service, not necessarily accompanied by the power to satisfy it. Synonymous with *need* in the behavioral sciences.

warehouse receipt
A document, serving as evidence of title, given to the owner of goods that have been placed in a public warehouse. Warehouse receipts are governed by the Uniform Warehouse Receipts Act, in effect in most of

the United States. Transfer of title is effected by assignment of the receipt.

warrant
In securities trading, a certificate giving the right to purchase securities at a stipulated price within a specified time period; may be offered with the purchase of securities as an inducement to buy. Sometimes no time period limitation is placed on the warrant. See RIGHTS and SUBSCRIPTION RIGHT.

In legal proceedings, an order written in the name of the state and signed by a magistrate that commands an officer of the court to arrest a person.

In procurement, a document authorizing the payment for goods or services received.

warranty
In insurance, there are two types: (1) a *promissory warranty* is an absolute guarantee on the part of the insured that he or she will perform some duty in the future (for example, in obtaining theft insurance, a promise has been made that a burglar alarm system will be installed and in continuous operation); (2) an *affirmative warranty* is a guarantee as to the absolute accuracy of some statement or condition. If an affirmative warranty is proven to be untrue in the slightest, the insurance company has the right to void the policy. For ocean marine insurance, see IMPLIED WARRANTY.

In marketing, a written guarantee of the integrity of a product and of the manufacturer's responsibility for the repair or replacement of defective parts under specified conditions and for limited time periods. The warranty is usually also explicit about the limitations of the manufacturer's liabilities with respect to the performance or nonperformance of the product.

warranty deed
See DEED, WARRANTY.

war risk
Policies in all lines of insurance offered by American firms exclude this as an uninsurable hazard. During World War II, war-damage insurance was issued by the federal government.

wash
In accounting, a transaction that is reversed or offset by another transaction in a short period of time.

Washington Agreement
A 1945 agreement between the United States and Great Britain under which $25 billion of Lend-Lease aid to the Commonwealth was written off and the United Kingdom was granted a long-term loan of $3.75 billion.

wash sale
The sale and purchase of substantially identical securities within a 30-day period. Losses from such transactions are not legal deductions from income subject to federal income taxes.

waste
In economic theory, resources of labor or material consumed or produced in a given operation and not returning an economic benefit.

wasting asset
A fixed asset with a limited useful life and subject to depreciation. Examples include assets from which natural products such as ore, oil, and timber are extracted at a rate exceeding the natural replacement rate, thereby causing a gradual diminution of the value of the asset.

water damage
Covered by many casualty policies. Fire insurance policies generally cover such damage as a proximate cause in hostile fires. An extended coverage endorsement may be made part of a policy to cover damage by wind-driven rain if there is reasonable evidence that the wind made an opening in the structure and the rain entered through this opening.

watered capital
The excess of capital stock issued, at its par or stated value, over the fair value of the assets contributed in exchange. See WATERED STOCK.

watered stock
Any class of the capital stock of a corporation containing watered capital. See CAPITAL STOCK and WATERED CAPITAL.

water right
See RIPARIAN RIGHT.

WATS
See WIDE AREA TELEPHONE SERVICE.

wave theory
See KONDATRIEFF CYCLE.

waybill
Issued by a carrier to the shipper, a record of details describing a unit of freight. Copies may be provided to all interested agents of the carrier.

way of necessity
The statutory right of an owner to enter and leave his or her land.

WCL
See WORLD CONFEDERATION OF LABOR.

wealth
In economic theory, an individual's total stock or inventory of tangible or intangible possessions having a definable market value and capable of being exchanged for money or other goods through a transfer of ownership. The same principle may be applied both to a business firm and to an economy as a whole, measured at a single instant in time.

Wealth of Nations, The
The popular name for *An Inquiry into the Nature and Causes of the Wealth of Nations* (1776), written by the Scottish economist Adam Smith. See SMITH, ADAM.

Webb-Pomerene Act
Passed by Congress in 1916, the act specifies that small businesses electing to form conferences or associations for the purpose of doing foreign trade may set prices for a product to be sold on the international market. The law is written to protect small businesses from conglomerates. For example, if a group of shippers in international commerce form an association, they may mutually establish a tariff rate that each and every exporter who uses their services must agree to recognize.

Weber, Max (1864–1920)
A German economist and sociologist, Weber studied law at Heidelberg, Berlin, and Göttingen. His interest centered on economics, of which he became a professor at Freiburg and later at Heidelberg. He was also a visiting professor at Vienna and Munich. In his published works, Weber rejected Karl Marx's theory of economic determinism and stressed the importance of ethical and religious factors in the for-

mation of capitalism. The University of Heidelberg established the Max Weber Institute in his honor.

weighted average method

A method of costing inventory based on the assumption that costs should be charged against revenue on the basis of an average, taking into consideration the number of units acquired at each price. The same average unit cost is employed in computing the cost of goods remaining in inventory. The weighted average is determined by dividing the total costs of a commodity available for sale by the total number of units of that commodity available for sale. For businesses in which various purchases of identical units of a commodity are mingled, the weighted average method has some relationship to the physical flow of inventory. See FIFO and LIFO.

welfare state

A social system based on the government's assumption of responsibility for providing unemployment compensation, medical care, old-age pensions, and income for families unable to participate in the productive process.

WEMA

Initials for *Western Electronic Manufacturers Association*. Name changed to *American Electronics Association* (AEA) in 1978.

wetback

A colloquialism sometimes applied to migrant laborers from Mexico who enter the United States illegally by crossing the Rio Grande.

WFTU

See WORLD FEDERATION OF TRADE UNIONS.

wharfage

A charge assessed by a pier or dock owner against freight handled at the pier or dock, or against a steamship company for the use of the pier or dock.

wharfinger

A person who maintains a wharf at which goods are stored for compensation. A wharfinger is not an insurer of the goods possessed, and is not liable to the bailor for loss or damage to the goods unless negligent. The wharfinger must exercise ordinary care, such as keeping the wharf in a state of repair and keeping the waters surrounding the wharf free from obstructions that might cause damage to approaching vessels.

Wheeler-Lea Act
A 1938 amendment to the Federal Trade Commission Act of 1914. Passed primarily for the benefit of consumers rather than business competitors, it protects them from unfair, deceptive, dishonest, or injurious methods of competition. Thus injured consumers are given equal protection with injured merchants before the law.

where-used file
In manufacturing, a file that records the assembly or subassembly in which each part or assembly is used.

where-used report
In manufacturing, a report that displays, for each part, all assemblies that contain the part in their single-level bill of material.

whip
A fast worker introduced by management as a pacesetter for other workers on a production line. See PACER.

whirlybird
In data processing, a colloquial expression for some types of disk-pack equipment.

WHO
See WORLD HEALTH ORGANIZATION.

whole life insurance
See STRAIGHT LIFE INSURANCE.

wholesale life insurance
Life insurance for individual members of a group that is smaller than the minimum required for a group life insurance policy.

wholesale merchants
See MERCHANT WHOLESALER.

wholesale price index
A measure of the average prices of commodities purchased in large quantities in transactions between firms.

wholesaler
See MERCHANT WHOLESALER.

Wicksell, John Gustav Knut (1851–1926)
A Swedish economist acknowledged by Keynes himself as an important predecessor of the Keynesian type of thinking. He concentrated his attention on analyses of changes occurring in the real world over time—the cycles of generally rising and generally falling prices, and the effects of supply and demand.

wide area data service (WADS)
Similar in concept to wide area telephone service (WATS), but intended for use with relatively low-grade telephone circuits, which are nonetheless adequate for the transmission of data.

wide area telephone service (WATS)
A system of interstate long-distance telephone lines offered for rental and in effect providing price-discounted service to the renter.

wildcat strike
An unofficial labor strike called on short notice or without notice and without going through contractual procedures for settling grievances.

windfall profit
An unexpected or unbudgeted profit from sources over which the recipient had exercised little or no control.

Windom Report
In 1872 the Senate appointed a special committee—known as the Windom Committee—to investigate the possibility of securing less expensive transportation than existed at the time between the interior and the seaboard. The committee made its report to the Senate in 1874. The defects and abuses of the existing transportation system were listed by the committee as "insufficient facilities, unfair discriminations, and extortionate charges." The report made recommendations concerning facilities and charges but offered little with respect to discriminatory practices. No action was taken on the Windom Report. See CULLOM REPORT.

WIP
See WORK IN PROCESS.

wire-mesh conveyor
Same as a belt conveyor, except that its moving bed is a continuous belt of wire mesh suspended between two strands of continuous chain. It is generally used in conveying materials involved in immersion, draining, or washing operations. See BELT CONVEYOR.

with average (WA)
In ocean marine insurance, the coverage of partial loss. WA is sometimes known as WPA, *with particular average.*

withdrawal account
A type of mutual fund account that pays a certain amount of money periodically to the owner of the account; often used by retired persons as a source of income.

withdrawal provisions
In a savings plan and occasionally in a qualified profit-sharing plan, the timing and terms under which either individual contributions or a portion of the accrued company contributions can be withdrawn by the participant.

withholding
In business accounting, the process of automatically deducting from salaries or wages the amounts of money specified by law or regulation, as in the case of government income taxes, and specified by contract with the employee, as in the case of voluntary contributions to pension or employee stock purchase plans.

WOM
Initials for *write-only memory.*

won
The basic unit of currency in North Korea and South Korea.

wonderlic
A general learning ability test developed in the 1960s for use with personnel in industry and business. It lasts 12 minutes and is derived partly from the Otis self-administering test of mental ability designed originally for use in schools.

woolly backs
Used particularly among miners in the U.K. coal-mining industry, an expression for employees who have a complacent and nonmilitant ap-

proach to industrial relations and are seen by the more militant employees as behaving like sheep in their relations with employers.

word

In data processing, an ordered set of characters occupying one storage location and treated by the computer circuits as a unit and transferred as such. Ordinarily, a word is treated by the control unit as an instruction, and by the arithmetic unit as a quantity. Word lengths may be fixed or variable, depending on the particular computer.

wordcom

A short expression for *fixed-word-length computer*. Wordcom is designed as a simplified machine to present machine language programming for computer communications. It has arithmetic, control, and storage units and input–output units; 1,000 words of sign and seven alphanumeric characters each in a high-speed storage (addresses are 000 through 999); accumulator and M-Q registers of sign and seven characters each; an instruction counter and three index registers; one card read-punch machine and up to ten magnetic-tape units; and the capability of executing 24 different single-address instructions.

workable competition

An approach to the preservation of competition within the economy that stresses the realistic rather than the idealistic concept of competition.

work analysis

See MOTION STUDY.

work center

See LOAD CENTER.

working asset

Any asset other than a capital asset. See CAPITAL ASSET.

working capital

Capital in current use in the operation of a business; the excess of current assets over current liabilities or net assets. One of the many methods by which the performance of management or of a business may be measured. Often considered a test of credit and a measure of the ability of a company to meet its current debts. Also known as *net current assets*.

working-capital ratio
The ratio of current assets to current liabilities. One of many ratios by which the performance of management or of a business may be measured.

working-capital turnover
The ratio of net sales to working capital. One of many ratios by which the performance of management or a business may be measured.

working control
Theoretically, control of a corporation requires ownership of 51 percent of the corporation's voting stock. In practice, effective (working) control may be exercised through ownership, individually or by a group acting as one, of less than 50 percent.

work in process (WIP)
The partially finished product or component of a manufacturer's output. Also known as *materials-in-process, goods-in-process,* and *in-process inventory.*

workmen's compensation insurance
An employer's liability contract covering all those liabilities imposed on an employer by the state workmen's compensation act, and applicable to accidents and occupational diseases for which an employer may be held legally responsible but which are not covered by the state workmen's compensation act.

work order
In business and industry, an internal document that authorizes the performance of a specific task or job. Also known as *work ticket.*

Work Projects Administration
See WORKS PROGRESS ADMINISTRATION.

works
In many countries outside the United States equivalent to the word *factory.*

work sampling
In manufacturing, a technique of work study and measurement in which a series of measurements of time/output relationships or of observations of the work activity are made at random intervals of time.

Used to determine manpower requirements for a particular phase of production or processing, as well as in developing statistically correct standard time values. Also, see RATIO-DELAY TECHNIQUE.

Works Progress Administration (WPA)
Established by executive order in 1935 under the authority of the Emergency Relief Appropriations Act of 1935 and continued by subsequent yearly Emergency Relief Appropriations Acts to operate a program of useful public works projects and to aid employable needy persons by providing work on such projects. The name was changed to Work Projects Administration in 1939 and the activity was consolidated into the Federal Works Agency. The WPA was dissolved in 1942 by direction of the president.

work study
British term for TIME AND MOTION STUDY.

work ticket
See WORK ORDER.

World Bank
Composed of a group of three institutions, the International Bank for Reconstruction and Development, the International Development Association, and the International Finance Corporation. The common objective of these institutions is to help raise the standards of living in developing countries by channeling financial resources from developed countries to the developing world. Established in 1945, the bank makes loans at a rate calculated in accordance with a formula related to its cost of borrowing.

World Confederation of Labor (WCL)
Founded in 1920 as the International Foundation of Christian Trade Unions, the WCL changed to its present name in 1968 and claims member trade unions in approximately 80 countries.

World Federation of Trade Unions (WFTU)
Established in 1945 by trade union organizations from approximately 50 countries. The American Federation of Labor refused to join, claiming that member trade unions from Communist countries were not democratic and independent. In 1949, the U.S. based Congress of Industrial Organizations and organizations from several other countries withdrew from the WFTU to form the International Confederation of Free Trade Unions.

World Health Organization (WHO)
A specialized agency of the United Nations, established in 1948 and headquartered in Geneva, Switzerland. Its primary purpose is to improve health conditions throughout the world through the collection and dissemination of scientific and statistical information on an international scale.

WPA
Initials for *with particular average;* see WITH AVERAGE. Also see WORKS PROGRESS ADMINISTRATION.

WPM
Initials for *words per minute,* a measure of speed in data transmission and telegraph systems.

wraparound mortgage
An arrangement whereby a borrower enters into a second mortgage for development purposes without refinancing the first mortgage, since the refinancing would probably have to be done at substantially higher current interest rates.

writ
A document in writing and under seal in the name of the state, issued by a court of justice at the start of, or during, a legal proceeding, directed to an officer of the court and commanding that officer to do some act, or requiring some person to do or refrain from doing some act, that is pertinent or related to the case being tried.

write-down
The transfer of a portion of an asset account to an expense account; The deliberate reduction of the book value of an asset.

write-off
The transfer of the remainder of the value of an asset to an expense account; The act of reducing book value.

write-up
The recording of an increase in the book value of an asset without incurring additional outlays of cash or other property and without producing an inflow of cash; the act of setting down an unduly high value.

WTL
Initials for *Western Trunk Line*.

W-2 form
A statement or document in a standardized format that all U.S. employers must give to their employees. The form contains the dollar amounts of wages and other compensation paid to the employee, contributions to Social Security (FICA tax), federal taxes withheld, state taxes withheld (where applicable), and a "yes" or "no" as to whether the employee participated in a qualified pension plan. A copy of the W-2 form must be attached to the employee's income-tax reports to the federal and state governments. The data given on the W-2 form cover the calendar year for the tax return.

x-axis
In a Cartesian coordinate system, the horizontal axis on a graph. See Y-AXIS.

X² distribution
See CHI-SQUARE DISTRIBUTION.

Yaoundé Convention
First drawn in 1964 and updated periodically, an agreement between member states of the Common Market and ten African states to provide aid for certain developing countries. The convention set up the European Development Fund.

y-axis
In a Cartesian coordinate system, the vertical axis on a graph. See x-axis.

year-end adjustment
Where indicated, a review and modification of a ledger account at the close of a fiscal year. Not related to corrections of clerical errors, but referring to adjustments made necessary by accruals, prepayments, changes in accounting policies, inventory data, or other transactions that may have occurred without being completely recorded.

yellow-dog contract
An agreement between an employer and an employee whereby the employee disavows membership in and pledges not to join a union during the period of employment. Outlawed in the United States by the Norris–La Guardia Act of 1932.

yen
The basic unit of currency in Japan.

yield
The dividends or interest paid by a company expressed as a percentage of the current price of a security or, if the security is already owned by an investor, as a percentage of the price originally paid for the security.

A stock yield is calculated by dividing the total of dividends paid in the preceding 12 months by the current market price or, if the security is already owned, by the price originally paid by the owner. The yield on a bond is calculated in the same way. Also known as a *return*. See COUPON YIELD, CURRENT YIELD, and YIELD TO MATURITY.

yield to maturity
A yield calculation that takes into account the relationship between a security's maturity value, time to maturity, current price, and coupon yield. The calculation allocates bond premium or discount over the life of the security and is the most accurate type of yield calculation. See YIELD, COUPON YIELD, and CURRENT YIELD.

Young Plan
Named for Owen D. Young, chairman of the committee that devised it, the plan became effective in 1929 and superseded the Dawes Plan. It reduced the total amount of reparations to be paid by Germany under the Treaty of Versailles, and did away with most of the supervisory controls on Germany's economy. Following a 1932 meeting of creditor powers at Lausanne, Germany paid no reparations and defaulted on her obligations under the Young Plan. See DAWES PLAN.

yo-yo option
See VARIABLE PRICE OPTION.

yuan
The basic unit of currency in the Republic of China (Taiwan) and the People's Republic of China.

zaire
The basic unit of currency in Zaire.

Zangerle curve
In real estate, a graph devised by John A. Zangerle for use in appraising corner lots. For any given main-street frontage, the graph shows the percentage of the side-street value to be added as corner influence to the value of the lot computed as an inside lot fronting on the main street.

zatacode indexing
In data processing, a unique library system of indexing individual documents by descriptors of equal rank so that a library can be searched for a combination of one or more descriptors. Also, an indexing scheme by which descriptors may be correlated or combined to show any interrelationships wanted for purposes of more precise information retrieval.

ZBB
See ZERO-BASE BUDGETING.

zero-base budgeting (ZBB)
An innovative general management tool intended to provide a systematic methodology for the evaluation of operations and programs applicable to the public and private sectors. The practice of zero-base budgeting is in its evolutionary stages. The basic assumption is that past or current experiences with a specific budget may be ignored as the basis for developing a new or replacement budget. This allows a comprehensive reexamination of all elements within the specific budget, and the equitable comparison of several budgets for the same

or for related activities. ZBB is considered a means for establishing a working structure to recognize priorities and performance measures for current or future plans, for redirecting resources into the highest-priority programs, and for explicitly identifying trade-offs among long-term growth, current operations, budgetary needs, and, where applicable, profit needs.

zero-minus tick
See DOWN TICK.

zero-plus tick
See UP TICK.

zero-sum game
In the theory of games, a situation in which the players are considered to be in pure conflict. For every possible choice of strategy in this situation, the gains and losses equalize each other, sum to zero. For example, in a hypothetical game played by two companies that between them control 100 percent of the market for a specific good or service, any increase attained by company A is at the expense of an equivalent loss sustained by company B; the sum of the two events is zero.

zloty
The basic unit of currency in Poland.

Zollverein
A German word meaning "customs union." In 1833 customs unions were formed between Prussia and a number of independent German states. It was agreed that no tariff duties would be imposed on members of the Zollverein, and the uniform duties adopted were applicable to all other states and nations.

zone
An area or district established for defining parcel post or freight rates or for defining time with respect to local areas.

zone time
Standard time references in which the surface of the globe is divided into 24 zones of 15° or one hour each. The 0 zone extends 7½° east and west of the meridian of Greenwich, England. The zones are designated by the number of hours that must be applied to the local time to obtain Greenwich time.

zoning ordinance
An ordinance passed by a city council by virtue of its police power and used to regulate and prescribe the kind of buildings, residences, or businesses that shall be constructed and put into service and use within the city's geographical limits.